ADVANCES IN

EXPERIMENTAL
SOCIAL PSYCHOLOGY

VOLUME 11

CONTRIBUTORS TO VOLUME 11

Thomas D. Cook

Fred E. Fiedler

Susan T. Fiske

Brian R. Flay

Andy Kukla

Helmut Lamm

David G. Myers

Janet E. Stockdale

Shelley E. Taylor

Abraham Tesser

ADVANCES IN

Experimental
Social Psychology

EDITED BY

Leonard Berkowitz

DEPARTMENT OF PSYCHOLOGY
UNIVERSITY OF WISCONSIN
MADISON, WISCONSIN

VOLUME 11

ACADEMIC PRESS
New York   San Francisco   London   1978
A Subsidiary of Harcourt Brace Jovanovich, Publishers

ACADEMIC PRESS, INC.
111 Fifth Avenue, New York, New York 10003

United Kingdom Edition published by
ACADEMIC PRESS, INC. (LONDON) LTD.
24/28 Oval Road, London NW1 7DX

LIBRARY OF CONGRESS CATALOG CARD NUMBER: 64–23452

ISBN 0–12–015211–8

PRINTED IN THE UNITED STATES OF AMERICA

CONTENTS

Group-Induced Polarization of Attitudes and Behavior

Helmut Lamm and David G. Myers

Crowding: Determinants and Effects

Janet E. Stockdale

Salience, Attention, and Attribution: Top of the Head Phenomena

Shelley E. Taylor and Susan T. Fiske

Self-Generated Attitude Change

Abraham Tesser

CONTRIBUTORS

Numbers in parentheses indicate the pages on which the authors' contributions begin.

Thomas D. Cook, *Psychology Department, Northwestern University, Evanston, Illinois 60201* (1)

Fred E. Fiedler, *Department of Psychology, Guthrie Hall, University of Washington, Seattle, Washington 98198* (59)

Susan T. Fiske, *Department of Psychology and Social Relations, Harvard University, Cambridge, Massachusetts 02138* (249)

Brian R. Flay, *Psychology Department, Northwestern University, Evanston, Illinois 60201* (1)

Andy Kukla, *Department of Psychology, University of Toronto, Toronto, Ontario, Canada* (113)

Helmut Lamm, *Lehrstuhl für Psychologie III, Padagogische Hochschule, Köln, West Germany (145)*

David G. Myers, *Department of Psychology, Hope College, Holland, Michigan 49423* (145)

Janet E. Stockdale, *Department of Social Psychology, London School of Economics and Political Sciences, London WC2A, England* (197)

Shelley E. Taylor, *Department of Psychology and Social Relations, Harvard University, Cambridge, Massachusetts 02138* (249)

Abraham Tesser, *Institute for Behavioral Research, and Department of Psychology, University of Georgia, Athens, Georgia 30602* (289)

THE PERSISTENCE OF EXPERIMENTALLY INDUCED ATTITUDE CHANGE[1]

Thomas D. Cook

and

Brian R. Flay

NORTHWESTERN UNIVERSITY
EVANSTON, ILLINOIS

Contents

[1]We would like to thank Richard Bootzin, Milton Rokeach, and William A. Watts for comments on earlier drafts. During preparation of this chapter Brian Flay, who is now at the University of Waterloo, was partially supported by a Fulbright/Hays Fellowship.

I. Introduction

A. WHY STUDY THE PERSISTENCE OF ATTITUDE CHANGE?

Hovland, Janis, and Kelley (1953) considered five factors to be important for a comprehensive understanding of the effects of persuasion attempts. The first two are process variables—attending to a message and learning from it—while the others are outcome variables—immediate attitude change, the generalization of such change to overt behaviors, and the long-term persistence of change. Most researchers have focused on the determinants of *immediate* attitude change, although there has been a recent upsurge of interest in the generalization of belief changes to behavior (e.g., Calder & Ross, 1973; Fishbein & Ajzen, 1972, 1975; Wicker, 1969). However, there has been no corresponding interest in studying the conditions under which attitude change *persists* over time. Indeed, there is no comprehensive review of the persistence literature other than short lists of relevant experiments up to 1969 (Cook & Insko, 1968; McGuire, 1969; Watts & McGuire, 1964). We hope that the present critical chapter will fill the gap and perhaps expand the scope of future attitude research.

Several theoretical benefits might be expected from a review of the persistence literature that has slowly and unsystematically accumulated in experimental social psychology. Just as theories of long-term memory stress different concepts from theories of short-term memory, so theories of persistence may employ different concepts from theories of initial attitude change. Given the past lack of emphasis on persistence, it might be useful to highlight the constructs that are unique to persistence theories and are not part of current analyses of initial attitude change.

A critical review of the persistence literature should also indicate how well current procedures leading to initial attitude change succeed in producing persistent attitude change. The concern for predicting persistence can be expressed at several theoretical levels. For instance, R. L. Miller, Brickman, and Bolan (1975) tested the relative merits of persuasion and attribution strategies for causing long-lasting modifications in attitudes. Thus, their interest was in general approaches to attitude change rather than in how specific theories of persuasion or attribution related to change. At the level of specific theories, one could compare the level of persistence conferred by, say, a dissonance manipulation with the level of persistence created by manipulations derived from some other consistency framework. Finally, at an even more specific level, one might compare the persistence that results from learning specific message details (e.g., the conclusion) as opposed to, say, the persistence produced by message-relevant details which were not in a persuasive message but which subjects generated for themselves. The point is that one can compare different perspectives or theories about attitude change (rather than persistence) in order to examine which ones confer more or less persistence.

Reviewing the persistence literature may also help determine whether "attitude" really changes in laboratory experiments on attitude change. Most definitions of attitude have as a central component either *"consistency* in responding" to an attitude object, or a *"stable* predisposition to respond" to the object. Such consistency or stability can be defined operationally as a correlation between item responses at a single point in time. This leads to multiitem attitude scales. However, consistency can also be defined operationally as an observed consistency in behavior across response modes. This definition calls for collecting affective, cognitive, and behavioral data from each subject and then determining whether the response modes are correlated. Neither of the foregoing operations differentiates stable dispositions from temporary states, and one could not use them to distinguish between whether John Doe has a positive attitude toward X or whether he indicates a belief in X only under certain conditions— perhaps because he has just heard a persuasive message (Anderson & Farkas, 1973) or because he perceives "demand characteristics" or other social pressures in the research setting. Indeed, recent research on anticipatory attitude change suggests that much of what was labeled "attitude" change in past experiments may have been nothing more than short-lived and situationally determined "elastic shifts" in response (e.g., Cialdini, Levy, Herman, Kozlowski, & Petty, 1976; Hass & Mann, 1976). "Elastic shift" can be differentiated from a stable "attitude" only if attitude change data are collected from the same person (or comparable persons) *at.two or more times* and if a reliable attitude test is used.[2] Thus, persistence data are crucial for scholars who take seriously the notion that attitudes are by definition temporally stable.

The present chapter has three purposes: (*a*) to assess the validity of predictions from explicit persistence theories, (*b*) to examine how well theories of

[2]Actually, persistence experiments can permit an even more comprehensive validation of "attitude." Delayed measures can be taken in the subjects' own environment, by persons who are unconnected with earlier manipulations, who are ignorant of any experimental hypotheses, and who use different instruments from those employed earlier. It can then be inferred that changes which persist across times, measurement contexts, and settings are not likely to reflect "demands" and may, instead, reflect what is descriptively called "internalization" (Kelman, 1958) or a "basal" (as opposed to "surface") component of attitude (Anderson, 1974).

initial attitude change predict persistence, and (c) to test the construct validity of "attitude" change.

B. CONCEPTUALIZING PERSISTENCE

Several types of persistence have been described in the literature. A *sleeper effect* refers to an increase in attitude change which occurs in a single experimental group some time after an experimental treatment. *Total persistence* denotes an initial change that remains at the same level over time, neither increasing nor decreasing. *Partial persistence* has to do with an initial change that subsequently decays but is not completely eliminated. And *nonpersistence* denotes an initial change that is no longer observable by the end of an experiment.

A distinction has also been made between *absolute* and *relative* persistence (Watts & McGuire, 1964). The former refers to what happens over time in a single experimental group, while the latter is inferred from the difference in time trends between two experimental groups.

Absolute persistence is usually inferred in one of two ways. The first is from a within-group comparison of means at two or more intervals following a change attempt, the purpose being to test whether the attitude change is increasing or decreasing. The second is by comparing attitude at a final delay interval with an estimate of what it would have been at that time if there had been no manipulations or persuasive communications. The "no-cause baseline" is often inferred from pretest scores, but the final posttest mean from a no-message control group is obviously better since it is more sensitive to experimental artifacts like history, maturation, or testing.

Some patterns of absolute persistence are graphically illustrated in Fig. 1. The first row illustrates data patterns using the first criterion—the attitude in a single group is contrasted at different posttest measurement sessions. The second row illustrates data patterns when an experimental group is compared with a no-treatment control group over time and there are no pretests.

Relative persistence requires a comparison of different experimental groups over time. Various patterns of relative persistence are illustrated in Fig. 2, where they are combined with different patterns of absolute persistence. The first column shows *relative sleeper effects*. Here, the defining attribute is that the attitude trends diverge over time. (To understand why this is a "sleeper effect" one need only plot the simple difference between the two trends, and this will resemble an absolute sleeper effect.) The second column depicts patterns of *total relative persistence*. Here, the time trends are parallel. Patterns of *partial relative persistence* are illustrated in column 3, where the crucial attributes are converging time trends and a statistically significant difference between groups at the final delayed testing. *Relative nonpersistence* occurs when time trends converge and the final difference between groups is not reliable (column 4).

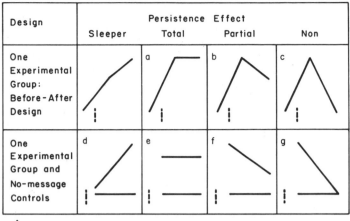

i = time when an independent variable is presented to subjects

Fig. 1.   Patterns of absolute persistence.

The usefulness of a distinction between absolute and relative persistence can be quickly seen if we look at the sleeper effect columns in Figs. 1 and 2. An *absolute sleeper effect* requires what is, in essence, a within-group increase in attitude change over time. But, as can be seen from the first column of Fig. 2, a *relative sleeper effect* can be inferred from a slower rate of absolute *decay*. If the "sleeper effect" label is widely understood to denote an absolute increase in attitude—as it seems to be—then labeling the slower rate of decay as a "sleeper effect" would be misleading. Indeed, we shall see later that conceptualizing the sleeper effect in absolute terms but testing for it statistically with a relative criterion causes much of the confusion surrounding the question of whether a sleeper effect results when a low credibility source is dissociated from a message.

A number of important points have to be borne in mind when using the descriptive labels introduced above. First, all patterns of relative partial persistence are characterized by converging time trends, and we do not know how these trends would continue if the delay intervals were extended. The longer time period might lead to total convergence which would suggest relative nonpersistence instead of relative partial persistence. Or the trends might even "cross over," suggesting initial partial persistence and a later relative sleeper effect. Although the descriptive labeling of relative partial persistence is particularly problematic and time-bound, we want to stress that changing the length of the final delay interval could change *any* verbal conclusion about the type of persistence obtained in a particular study.

Second, while Fig. 2 depicts trends for two groups at two times, some past designs have involved more groups and more delay intervals. This makes possi-

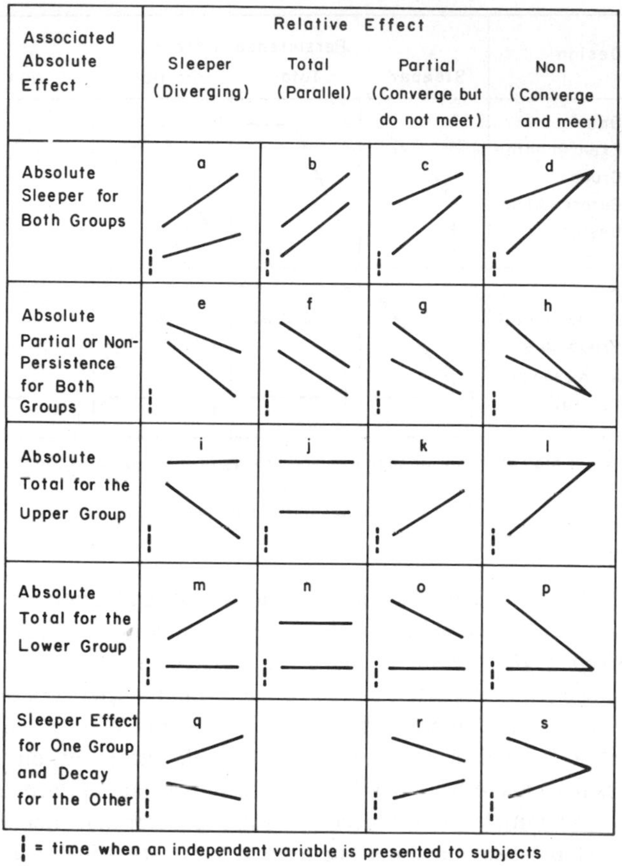

Associated Absolute Effect	Relative Effect			
	Sleeper (Diverging)	Total (Parallel)	Partial (Converge but do not meet)	Non (Converge and meet)
Absolute Sleeper for Both Groups	a	b	c	d
Absolute Partial or Non-Persistence for Both Groups	e	f	g	h
Absolute Total for the Upper Group	i	j	k	l
Absolute Total for the Lower Group	m	n	o	p
Sleeper Effect for One Group and Decay for the Other	q		r	s

⫶ = time when an independent variable is presented to subjects

Fig. 2. Patterns of relative persistence.

ble many statistical tests of trend differences and of differences between delayed posttest means. Obviously, such a plethora of tests can lead one to draw too many positive conclusions about effects unless corrective measures are taken.[3]

A third issue concerns the fact that the time trends in Figs. 1 and 2 are all linear. However, linearity should be rare in well-planned persistence studies, for it implies that the experiment was too short-lived to determine the level at which

[3]To avoid this trap we shall ignore all group mean differences that emerged at one delayed testing but not at earlier or later ones, and we shall examine slope differences only if they are associated with a statistically significant global interaction of all the experimental groups and the time of delayed testing. In this last respect it is worth noting that the failure to find a statistically significant interaction of treatments and time requires concluding that all initial group differences have totally persisted. Since such an inference depends on accepting the null hypothesis, special caution has to be exercised before inferring total relative persistence.

the attitude change finally stabilized. Multiple delayed measures of attitude are obviously required for learning about asymptotes. But they are rare in persistence studies (McGuire, 1969), and their absence makes it easy to mislabel effects.

We are not aware of any acceptable way to avoid the limitations of descriptive persistence labels. This is because most of the available alternatives require unrealistic assumptions; for example, estimates of the rate at which attitude change decays or increases per week assume linear posttest trends. While pictorial plots of time trends would illustrate persistence results most comprehensively, space constraints prevent us from presenting plots here. Instead, we shall use the flawed descriptive labels introduced above,[4] with the warning that they should be treated as tentative and time-contingent.

C. TIME AS AN EXPLANATORY CONSTRUCT

A recurring problem with persistence studies is that time is not a psychological construct. Rather, it is one kind of locator variable for interpersonal or intrapersonal processes which take place in time and directly mediate attitude change and its persistence. Thinking of time in this way stresses the importance of designing studies around the processes that mediate effects rather than around time *per se,* and it is obviously desirable to measure or manipulate these processes directly. Unfortunately, delayed measures seem to have been added to many past experiments "just to see what happens" rather than to examine processes that occur in time and might affect persistence. It is not surprising, therefore, that many studies are more useful for indicating persistence effects that need explaining than for explaining the effects that were obtained.

The fact that time is not a psychological variable means that it is irrelevant to ask how long a persistence experiment lasts, for the same events can often be packed into 1 year, 1 month, 1 week, or even 1 day (c.f., Ronis *et al.,* 1977). But although no single temporal dividing point can be justified for classifying studies as relevant or irrelevant to persistence, such a cutting point has to be specified for purely practical reasons. The choice of a point depends on one's reasons for studying persistence. To argue by analogy with current practice concerning test–retest reliability, the construct validity of "attitude" should be enhanced if the final posttest takes place about 1 week after a treatment. Recall of prior attitude responses might be low by then, and yet attitudes should not have had time to change for reasons that are irrelevant to the manipulations. However, someone interested in the power of attitude change theories for predicting persistence might think in terms of an influence lasting months or years, and final delay

---

[4]Readers who are interested in more detailed descriptions of most of the persistence studies reviewed, and graphs of persistence findings, should see an earlier draft of this chapter (Cook & Flay 1974).

intervals of only a week would be considered somewhat trivial. Since we are interested in persistence for construct validity reasons, we shall include in this review all studies having a final delay interval of 1 week or more. But for persons who find 1 week to be insufficient, we shall also note the length of the period between the treatment and the final delay interval as well as the findings obtained at the later time.

D. SCOPE OF THIS CHAPTER

In this chapter we shall concentrate on four topics which we think may be of interest to most experimental social psychologists: (a) Kelman's theory of social influence, which makes specific predictions about time trends; (b) the dissociative and discounting cue hypotheses, which lead to explicit predictions about relative and absolute persistence; (c) various kinds of message learning factors which might cause persistence; and (d) a variety of consistency approaches which lead to long-term attitude change. After reviewing these areas we will attempt to integrate and synthesize the findings.

Some other issues are important for a comprehensive understanding of persistence but will not be reviewed here because of space limitations. These include how persistence is related to social support, the adoption of innovations, and the effects of therapeutic interventions.

Space also prevents us from dealing in any comprehensive fashion with some important ethical and methodological issues. On the ethics side is the issue of control over people's behavior that might be available if we know all the conditions necessary for producing persistent changes (Bandura, 1977, pp. 113–114). Methodologically, it is important to note that some of the experimental designs used in persistence research require each subject to provide attitude data at several delayed posttest sessions, while other designs have independent groups at each session. Although repeated attitude measurement may well have important consequences for the given attitude, we do not yet know whether it does. It should also be noted that some experiments have only two delay intervals, one immediately after an influence attempt and the other some weeks later. Such designs do not permit us to describe time trends or to compare results across experiments meaningfully. Persistence studies almost inevitably involve subject attrition. If equal across experimental conditions, attrition affects only external validity. But if it is higher in one condition than another, it is more of a problem and constitutes a threat to internal validity. Attrition rates have not always been carefully analyzed in the past, and there are instances of treatment-correlated attrition in which no attempt was made to assess the plausibility or magnitude of any resultant biases. Finally, it is often easy for subjects in persistence experiments to talk to each other after the initial treatments have been manipulated. However, it is not yet clear how often this occurs and what effects it has. Although we will not deal with these methodological issues in this chapter, the reader should note that each of them can be examined empirically. Should subsequent research indicate that these problems are prevalent, then some of the conclusions reached in this chapter might have to be revised.

For the purposes of this chapter we shall define attitudes very broadly to include beliefs, values, feelings, and overt behaviors. While there is reason to believe that these different kinds of variables will sometimes be correlated when measured together, this does not necessarily imply that a change in the observed mean level of one will involve a corresponding change in the other. We shall take care, therefore, to note the class (or classes) of attitude measures involved in particular experiments, and we hope to reach conclusions about independent variables whose observed effects to date are limited to certain response classes (say, beliefs) or can be generalized across more than one such class (say, beliefs and behaviors).

II. Kelman's Theory of Compliance, Identification, and Internalization

Kelman (1958, 1961) is one of the few attitude theorists to have developed an explicit theory of attitude persistence. It is based on specifying the antecedents and consequences of three attitude change processes. *Compliance* is said to cause a lasting change in attitude if, and only if, persons who control means that are important to respondents observe the respondents' expression of attitude and the respondents believe that their compliance with such powerful persons will bring rewards. *Identification* presumably causes persistence if, and only if, a respondent's relationship to an attractive person remains salient and permits the respondent to define himself on the basis of the relationship in some satisfying way. *Internalization* is supposed to occur when respondents are concerned with the congruence between their values and behavior, and this is presumed to happen when information from a credible source leads respondents to reorganize means–end relationships and to see their acceptance of the message as helping to realize important values. Any change resulting from internalization supposedly persists independently of surveillance (which is necessary for compliance to cause persistence) and of the salience of role relationships (which is necessary for identification to cause persistence).

A. THE ONE DIRECT TEST

To our knowledge only one direct test of these persistence predictions has been published (Kelman, 1958). It resulted in what we interpret to be marginal support for the persistence predictions. In the experiment, the communicator in the *means–control* condition was portrayed as someone whose decision to provide funds to the subjects' school depended on whether the subject agreed with his opinions. This manipulation was intended to motivate compliance. The communicator in the *attractiveness* condition was a popular peer, and this manipulation was intended to motivate identification. The communicator in the *credibility* condition was a noted and unbiased authority on the topic, and this was meant to facilitate internalization. Attitude was assessed three times for the same subjects: immediately after the message when the source was made salient and subjects thought he would see their replies (the surveillance manipulation); next, a few minutes later at the same session when the source was salient but no surveillance was apparent; and again, at a session 1 to 2 weeks later when neither salience nor surveillance were present.

To examine the time effects, Kelman conducted analyses within the means-control, credibility, and attractiveness groups. He found (a) that attitude in the means-control condition was more favorable at the first testing when there was surveillance than at the two later times when there was no surveillance; (b) that the three attitude means did not differ in the credibility condition, suggesting that any initial attitude change persisted even though there was neither surveillance nor a salient source; and (c) that the first two attitude means in the attractiveness condition did not differ from each other but differed from the delayed mean when the source was presumably not salient. Kelman interpreted these results as supporting his hypotheses.

However, the data can be looked at rather differently. First, there was most initial attitude change in the means-control condition, and it appeared to decay over time without totally dissipating. While the decay is in line with Kelman's compliance prediction, the absolute partial persistence is not—unless it is assumed that some subjects spontaneously reinstated the source's surveillance at the delay interval. Second, there is no statistically significant decay in the credibility condition. This conforms with Kelman's prediction. However, there also seems to be no difference in decay slope between the means-control and credibility conditions, irrespective of whether one judges from the first or second immediate measure. Yet such a difference would be expected from the theory. Third, there is presumably a total decay of change in the attractiveness condition, and this is in line with Kelman's hypothesis if it is assumed that the source was not linked to the message at the delay interval. But an obvious difficulty in interpreting this decay is that it may be due to the message's effects dissipating with time—a frequent finding—rather than to the source's effects dissipating because linkage with the message was lost.

B. COMPLIANCE

The term "compliance" is used in many ways in social psychology. To evaluate Kelman's compliance predictions by means of experiments that were not designed as explicit tests requires us to be exact in specifying the types of experiments that are relevant to his predictions. Kelman claims that compliance is aroused when subjects believe that their agreement with the opinions of others will bring extrinsic rewards or avoid punishment. This being so, experiments on the attitudinal and behavioral consequences of response-contingent reinforcement are relevant. But the "forced compliance" literature is not relevant because the very dilemma of subjects in these experiments is that their compliance cannot be justified by the small rewards offered them. Equally irrelevant is work on "forward" and "backward" conditioning (McGuire, 1957; Rosnow, 1966), for subjects in this research do not perceive that their rewards depend on agreeing with others.

Let us turn now to the relevant literature which has been invoked to support Kelman's theorizing about compliance. The persuasive message of Schopler, Gruder, Miller, and Rousseau (1968) came from a source they described as "gruff and stern" in his dealings with subordinates, and Kelman's "compliance" idea was invoked to explain why the initial change produced by this source failed to last over 1 week.[5] However, this explanation requires us to assume that subjects anticipated that they too would be treated gruffly and sternly if they did not agree with the communicator. There is no independent evidence of this. In a nonexperimental study, Schein (1958) claimed that there was a high degree of compliance with Chinese prison officials by American POWs, but that this compliance ceased as soon as the Korean War ended and the fear of external punishment was removed. Reviews of the "token economy" literature by O'Leary and Drabman (1971), Kazdin and Bootzin (1972), and Kazdin (1975) have each commented on the dearth of relevant follow-up studies. Kazdin and Bootzin (1972) interpreted the few studies that are available as generally showing that the "removal of token reinforcement results in decrements in desirable responses and a return to baseline or near-baseline levels of performance" (p. 359), although the view now seems to be that maintenance might be possible if systematic fading procedures and/or reprogramming of the environment are instituted (e.g., Jones & Kazdin, 1975; Kazdin, 1975; Walker, Hops, & Johnson, 1975), or if minimal or unexpected rewards are given (e.g., O'Leary, Drabman, & Kass, 1973; Resick, Forehand, & Reed, 1974). Verbal operant conditioning is also relevant to compliance in that behavior is shaped by external rewards. In the

---

[5]Schopler *et al.* cite a study by Kipnis (1958) which also deals with the temporal effects of reward and coercive power. But the results are difficult to interpret. The procedure required telling fifth- and sixth-grade children that some of them would get movie tickets in 3 weeks but others would not, and it is not clear whether subjects believed that their responses at the final delay interval would affect whether they did or did not get a movie pass. Since such a belief is crucial for "compliance" we shall not consider the Kipnis experiment further.

only experiment of this type we could find with delayed measures (Insko, 1965),[6] absolute partial persistence was obtained over 1 week, but was only just significant. It is not clear, therefore, whether this effect would have persisted over a longer period. To date, then, there is no compelling evidence of the absolute persistence of the initial changes in belief or behavior that were caused by obtrusive, response-contingent, positive reinforcements.

If response-contingent rewards are so ineffective in inducing persistence, what about response-contingent punishment? Reviews by Hunt and Matarazzo (1973), and McFall and Hammen (1971) have each shown that aversive counterconditioning does not produce compliance that has long-term effects of great significance.[7]

If compliance, token economies, and response-contingent reward and punishment are so ineffective in facilitating persistence, what happens if rewards are dispensed after a delay or according to a partial reinforcement schedule? To argue by analogy with the literature on resistence to extinction, persistence should be facilitated by such features provided that a response has been acquired. Unfortunately, we know of no experiments in the attitude change or behavior modification literature which vary the percentage or delay of reinforcement. This is surprising given that attitude-oriented reinforcement theorists would presumably predict persistence best by applying to attitudes the well-known principles of behavior *maintenance* as opposed to principles of behavior *acquisition*.

C. IDENTIFICATION

Schopler *et al.* showed that the attitude change caused by a source who treated others pleasantly partially persisted over at least 1 week. This partial persistence was attributed to "identification," but since there is no indication of whether the attractive source was still salient to subjects at the delay interval, we cannot be sure that the effect is due to this process. Kelman (1961) himself described the findings from an unpublished experiment in which subjects received "information . . . designed to spell out the implications of the induced opinions for the subjects' relationship to certain important reference groups" (p. 73). This was called the role orientation manipulation, and Kelman reported that

[6]Scott (1959) had judges tell subjects that they had won or lost a debate on the basis of the style of their presentation. The winners changed belief in the direction they advocated in the debate, and the change seemed to persist over 10 days. However, the delayed testing took place immediately after a second debate on an unrelated issue which subjects won or lost *according to individual merit and not random assignment,* and nearly all the persistence seems to be due to subjects who won their two debates. This makes the effects of winning or losing at the first session difficult to assess.

[7]More supportive conclusions were reached by Rachman and Teasdale (1969) and Eysenck and Beech (1971). However, all the studies they cited involved complex treatment packages of which aversive counterconditioning was only a part, making it difficult to attribute effects to aversive counterconditioning alone.

some of the original attitude change was lost over a period of "a few weeks" and that the source was not noticeably salient at the delayed interval.

It is difficult to draw firm conclusions about the identification at this time because there is little relevant evidence from studies in which the crucial variable of saliency was explicitly manipulated or measured at delay intervals.[8] However, the available evidence, weak as it is, does not at all contradict the conclusion that identification might facilitate partial persistence over short periods under some conditions.

D. INTERNALIZATION

Kelman manipulated source credibility in order to vary internalization and found that total absolute persistence resulted over 1 or 2 weeks when the source was highly credible. This effect has been replicated in an experiment with a 1-week delay interval (Johnson, Torcivia, & Poprick, 1968) but not in nine other studies with longer final delays (Falk, 1970; Gillig & Greenwald, 1974; Hovland & Weiss, 1951; Papageorgis, 1963; Schulman & Worrell, 1970; Watts & McGuire, 1964; Weber, 1971; Weiss, 1953; Whittacker & Meade, 1968). Although partial absolute persistence was found in most of these studies, the larger body of data seems to disconfirm the internalization prediction of total absolute persistence. However, it should not be forgotten that credibility is only one antecedent of internalization. The establishment of the communicator's credibility does not necessarily mean that subjects will believe that accepting his message will help realize their important personal values, which is the essence of "internalization." Hence, manipulating credibility does not necessarily provide a test of internalization.

There is one special context, however, where the attitude change caused by a highly credible source has totally persisted over periods longer than 1 week. This is when the credible source of the message is initially repeated many times or is reinstated to subjects at delay intervals (Johnson & Watkins, 1971; Kelman & Hovland, 1953; Weber, 1972). Once again, we cannot be sure whether internalization was involved in these experiments, because there were no measures of cognitive reorganization and value linkage—measures that would be required for corroborating the link between credibility, internalization, and persistence. However, it does not seem intuitively plausible to us that reinstating the source at the delay interval (Kelman & Hovland, 1953) or mentioning the source 22 times during the message (Weber, 1972) should facilitate internalization, although repeating the message five times (Johnson & Watkins, 1971) might.

[8] Stotland and Patchen (1961) manipulated "identification" by presenting subjects with information about someone similar or dissimilar to themselves. This procedure invites subjects to identify with the person described in the persuasive communication rather than, as in Kelman's work, with the person who gives the communication.

Some experiments have manipulated other antecedents of internalization. Cook and Insko (1968) and Katz, Sarnoff, and McClintock (1956) varied the value relevance of persuasive information and did not find persistence over 11 days or 6 weeks, respectively. On the other hand, Kelman (1961) reported an unpublished study in which subjects learned that experimentally induced opinions were related to accepting personal responsibility for their actions, and he claimed that this type of value linkage resulted in absolute total persistence as well as in a generalized effect to other issues and situations. Katz *et al.* (1956), Katz, McClintock, and Sarnoff (1957), Stotland, Katz, and Patchen (1959), and Stotland and Patchen (1961) devised a "self-insight" procedure which they thought would vary Kelman's internalization (Katz *et al.*, 1956, p. 57). This procedure has twice resulted in absolute persistence over periods up to 7 weeks (Katz *et al.*, 1956; Stotland *et al.*, 1959),[9] although only among persons low or moderate in ego defensiveness. A crucial theoretical problem is that it is difficult to ascertain the degree to which the multifactorial self-insight procedure of Katz and his associates corresponds with Kelman's notion of internalization. Katz and his associates assume that their subjects learn about the emotional bases of racial prejudice and come to believe that the value of mental health cannot be achieved by prejudiced persons. If subjects do think like this, then the process would be akin to internalization and the Katz results would largely support Kelman's hypothesis.

For a quasi-experimental test of Kelman's persistence predictions Smith (1976) classified sensitivity group trainees as internalizers or externalizers (compliers or identifiers) on the basis of a pencil and paper measure he designed for the purpose. Smith reasoned that externalizers should attribute any change arising from sensitivity training to the influential and/or attractive group leader. Such change would not be expected to persist when the group leader was no longer salient. Internalizers, on the other hand, should attribute any change to themselves and such change should persist over time and generalize to new situations. While Smith did not provide any evidence that internalizers actually saw themselves as the origins of changes resulting from sensitivity training, he did find, as expected, that such change totally persisted for up to five months on self-report measures for internalizers but significantly decayed for externalizers. This finding is of considerable theoretical importance but still needs to be replicated in true experiments. Indirect evidence for the internalization explanation of the persistence of change arising from sensitivity groups comes from a study by Allen reported in Lieberman, Yalom, and Miles (1973). Allen found that former

---

[9]The Scotland and Patchen (1961) data are difficult to interpret since not all of the pretest and immediate posttest data are reported, and the possibility of statistical regression artifacts cannot be ignored.

sensitivity training group participants who had maintained change engaged in activities that would theoretically be expected of internalizers (e.g., taking personal initiatives) while those who failed to maintain change stressed the reactions of important others as would be expected of externalizers.

Overall, the evidence for Kelman's persistence predictions from his concept of internalization while promising, is, nonetheless, still equivocal. This is partly because of the difficulty of measuring the cognitive reorganization that is supposed to buttress internalization. The existing studies do not include such measures. Rather, they rely on manipulating presumed antecedents of internalization. This would be acceptable if all the antecedents were varied simultaneously, but in no existing study is this the case.

III.   Dissociative and Discounting Cue Hypotheses

The most crucial assumption of the work on persuasion by Hovland and by McGuire is that attitude change can usefully be conceptualized as a two-factor process. The first factor involves learning a persuasive message, and the second involves associating the message with a cue that leads subjects to accept or reject the message. (Rejection cues are sometimes called discounting cues.)

The basic notion underlying this approach comes from paired-associate learning, and relative persistence is predicted under two conditions: first, when an acceptance cue is initially linked to a message and remains associated with it over time versus when the association is forgotten; and second, when a rejection cue is initially associated with a message but later becomes dissociated from it versus when the association remains. Thus, the same process of initial association and subsequent dissociation should *inhibit* relative persistence when message-acceptance cues are eventually dissociated from a message, and should *facilitate* persistence when rejection cues are dissociated. Traditionally, the process common to both the message-acceptance and message-rejection cases is called the *dissociative cue hypothesis*, while the prediction for the message-rejection case alone is called the *discounting cue hypothesis*.

The discounting cue hypothesis has evoked most interest in the past, largely because Hovland, Lumsdaine, and Sheffield (1949) used it as one possible explanation of what they claimed was a "sleeper effect." They reasoned that a discounting cue will initially inhibit the attitude change caused by a persuasive message, but that once the message and cue are dissociated this inhibition will be removed and delayed attitude will come to be under the control of the message. Hence, when the discounting cue is dissociated, attitude should revert upward over time to the level of attitude change produced by the message, thereby resulting in an absolute sleeper effect.

A. DISSOCIATIVE CUE HYPOTHESIS

Two direct tests of the general dissociative cue hypothesis exist, and each provided supporting results (Kelman & Hovland, 1953; Weber, 1972). Kelman and Hovland (1953) had subjects learn a persuasive message, and their attitude was assessed immediately afterward and 3 weeks later. The authors varied source credibility (high vs. low)[10] as the message-acceptance and rejection-cues, and these cues were or were not reinstated at the delay interval. Attitude change decayed less when the high credibility source was reinstated than when it was not.

Since the reinstatement of the source may have reinstated any "demand characteristics" associated with the initial manipulation of credibility, Weber (1972) varied the associative strength of the message and cue during initial exposure to a persuasive message. He also obtained the delayed attitude measurement in the subject's home environment using testers who were ignorant of the experimenter's hypothesis. His design involved two levels of source credibility, mentioning the source's name two or 22 times during or after reading a persuasive message, and having each subject's attitude assessed immediately after the message and either 3 or 7 weeks later. A statistically significant three-way interaction of source credibility, associative strength, and time of testing resulted. When the source was mentioned twice, the decay of attitude change was greater in the high credibility condition than in the low credibility condition, but when the source was mentioned 22 times the opposite relationship was obtained. This is what the dissociative cue hypothesis predicts.

The results from these two studies suggest that the basic dissociative theory which led to predicting the absolute sleeper effect is probably not wrong.

B. DISCOUNTING CUE HYPOTHESIS AND ABSOLUTE SLEEPER EFFECT

The greater *relative* persistence found in the low credibility conditions where there was more *versus* less source–message dissociation (Kelman & Hovland, 1953; Weber, 1972) suggests that an absolute sleeper effect could result from the discounting cue process. However, the appropriate time trend was not even in the required direction in Weber's study, and it was not statistically different from zero in Kelman and Hovland's study. Thus, the studies that supported the dissociative cue hypothesis and hence the discounting cue hypothesis did not support the hypothesis that there would be an absolute sleeper effect in the discounting cue condition.

In a review of the pre-1978 literature, Cook et al. (1978) found 13 other

[10]Kelman and Hovland (1953) actually had positive, neutral, and negative communicators, but the final delay means for the neutral communicator were not presented.

papers reporting studies involving discounting cue manipulations, some of which included the results from several different experiments or from several discounting cue variations within the same experiment[11] (Falk, 1970; Gillig & Greenwald, 1974; Holt & Watts, 1973; Hovland & Weiss, 1951; Johnson et al., 1968; Johnson & Watkins, 1971; Kelman, 1958; Papageorgis, 1963; Schulman & Worrell, 1970; Watts & McGuire, 1964; Weber, 1971; Weiss, 1953; Whittacker & Meade, 1968). In these 13 papers trends toward an absolute sleeper effect were obtained in seven (Falk, 1970; Gillig & Greenwald, 1974; Holt & Watts, 1973; Hovland & Weiss, 1951; Kelman, 1958; Kelman & Hovland, 1953; Papageorgis, 1963). Where tests could be carried out, only one of these was statistically significant (Holt & Watts, 1973), and interpretation of this finding is somewhat obscure because retention of the message was higher in the discounting cue condition. Thus, there is little evidence to date that the discounting cue process often results in absolute sleeper effects.

However, the sleeper effect that is predicted from the dissociative cue hypothesis may not have been strongly tested as yet. A failure to obtain the effect would only invalidate the discounting cue hypothesis from which it was derived if all the theory-specified conditions necessary for the effect had demonstrably been present in the experimental tests. The necessary conditions for the effect have been derived by Cook (1971; Cook et al., 1978). First, the message must by itself be capable of causing considerable amounts of attitude change. Second, the discounting cue should be so powerful that it significantly inhibits the attitude change that the message would otherwise have caused. Third, the discounting cue and message should be dissociated by the time of delayed attitude measurement. And fourth, the level of attitude in a message only group at the delayed measurement must be higher than the level found in the discounting cue group immediately after exposure to the message. This last condition is the most crucial, for it defines the maximum distance that attitudes in the discounting cue group can increase over time if they are to cause a sleeper effect by changing—as theory predicts—to the level found in a message only group after dissociation. The fourth condition will be facilitated (a) if the initial attitude change in the

---

[11]Where discounting cues are presented at different points in an experiment we shall report findings from the condition where the cue is presented before the message; and where several experiments are reported in a single paper we shall report findings from a composite. In making such selections we omitted no individual conditions or experiments which appear to result in an absolute sleeper effect. Low credibility provides the discounting cue in all but three experiments. Weiss (1953) used a brief countermessage attached to the basic persuasive communication; Papageorgis (1963) did or did not insert qualifying statements into a message; while Holt and Watts (1973) prewarned half of their subjects that the message was designed to change attitude. Only the first and last of these papers were designed as explicit tests of the sleeper effect. The prediction for the second experiment was couched in terms of arresting decay rather than increasing change.

message only group decays slowly, and (b) if the discounting cue dissociates rapidly from the message.

These necessary conditions for a test of the absolute sleeper effect are derived from the discounting cue hypothesis. They do not by themselves guarantee a statistically powerful test of the sleeper effect because they make no reference to variability. The Sleeper Effect Ratio (SER) below provides a convenient summary of the theoretical conditions conducive to a powerful *statistical* test of the absolute sleeper effect. The numerator of the formula is based on the crucial fourth condition just described and the denominator is an estimate of the standard error that will be used for actually testing a sleeper effect. Taken together, the numerator and denominator indicate whether the maximum distance over which attitude in a discounting cue group can change over time is large enough, given the variability, that a sleeper effect could be statistically corroborated if one occurred. A minimal requirement for a strong test, therefore, is that SER exceed the t-value associated with the alpha level and degrees of freedom that are to be used in direct tests of the mean change which would indicate whether a sleeper effect had taken place. The formula is:

$$SER = \frac{\overline{X}_{PD \cdot MO} - \overline{X}_{I \cdot DC}}{\text{Particular standard error used for directly testing the absolute sleeper effect}}$$

where:

$\overline{X}_{PD \cdot MO}$ = the attitude mean at the post-dissociation testing (PD) in a message only group (MO);

$\overline{X}_{I \cdot DC}$ = the attitude mean at the immediate post-message testing (I) in a discounting cue group (DC).

SER can be computed in any experiment to test whether the theoretically specified necessary conditions for a strong test of the sleeper effect have been met, and whether a statistical test powerful enough to detect the effect, if it exists, can be conducted. Of course, SER can somewhat over- or under-estimate the power of any subsequent test of the absolute sleeper effect because sampling error entails that the means in the numerator will randomly deviate from their population values. Unfortunately, the SER formula is not as useful as it should be for examining whether past studies have been strong tests of the sleeper effect, because it is crucial to know whether dissociation has taken place. But dissociation measures were rare in the past. Moreover, the discounting cue hypothesis is not specific as to the aggregate level of dissociation that must occur in any experimental condition before it is warranted to claim that "enough" dissociation has taken place. Keeping these limitations in mind, Cook *et al.* (1978) used SER to provide an approximate indicator of whether past studies met conditions for a powerful test of the absolute sleeper effect, and they concluded that the conditions were probably not met in most past experiments.

Testing the sleeper effect requires more than demonstrating that the theory-derived necessary conditions for a strong test have been met. It also requires that all countervailing forces have been ruled out. A major countervailing force in many persistence studies is the immediate attitude change that is found in a discounting cue group. We would expect this change to *decay* with time, and so countervail against obtaining an absolute *increase* in change over time. Thus, it is possible that, even if all the previously discussed conditions for a strong test of the sleeper effect were met, the failure to suppress initial attitude change in a discounting cue group would nonetheless prevent an absolute sleeper effect from occurring. In fact, Cook *et al.* (1978) were able to show that in the few sleeper effect experiments where SER may have been sufficiently high, there was nonetheless some immediate attitude change in all the discounting cue groups. This change should have worked against obtaining a sleeper effect, and it suggests that the sleeper effect was not strongly tested in any study prior to 1978.

Failure to obtain the absolute sleeper effect in strong tests would suggest that the paired-associate approach to attitude change favored by Hovland and by McGuire could not be generalized to account for the forgetting of message-cue associations. Instead, it might have to be limited to contexts of immediate attitude change where the *learning*, rather than the retention of message-cue associations is at issue. Fortunately, *demonstrably* strong tests of the absolute sleeper effect have recently been conducted (Gruder *et al.*, 1978), and they *repeatedly* resulted in absolute sleeper effects. In one experiment subjects read a persuasive message about either the disadvantages of a four-day work week or the disadvantages of permitting right turns when traffic lights are red. Each message was or was not accompanied by a brief statement which suggested that the information in the message was ''false.'' Subjects' attitudes were assessed both immediately after the message and five weeks later at an unrelated experimental session. The data showed that for one topic but not the other, SER was probably large enough and the discounting cue manipulation suppressed all attitude change. Thus, the conditions for a strong test of the absolute sleeper effect were clearly met for one message and not for the other. Analysis of the attitude data showed a statistically significant sleeper effect where the conditions were met and no such effect where they were not met.

A second experiment was designed to replicate and extend the first by linking the four-day work week message to five different discounting cues that varied in strength and kind. Half the subjects' attitudes were measured immediately after the message, and all the subjects' attitudes were measured by phone six weeks later by persons who did not know the subjects' experimental condition. Analyses of the data relevant to the conditions for a strong test showed that (a) there was no initial attitude change in three of the five discounting cue groups; (b) SER was large enough for these three conditions; and (c) direct measures of dissociation revealed that over 75% of the subjects in each cue group dissociated the cue and the message. Thus, the conditions for a strong test were clearly met for three cue groups and were not met for the other two. Absolute sleeper effects were reliably obtained in the three cue groups where the conditions for a strong test were met, and no such effects were obtained in the two cue groups where the conditions were not met.

These studies demonstrate that the absolute sleeper effect that is predicted from the discounting cue hypothesis is both reliable and valid. It is reliable in the sense that it has been replicated across experiments, discounting cues within experiments, repeated versus independent delayed attitude assessment, and two different techniques of delayed measurement (in an experimental session and by telephone at home). Though replication with different messages, in different laboratories, and with different orders of presenting the message and cue are still needed, it does seem that the absolute sleeper effect is valid by criteria of both convergent and divergent validity insofar as the effect occurred when the theory-derived conditions for a strong test were demonstrably met, and did not occur when these conditions were demonstrably not met.

IV. Retention of Message Details

This section examines data relevant to the hypothesis that the retention of details from a persuasive message facilitates persistence. It is divided into two sections dealing with the relationship of persistence to: (a) the retention of the combined details from a message; and (b) the retention of specific details that are in a message or are generated about it.

A. RETENTION OF ALL MESSAGE DETAILS COMBINED

Five strategies have been used for examining how the duration of attitude change is related to the retention of global details from a persuasive message. These involve (a) varying the frequency of exposures to a message in order to manipulate the *degree* of initial message learning; (b) varying the amount of persuasive material made available to subjects in order to manipulate the *amount* of initial learning; (c) examining attitude and retention time trends in order to ascertain the degree of isomorphism; (d) correlating measures of delayed or changed attitude with measures of retention in order to assess the degree of association; and (e) testing the fit between observed data patterns and specific complex patterns that would be predicted if retention and persistence were simply related to each other.

Of these strategies, the first is clearly the most efficient. By varying the number of exposures to a message, equal initial learning and comparable levels of immediate attitude change can be ensured while creating differences in retention. Other means of studying retention confound differences in retention with differences in initial learning or "selection," or else retention is inferred without being directly manipulated or measured. The fifth strategy is particularly weak in this last respect.

1. Direct Manipulation of the Degree of Initial Message Learning

Degree of initial learning has been manipulated by repeated exposure to a message. Repeated exposure has twice facilitated persistence: once when subjects heard a message five times (Johnson & Watkins, 1971), and once when some arguments in a court case were repeated three times while the opposite side was presented only once (Wilson & Miller, 1968).

There is one study in which the degree of initial message learning appears not to have facilitated persistence (Greenwald, 1968). Greenwald manipulated the degree of initial message learning by having half his subjects rehearse six underlined arguments in favor of a proposition while the other half rehearsed the arguments against the proposition. A week later each group remembered more of the arguments that it had rehearsed, but there was no corresponding difference in delayed attitude. The absence of delayed attitude differences is hard to interpret, especially in light of the Johnson and Watkins (1971) and Wilson and Miller (1968) findings. One possibility is that Greenwald's manipulation of differences in retention was not strong enough to cause differences in delayed attitude. Also, the self-paced rehearsal of persuasive material might have different consequences for attitudes than forced multiple exposure to persuasive material.

It is not clear from the two experiments where repeated message exposure was related to persistence whether or not the relationship was causal in any simple way. For instance, repeated message exposure might have induced subjects to regard the message as more convincing. Alternatively, responding to an attitude scale after being repeatedly exposed to a message on the same topic may set up "demands" to respond in the same way when the same measure is later readministered at a delayed session of the experiment. Despite these problems of interpretation, it would be premature at this time to suggest that persistence is not related to the retention of the combined details from a persuasive message as Greenwald (1968) or McGuire (1969) have done on the basis of earlier studies where the degree of initial message learning was not deliberately varied.

2. Direct Manipulation of the Amount of Initial Learning

It is easy to vary the amount of persuasive material in a message, and two experiments indicate that persistence is positively related to the number of points in a message which support its general conclusion (Calder, Insko, & Yandell, 1974; Leventhal & Niles, 1965). Thus, the basic pattern of results parallels the predominant pattern found in studies which manipulated the degree of initial learning.

Two features are worth noting about the experiments on the amount of learning. First, a deliberate attempt was made in each case to select units of learning (e.g., a lawyer's argument) which might be assumed to be sufficient for persuasion. This is quite different from measuring other units of message learning which, while they may measure attention to a message, do not necessarily measure comprehension of its crucial change-inducing points. What would be gained from learning more of the information in a message if this information does not change attitudes? Second, varying the amount to be learned virtually guarantees differences in retention. Unfortunately, it usually also varies the message's credibility, as well as assuring that retention is confounded with initial learning and with initial attitude change.

3. Comparisons of Attitude and Retention Time Trends

Papageorgis (1963) exposed subjects to a message, and then randomly assigned them to having attitude and retention measured immediately after the message or after delays of 2 days, 2 weeks, or 6 weeks. The retention data seem to have followed the classical forgetting curve. But the attitude change data were not related to time in the same way, for the change totally persisted over 2 weeks but then decayed between 2 and 6 weeks. A similar nonisomorphism of retention and attitude time trends is evident in the experiment of Watts and McGuire (1964) where each subject's attitude was measured at each of three delay intervals. It seems unlikely, therefore, that the absolute persistence of attitude change is dependent in any *simple* way on the retention of broad message details after a single exposure to a persuasive message.

4. Correlations Between Attitude and Retention

Many investigators have presented correlational evidence about the relationship of attitude and retention. These have either been within-cell, product-moment correlations, or impressions gleaned from "eyeballing" the association between mean attitude and recall in different experimental groups. To give an instance of this last point, Hovland and Weiss (1951) demonstrated that high and low source credibility conditions did not differ in the delayed recognition of message details but that the conditions did differ in the percentage of persons whose attitude changed from the immediate to the delayed posttest. Thus, retention and attitude *change* means do not seem to have been related.

Most researchers have favored correlating attitude and retention at each delay interval rather than computing attitude change scores. Such scholars have asked whether knowledge of a message is differently correlated with attitude states at different points in time. Both N. Miller and Campbell (1959) and Watts and McGuire (1964) answered "yes" to this question, since they found positive correlations between retention and attitude immediately after a message but negative correlations later. Other scholars have not replicated this pattern of findings, but have produced at best very modest positive correlations at delayed testings (e.g., Insko, 1964; Wilson & Miller, 1968). It seems unlikely that retention of message details and delayed attitude are related in any simple way, though they may be related in complex ways.

5. Predictions Assuming Isomorphism Between Retention and Persistence

There have been two experimental traditions assuming a causal relationship between retention and persistence. N. Miller and Campbell (1959) used Ebbinghaus's forgetting curve to make predictions about retention when a two-sided message was presented to subjects. One prediction was that, when a week intervened between exposure to the two sides of the message, the side learned last would be better recalled immediately after it was presented, but its superiority would decrease the longer the time interval between presenting the second side of the message and measuring retention. The assumption here is that a recency effect initially occurs but then wears off. Given this, and further assuming that retention and attitude are closely related, Miller and Campbell predicted that the increase in attitude change caused by the argument presented last should decrease as the interval between presenting the second side and measuring delayed attitude increased. This hypothesis was corroborated by N. Miller and Campbell (1959), Insko (1964), and Wilson and Miller (1968).

Miller and Campbell made a different retention prediction for the situation where two sides of an argument are presented immediately after each other. They hypothesized that the side presented first would reach a higher asymptote for forgetting and that the side presented first would therefore have an advantage in attitude change at the final delay interval (the so-called primacy effect). The primacy effect prediction is weaker than the recency one, since it depends on the assumption of differential asymptotes which is hard to justify. It is perhaps because of this that the persistence effect predicted and obtained by Miller and Campbell (1959) has not been replicated (Insko, 1964; Richey et al., 1966; Thom et al., 1961; Wilson & Miller, 1968), although some writers have claimed a slight (but statistically nonsignificant) trend toward primacy (e.g., Beigel, 1973, Luchins & Luchins, 1970). Thus, the experiments on primacy and recency stimulated by Miller and Campbell do not offer unequivocal support for the hypothesis that the retention of message details causes persistence.

The second experimental tradition assuming a causal connection between retention and persistence is concerned with "forward" and "backward" conditioning. McGuire (1957) varied the order of presenting desirable or undesirable information and found relatively more initial attitude change when the desirable information came first. He explained this in terms of the desirable information causing subjects to pay greater attention to the later part of the two-sided message and this greater attention causing greater learning. Though there was absolute partial persistence over 1 week in both order conditions, the crucial finding was that the initial difference between the order conditions was maintained over time. Rosnow (1966) conducted a second experiment on forward conditioning. He had some subjects believe that the rewards or punishments they received after improvising arguments depended on the quality of their improvisation. For other conditions, the rewards or punishments were associated with other arguments not yet improvised. Thus, there were four experimental groups: "forward reward" where positive information is presented first and is meant to increase the attention to later information; "forward punishment" where less desirable information is presented first and is meant to decrease attention to later information; "backward reward" where desirable information that comes later is meant to positively affect opinions derived from earlier information; and "backward punishment" where undesirable information that comes later is meant to negatively affect opinions derived from earlier information. A complicated data analysis revealed that over 17 days the "forward" effects of reward totally persisted, the "forward" effects of punishment totally decayed, and the "backward" effects of both reward and punishment may have partially persisted. Thus, presenting positive information first seems to facilitate relative persistence. Unfortunately, Rosnow did not measure the amount of learning that took place in his different conditions.

Taken together, the McGuire (1957) and Rosnow (1966) experiments are suggestive of an isomorphism between retention and delayed attitudes. However, they cannot be taken as definitive on the issue because alternative explanations of the basic findings are possible. For example, desirable or rewarding topics may reinforce the response of agreeing with later messages without necessarily affecting long-term retention. Rewarding messages may also cause subjects to feel better and it may be this elevation of hedonic tone which conditions "forward," again without necessarily influencing long-term retention. While the McGuire and Rosnow experiments are suggestive, a learning explanation of why the "forward" conditioning of attitudes appears to cause relatively more persistence than "backward" conditioning is not the only one possible.

6. Summary of Five Traditions Devoted to the Retention–Persistence Relationship

We can briefly summarize the major implications of these five different traditions devoted to examining the relationship between persistence and the retention of all message details combined. Varying the frequency of exposures to all or part of a message demonstrably facilitates retention and also, under some conditions, the persistence of attitude change. Varying the amount of persuasive material to which subjects are exposed also seems to cause persistence. Thus far, the evidence seems clear. However, the correlational evidence implies that persistence is not simply related to the amount learned after one exposure to a message, and this conclusion is also suggested by the nonisomorphism of attitude and recall time trends. Finally, although some predictions about persistence that are based on differences in message learning have been corroborated, the experiments are not definitive in ruling out other interpretations of the findings.

Overall, then, persistence seems to be related to the strongest manipulations of the retention of message details (variations in the number of message exposures or in the amount of information initially learned), but is not so clearly related when weaker correlational evidence is considered or when indirect manipulations of retention are involved. Although the evidence is equivocal, there are indications of a causal relationship, and it would be premature to suggest that persistence is not at all related to the retention of broader details of a persuasive communication.

We wonder, however, whether it might not be more fruitful in the future to modify the style of research on learning and persistence. For instance, we might use parametric designs to study the temporal effects of different numbers of message exposures. This would be an improvement on the simpler designs of the past which had only two levels of exposure and two delay intervals, or which had no direct manipulations at all and instead manipulated retention indirectly or computed correlations. More radically, we might want to assume that the whole retention–persistence problem is naively posed and may not be worth pursuing. After all, it is difficult to establish a theoretically compelling unit of recall. Should one measure recall of each of a message's basic arguments, or is recall of its factual details better? What is an argument or fact, anyway? Since not all facts and arguments are equally "persuasive" initially, why should they be assigned equal weights in retention tests, as they typically are? Would a time trend of the number of weighted persuasive arguments that subjects remember be as unrelated to attitude time trends as the recall of unweighted global arguments seems to be (Papageorgis, 1963; Watts & McGuire, 1964)? Are there particular message factors other than the arguments or facts in a message that are crucial for determining persistence if they are retained?

B. RETENTION OF SPECIFIC DETAILS

As we have just noted, it is important to determine what elements of a message may be most crucial for determining persistence. In this section we will examine how persistence is related to: (a) information that contradicts a basic message; (b) specific details of the message, especially the conclusion; and (c) information about a message that subjects have generated for themselves.

1. Arguments Countering a Persuasive Message

McGuire's (1964) theory of resistance to persuasion is based on an analogy with biological inoculation, and the theory has given rise to ingenious tests of some of its complex hypotheses. McGuire assumes that the persistence of resistance to persuasion is determined first by what one learns before a persuasive message is heard, and second by how one learns the contents of the message. He has worked mostly with three ways of defending beliefs. *Supportive* defenses involve bolstering the subject's existing beliefs with rational arguments which he reads before exposure to a persuasive message. McGuire assumes that supportive arguments will be quickly forgotten in accordance with the classical forgetting curve. *Refutational-different* defenses involve subjects learning arguments which will refute points different from those that will appear in a later message attacking their beliefs. Such defenses signal to subjects that their prior belief is vulnerable. But defending their belief will be difficult since few environments contain cogent information about the cultural truisms that McGuire used as the topics of his messages. It was this lack of ways to defend a belief which prompted McGuire to conclude that any resistance conferred by the refutational–different defense should be due to motivational rather than cognitive forces. Such a "motivating threat" mechanism, he predicted, would result in a monotonic decay trend because subjects would need time to accumulate defensive material and because their motivation to find such material would be high at first but would decrease as time passed and no attack followed. *Refutational-same* defenses inform subjects how to refute the very attack they will later receive. It is assumed that the persistence of resistance conferred by refutational–same defenses depends both on the retention of specific refutational arguments and also on the motivating threat mechanism described above. Weighing the persistence conferred by each of these sources equally, as McGuire does, results in a time trend where the decay in a refutational–same condition continuously increases, with more decay being expected between later time intervals than earlier ones.

McGuire's theory is important because it postulates that the learning of different kinds of message content may be important for understanding persistence in environments *hostile to beliefs.* Most of the other learning approaches we examine implicitly assume a neutral postmessage environment—an assumption that restricts the range of their applicability and also obscures the question of whether learning factors differ in importance when the postmessage environment can be grossly characterized as supportive, neutral, or hostile to a new attitude. Moreover, McGuire's work exemplifies theorizing that makes specific predictions about the form of time trends, and such specificity is one way of increasing our confidence that the data corroborate a particular theory.

Four studies (McGuire, 1961, 1963; McGuire & Papageorgis, 1961; Rogers & Thistlethwaite, 1969) indicate that: (*a*) passively read refutational defenses confer relatively more persistent resistance than supportive material; (*b*) passively read refutational–same and refutational–different defenses do not significantly differ over 2 or 7 days in the amount of absolute partial persistence they cause; and (c) self-generated refutational–same defenses confer less resistance than passively acquired defenses initially, but almost as much after 2 or 7 days— that is, active defenses show a relative sleeper effect and a (nonsignificant) trend toward an absolute sleeper effect.[12]

The similarity between the refutational conditions suggests that the learning variable most strongly related to persistence is knowledge that *a* defense of *an* attack is possible. It does not seem to be especially important that subjects can recall arguments that specifically counter the content of a persuasive message. The crucial factor seems to be: "I've heard some defense of that belief" rather than "I know how to refute that argument." Further support for this explanation is provided by Rogers and Thistlethwaite (1969) who found that for refutational– same defenses subjects' beliefs were more closely related to their global evalua- tion of a message than to the retention of its details. Thus, tests of McGuire's theory of resistance to persuasion suggest the importance of knowing that a position can be defended as opposed to knowing how to defend it.

2. Conclusion of a Message

The conclusion of a message should serve as a convenient summary of the topic and side taken in a persuasive message. It is probably more easily retrieved than any other message detail because it is likely to be repeated more often or used as the global index under which message details are stored. Four studies provide some evidence that persistence is related to the retention of the conclu- sion.

Cook and Insko (1968) found total absolute persistence when a conclusion was reinstated to subjects several days after they had originally learned it. Cook and Wadsworth (1972) found the same when the conclusion was repeated seven times during a message and could later be related to the belief that most of one's peers thought that the original persuasive message was convincing.[13]

There are two studies in which subjects were partitioned after the fact into those who could and could not remember the conclusion—the topic and the side taken—of a message (Watts, 1967; Watts & McGuire, 1964). Although the

---

[12]This pattern of results was also replicated in a composite trend that McGuire (1962) con- structed by combining data from different experiments with different delay intervals. We must, however, be careful not to overgeneralize this effect, for in an opportunistic study of some relevance to the issue Janis, Lumsdaine, and Gladstone (1951) found that a supportive defense conferred some resistance to an attack 3 months later. The attack was the reporting of Russia's first A-bomb explosion, which an earlier message had argued would not occur in the next 5 years. While the study of Janis *et al.* is not definitive, it nonetheless reminds us that McGuire's contrary-appearing results have been obtained only with cultural truisms.

[13]In Cook and Wadsworth's (1972) study, simply repeating the conclusion seven times was not sufficient for persistence. It was only when this manipulation was yoked to the social support manipulation that persistence resulted.

partitioning introduces selection confounds that limit interpretation, partial relative persistence was found by Watts and McGuire for those subjects who could recall the side taken and who also had the message topic reinstated, and by Watts for those subjects who improvise their own persuasive message. Hence, recall of the conclusion was related to persistence, but only under some experimental conditions.

Overall, the four studies indicate that the retention of a conclusion can *sometimes* facilitate persistence. As yet, however, there are too few studies to be certain of the conditions under which this occurs, although it seems that persistence is more likely to be obtained if the message is actively acquired or if the topic or conclusion is actually reinstated or yoked to social support factors.

3. Self-Generated Message Details

The retention of thoughts about the message which subjects have generated for themselves is sometimes related to the persistence of attitude change. The strongest evidence for this comes from Greenwald (1968) and Watts (1967).

Greenwald (1968) measured subjects' beliefs at a pretest. He then asked them to read a message containing three main arguments, to write after each argument comments that they generated for themselves, and to rate their beliefs about the topic. Beliefs about the topic were assessed again 1 week later, when measures of retention of both the actual message content and self-generated cognitive reactions were also taken. An index of the self-generated cognitive reactions (collected during the message) was correlated about .50 with both the immediate and delayed beliefs after partialing on pretest belief. More importantly, the delayed retention of self-generated reactions was positively correlated with delayed belief, but there was no significant relationship between immediate beliefs and immediate cognitive reactions, or between delayed belief and the retention of details from the actual persuasive message. This pattern of data suggests that persistence may be more strongly related to thoughts about a topic that subjects have generated for themselves than to passively acquired details from a message.

Such evidence, while suggestive, is not conclusive. This is because: (a) it is entirely correlational; (b) the measure of retention was restricted in range, from 0 to 4; (c) the correlation of belief and self-generated thoughts at the immediate posttest was probably not significantly different from the correlation at the delayed posttest; and (d) Calder *et al.* (1974) found that recipient-generated thoughts were no more closely related to belief than were details from the persuasive message. In this last respect it is worth noting that the materials of Calder *et al.* involved prosecution or defense arguments from a legal case with which the subjects were presumably not acquainted, whereas Greenwald's materials dealt with admitting Puerto Rico as the fifty-first state or advocating popular election of the Secretary of State. Hence, the different results suggest that the role of self-generated thoughts in mediating persistence may depend on how much prior information subjects have—the more prior information, the more likely cognitive reactions will be congruent with beliefs and the more likely beliefs will remain stable over time.

Watts (1967) provided a direct experimental test of the relative effectiveness of generating one's own message as opposed to passively learning a message provided by an external source. He did this by having some subjects write a message by themselves, while others read a message. The reading and writing manipulations did not cause different amounts of initial attitude change, but the writing condition was clearly superior after 6 weeks. Watts also found that subjects in the writing condition better recalled the topic and side taken, reported greater subsequent discussion of the topic with others, and also tended to report more reading about the topic. In addition, the subjects who reported more subsequent discussion and reading tended to show more change at each delay interval. Thus, the experiment indicates one kind of active acquisition which causes absolute persistence and relatively more persistence than is found after passive reading of a message. The study also indicates that the effects of active acquisition may come about either because self-generation of a message motivates subjects to seek out persons or other information sources that are relevant to a topic, or because self-generation helps subjects better retain the conclusion of a message.

Active acquisition of information is not always more effective than passive acquisition. McGuire and Papageorgis (1961), McGuire (1961, 1963), and Rogers and Thistlethwaite (1969) found that the passive acquisition of refutational–same defenses was superior over time to the active acquisition of such defenses. However, the cultural truisms used in these experiments clearly represent a special case for understanding passive–active acquisition processes. This is because the novel topics make it difficult for subjects to generate relevant information for themselves. Self-generated messages are also involved in the counterattitudinal advocacy literature. However, we know of only two experiments in this area with delayed measures (Collins & Hoyt, 1972; Nuttin, 1975), and each was more concerned with effects of payment levels than with comparing active advocacy and passive reading. In both cases the active and passive groups did not differ in either immediate or delayed attitudes, except when low payment was given for a personally relevant message that had important consequences for the subject. These experiments were unusual, however, in that there were no generalized initial attitude effects due to the counterattitudinal advocacy itself. This is unlike the case with other studies of self-generated persuasive information and suggests that strong conclusions about persistence and active versus passive advocacy may not be justified from the counterattitudinal advocacy studies. Certainly, neither Nuttin nor Collins and Hoyt attempted to draw such conclusions.

It is clear that the self-generation of information sometimes facilitates absolute persistence, but it does not invariably do so. The conditions under which it does are not yet known, but Greenwald's (1968) results, when compared with those of the other studies reviewed in this section, suggest that self-generated cognitive reactions to a message may be more closely related to persistence when subjects have some prior information on the topic and the topic of the message is not strongly counterattitudinal.

4. Summary of Approaches to the Relationship Between the Retention of Specific Details and Persistence

The major question of this section was concerned with which message details, if they are retained, might be related to the persistence of attitude change. The studies reviewed suggest that: (a) knowing that a belief can be defended seems to be more important than knowing any detail about how it can be defended; (b) the retention of the conclusion to a message can sometimes facilitate persistence, although the effect may be limited to conditions where the conclusion is reinstated or is yoked to social support factors; and (c) the retention of self-generated thoughts about a message is sometimes related to persistence. However, further research is needed before we can specify the conditions under which each one of these statements holds. Moreover, there are probably other details of a message which we have not yet studied but that might be related to persistence.

V. Consistency Approaches

Although persuasion experiments use messages to create inconsistencies between the subjects' prior attitudes and the position advocated in a message, these approaches are rarely based on explicit consistency theorizing. We have grouped together six other approaches to attitude change under the general heading of "consistency approaches" because (a) they are derived from explicit consistency theory frameworks, (b) they involve explicit consistency manipulations, or (c) they involve salient discrepancies between two or more behaviors. The approaches are: (a) McGuire's syllogistic theory, which involves inconsistencies between two related beliefs; (b) the symbolic psycho-logic approach of Abelson and Rosenberg (1958), which involves inconsistencies between affect and beliefs; (c) Rokeach's procedure for confronting value discrepancies, which involves inconsistencies between two terminal values or, alternatively, between cognitions about oneself and one's value–attitude system; (d) the "self-insight" procedure of Katz and his associates, which involves inconsistencies between cognitions about one's ideal and real self; (e) dissonance theory, which involves an inconsistency between attitudes and behavior; and (f) approaches based on the observation of discrepant behaviors, which involve inconsistencies between how one behaves and how one wants to behave.

A. McGUIRE'S SYLLOGISTIC THEORY

McGuire (1960a, 1960b, 1960c) postulated that cognitions can be heuristically ordered into "Barbara"-type syllogisms and that, if a persuasive communication altered the minor premise of an argument, then the truth value of a nonmentioned and remote conclusion would have to change if logical consistency were to be restored. He also postulated that there is "inertia" in cognitive systems so that the conclusion should change less than would be logically required for consistency. Since syllogistically related cognitive elements are supposed to be structurally interdependent, McGuire hypothesized

> that inertia would also result in temporal effects, such that the impact of the message on the remote issue occurs only gradually, the opinion on the remote issue continuing to change in the logically required direction for some time after the receipt of the persuasive message [McGuire, 1960a, pp. 345–346].

The clear implication here is of some kind of sleeper effect, caused not by the forgetting of message-cue associations as we have discussed earlier, but by the transmission of influence from one related cognition to another.

McGuire (1960a) showed that belief in a minor premise was changed by a message and that this change partially persisted—in an absolute sense—over 1 week. As far as the unmentioned conclusion is concerned, the predicted initial change was found. Moreover, there was a relative sleeper effect in the sense that the initial change in the minor premise decayed 60% as compared with only 25% for the conclusion. McGuire explained the less-than-expected decay in the remote conclusion in terms of partial "seepage" from the changed premise to the conclusion. However, the expected absolute sleeper effect for the unmentioned conclusion was not obtained. McGuire explained this absence in terms of the immediate change in the conclusion setting up a decay force that countervailed against an absolute sleeper effect. Unfortunately, neither McGuire (1960b) nor Dillehay, Insko, and Smith (1966) were able to replicate the relative sleeper effect pattern at acceptable levels of statistical significance, and no absolute sleeper effects were found.

Two other studies have been cited as support for McGuire's "inertia" and "seepage" effects, though neither study was explicitly designed as a test of these concepts. Stotland et al. (1959) found a sleeper effect 3 to 4 weeks after subjects underwent their "self-insight" procedure. In a quasi-experimental analysis of the effects of a dramatic event on attitudes, Riley and Pettigrew (1976) found that attitudes toward formal and informal contact with blacks changed within a few weeks of the assassination of Dr. Martin Luther King and that this change persisted for three months. However, attitudes toward intimate contact showed no immediate change, but an absolute sleeper effect was observable at the delayed posttest. In neither of these studies was a specific causal chain postulated that was based on McGuire's reasoning about the temporal flow of influence from one cognition to another. Consequently, the presumed causal links were not measured, and it is not clear that the delayed change could *only* have been caused by the immediate change in a related cognition.

The equivocal evidence for McGuire's logic-based "seepage" predictions has to be seen in the context of three mitigating factors. The first is that most of the nonsignificant time trends were in the predicted direction. The second is that there may not yet have been a strong test of the absolute sleeper effect prediction. Such a test requires (*a*) that there should be no immediate change in belief in the remote conclusion, and (*b*) that there be an initial change in belief in the minor premise which totally persists. Without such features, countervailing forces are set up (see the earlier section on the discounting cue hypothesis). The third point to be noted is that when McGuire made the premise and the conclusions salient without manipulating them, he found that they became more closely related to each other over time. McGuire called this increase in consistency the "Socratic effect," and it has been replicated by Dillehay *et al.* (1966), by Wyer and his associates (e.g., Rosen & Wyer, 1972; Wyer, 1974; Wyer & Goldberg, 1970), and in the field study of Riley and Pettigrew (1976). Unfortunately for the theory, there are some indications that this increase in consistency is obtained during exposure to inconsistencies (Henninger & Wyer, 1976) or shortly afterward (Watts & Holt, 1970), and may not depend to a large extent on the time-bound "seepage" of influence from one cognitive element to another. Nonetheless, it must be stressed that a persistent increase in consistency between related beliefs has been obtained and that not all of it may be accounted for by short-term shifts.

B.   ROSENBERG'S "PSYCHO-LOGICAL" APPROACH

Abelson and Rosenberg's (1958) theory of symbolic "psycho-logic" provided the rationale for Rosenberg's (1960) test of whether a change in the affect associated with an attitude object would result in changed beliefs about that object. He hypnotized susceptible subjects and told them they would feel bad whenever they thought or heard about the giving of foreign aid. He then measured some variables tapping cognitive structure and feelings about foreign aid. The cognitive structure measures required rating the importance of values that might be promoted by giving foreign aid and then rating the extent to which subjects believed that giving foreign aid would facilitate or hinder attaining these values. A cognitive structure index was then computed by taking the product of the importance and instrumentality ratings for each value and summing these across the values. Measures of cognitive structure and feelings about foreign aid were measured six times for each subject: once before hypnosis, and then 2, 4, 7, 11, and 18 days later. The amnesia was removed after 7 days, thus permitting a test of persistence during amnesia and after it. Subjects felt that foreign aid was less desirable during amnesia, but the effect decayed afterward. However, the cognitive structure index showed a change, which totally persisted during amnesia and, unlike with feelings about foreign aid, seems to have partially persisted for the 10 days after amnesia removal.

C. ROKEACH'S PROCEDURE FOR CONFRONTING VALUE DISCREPANCIES

According to Rokeach (1973) values are beliefs about "modes of conduct or end states of existence that are personally or socially preferable to an opposite or converse mode of conduct or end state of existence" (p. 5). Rokeach assumes that values are self-justifying, temporally enduring, and cognitively central. He also assumes that they are related to attitudes and beliefs in such a way that a change in values is more likely to affect related attitudes, beliefs, and behaviors than a change in attitudes, beliefs, or behaviors is likely to affect related values.

Rokeach has developed a value confrontation procedure which involves giving subjects feedback about their own and others' values, attitudes, and behavior in order to make them consciously aware that some of their values are discrepant with others, or are discrepant with the subjects' self-esteem or conception of themselves. To achieve this awareness, Rokeach has usually confronted subjects with the different implications of their rankings of the values of freedom and equality, and has obtained value changes that persist over periods as long as 2 years. Most of the experiments have been by Rokeach and his associates or students (e.g., Greenstein, 1976; Penner, 1971; Rokeach, 1968, 1971, 1973, 1975; Rokeach & Cochrane, 1972; Rokeach & McLellan, 1972; Sherrid & Beech, 1976). The only relevant, independent, and published study known to us (Hamid & Flay, 1974) reported a significant change in the ranking of equality by students after 2 weeks, but the final ranking was not significantly different from a control group's final ranking. Thus, the evidence from the sole independent published replication is partly encouraging but not totally so.

The evidence concerning the generalization of change from the target values to other values or related attitudes is mixed. For example, Tables 10.2, 10.3, and 10.5 of Rokeach (1973) reveal few instances of statistically significant differences between the experimental and control groups at the delayed measure, and there is no obvious pattern of replication across either samples or confrontation conditions.[14] This leads us to conclude that the statistical evidence for the

[14]These conclusions about generalization are more cautious than Rokeach's. This is mostly because he relies on statistical tests of the difference between pretest and delayed posttest measures within experimental groups. We prefer tests of this same difference relative to that in the no-treatment control group, since such a comparison does not capitalize upon history, maturation, or testing. We also rely more heavily than Rokeach on replication as one means of reducing the error rate problem. For instance, Rokeach (1973) statistically compared pretest–posttest differences (a) within experimental groups, and (b) between experimental and control groups, for multiple individual values, at three time intervals, in three experiments. It should also be noted that a small degree of "generalization" across values is inevitable because the ranking scale is ipsative.

generalization of value change to other values and related attitudes is weak. However, the trends are promising—the more so because they suggest that the confrontation manipulation may have made subjects more conscious of social values as opposed to self-oriented ones.

With regard to generalization to overt behavior, the data indicate that persons who experienced the value confrontation procedure 90 weeks earlier are more likely than controls to respond to direct solicitations to join the NAACP or to take ethnic courses in college (Rokeach, 1973). These results are impressive since they come from completely unobtrusive substudies with random assignment, and because the NAACP effect was replicated across two experiments. However, no such generalization was found with other behavioral variables in those studies, nor in other studies where behavior generalization was expected (Sherrid & Beech, 1976). Although generalization has been claimed for other studies (Penner, 1971; Rokeach & McLellan, 1972), methodological considerations lead us to be skeptical.[15]

Rokeach's findings have important practical, theoretical, and ethical implications. This being so, we believe that they need further independent replication, using confrontation between other sets of values, and using experimental procedures that differ from those of Rokeach. Another need is to discover which aspects of the complex value confrontation procedure mediate effects. Rokeach (1973, chapter 12) has discussed many possible interpretations of his findings, and his preference is to explain them in terms of subject's feelings of self-dissatisfaction rather than in terms of the inconsistency between values (cf., Grube, Greenstein, Rankin, & Kearney, 1977). The self-dissatisfaction and inconsistency interpretations are not necessarily contradictory, since dissatisfaction with oneself can result from many kinds of inconsistency. Nonetheless, a test of Rokeach's interpretation requires long-term experiments that arouse self-dissatisfaction but do not cause value discrepancies. This will not be easy.

Overall, the work based on Rokeach's self-confrontation procedure shows that persisting change can be obtained from confronting subjects with inconsistencies in their system of values. Moreover, these changes may sometimes generalize and cause absolutely persisting changes in related attitudes and behaviors. But we do not yet know *when* such generalizations occur.

---

[15]Penner (1971) used questionable adjustment procedures in order to equate the control and experimental groups on the pretest ranking of equality before testing for difference in behavior changes. Rokeach and McLellan (1972) found no difference in the number of experimental and control subjects responding to a solicitation from a Committee to End Racism, although there may have been a strengthening of the level of commitment of individuals already predisposed to respond. Greenstein (1976) included information about his behavioral dependent variable in the self-confrontation procedure, so that the behavior changes he obtained may have been results of the manipulation rather than generalization.

D. "SELF-INSIGHT" PROCEDURE OF KATZ AND ASSOCIATES

Katz *et al.* (1956) compared the effects of an informational and interpretational appeal on the racial prejudice of persons who differed in ego defensiveness. The informational appeal involved telling subjects about the cultural relativity of prejudice, while the interpretational appeal involved giving subjects "self-insight" about the unhealthy psychodynamic origins and functions of prejudice. Results from measures of social distance and stereotyping indicated that 6 weeks later more persons who heard the interpretational appeal had changed attitudes than persons who heard the informational appeal. However, this effect held only among persons who were low and moderate in ego defensiveness. The authors reasoned that the interpretation manipulation made salient discrepancies between the subjects' ideal and actual selves, which could be worked through only by persons who were low or moderate in ego defensiveness. They reasoned that persons high in defensiveness would not be able to contemplate the inconsistency, much less work through it, and that the informational and interpretational appeals should make no difference to them.

In a later experiment, Stotland *et al.* (1959) attempted to refine the meaning of their interpretation construct. Some subjects first read material about the psychodynamics of prejudice and then underwent three additional experiences: First, they ordered statements about psychodynamics into cause and effect relationships—the so-called *self-activity component;* second, they were told about the high relevance between the psychodynamic material and the attitudes that they were expected to change—the so-called *relevance component;* and third, they were taught about the importance of understanding the emotional basis of behavior if they were to avoid irrational behavior in the future—the so-called *self-consistency component.* Three control groups underwent the same procedure, but each group lacked one of the three components so as to test which component was responsible for any effects attributable to the global interpretational appeal. Stereotyping declined in the major experimental group and in the one control group where the self-activity component was omitted. Indeed, over 3–4 weeks, there was an absolute sleeper effect in the former case and total absolute persistence in the latter. The sleeper effect found here provides some indirect support for McGuire's (1960a, 1960b, 1960c) contention that there is inertia in the cognitive system, and that only after time has allowed for information processing does the impact of a communication filter down to affect more remote implications. Stotland *et al.* (1959) also replicated the finding of Katz *et al.* (1956) that persons low in ego defensiveness were more responsive to the self-insight procedure. This suggests that persons who are less defensive are better able to process information about discrepancies between their ideal and real selves which the self-insight procedure may bring about. It is interesting to speculate on whether or not this would be the case with all "seepage" effects.

E. DISSONANCE AND RELATED ATTRIBUTION THEORIES

Cognitive dissonance theory provided the dominant orientation to social psychological research in the 1960s. Attempts have been made to reformulate the theory in attributional terms (Bem, 1972), and there does not yet seem to be any well recognized way of distinguishing dissonance theory from attribution theory in studies where cognitive or behavioral dependent variables are measured. Hence we shall not distinguish the interpretations here.

Few dissonance or attribution theorists have been interested in persistence, except with respect to "regret" (Walster, 1964) and those parts of the forced compliance literature where the time interval between manipulating payment and measuring attitude was deliberately or inadvertently varied (Carlsmith, Collins, & Helmreich, 1966; Cook, 1969; Rosenberg, 1968). However, we shall not consider the forced compliance or regret studies here, since they all involved final delay periods of 90 minutes or less.

Dissonance theory has been used to predict that mild threats should be more effective than severe ones for creating resistance to temptation. Three studies in this area have varied the time period between the threat and attitude measurement (Aronson & Carlsmith, 1963; Freedman, 1965; Lepper, 1973), and all resulted in persistent changes in behavior, some of which were evident 45 days after the original influence attempt. It is clear, therefore, that mild threats sometimes have persistent prosocial consequences. What is less clear is whether these changes are due to the postulated cognitive mechanisms, for in the experiments under discussion the results from direct measures of these processes were less confirmatory than the results from the theoretically more remote attitude or behavior-dependent variables.

When subjects perform a counterattitudinal task for low payment, it is assumed that dissonance is aroused and that, since the payment cannot justify the behavior, it will have to be justified in some other way—perhaps by subjects coming to believe that they are performing the task because they like it or support the viewpoints they expound during the task. It is now apparent that low payment reliably increases attitude change only when subjects perceive that they freely choose to perform a counterattitudinal task, and also perhaps if it has important consequences for which they take personal responsibility. Fortunately, the forced compliance experiments with delay intervals of a week or more (Collins & Hoyt, 1972; Nuttin, 1975) varied choice, consequences, and responsibility or can be reasonably presumed to have held them constant at "high" levels. Most immediate attitude change resulted when all of them were linked to low payment, and this change absolutely persisted over 2 (Collins & Hoyt, 1972) or 5 weeks (Nuttin, 1975). However, the sample giving posttest data in the Collins and Hoyt experiment included only about half of the original subjects (i.e., about six per cell), and the complex Nuttin study produced some findings which cast doubt on the generalizability of the effect. In particular, Nuttin included one experimental condition where attitude was assessed *only* at the 5-week delay interval, and in this condition there was no sign of the persistence that was obtained when attitude was repeatedly measured. Also, when Nuttin measured delayed attitude with an item that was not in his immediate attitude test but appears to be highly related to the immediate attitude items, there was again no indication of delayed change. Such findings suggest that Nuttin's effects (and those of Collins and Hoyt?) may be situation- and measurement-specific, or may be due to demand characteristics.

The dissonance/attribution approach has implications for the effects of overpayment as well as underpayment. Just as underpayment is presumed to enhance one's sense of intrinsic motivation for performing a task, so overpayment is assumed to decrease intrinsic motivation—at least initially—since subjects can come to believe that they are working for a reward and not because they enjoy the task or believe in any attitudinal issues to which it relates. Experiments by Lepper, Greene, and Nisbet (1973), Lepper and Greene (1975), and Greene, Sternberg, and Lepper (1976) suggest that the general justification/dissonance/attribution framework is successful in predicting when children will think that they are not working for intrinsic reasons. More importantly for our purposes, they also showed that this perception can remain at a reduced level for up to 3 weeks. Reiss and Sushinsky (1975, 1976) and others have challenged the interpretation of these findings. However, it is clear that whether extrinsic rewards increase, reduce, or do not affect interest in particular activities depends upon the activities involved and the way in which rewards are used (e.g., Anderson, Manoogian, & Reznick, 1976; Calder & Staw, 1975; Condry, 1977; Kruglanski, 1975; Reiss & Sushinsky, 1975, 1976; Ross, 1976). The crucial point to be noted here is that extrinsic rewards can sometimes undermine behavior and that this undermining can persist over time.

Other persistence data have been interpreted in terms of low or high rewards causing people to change the intrinsic value of institutions or objects. Notz, Staw, and Cook (1971) and Staw, Notz, and Cook (1974) found 6 months after the 1969 and 1970 draft lotteries that men whose number would have exempted them from military service were more opposed than others to the Vietnam war. They interpreted this relationship in terms of the perception that a large reward (freedom from the draft) had been unfairly obtained (because of random assignment), and they further reasoned that one way of justifying the unfair large reward would be to have as few persons as possible serve in Vietnam. Staw (1974) extended this reasoning. In a study of men legally bound to enter ROTC, he found that ROTC grades were negatively related to the likelihood of being drafted, and that this relationship could be observed for 6 and perhaps 12 months after the lottery. A survey of attitudes toward ROTC taken about a year after the lottery indicated a similar negative relationship. Staw's interpretation of these results was that dissonance was created in men who were legally bound to enter the service and whose draft numbers would have exempted them from service, and that this dissonance could be reduced by coming to like ROTC more and performing better in it. In another naturalistic study, Doob, Carlsmith, Freedman, Landauer, and Tom (1969) found that discounting goods in a store led to a later decrease in sales of these goods—a decrease that totally persisted for at least 14 weeks. They interpreted this finding in terms of shoppers thinking that they had bought the discounted goods because they were cheap rather than because they were intrinsically worth buying.

Lepper (1973) interpreted his previously reported findings about the consequences of mild threat in terms of the children labeling themselves as "good boys or girls" because they had desisted from engaging in rewarding behaviors when there was no obvious reason for desisting. He took his interpretation from Freedman and Fraser (1966) who found that compliance with a small request facilitated compliance with a larger request 2 weeks later. In a replication of the "foot-in-the-door" technique, as it is known, Seligman, Bush, and Kirsch (1976) found that compliance with the first request will generalize to compliance with further requests only when the first request is large enough to motivate individuals to develop the self-perception that they are "doers." An implication of this "self-labeling" interpretation is that attributions about self can change, sometimes in order to solve cognitive dilemmas, and that such changes may persist and even generalize over time. Similar reasoning is apparent in R. L. Miller et al. (1975) whose self-attribution manipulations had effects that persisted for up to 17 days while their persuasion manipulation did not have persistent effects. Davison and Valins (1969), Davison, Tsujimoto, and Glaros (1973), Dutton and Lennox (1974), and Lau, Lepper, and Ross (1976) have also claimed that "self-labeling" can result in absolute persistence.[16]

Several notes about persistence and the dissonance/attribution literature need to be made before any conclusions can be drawn. First, a higher proportion

[16]A form of "self-labeling" can also be used to explain Rodin and Langer's (1977; Langer and Rodin, 1976) finding that elderly institutionalized persons who might have labeled themselves as having some control over their environment were significantly happier and more active than a comparison group who might not have labeled themselves in this way. This change in attitudes appears to have partially persisted for 18 months. For a variety of methodological reasons, these results must be considered tentative, and independent replication is needed. Schulz (1976, 1978, in press) conducted a replication using different procedures and found that the attitude change induced by a treatment designed to increase the sense of control decayed rapidly to a level below that of a comparison group. However, Schulz's manipulation was not designed to provide a continuous sense of enhanced control, and either this or a failure to replicate may explain the discrepant temporal findings. The social implications of these experiments are very important. However, it would be naive at this time to believe that subtle manipulations designed to have people label themselves as having control over parts of their environment will invariably lead to positive changes in belief and behavior that persist over time.

of the studies derived from explicit attributional orientations contain long-term measures than is true of studies derived from an explicit dissonance orientation. Second, there is still no information about the temporal consequences of some reliable dissonance phenomena such as the effects of effort, forced choice dilemmas, and discrepancies between body states and cognitions. Third, many of the designs used to date involve a single delayed measure with no measurement being made immediately after the first experimental session (the Greene *et al.*, 1976 study provides a notable exception). This makes it impossible to describe time trends and, in particular, to assess whether absolute sleeper effects occur. Fourth, some of the studies were carried out with children, and it is not obvious that the subjects' cognitive repertoires are adequate for the reasoning attributed to them by some theoreticians. Fifth, there is in general better support for the behavioral outcomes that are assumed to result because cognitions have changed than there is for the cognitive changes that were assumed to mediate the behavioral effects! This may be due to a number of factors including, on the one hand, special reliability and validity problems which operate in the cognitive domain, and on the other hand, in most experiments a number of cognitive changes could be used to restore consistency, and few experiments measure all of the possible changes.

Despite these difficulties, the available evidence indicates that a persistent change in behavior can result from mild threats and, under certain conditions, from unexpectedly low or high rewards. These findings are all the more important because the change persists in the presence of the very environmental forces that may have maintained the behavior in the past. For example, in experiments to test whether mild threats decrease the time spent playing with attractive toys, we might expect the more popular toys to be played with once a mild threat was no longer present, simply because these toys are more attractive than the alternatives. Similarly, subjects in the Collins and Hoyt (1972) and Nuttin (1975) experiments were chosen because they strongly believed a point of view opposite to the one they agreed to advocate. More importantly, most of their peers also disagreed with the stand subjects took in the experiments, which suggests that the subjects' change in attitude persisted *despite environmental opposition to it*. Indeed, most dissonance manipulations lead subjects to adopt seemingly counterhedonic beliefs and behaviors, and it is therefore all the more striking that the effects obtained in these studies have repeatedly persisted over long time periods.

F. OBSERVATION OF DISCREPANT BEHAVIORS

Many experiments in social psychology and behavior modification require subjects to perform behaviors that are inconsistent with their normal attitudes or their normal behavior patterns (but usually not both). In other experiments, subjects are asked to imagine themselves performing inconsistent behaviors or to watch others behaving inconsistently. Experiments of this type are interesting because subjects are not provided with information from external sources about cognitive inconsistencies. Rather, they are provided with experiential (or vicarious) knowledge about the consequences of specific behaviors which are not in their active repertoire, although they may wish them to be—as with smokers who wish to stop smoking, or snake phobics who wish to lose their fear of snakes.

This is not the place to try to review in detail the literature on techniques which involve the observation of one's own or others' inconsistent behavior. However, we do want to briefly outline conclusions about persistence that have been derived from reviews of studies using techniques such as behavior rehearsal, systematic desensitization, and modeling. Before doing this, we want to note that the behavior to be changed in such studies is usually a specific discrete behavior that subjects should adopt or toward which their beliefs or affect should change. Unlike the previous literature we have reviewed, there is no stress on abstract issues or the attempt to create a generalized, cognitively anchored change. Furthermore, the subjects in the experiments we shall review here were often volunteers or clients who were already aware of the inconsistency between the behaviors they wanted to perform and the behaviors they actually performed. Such high levels of awareness and desire to change are not characteristic of most of the studies we have examined thus far.

Behavior rehearsal is involved when subjects physically role-play behaving in novel ways. Most of these studies are about emotional role play, and are highly involving for subjects. These role-play studies usually cause absolute total persistence for periods as long as 18 months. The relevant evidence comes from experiments on role-playing disabled persons (Clore & Jeffrey, 1972), role-playing persons who were suffering or dying because of smoking (Elms, 1966; Janis & Mann, 1965; Lichtenstein, Kentzer, & Himes, 1969; Mann, 1967; Mann & Janis, 1968). The evidence also comes from research on psychodrama, as when subjects in a changing and previously all-white community were asked to work through their antagonisms toward blacks (Culbertson, 1957); from research with phobics on "live modeling with participation" (Bandura, Blanchard, & Ritter, 1969; Bandura, Adams, & Beyer, 1977); and from studies where role play plus modeling was used to increase assertiveness (Friedman, 1971) or reduce dating anxiety (Curran & Gilbert, 1975).

Relatively more change and persistence result from performing target behaviors for oneself as opposed to imagining or watching others perform them. The evidence for this proposition comes from Bandura *et al.* (1969) as well as from the subjects in emotional role-play studies who were *passively* exposed to actors role playing and who did not themselves perform the target actions (e.g., Culbertson, 1957; Elms, 1966; Friedman, 1971; Mann & Janis, 1968). In these studies, the observer controls changed less and usually showed less persistence than the experimental subjects, but nonetheless there was some absolute persistence in all of them except Clore and Jeffrey (1972). It is not clear why the results were different in this one experiment from those in the other experiments.

The basic hypothesis that behaviors will be adopted, changed, or repressed as a consequence of observing others has also been well-documented in the modeling literature (see Bandura, 1969, 1977; Flanders, 1968). Moreover, experiments have shown that modeling effects largely persist over time (e.g., Bandura *et al.*, 1977; Bandura, Grusec, & Menlove, 1967; Bandura & Menlove, 1968; Chittenden, 1972; Friedman, 1971; Kazdin, 1973; Leyens, Camino, Parke, & Berkowitz, 1975; O'Conner, 1972; Rice & Grusec, 1975; Rushton, 1975; Spiegler, Liebert, McMains, & Fernandez, 1969).[17] The temporal effects of imagining someone else modeling a behavior (i.e., covert modeling) were assessed by Kazdin (e.g., Kazdin, 1973, 1974, 1976), and the absolute total persistence of avoidance behavior has been obtained, as has a persistent increase in assertiveness. Variables which enhance the persistence effects of vicarious modeling include model similarity, whether the models are ''copers'' or ''masters,'' and whether there is one or many models. Such findings suggest that a persistent change in behavior can result from merely imagining others behave in ways that are not in the subject's overt repertoire.

In systematic desensitization subjects are asked to imagine performing a hierarchy of graded behaviors that they would not normally perform. In this way they must face inconsistencies between the way they behave and the way they wish to behave. Systematic desensitization has consistently caused behavior changes which have absolutely and totally persisted over as long as 2 years (e.g., Paul, 1966, 1967, 1968; see reviews by Kanfer & Phillips, 1970; Lang, 1969). The effects of systematic desensitization have been large and very persistent, so it is not surprising that there have been attempts made to understand why it works (see the above cited reviews). However, the most recent work has not yet definitely isolated the parts of the global systematic desensitization procedure that are necessary and sufficient for its effects. Indeed, it is still not clear whether the effects are due to desensitization or subject expectancy (Kazdin & Wilcoxon, 1976). Though further theoretical investigation is still warranted, the bulk of the data strongly suggests that under some conditions systematic desensitization procedures cause persistent changes in attitude and behavior.

[17]There are some factors that seem to increase the long-term effects of modeling. For instance, when exposure takes place in a relaxed atmosphere (e.g., Bandura *et al.*, 1967; Spiegler *et al.*, 1968), when there are multiple models (Bandura & Menlove, 1968), when the models are live (as opposed to on film) (Bandura, 1969), when judgments of moral dilemmas are according to actors' intentions rather than according to consequences of actions (Cowen, Langer, Heavenrich, & Nathanson, 1969; Glascow, Milgram, & Youniss, 1970; Sternlieb & Youniss, 1975), or when the model's actions are free of explicit preaching as opposed to when he preaches either generosity or selfishness (Rushton, 1975). In addition, the effect of modeling can be enhanced by linking it to other procedures that cause persistence such as behavior rehearsal or desensitization.

The literature on emotional role play, behavior rehearsal, modeling, and systematic desensitization clearly shows that these approaches can produce belief and overt behavior changes that absolutely and totally persist over long periods. Confidence in these findings is increased because: first, the delayed measures in some of these studies were collected using procedures with few obvious demand characteristics (e.g., Clore & Jeffrey, 1972; Elms, 1966); second, though there has been a heavy reliance on individual reports of behavior by subjects, there have also been experiments with direct behavioral measures (e.g., Bandura *et al.*, 1969; Curran & Gilbert, 1975; Friedman, 1971); and third, though there has been a heavy reliance on volunteer subjects who wanted to have their specific behavioral symptoms alleviated, this use of cooperative volunteers has not been universal (e.g., Clore & Jeffrey, 1972; Elms, 1966).

G. SUMMARY OF CONSISTENCY APPROACHES

The research reviewed in this section was concerned with manipulating inconsistencies between: two related beliefs (McGuire); affect and related beliefs (Rosenberg); two terminal values, or cognitions about oneself and one's values and attitudes (Rokeach); cognitions about real and ideal self (Katz); attitudes and behaviors (dissonance theory); and how one behaves and how one wants to behave. The saliency of the inconsistencies used in these studies has varied from very low (McGuire; Rosenberg) to very high (the behavioral approaches; Katz; Rokeach), and the specificity of the elements assumed to be in conflict has varied from very specific (McGuire; Rosenberg) to relatively unspecific (Katz). It is probably fair to conclude that, for nearly all the elements in conflict and for nearly all the levels of specificity, inconsistency has resulted in persistent changes in belief and behavior.

A major problem is to understand the conditions under which inconsistencies produce these effects. It is unlikely that specificity of conflicting elements is necessary for persistence, since persistence was obtained both in studies where specificity seemed high and low. Perhaps a more important condition is the "saliency of the discrepancy," for it is our impression that larger effects tended to result when the saliency was high (e.g., the behavior studies of Rokeach) as opposed to when it was low (McGuire).

VI. Implications of This Chapter

We began this review by outlining three benefits that might be expected from reviewing the persistence literature. These were: (*a*) to explicate persistence theories and hypotheses and assess how well data corroborate them; (*b*) to evaluate how well theories of initial attitude change predict persistence; and (*c*) to estimate how well the construct of attitude change was validated by the criterion of demonstrated temporal consistency in attitude responses. We shall now consider each of these potential benefits in turn.

A. SPECIFIC PERSISTENCE PREDICTIONS

Kelman's is probably the only theory of the temporal persistence of attitude change in social psychology today. However, this does not mean that it is the only source of specific predictions about persistence. For instance, crucial hypotheses derived from McGuire's work on syllogisms and on resistance to persuasion can be tested only with persistence designs. This is also true for predictions derived from what we know about the long-term retention of meaningful verbal material—for example, the work of Miller and Campbell that was based on the theorizing of Ebbinghaus. Persistence designs are also necessary to test predictions derived from extensions of well-tested theories of immediate attitude change. An example of this is the paired-associate learning perspective of Hovland which was extended to cover the forgetting of message–cue associations and led to the dissociative cue hypothesis. But though there are these exceptions, the paucity of explicit persistence predictions is striking. Our suspicion is that most of the experiments with delayed measures included them solely in order to test what would happen to attitude change over time. We doubt whether the measures were included to test specific hypotheses about intrapersonal or interpersonal processes that could happen in time and mediate persistence.

With the exception of McGuire's propositions about resistance to persuasion, explicit persistence predictions have not fared well in empirical tests (e.g., the Ebbinghaus-inspired retention predictions, some aspects of McGuire's syllogistic theory), or they have not yet been adequately tested (e.g., Kelman's theory, some specific predictions from McGuire's syllogistic theory). Other predictions have been supported but not yet independently replicated (e.g., the sleeper effect predicted from the discounting cue hypothesis; the "sleeper effect" that Katz and his associates predicted to result from their "self-insight" procedure). Consequently, past direct tests of persistence hypotheses have not been very informative for specifying reliable determinants of long-term attitude change.

This pessimistic conclusion may reflect the fact that most of the past direct tests of specific persistence hypotheses took place within a persuasion context—a context that has usually not been conducive to persistence.[18] It may also reflect the

---

[18]We do not mean to imply by this that persistence has not been obtained in persuasion contexts. It has sometimes. We mean to suggest only that persistence is less common than nonpersistence.

fact that most persuasion studies have assumed the postmessage environment to be supportive or indifferent to the newly changed attitude. This may not always have been the case, but it is obvious that persistence will be more likely if the post-message environment supports a newly changed attitude, or is indifferent to it, as opposed to when it contradicts the attitude. Finally, the pessimistic conclusions may also reflect the fact that most persuasion experiments have placed major stress on how information was presented to subjects, rather than on the manner in which information was encoded or stored. The current stress may be misplaced. For instance, McGuire's work on resistance to persuasion suggests that knowing that a persuasive message can be refuted may be more important than knowing the specific arguments which refute the message. Likewise, tests of the discounting cue hypothesis suggest that persistence might be influenced less by recall of the message than by whether the source of the message can be retrieved in a way that is linked with some content factor.

B. HOW WELL DO CURRENT THEORIES OF ATTITUDE CHANGE PREDICT PERSISTENCE?

We want now to draw some general conclusions about studies that had long-term measures of attitude but were not designed to test specific theories of persistence. We shall discuss first experiments stressing persuasion and next experiments involving manipulations of attitudinal inconsistencies. A clear distinction between persuasion and consistency approaches to attitude change cannot be made in any simple fashion. This is because so-called persuasion studies attempt to create an inconsistency between the subject's preexperimental attitudes and the attitude advocated in the message, while tests of some consistency approaches have involved persuasive messages in some form or another (e.g., McGuire's work on syllogisms and Katz' work on prejudice). We will, therefore, make loose distinctions based on traditional usage in social psychology.

1. Persuasion Approaches

Few experiments with persuasive messages resulted in absolute persistence. Moreover, when persuasion strategies were experimentally pitted against other strategies—such as writing one's own counterattitudinal message, emotional role play, the Katz "self-insight" procedure, or attribution approaches—the persuasion manipulations invariably resulted in less persistence.[19]

It is important to remember that persistence is related to the *repetition* of a message or source. This implies that persistence can sometimes be obtained in

___

[19]However, it is difficult to compare qualitatively different attitude change techniques, like persuasion versus consistency, because we rarely know the strength of each manipulation, and so do not know if the same results would have been obtained if the relative strengths of the manipulations had been different.

specific persuasion contexts. However, we have not yet explored the effect of repetition in any systematic way. This is sad because it means that the attributes of persuasive messages most germane to persistence have not yet been detailed even though in everyday life many messages are heard frequently and come from multiple sources, each of which uses different kinds of persuasive arguments. Moreover, the repetition and distribution of information play crucial roles in various learning approaches to the acquisition and maintenance of skills, and it is reasonable to assume that they might be just as important for attitudes. Indeed, Kelley's (1967) attribution theory predicts that they will be, for he maintains that subjects are likely to believe that a conclusion ''is true'' if they hear arguments in favor of it from different kinds of persons, with different presumed biases, in different settings, at different times, and across different modalities. Given all of this, it is surprising that the frequency and distribution of exposures has not claimed more research attention.

Research into the conditions under which persuasion techniques results in persistence is all the more needed because persuasive communications can be flexible enough to incorporate many of the persistence-causing variables that emerge from research using nonpersuasion strategies. For instance, one can imagine persuasion strategies based on communicators asking questions of an audience so that listeners generate their own answers which then change their own attitudes. Or communicators might design their messages so as to arouse the types of inconsistency that produce persistence, much as Rokeach does. Alternatively, communicators might organize their messages so as to gradually reach positions that are distant from the initial stand of individuals or groups, as is done in systematic desensitization. Of course, there are practical restrictions to the flexibility of the persuasion paradigm. Moreover, the translation of other techniques into the persuasion paradigm may lead to a decrease in effectiveness. After all, observing emotional role play does not result in as much relative persistence as actively engaging in such role play. Hence, even if a communicator could effectively instruct subjects to covertly symbolize the events that would take place in role play, it is unlikely that this would be as effective in modifying attitudes as role playing itself.

Overall, persuasion approaches have not often led to absolute persistence, and where they have it is not clear what the mediating variables might have been. But since there are few studies devoted to the variables which learning theories and Kelley's attribution theory suggest are most likely to mediate persistence, it would be premature to conclude that the rarity of persistence effects is because persuasion contexts necessarily preclude persistence.

2. Consistency Approaches

One of the most heartening findings of this review was that most of the experiments we labeled as ''consistency'' experiments resulted in absolute persistence. The approaches involving inconsistencies with behavior (emotional role play, behavior rehearsal, modeling) or inconsistencies with cognitions about self (Katz; Rokeach) seem to have produced greater and more persistent change than approaches involving inconsistencies between more peripheral cognitive elements (McGuire's syllogistic theory; Rosenberg). Moreover, most of the effects involving inconsistencies with behavior have been replicated by more than one independent investigator using very different procedures, whereas the effects involving inconsistencies with cognitions about self have not yet been unambiguously replicated by independent researchers, and some predicted effects from approaches involving more peripheral cognitive elements have not yet been strongly tested at all (e.g., the "sleeper effect" prediction from the work of McGuire).

A stronger test of how well different approaches confer persistence requires that they be compared within one experiment. Few such experiments exist. Those that do indicate that: observing one's own behavior usually causes greater and more persistent change than observing others behave in some counternormative way (e.g., Bandura *et al.,* 1969; Mann & Janis, 1968); an attribution manipulation causes more persistence than a persuasive message (R. L. Miller *et al.,* 1975); and writing one's own counterattitudinal message sometimes causes more persistence than passively reading a message (e.g., Watts, 1967).

Some of the long-term changes caused by consistency approaches are obviously prosocial: for instance, increases have been reported in the importance attached to freedom and equality (Rokeach); children have been taught self-control and honesty in ways that caused persistence for periods up to 6 weeks (Freedman, 1965; Lepper, 1973); reductions in smoking have been reported over 18 months (Mann & Janis, 1968); decreases in ethnocentrism (directed toward the physically handicapped) have absolutely totally persisted over 4 months (Clore & Jeffrey, 1972); and reductions in phobic behaviors of many kinds have lasted as long as 2 years for as many as 85% of clients (systematic desensitization). Seen as a whole the long-term changes resulting from consistency approaches are catholic—some influencing cognitive measures, others affective, and yet others influencing measures of reported or overt behavior. Though most of the changes were observed in target-dependent variables, there are hints that cognitive effects may *sometimes* generalize to behavior (e.g., Rokeach).

Most past change attempts have been aimed at modifying neutral beliefs, at inducing new attitudes that would be supported in the subject's normal environment, or at modifying target behaviors that most people, including the volunteer clients in some experiments, would like to see changed (e.g., smoking or phobic behavior). There is, though, a sense in which almost all the past changes were maintained *despite the environment.* If we assume that the level of preexperimental attitude is partly due to environmental forces, then any change from this level must to some extent counteract environmental forces. More important than this, though, are two dramatic examples of consistency-induced change that have persisted despite environmental hostility to the change. Collins and Hoyt (1972) found that students changed a belief that 90% of their peers had initially agreed with, while the children in Freedman's (1965) and Lepper's (1973) experiments played less often with toys that were deliberately chosen as intrinsically attractive to them. Thus, some changes have been maintained in the face of environments that were earlier perceived to be hostile.

3. Synthesizing the Findings

It would be unrealistic to expect to derive an elegant theory of persistence from the heterogeneous collection of consistency studies that we have reviewed. Few of them included the direct measurement of potential mediating processes, and even fewer were specifically designed as persistence studies. At most, we can hope to isolate some tentative points of communality in the findings in order to suggest some data-relevant directions that future persistence research might take.

Four general factors seem to have been present in most of the past experiments where absolute persistence was obtained. First, most seem to have presented subjects with a *behavioral dilemma*. For example, how do I justify not playing with a toy that I like? Why am I not approaching a snake when others can do so and I know that I'm free to stop approaching it whenever I get too frightened? Second, most experiments seem to have generated considerable *emotional affect*, especially when compared with persuasion experiments. A third and related factor is that most experiments seem to have had a high degree of *personal relevance* for subjects. Finally, there were usually *rather obvious ways available for reducing the self-relevant dilemma* and its related arousal state.

One *ex post facto* way of approximately testing the validity of this interpretation is to compare experiments where the four factors were probably present with experiments where one or more of them was missing. Let us note, first, that McGuire's syllogistic theory was the sole manipulation of inconsistency that did not result in persistence. His work was also the least likely to have aroused behavioral dilemmas, and his message topics concerned less personally relevant beliefs than did the work of other consistency theorists (e.g., Collins & Hoyt; Freedman; Katz; Lepper; Rokeach; Rosenberg; Staw). Note next the finding of Collins and Hoyt (1972). They discovered that low payment produced a persistent attitude change only when subjects perceived that they freely chose to write a counterattitudinal essay that would have important consequences for which they took personal responsibility. It is possible that the consequences and responsibility manipulations, so necessary for the effect, increased what we have called personal relevance and/or arousal. Personal relevance may also explain why persistence is sometimes more related to self-generated cognitive work and active information processing than the information provided by experimenters. Katz and his associates found that their self-insight procedure was effective only with persons whose low defensiveness permitted them to work through the disquieting information. It may be that only such persons are capable of considering the personal relevance of the message and finding ways to reduce disquieting arousal. Finally, consider the research which has shown that observing both role play and modeling causes some absolute persistence, albeit less than when active participation is involved. In nearly all the relevant experiments, the observers were addicts or phobics who could "identify" with the similarly afflicted persons they were observing. They may well have come to realize that there was an obvious way of reducing their discomfort by themselves acting like the persons they observed.

Concepts like "behavioral dilemma," "arousal," "self-relevance," and "obvious ways of reducing arousal" are somewhat vague. This, plus the natural latitude of all *ex post facto* explanations, makes our analysis tentative, aimed more at indicating concepts which, after rigorous explication, are probably most worth further investigation than at presenting an integrated set of apparently definitive relationships. While we would have liked to develop an integrated set of findings, we believe that neither the current "state of the art" in the persistence area, nor the data examined, warrant any more definitiveness than we have indicated.

In the preceding paragraphs we stressed variables derived from consistency theories. This should not blind us to the multiply replicated relationship between persistence and the frequency of presenting a message or a source. This relationship suggests a second avenue of possibly fruitful research—one based on using analogs to the concepts that experimental psychologists have found useful for understanding the long-term retention of novel behaviors over time.

C. VALIDATION OF ATTITUDE

Consistency in responding to an attitude object can be interpreted in terms of the consistency between mean attitude ratings at two or more time intervals. Only if there is evidence of such consistency can we begin to infer that some stable "attitude" attribute has been tapped. If attitude is also defined to have affective, cognitive, and behavioral components, then a consistency across these components is required as well as a consistency across time. But the validation of a construct requires not only that a convergence criterion be met (Campbell & Fiske, 1959). It also requires that a divergence criteria be met so that the construct under consideration can be differentiated from its cognates. It would be easy to demonstrate divergence if we were only interested in validating, say, whether a belief has changed. We could simply measure belief in multiple ways and then test whether these measures were affected by an experimental manipulation and remained changed over time, while measures of the nontarget constructs (say, affect) were not influenced by the manipulations. It is difficult to meet the divergence criterion for a global construct like attitude, since it is not operationally clear which variables have to be differentiated from it.[20]

Although the divergence criterion cannot be met, the convergence criterion can be. The experiments we reviewed which had both cognitive (usually belief) and behavioral measures nearly always resulted in a correspondence between the two. This was either in the sense that each was similarly related to a treatment at the delay interval (e.g., Rokeach; Staw), or in the sense that one of them was related to a statistically significant degree while the other only tended to be related but not to a statistically significant degree (e.g., Aronson & Carlsmith; Freedman; Lepper). In addition, there were experiments in which beliefs and reported or intended behaviors were similarly related to treatments at each delay interval or at the final delay interval (e.g., Elms; Levanthal & Niles; Watts). Perhaps most importantly of all, we found no cases of reported discrepancies between beliefs and behavior. That is, beliefs were never related to treatments in one way at one delay interval (or across a series of delay intervals) while behaviors, reported behaviors, or intended behaviors were related to the treatments, or tended to be related to them, in the opposite way. We should also not forget that subjects in systematic desensitization and modeling studies not only behaved differently with respect to feared objects, but also reported less fear (e.g., Bandura et al., 1969) and greater self-efficacy (Bandura et al., 1977).

While the evidence consistently suggests that the cognitive and behavioral dimensions of attitude were related in persistence experiments, three qualifying points should be remembered. First, the evidence is obviously confined to the minority of experiments which had measures of each construct. Second, in some instances, the evidence is based on statistically nonsignificant trends. And third, the relationship between cognitions and behavior does not necessarily imply that any belief changes have preceded, or mediated, behavior changes.

Considerable evidence exists which permits us to assess the degree of convergence between two belief (or behavior) measures taken at different time intervals. Since so many persuasion studies failed to find persistence, we have to conclude that convergence was seldom demonstrated. This means that doubt has to be raised about whether many past persuasion studies really resulted in a change in "attitude," and whether it might not be more accurate to label the observed change as "a temporary accommodation to new information." However, by the same criterion, most of the consistency approaches probably did result in a new "consistency in responding" or a new "stable predisposition." Given the stress on "consistency" and "stability" in defining the concept of attitude, it is surprising to us that delayed measures of attitude are not more common. Indeed, they would seem to be necessary in any study that purports to

---

[20]For example, Campbell (1963) gives a long list of related, but perhaps different, constructs. Among others, his list includes expectation, habit, and predisposition.

be about attitudes, and they are indispensable if we are to learn about "internalized" change as opposed to "compliance" (Kelman, 1958), or if we are to learn about the "basal" component of attitudes as opposed to their "surface" component (Anderson, 1974).

REFERENCES

Abelson, R. P., & Rosenberg, M. J. Symbolic psycho-logic—a model of attitudinal cognition. *Science*, 1958, **3,** 1–13.

Anderson, N. H. Information integration theory: A brief survey. In D. H. Krantz, R. C. Atkinson, R. D. Luce, & P. Suppes (Eds.), *Contemporary developments in mathematical psychology.* Vol. 2. San Francisco, Freeman, 1974.

Anderson, N. H.. & Farkas, A. J. New light on order effects in attitude change. *Journal of Personality and Social Psychology,* 1973, **28,** 88–93.

Anderson, R., Manoogian, S. T., & Reznick, J. S. The undermining and enhancing of intrinsic motivation in preschool children. *Journal of Personality and Social Psychology,* 1974, **34,** 915–922.

Aronson, E., & Carlsmith, J. M. Effect of the severity of threat on the devaluation of forbidden behavior. *Journal of Abnormal and Social Psychology,* 1963, **66,** 584–588.

Bandura, A. *Principles of behavior modification.* New York: Holt, 1969.

Bandura, A. *Social learning theory.* Englewood Cliffs, N.J.: Prentice-Hall, 1977.

Bandura, A., Adams, N. E.. & Beyer, J. Cognitive processes mediating behavioral change. *Journal of Personality and Social Psychology,* 1977, **35,** 125–139.

Bandura, A., Blanchard, E. B., & Ritter, B. The relative efficacy of desensitization and modeling approaches for inducing behavioral, affective, and attitudinal changes. *Journal of Personality and Social Psychology,* 1969, **13,** 173–199.

Bandura, A., Grusec, J. E., & Menlove, F. L. Vicarious extinction of avoidance behavior. *Journal of Personality and Social Psychology,* 1967, **5,** 16–23.

Bandura, A., & Menlove, F. L. Factors determining vicarious extinction of avoidance behavior through symbolic modeling. *Journal of Personality and Social Psychology,* 1968, **8,** 99–108.

Beigel, A. Resistance to change in differential effects of favorable and unfavorable communicators. *British Journal of Clinical and Social Psychology,* 1973, **12,** 153–158.

Bem, D. J. Self-perception theory. In L. Berkowitz (Ed.), *Advances in experimental social psychology.* Vol. 6. New York: Academic Press, 1972.

Calder, B. J., Insko, C. A., & Yandell, B. The relation of cognitive and memorial processes to persuasion in a simulated jury trial. *Journal of Applied Social Psychology,* 1974, **4,** 62–93.

Calder, B. J., & Ross, M. *Attitudes and behavior.* New York: General Learning Press, 1973.

Calder, B. J., & Staw, B. M. Self-perception of intrinsic and extrinsic motivation. *Journal of Personality and Social Psychology,* 1975, **31,** 599–605.

Campbell, D. T. Social attitudes and other acquired behavioral dispositions. In S. Koch (Ed.), *Psychology: A study of a science.* Vol. 6. New York: McGraw-Hill, 1963.

Campbell, D. T., & Fiske, D. W. Convergent and discriminant validation by the multitrait-multimethod matrix. *Psychological Bulletin,* 1959, **56,** 81–105.

Carlsmith, J. M., Collins, B., & Helmreich, R. L. Studies in forced compliance: I. The effect of pressure for compliance on attitude change produced by face-to-face role playing and anonymous essay writing. *Journal of Personality and Social Psychology,* 1966, **4,** 1–13.

Chittenden, G. E. An experimental study in measuring and modifying assertive behavior in young children. *Monographs of the Society for Research in Child Development,* 1972, 7(1, Serial No. 31).

Cialdini, R. B., Levy, A., Herman, C. P., Kozlowski, L. T., & Petty, R. Elastic shifts: Determinants of direction and durability. *Journal of Personality and Social Psychology,* 1976, **34,** 663–672.

Clore, G. L., & Jeffrey, K. McM. Emotional role playing, attitude change, and attraction toward a disabled person. *Journal of Personality and Social Psychology,* 1972, **23,** 105–11.

Collins, B. E., & Hoyt, M. F. Personal responsibility-for-consequences: An integration and extension of the "forced compliance" literature. *Journal of Experimental Social Psychology,* 1972, **8,** 558–593.

Condry, J. Enemies of exploration: Self-initiated versus other initiated learning. *Journal of Personality and Social Psychology,* 1977, **35,** 459–477.

Cook, T. D. Temporal mechanisms mediating attitude change after underpayment and overpayment. *Journal of Personality,* 1969, **37,** 618–635.

Cook, T. D. The discounting cue hypothesis and the sleeper effect. Unpublished manuscript, Northwestern University, 1971.

Cook, T. D., & Flay, B. R. The temporal persistence of experimentally induced attitude change: An evaluative review. Unpublished manuscript, Northwestern University, 1974.

Cook, T. D., Gruder, C. L., Hennigan, K. M., & Flay, B. R. The sleeper effect in the context of the discounting cue hypothesis: A living phenomenon. Unpublished manuscript, Northwestern University, 1978.

Cook, T. D., & Insko, C. A. Persistence of induced attitude change as a function of conclusion re-exposure: A laboratory-field experiment. *Journal of Personality and Social Psychology,* 1968, **9,** 328.

Cook, T. D., & Wadsworth, A. Persistence of induced attitude change as a function of overlearned conclusions and supportive attributions. *Journal of Personality,* 1972, **10,** 50 61.

Cowen, P. A., Langer, J., Heavenrich, J., & Nathanson, M. Social learning and Piaget's cognitive theory of moral development. *Journal of Personality and Social Psychology,* 1969, **11,** 261–274.

Culbertson, F. M. Modification of an emotionally held attitude through role playing. *Journal of Abnormal and Social Psychology,* 1957, **54,** 230–233.

Curran, J. P., & Gilbert, F. S. A test of the relative effectiveness of a systematic desensitization program with date-anxious subjects. *Behavior Therapy,* 1975, **6,** 510–521.

Davison, S. C., Tsujimoto, R. N., & Glaros, A. S. Attribution and the maintenance of behavior change in falling asleep. *Journal of Abnormal Psychology,* 1973, **82,** 174–133.

Davison, S. C., & Valins, S. Maintenance of self-attributed and drug-attributed behavior change. *Journal of Personality and Social Psychology,* 1969, **11,** 25–33.

Dillehay, R. C., Insko, C. A., & Smith, M. B. Logical consistency and attitude change. *Journal of Personality and Social Psychology,* 1966, **3,** 646–654.

Doob, A. N., Carlsmith, J. M., Freedman, J. L., Landauer, T. K., and Tom, S., Jr. Effect of initial selling price on subsequent sales. *Journal of Personality and Social Psychology,* 1969, **11,** 345–350.

Dutton, D. G., & Lenox, V. L. Effect of prior "token" compliance on subsequent interracial behavior. *Journal of Personality and Social Psychology,* 1974, **29,** 65–71.

Elms, A. C. Influence of fantasy ability on attitude change through role-playing. *Journal of Personality and Social Psychology,* 1966, **4,** 36–43.

Eysenck, H. J., & Beech, R. Counterconditioning and related methods. In A. E. Bergen & S. L. Garfield (Eds.), *Handbook of psychotherapy and behavior change.* New York: Wiley, 1971.

Falk, D. I. The effects on attitude change of manipulating antecedents of Kelman's internalization process. Unpublished master's thesis, Northwestern University, 1970.

Fishbein, M., & Ajzen, I. Attitudes and opinions. *Annual Review of Psychology,* 1972, **23,** 487–544.

Fishbein, M., & Ajzen, I. *Belief, attitude, intention and behavior: An introduction to theory and research.* Reading, Mass: Addison-Wesley, 1975.

Flanders, J. P. A review of research on imitative behavior. *Psychological Bulletin,* 1968, **69,** 316–337.

Freedman, J. L. Long-term behavioral effects of cognitive dissonance. *Journal of Experimental Social Psychology,* 1965, **1,** 145–155.

Freedman, J. L., & Fraser, S. C. Compliance without pressure: The foot-in-the-door technique. *Journal of Personality and Social Psychology,* 1966, **4,** 195–202.

Friedman, P. H. The effects of modeling and role-playing on assertive behavior. In R. D. Rubin, H. Fensterheim, A. A. Lazarus, & C. M. Franks (Eds.), *Advances in behavior therapy, 1969.* New York: Academic Press, 1971.

Gillig, P. M., & Greenwald, A. G. Is it time to lay the sleeper effect to rest? *Journal of Personality and Social Psychology,* 1974, **29,** 132–139.

Glascow, J., Milgram, N. A., & Youniss, J. The stability of training effects on intentionality of moral judgment in children. *Journal of Personality and Social Psychology,* 1970, **14,** 360–365.

Greene, D., Sternberg, B., & Lepper, M. R. Overjustification in a token economy. *Journal of Personality and Social Psychology,* 1976, **34,** 1219–1234.

Greenstein, T. Behavior change through self-confrontation: A field experiment. *Journal of Personality and Social Psychology,* 1976, **34,** 254–262.

Greenwald, A. G. Cognitive learning, cognitive response to persuasion, and attitude change. In A. G. Greenwald, T. C. Brock, & T. M. Ostrom (Eds.), *Psychological foundations of attitudes.* New York: Academic Press, 1968.

Grube, J. W., Greenstein, T. N., Rankin, W. L., & Kearney, K. A. Behavior change following self-confrontation: A test of the value mediation hypothesis. *Journal of Personality and Social Psychology,* 1977, **35,** 212–216.

Gruder, C. L., Cook, T. D., Hennigan, K. M., Flay, B. R., Alessis, C., & Halamaj, J. Empirical tests of the absolute sleeper effect predicted from the discounting cue hypothesis. *Journal of Personality and Social Psychology,* (1978).

Hamid, P. N., & Flay, B. R. Changes in locus of control as a function of value modification. *British Journal of Social and Clinical Psychology,* 1974, **13,** 143–150.

Hass, R. G., & Mann, R. W. Anticipatory belief change: Persuasion or impression management? *Journal of Personality and Social Psychology,* 1976, **34,** 105–111.

Henninger, M., & Wyer, R. S., Jr. The recognition and elimination of inconsistencies among syllogistically related beliefs: Some new light on the "Socratic Effect." *Journal of Personality and Social Psychology,* 1976, **34,** 680–693.

Holt, L. E., & Watts, W. A. Immediate and delayed effects of forewarning of persuasive intent. *Proceedings of the 81st Annual Convention of the American Psychological Association,* 1973, 361–362.

Hovland, C. I., Janis, I. L., & Kelley, H. H. *Communication and persuasion.* New Haven, Conn.: Yale University Press, 1953.

Hovland, C. I., Lumsdaine, A. A., & Sheffield, F. D. *Experiments on mass communication.* Princeton, N.J.: Princeton University Press, 1949.

Hovland, C. I., & Weiss, W. The influence of source credibility on communication effectiveness. *Public Opinion Quarterly,* 1951, **15,** 635–650.

Hunt, W. A., & Matarazzo, J. D. Three years later: Recent developments in the experimental modification of smoking behavior. *Journal of Abnormal Psychology,* 1973, **81,** 107–114.

Insko, C. A. Primacy versus recency in persuasion as a function of the timing of arguments and measures. *Journal of Personality and Social Psychology,* 1964, **69,** 381–391.

Insko, C. A. Verbal reinforcement of attitude. *Journal of Personality and Social Psychology,* 1965, **2,** 621–623.

Janis, I. L., Lumsdaine, A. A., & Gladstone, A. I. Effects of preparatory communications on reactions to a subsequent news event. *Public Opinion Quarterly,* 1951, **15,** 487–518.

Janis, I. L., & Mann, L. Effectiveness of emotional role-playing in modifying smoking habits and attitudes. *Journal of Experimental Research in Personality*, 1965, **1**, 84–90.

Johnson, H. H., Torcivia, J. M., & Poprick, M. A. Source credibility, authoritarianism and attitude change. *Journal of Personality and Social Psychology*, 1968, **9**, 179–183.

johnson, H. H., & Watkins, T. A. The effects of message repetitions on immediate and delayed attitude change. *Psychonomic Science*, 1971, **22**, 101–103.

Jones, R. T., & Kazdin, A. E. Programming response maintenance after withdrawing token reinforcement. *Behavior Therapy*, 1975, **6**, 153–164.

Kanfer, F. H., & Phillips, J. S. *Learning foundations of behavior therapy*. New York: Wiley, 1970.

Katz, D., McClintock, C., & Sarnoff, I. The measurement of ego defense as related to attitude change. *Journal of Personality*, 1957, **25**, 465–474.

Katz, D., Sarnoff, I., & McClintock, C. Ego defense and attitude change. *Human Relations*, 1956, **9**, 27–45.

Kazdin, A. E. Covert modeling and the reduction of avoidance behavior. *Journal of Abnormal Psychology*, 1973, **81**, 87–95.

Kazdin, A. E. Covert modeling, model similarity, and reduction of avoidance behavior. *Behavior Therapy*, 1974, **5**, 325–340.

Kazdin, A. E. Recent advances in token economy research. In M. Hersen, R. M. Eisler, & P. M. Miller (Eds.), *Progress in behavior modification*. Vol. 1. New York: Academic Press, 1975. Pp. 233–275.

Kazdin, A. E. Effects of covert modeling, multiple models, and model reinforcement on assertive behavior. *Behavior Therapy*, 1976, **7**, 211–222.

Kazdin, A. E., & Bootzin, R. R. The token economy: An evaluative review. *Journal of Applied Behavior Analysis*, 1972, **5**, 343–372.

Kazdin, A. E., & Wilcoxon, L. A. Systematic desensitization and non-specific treatment effects: A methodological evaluation. *Psychological Bulletin*, 1976, **83**, 729–758.

Kelley, H. H. Attribution theory in social psychology. In D. Levine (Ed.), *Nebraska Symposium on Motivation*. Lincoln: University of Nebraska Press, 1967.

Kelman, H. C. Compliance, identification, and internalization: Three processes of opinion change. *Journal of Conflict Resolution*, 1958, **2**, 51–60.

Kelman, H. C. Processes of opinion change. *Public Opinion Quarterly*, 1961, **25**, 57–78.

Kelman, H. C., & Hovland, C. I. "Reinstatement" of the communicator in delayed measurement of attitude change. *Journal of Abnormal and Social Psychology*, 1953, **48**, 327–335.

Kipnis, D. The effects of leadership style and leadership power upon the inducement of attitude change. *Journal of Abnormal and Social Psychology*, 1958, **57**, 173–180.

Kruglanski, A. W. The endogenous-exogenous partition in attribution theory. *Psychological Review*, 1975, **82**, 387–406.

Lang, P. J. The mechanics of desensitization and the laboratory study of human fear. In C. M. Franks (Ed.), *Behavior therapy: Appraisal and status*. New York: McGraw-Hill, 1969.

Langer, E. J., & Rodin, J. The effects of choice and enhanced personal responsibility for the aged: A field experiment in an institutional setting. *Journal of Personality and Social Psychology*, 1976, **34**, 191–198.

Lau, R., Lepper, M. R., & Ross, L. Persistence of inaccurate and discredited personal impressions: A field demonstration of attributional perseverance. Paper presented at the 56th Annual Meeting of the Western Psychological Association, Los Angeles, April, 1976.

Lepper, M. R. Dissonance, self-perception, and honesty in children. *Journal of Personality and Social Psychology*, 1973, **25**, 65–74.

Lepper, M. R., & Greene, D. Turning play into work: Effects of adult surveillance and extrinsic rewards on children's intrinsic motivation. *Journal of Personality and Social Psychology*, 1975, **31**, 479–486.

Lepper, M. R., Greene, D., & Nisbet, R. E. Undermining children's intrinsic interest with extrinsic reward—a test of the "overjustification" hypothesis. *Journal of Personality and Social Psychology*, 1973, **28**, 129–137.

Leventhal, H., & Niles, P. Persistence of influence for varying durations of exposure to threat stimuli. *Psychological Reports*, 1965, **16**, 223–233.

Leyens, J. P., Camino, L., Parke, R. D., & Berkowitz, L. Effects of movie violence on aggression in a field setting as a function of group dominance and cohesion. *Journal of Personality and Social Psychology*, 1975, **32**, 346–360.

Lichtenstein, E., Kentzer, C. S., & Himes, K. H. "Emotional" role-playing and changes in smoking attitudes and behaviors. *Psychological Reports*, 1969, **25**, 379–387.

Lieberman, M. A., Yalom, I. D., & Miles, M. B. *Encounter groups: First facts*. New York: Basic Books, 1973.

Luchins, A. S., & Luchins, E. H. The effects of order of presentation of information and explanatory models. *Journal of Social Psychology*, 1970, **80**, 63–70.

Mann, L. The effects of emotional role playing on desire to modify smoking habits. *Journal of Experimental Social Psychology*, 1967, **3**, 334–348.

Mann, L., & Janis, I. L. A follow-up study on the long-term effects of emotional role playing. *Journal of Personality and Social Psychology*, 1968, **8**, 339–342.

McFall, R. M., & Hammen, C. L. Motivation, structure, and self-monitoring: Role of nonspecific factors in smoking reduction. *Journal of Consulting and Clinical Psychology*, 1971, **37**, 80–86.

McGuire, W. J. Order of presentation as a factor in "conditioning" persuasiveness. In C. I. Hovland (Ed.), *Order of presentation in persuasion*. New Haven, Conn.: Yale University Press, 1957.

McGuire, W. J. Cognitive consistency and attitude change. *Journal of Abnormal and Social Psychology*, 1960, **60**, 345–353. (a)

McGuire, W. J. Direct and indirect persuasive effects of dissonance-producing messages. *Journal of Abnormal and Social Psychology*, 1960, **60**, 354–358. (b)

McGuire, W. J. A syllogistic analysis of cognitive relationships. In M. J. Rosenberg and C. I. Hovland (Eds.), *Attitude organization and change*. New Haven, Conn.: Yale University Press, 1960. (c)

McGuire, W. J. Resistance to persuasion conferred by active and passive prior refutation of the same. and alternative counterarguments. *Journal of Abnormal and Social Psychology*, 1961, **63**, 326–332.

McGuire, W. J. Persistence of the resistance to persuasion induced by various types of prior belief defenses. *Journal of Abnormal and Social Psychology*, 1962, **64**, 241–243.

McGuire, W. J. Comparative persistence of actively and passively conferred resistance to persuasion. Unpublished manuscript, Yale University, 1963. Discussed in McGuire (1964).

McGuire, W. J. Inducing resistance to persuasion. In L. Berkowitz (Ed.), *Advances in experimental social psychology*. Vol. 1. New York: Academic Press, 1964.

McGuire, W. J. The nature of attitudes and attitude change. In G. Lindzey & E. Aronson (Eds.), *The handbook of social psychology*. (2nd ed.) Vol. 3. Reading, Mass.: Addison-Wesley, 1969.

McGuire, W. J., & Papageorgis, D. The relative efficacy of various types of prior belief-defense in producing immunity against persuasion. *Journal of Abnormal and Social Psychology*, 1961, **62**, 327–337.

Miller, N., & Campbell, D. T. Recency and primacy in persuasion as a function of the timing of speeches and measurement. *Journal of Abnormal and Social Psychology*, 1959, **59**, 1–9.

Miller, R. L., Brickman, P., & Bolan, D. Attribution versus persuasion as a means for modifying behavior. *Journal of Personality and Social Psychology*, 1975, **31**, 430–441.

Notz, W. W., Staw, B. M., & Cook, T. D. Attitude toward troop withdrawal from indochina as a function of draft number: Dissonance or self-interest? *Journal of Personality and Social Psychology*, 1971, **20**, 118–126.

Nuttin, J. M., Jr. *The illusion of attitude change: Toward a response contagion theory of persuasion.* London: Academic Press and Leuven University Press, 1975.

O'Connor, R. D. Relative efficacy of modeling, shaping and the combined procedures for modification of social withdrawal. *Journal of Abnormal Psychology,* 1972, **79,** 327–334.

O'Leary, K. D., & Drabman, R. Token reinforcement programs in the classroom: A review. *Psychological Bulletin,* 1971, **75,** 379–398.

O'Leary, K. D., Drabman, R., & Kass, R. E. Maintenance of appropriate behavior in a token program. *Journal of Abnormal Child Psychology,* 1973, **1,** 127–138.

Papageorgis, D. Bartlett effect and the persistence of induced opinion change. *Journal of Abnormal and Social Psychology,* 1963, **67,** 61–67.

Paul, G. L. *Insight vs. desensitization in psychotherapy.* Stanford, Calif.: Stanford University Press, 1966.

Paul, G. L. Insight vs. desensitization in psychotherapy two years after termination. *Journal of Consulting Psychology,* 1967, **31,** 333–348.

Paul, G. L. Two-year follow-up of systematic desensitization in therapy groups. *Journal of Abnormal Psychology,* 1968, **73,** 119–130.

Penner, L. A. Interpersonal attraction toward a black person as a function of value importance. *Personality,* 1971, **2,** 175–187.

Rachman, S., & Teasdale, J. Aversion therapy: An appraisal. In C. M. Franks (Ed.), *Behavior therapy: Appraisal and status.* New York: McGraw-Hill, 1969.

Reiss, S., & Sushinsky, L. W. Overjustification, competing responses, and the acquisition of intrinsic interest. *Journal of Personality and Social Psychology,* 1975, **31,** 1116–1125.

Reiss, S., & Sushinsky, L. W. The competing response hypothesis of decreased play effects: A reply to Lepper and Greene. *Journal of Personality and Social Psychology,* 1976, **33,** 233–244.

Resick, P. A., Forehand, R., & Reed, S. Prestatement of contingencies: The effects on acquisition and maintenance of behavior. *Behavior Therapy,* 1974, **5,** 642–647.

Rice, M. E., & Grusec, J. E. Saying and doing: Effects on observer performance. *Journal of Personality and Social Psychology,* 1975, **32,** 584–593.

Richey, M. J., McClelland, L., & Shimkunas, A. M. Relative influence of positive and negative information in impression formation and persistence. *Journal of Personality and Social Psychology,* 1967, **6,** 322–327.

Riley, R. T., & Pettigrew, T. F. Dramatic events and attitude change. *Journal of Personality and Social Psychology,* 1976, **34,** 1004–1015.

Rodin, J., & Langer, E. J. Long-term effects of a control-relevant intervention with the institutionalized aged. *Journal of Personality and Social Psychology,* 1977, **35,** 897–902.

Rogers, R. W., & Thistlethwaite, D. L. An analysis of active and passive defenses in inducing resistance to persuasion. *Journal of Personality and Social Psychology,* 1969, **11,** 301–308.

Rokeach, M. *Beliefs, attitudes and values.* San Francisco: Jossey-Bass, 1968.

Rokeach, M. Long-range experimental modification of values, attitudes, and behavior. *American Psychologist,* 1971, **26,** 453–459.

Rokeach, M. *The nature of human values.* New York: Free Press, 1973.

Rokeach, M. Long-term value change initiated by computer feedback. *Journal of Personality and Social Psychology,* 1975, **32,** 467–476.

Rokeach, M., & Cochrane, R. Self-confrontation and confrontation with another as determinants of long-term value change. *Journal of Applied Social Psychology,* 1972, **2,** 283–292.

Rokeach, M., & McLellan, D. D. Feedback of information about the values and attitudes of self and others as determinants of long-term cognitive and behavioral change. *Journal of Applied Social Psychology,* 1972, **2,** 236–251.

Ronis, D. L., Baumgardner, M. H., Leippe, M. R., Cacioppo, J. T., & Greenwald, A. G. In search of reliable persuasion effects: I. A computer-controlled procedure for studying persuasion. *Journal of Personality and Social Psychology,* 1977, **35,** 548–569.

Rosen, N. A., & Wyer, R. S. Some further evidence for the "Socratic Effect" using a subjective probability model of cognitive organization. *Journal of Personality and Social Psychology,* 1972, **24,** 420–424.

Rosenberg, M. J. An analysis of affective-cognitive inconsistency. In M. J. Rosenberg and C. I. Hovland (Eds.), *Attitude organization and change.* New Haven, Conn.: Yale University Press, 1960.

Rosenberg, M. J. Hedonism, inauthenticity and other goads toward expansion of a consistency theory. In R. P. Abelson, E. Aronson, W. J. McGuire, T. M. Newcomb, M. J. Rosenberg, and P. H. Tannenbaum (Eds.), *Theories of cognitive consistency: A sourcebook.* Chicago: Rand McNally, 1968.

Rosnow, R. L. "Conditioning" the direction of opinion change in persuasive communication. *Journal of Social Psychology,* 1966, **69,** 291–303.

Ross, M. The self perception of intrinsic motivation. In J. H. Harvey, W. J. Ickes, & R. F. Kidd (Eds.), *New directions in attribution research.* Hillsdale, N.J.: Lawrence Erlbaum Associates, 1976.

Rushton, J. P. Generosity in children: Immediate and long-term effects of modeling, preaching, and moral judgment. *Journal of Personality and Social Psychology,* 1975, **31,** 459–466.

Schein, E. H. The Chinese indoctrination program for prisoners of war: A study of attempted "brainwashing." In E. E. Maccoby, T. M. Newcomb, & E. L. Hartley (Eds.), *Readings in social psychology.* New York: Holt, 1958.

Schopler, J., Gruder, C. L., Miller, M., & Rousseau, M. O. The endurance of change induced by a reward and a coercive power figure. *Human Relations,* 1968, **20,** 301–308.

Schulman, S. I., & Worrell, C. Salience patterns, source credibility, and the sleeper effect. *Public Opinion Quarterly,* 1970, **34,** 371–382.

Schulz, R. Effects of control and predictability on the psychological well-being of the institutionalized aged. *Journal of Personality and Social Psychology,* 1976. **33,** 563–573.

Schulz, R. Aging and control. In J. Garber and M. E. P. Seligman (Eds.), *Human helplessness: Theory and applications.* New York: Academic Press, 1978.

Schulz, R. Long term effects of control and predictability enhancing interventions: Findings and ethical issues. Unpublished manuscript, Carnegie-Mellon University, 1978.

Scott, W. A. Attitude change by response reinforcement: Replication and extension. *Sociometry,* 1959, **22,** 328–335.

Seligman, C., Bush, M., & Kirsch, K. Relationship between compliance in the Foot-in-the-Door technique paradigm and size of first request. *Journal of Personality and Social Psychology,* 1976, **33,** 517–520.

Sherrid, S. D., & Beech, R. P. Self-dissatisfaction as a determinant of change in police values. *Journal of Applied Psychology,* 1976, **61,** 273–278.

Smith, P. B. Social Influence processes and the outcome of sensitivity training. *Journal of Personality and Social Psychology,* 1976, **34,** 1087–1094.

Spiegler, M. D., Liebert, R. M., McMains, M. J., & Fernandez, L. E. Experimental development of a modeling treatment to extinguish persistent avoidance behavior. In R. D. Rubin & C. Franks (Eds.), *Advances in behavior therapy, 1968.* New York: Academic Press, 1969.

Staw, B. M. The attitudinal and behavioral consequences of changing a major organizational reward. *Journal of Personality and Social Psychology,* 1974, **29,** 742–751.

Staw, B. M., Notz, N. W., & Cook, T. D. Attitude toward troop withdrawal from Indochina as a function of draft number: Replication, refinement, and extension. *Psychological Reports,* 1974, **34,** 407–417.

Sternlieb, J. L., & Youniss, J. Moral judgments one year after intentional or consequence modeling. *Journal of Personality and Social Psychology,* 1975, **31,** 895–897.

Stotland, E., Katz, D., & Patchen, M. The reduction of prejudice through the arousal of self-insight. *Journal of Personality,* 1959, **27,** 507–531.

Stotland, E., & Patchen, M. Identification and changes in prejudice and in authoritarianism. *Journal of Abnormal and Social Psychology,* 1961, **62,** 265–274.

Streltzer, N. E., & Koch, G. V. Influence of emotional role-playing on smoking habits and attitudes. *Psychological Reports,* 1968, **22,** 817–820.

Thomas, E. J., Webb, S., & Tweedie, J. Effects of familiarity with a controversial issue on acceptance of successive persuasive communications. *Journal of Abnormal and Social Psychology,* 1961, **63,** 656–659.

Walker, H. M., Hops, H., & Johnson, S. M. Generalization and maintenance of classroom treatment effects. *Behavior Therapy,* 1975, **6,** 188–200.

Walster, E. The temporal sequence of post-decisional processes. In L. Festinger (Ed.), *Conflict, decision, and dissonance.* Stanford, Calif.: Stanford University Press, 1964.

Watts, W. A. Relative persistence of opinion change induced by active compared to passive participation. *Journal of Personality and Social Psychology,* 1967, **5,** 4–15.

Watts, W. A., & Holt, L. E. Logical relationships among beliefs and timing as factors in persuasion. *Journal of Personality and Social Psychology,* 1970, **16,** 571–582.

Watts, W. A., & McGuire, W. J. Persistence of induced opinion change and retention of inducing message content. *Journal of Abnormal and Social Psychology,* 1964, **68,** 233–241.

Weber, S. J. Source primacy-recency effects and the sleeper effect. Paper presented at the annual meeting of the American Psychological Association, Washington, D.C., September 1971.

Weber, S. J. Opinion change as a function of the associative learning of content and source factors. Unpublished doctoral dissertation, Northwestern University, 1972.

Weiss, W. A sleeper effect in opinion change. *Journal of Abnormal and Social Psychology,* 1953, **48,** 173–180.

Whittaker, J. O., & Meade, R. D. Retention of opinion change as a function of differential source credibility: A cross-cultural study. *International Journal of Psychology,* 1968, **3,** 103–108.

Wicker, A. W. Attitudes versus actions: The relationship of verbal and overt behavioral responses to attitude objects. *Journal of Social Issues,* 1969, **25,** 43–78.

Wilson, W., & Miller, H. Repetition, order of presentation, and timing of arguments and measures as determinants of opinion change. *Journal of Personality and Social Psychology,* 1968, **9,** 184–188.

Wyer, R. S. *Cognitive organization and change: An information-processing approach.* Potomac, Md.: Lawrence Erlbaum Associates, 1974.

Wyer, R. S., & Goldberg, L. A. A probabilistic analysis of the relationships between beliefs and attitudes. *Psychological Review,* 1970, **77,** 100–120.

THE CONTINGENCY MODEL AND THE DYNAMICS OF THE LEADERSHIP PROCESS[1]

Fred E. Fiedler

UNIVERSITY OF WASHINGTON
SEATTLE, WASHINGTON

[1]This chapter is based on research conducted largely under contracts with the Office of Naval Research, the Advanced Research Projects Agency of the Department of Defense, the Office of the Chief of Naval Education and Training, and the Army Research Institute for the Behavioral Sciences, to all of whom I wish to express my sincere thanks for their support. I am also deeply appreciative of my colleagues and friends who saw this chapter in various stages of completion. I am particularly indebted to Alan R. Bass, Judith Fiedler, A. Korman, Gary Latham, Linda Mahar, Joseph McGrath, Gary Yukl, and Valann Valdeson, who gave me the benefit of their critical comments at various stages of the manuscript.

59

I.   Introduction

In the first volume of this series I described a contingency model of leadership effectiveness which was based on research conducted between 1951 and 1963 (Fiedler, 1964). This model made specific predictions about the way in which certain personality attributes would correlate with leadership and organizational performance under given conditions at a particular point in time. Since then, well over 300 studies have dealt with various aspects of this model's earlier formulation. The major task which now faces us is the development of a dynamic theory of leadership which adequately accounts for the changes in a leader's behavior and performance over time. This chapter proposes that the key for such a dynamic leadership theory is an understanding of the factors which change the leader's situational control and influence.

The first section of this chapter briefly reviews the model and major validation research; the second section presents a dynamic interpretation of the Contingency Model; the third discusses important methodological issues related to the situational control dimension and the main predictor, the Least Preferred Co-worker score (LPC). The final section describes a new approach to leadership training which is based on the Contingency Model as well as empirical studies which validate the method and thus provide further support for the dynamic interpretation which this chapter presents.

II.   The Contingency Model

The Contingency Model states that effectiveness of interacting[2] groups or organizations depends, or is contingent, upon the appropriate match between leader personality attributes, reflecting his or her motivational structure, and the degree to which the leader has situational control and influence. Specifically, task-motivated leaders perform best in situations in which their control is either high or relatively low; relationship-motivated leaders perform best when they have moderate control and influence.

A.   MOTIVATIONAL STRUCTURE

The leader's motivational structure is measured by means of a simple bipolar adjective scale which asks the individual to think of all the persons whom he

---

[2]The Contingency Model deals primarily with groups in which performance depends on the interaction and collaborative contribution of the members (e.g., as in basketball teams), rather than the relatively independent performance of coacting group members whose scores are summed to yield a team performance measure (e.g., bowling teams).

or she has ever known and then to describe the *one* person with whom it has been most difficult to work (the least preferred co-worker or LPC). The description, using a recently published scale (Fiedler, Chemers, & Mahar, 1976), is made on 18 bipolar items which follow the Semantic Differential format, for example,

$$\text{Pleasant} \quad :\underline{\ }:\underline{\ }:\underline{\ }:\underline{\ }:\underline{\ }:\underline{\ }:\underline{\ }:\underline{\ }: \quad \text{Unpleasant}$$
$$8\ 7\ 6\ 5\ 4\ 3\ 2\ 1$$

$$\text{Friendly} \quad :\underline{\ }:\underline{\ }:\underline{\ }:\underline{\ }:\underline{\ }:\underline{\ }:\underline{\ }:\underline{\ }: \quad \text{Unfriendly}[3]$$
$$8\ 7\ 6\ 5\ 4\ 3\ 2\ 1$$

An individual who describes the LPC in very negative, rejecting terms (low LPC score, i.e., less than about 57) is considered task-motivated. In other words, the completion of the task is of such overriding importance that it completely colors the perception of all other personality traits attributed to the LPC. In effect, the individual says, "If I cannot work with you, if you frustrate my need to get the job done, then you can't be any good in other respects. You are . . . unfriendly, unpleasant, tense, distant, etc."

The relationship-motivated individual who sees his or her LPC in relatively more positive terms (high LPC score, i.e., about 63 and above) says, "Getting a job done is not everything. Therefore, even though I can't work with you, you may still be friendly, relaxed, interesting, etc., in other words, someone with whom I could get along quite well on a personal basis." Thus, the high LPC person looks at the LPC in a more differentiated manner—more interested in the personality of the individual than merely in whether this is or is not someone with whom one can get a job done.

There is also a middle LPC group, consisting of perhaps 15–20% of the population, clustered around the population mean, which appears to differ in many respects from either the high or the low LPC. These individuals tend to be socially independent, less concerned about the way others evaluate them, and less eager to conform to the expectations of others or to take the leadership role (Fiedler, Chemers, & Mahar, 1976; Mai-Dalton, 1975). Some individuals in this middle category may also have mixed motivation or a combination of the two motivational patterns. We currently know relatively little about this group, which we have tentatively labeled "socioindependent." For the sake of easier presentation, we will deal primarily with high- and low-LPC leaders.

It is important to stress that the LPC score does not generally predict leader behavior. Thus, a high LPC score does not necessarily imply that a leader will be considerate, nor does a low LPC score imply more structuring behavior. In fact,

---

[3]The other item pairs are rejecting–accepting, tense–relaxed, distant–close, cold–warm, supportive–hostile, boring–interesting, quarrelsome–harmonious, gloomy–cheerful, open–guarded, backbiting–loyal, untrustworthy–trustworthy, considerate–inconsiderate, nasty–nice, agreeable–disagreeable, insincere–sincere, and kind–unkind.

as we shall discuss later in this chapter, leader behavior is itself the product of the interaction between the LPC score and the degree to which the situation provides the leader with control and influence.

B. SITUATIONAL CONTROL

The second major element in the Contingency Model is the degree to which the situation provides the leader with control and influence. (In previous publications this dimension usually has been called "situational favorableness," a term which has since been discarded because it is frequently confused with task difficulty.) A high degree of control and influence implies that the leader has correspondingly high certainty that his decisions and actions will have predictable results, and that they will achieve the desired goals and gratify the leader's needs in the situation. As we shall see, situational control and influence has emerged as the key to the development of a dynamic theory of leadership. The most common method of measuring situational control or favorableness has been by means of three subscales.

1. Leader–Member Relations

The first subscale indicates the degree to which *leader–member relations* are good, that is, the degree to which the leader enjoys the support and loyalty of group members. This dimension has been measured by such methods as the group members' preference ratings or evaluations of the leader, or by a "group atmosphere scale" which the leader fills out. The latter approach, which has been used most frequently, is a 10-item semantic differential scale which asks the leader himself to describe the atmosphere of the group in such terms as friendly–unfriendly, pleasant–unpleasant, etc. A number of studies (e.g., McNamara, 1968) have shown that the scale correlates highly with the group's loyalty and support of the leader but not with LPC (see Fiedler, 1967, p. 153; McNamara, 1968; Stinson & Tracy, 1974). A new scale (shown in Fig. 1) allows the leader to estimate leader–member relations with his own group as well as between subordinate managers and their groups. The correlation between this scale and the Group Atmosphere scale in a recent study was .88, $n = 26$.

The leader–member relations dimension is the most important of the three subscales, since a leader who enjoys the support and loyalty of group members can depend and rely on them. He can be certain that the group members will do their best to comply with his wishes and directions. A leader who cannot count on his group is, of course, in a very precarious position. He will need to be considerably more circumspect in his dealings with subordinates and continuously on guard to assure that his directions or policies are not subverted.

2. Task Structure

The second most important dimension is *task structure*. We generally do not

LEADER-MEMBER RELATIONS SCALE

Circle the number which best represents your response to each item.

	STRONGLY AGREE	AGREE	NEITHER AGREE NOR DISAGREE	DISAGREE	STRONGLY DISAGREE
1. The people I supervise have trouble getting along with each other.	1	2	3	4	5
2. My subordinates are reliable and trustworthy.	5	4	3	2	1
3. There seems to be a friendly atmosphere among the people I supervise.	5	4	3	2	1
4. My subordinates always cooperate with me in getting the job done.	5	4	3	2	1
5. There is friction between my subordinates and myself.	1	2	3	4	5
6. My subordinates give me a good deal of help and support in getting the job done.	5	4	3	2	1
7. The people I supervise work well together in getting the job done.	5	4	3	2	1
8. I have good relations with the people I supervise.	5	4	3	2	1

TOTAL SCORE [ ]

Fig. 1.   Leader–member relations scale. From Fiedler *et al.*, 1975. Reprinted by permission of John Wiley & Sons, Inc.

think of the task as providing the leader with control and influence. However, leaders who have a blueprint or detailed operating instructions are assured of the support of their organization in directing the job. They very rarely get any arguments from subordinates as to the course the group should take. In contrast, when the task is unstructured, as is the case with typical committee assignments or research and development work, the control which leaders can exercise over the task and the group is considerably diluted. Most committee chairpersons would find it extremely difficult to dictate the committee's decision or to predict the acceptability of the outcome of these decisions. Such a prediction is easily made when the leader has step-by-step instructions which guarantee an acceptable completed task if they are faithfully followed.

The degree of task structure has been measured in a number of ways, generally following four subcategories suggested by Shaw (1963). These are the task's decision verifiability, goal path multiplicity, goal clarity, and solution specificity. Thurstone scales for each of these four subscales have been developed by Hunt (1967) and have been described in previous publications (e.g., Fiedler, 1967; Fiedler & Chemers, 1974). Abbreviated scales also have been extensively used and generally serve the purpose quite well. By and large, line management, production supervisors, and military troop commanders have relatively structured tasks. Leaders of research and development groups, committees, boards, or organizations which require creative effort tend to have unstructured tasks. A recent task structure scale (Fiedler *et al.*, 1976) is shown in Fig. 2.

TASK STRUCTURE RATING SCALE   Circle one

	Usually True	Sometimes True	Seldom True
IS THE GOAL CLEARLY STATED OR KNOWN?			
1. Is there a blueprint, picture, model, or detailed description available of the finished product or service?	2	1	0
2. Is there a person available to advise and give a description of the finished product or service, or how the job should be done?	2	1	0
IS THERE ONLY ONE WAY TO ACCOMPLISH THE TASK?			
3. Is there a step-by-step procedure, or a standard operating procedure which indicates in detail the process which is to be followed?	2	1	0
4. Is there a specific way to subdivide the task into separate parts or steps?	2	1	0
5. Are there some ways which are clearly recognized as better than others for performing this task?	2	1	0
IS THERE ONLY ONE CORRECT ANSWER OR SOLUTION?			
6. Is it obvious when the task is finished and the correct solution has been found?	2	1	0
7. Is there a book, manual, or job description which indicates the best solution or the best outcome for the task?	2	1	0
IS IT EASY TO CHECK WHETHER THE JOB WAS DONE RIGHT?			
8. Is there a generally agreed understanding about the standards the particular product or service has to meet to be considered acceptable?	2	1	0
9. Is the evaluation of this task generally made on some quantitative basis?	2	1	0
10. Can the leader and the group find out how well the task has been accomplished in enough time to improve future performance?	2	1	0

TOTAL [   ]

Fig. 2.   Task structure rating scale. From Fiedler *et al.*, 1975. Reprinted by permission of John Wiley & Sons, Inc.

3. Position Power

The third dimension which defines situational control is *position power,* that is, the degree to which leaders are able to reward and punish, to recommend sanctions, or otherwise to enforce compliance by subordinates. Here again, a scale is available which provides norms for scoring (see Fig. 3) (Fiedler *et al.,* 1976).

Task structure and position power should be assessed by the leader's superiors. Self assessments are subject to distortion. In one study, for example, inexperienced high LPC leaders perceived their task structure and position power as very low. However, self-ratings are useful for training purposes, as we will see later.

POSITION POWER RATING SCALE

Circle the number which best represents your answer.

1. Can the leader directly or by recommendation administer rewards
    and punishments to his subordinates?

2	1	0
Can act directly or can recommend with high effectiveness	Can recommend but with mixed results	NO

2. Can the leader directly or by recommendation affect the promotion, demotion, hiring or firing of his subordinates?

2	1	0
Can act directly or can recommend with high effectiveness	Can recommend but with mixed results	NO

3. Does the leader have the knoweldge necessary to assign tasks to subordinates and instruct them in task completion?

2	1	0
YES	Sometimes or in some aspects	NO

4. Is it the leader's job to evaluate the performance of his subordinates?

2	1	0
YES	Sometimes or in some aspects	NO

5. Has the leader been given some official title of authority by the organization (e.g., foreman, department head, platoon leader)?

2	0	
YES	NO	

TOTAL. . . . .

Fig. 3.   Position power rating scale. From Fiedler *et al.*, 1975. Reprinted by permission of John Wiley & Sons, Inc.

4. Measuring Situational Control

The leader's situational control (or situational favorableness) is usually represented on an 8-point continuum. This is obtained first by dividing the groups into those falling above and below the normative cutting score on leader–member relations, then on task structure, and finally on position power. A continuous scale of situational control can also be constructed by weighting the standardized leader–member relations score by 4, the standardized task structure score by 2, and adding these to the standardized position power score (Nebeker, 1975). The formula thus reads:

Leader situational control = 4(leader–member relations) + 2(task structure) + (position power).

This system of weighting has recently been supported by a number of empirical studies which will be discussed in Section III of this chapter.

It must be pointed out, of course, that the three major subscales of leader–member relations, task structure, and position power by no means represent the only factors which determine the leader's situational control and influence. Other studies (e.g., Ayer, 1968; Meuwese & Fiedler, 1965) have pointed to situational stress as affecting the leader's control; cross-cultural studies (e.g., Fiedler, 1966; Fiedler, Meuwese, & Oonk, 1961; Fiedler, O'Brien, & Ilgen, 1969) have shown that linguistic and cultural heterogeneity also play a major role in determining leader control. And leader experience and training also increase control. In unusual cases this formula may thus require appropriate modification, and specific rules governing these modifications still need to be developed.

5. Leader–Situation Interaction

As already mentioned, task-motivated leaders tend to perform best in situations in which their control is either high or else relatively low, while the relationship-motivated leaders perform best in situations in which they enjoy moderate control. This relationship is seen in Fig. 4. The horizontal axis indicates the eight cells or octants of the situational control dimension. The vertical axis shows the correlations between the leader's LPC score and the group performance scores. The median correlations of the original studies are connected by the broken line on this graph.

Positive correlations, shown by median coefficients above the midline on the graph, show that the relationship-motivated (high-LPC) leaders performed better than did task-motivated (low-LPC) leaders. Negative median correlations (i.e., below the midline) indicate that the task-motivated leaders were superior. Thus, both the task- and the relationship-motivated leaders performed well under some conditions and poorly under others. This implies that it is not appropriate to speak of a "good leader" or a "poor leader." Rather, a leader may perform well in one situation and not another, depending on the proper match between leader motivational structure and situational control.

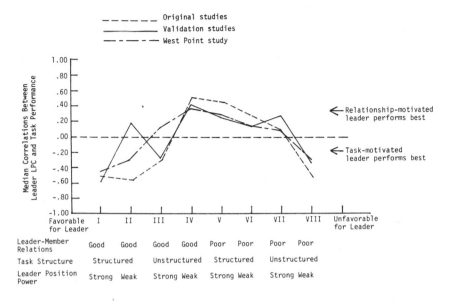

Fig. 4.   Median correlations between leader performance and group performance for the original studies, validation studies, and the West Point 1972 study. From Fiedler, 1977b. Reprinted with permission.

III.   Validation Evidence

The Contingency Model has been extensively tested in a wide variety of laboratory and field conditions. Most of these studies have supported the model. Since the Contingency Model makes different predictions for different situations, for example, for each of the eight octants or cells of the situational control dimension shown on Fig. 4, a sizable number of groups must be found which perform comparable tasks under each of these conditions. That is, the groups which are compared must have leaders who have (a) demonstrably good or poor relations with group members, (b) structured versus unstructured tasks, and (c) strong versus weak position power. Most validation studies have tested the Contingency Model only in some of these conditions.

Extensive reviews of the validation evidence have been presented in a number of publications (e.g., Fiedler, 1971b; Fiedler & Chemers, 1974; Mitchell, Biglan, Oncken, & Fiedler, 1970), and the research will be presented here in summary form.

Table I presents the correlation coefficients obtained in validation studies between 1963 and 1973 which dealt with interacting groups and tested the appropriate octant. That is, the methodology and design of each study was rated by four independent judges who had been given training in classifying groups. They

TABLE I

SUMMARY OF FIELD AND LABORATORY STUDIES
TESTING THE CONTINGENCY MODEL[a]

Field studies	Octant 1	Octant 2	Octant 3	Octant 4	Octant 5	Octant 6	Octant 7	Octant 8
Hunt (1967)	−.64		−.80		.21		.30	
	−.51	.60					−.30	
Hill (1969)		−.10	−.29			−.24	.62	
Fiedler et al. (1969		−.21		.00		.67[b]		−.51
O'Brien and Fiedler (unpublished)		−.46		.47		−.45		−.14
Tumes (1972)	−.47[c]			.62[c]				

Laboratory experiments[d]								
Belgian Navy (Fiedler, 1966)	−.72	.37	−.16	.08		.07	.26	−.37
	−.77	.50	−.54	.13	.03	.14	−.27	.60
Shima (1968)		−.26		.71[b]				
Mitchell (1970)		.24		.43				
		.17		.38				
Fiedler Exec.		.34		.51				
Chemers and Skrzypek (1972)	−.43	−.32	.10	.35	.28	.13	.08	−.33
Rice and Chemers (1973)						30		−.40
Sashkin (1972)			−.29[b]					
Schneier (1978)		−.55[e]						

	Octant 1	Octant 2	Octant 3	Octant 4	Octant 5	Octant 6	Octant 7	Octant 8
Median, all studies	−.59	−.10	−.29	.40	.19	.13	.17	−.35
Median, field studies	−.51	−.21	−.29	.47	.21	−.24	.30	−.33
Median, laboratory experiments	−.72	.21	−.23	.38	.16	.14	.08	−.35
Medians in original studies	−.52	−.58	−.33	.47	.42		.05	−.43

Number of correlations in the expected direction: 38[f]
Number of correlations opposite to expected direction: 9
p by biomial test: .01

[a]From Fiedler, 1971a. Copyright 1971 by the American Psychological Association. Reprinted with permission.

[b]$p < .05$.

[c]$p < .01$.

[d]An additional study by Shiflett and Nealey (1972) should have been included in this table. This laboratory experiment compared 3-man college groups with very high intellectual ability and with moderate ability on performance in creative tasks in octants 3 and 4 (weak and strong position power). The results of the moderate ability groups supported the prediction of the model (−.16, .34), while those of very high ability gave contradictory findings (.64, −.49, all ns = 8, and nonsignificant). These additional findings give rise to interesting speculations about high-ability college students but do not change the basic interpretation of the table.

[e]$p < .001$.

[f]Exclusive of octant 6, for which no prediction had been made.

were to determine whether the groups were interacting or coacting, and into which of the eight octants the various groups belonged. Groups were considered properly classified if three of the four judges agreed in their placement of the group. Most of the correlations are based on very small samples and were individually not significant. Thirty-eight (81%) of the 47 separate correlation coefficients were in the predicted direction. A binomial test of the proportion of correctly and incorrectly predicted correlations is highly significant.

The similarity in the pattern of correlations also provides evidence of the Contingency Model's predictive power. The median correlations obtained in the validation studies under laboratory and field conditions are indicated on Table II, as are the median correlations obtained in the original studies. The medians of the validation studies in Fig. 3 are connected by a solid line. The rank–order correlation between the corresponding medians is .75 ($n=7$) and statistically significant. As Table II also shows, the only discrepancy between the predicted median correlations and the validation study medians occurred in octant 2 of the laboratory studies, while the direction of the correlations in the field studies followed the prediction of the model. These findings suggest either that the prediction for octant 2 is incorrect or that the conditions of octant 2 are difficult to reproduce in

TABLE II

COMPARISON OF MEDIAN CORRELATIONS FROM ORIGINAL STUDIES WITH CORRESPONDING CORRELATIONS FROM VALIDATION STUDIES[a]

	Median correlations between leader LPC scores and group performance				
Octant	Original studies	All validation studies	Field studies	Laboratory studies	West Point
1[b]	−52	−59	−51	−72	−43
2	−58	−10	−21	21	−32
3	−33	−29	−29	−23	10
4	47	40	47	38	35
5	42	19	22	16	28
6		(13)	(−24)	(14)	(13)
7	05	17	30	08	05
8	−43	−35	−33	−35	−33

Rank correlations between medians of original studies and results of validation studies

All validation studies	.79	$p < .05$ (one-tailed)
Field studies	.75	$p < .05$ (one-tailed)
Laboratory studies	.46	n.s.
West Point study	.86	$p < .01$ (one-tailed)

[a]From Fiedler, 1973. Reprinted with permission.
[b]No predictions were made for octant 1.

laboratory research. The latter seems more likely, since laboratory studies are by their nature artificial. Moreover, situations in which the leader has low position power while the task is highly structured are rather rare in real life. It is even more unusual to find a leader who can manage a situation of this type unless he has the full support of his group. This may account in large part for the difficulty of finding such groups in real-life conditions.

Also reproduced are studies which permitted only an approximate classification of groups into those in which the leader had high, intermediate, and low situational control (or favorableness) (Table III). Here, 26 of the 35 (74%) correlation coefficients are in the predicted direction, and the binomial test is again highly significant.

This method of validation has been attacked on various grounds, e.g., because it interprets nonsignificant correlation coefficients and because some correlation coefficients are based on subsamples in the same study where one subsample might have had good and the other poor leader–member relations (Ashour, 1973; Graen, Alvares, Orris, & Martella, 1970). While the latter argument has some validity, the former does not (Fisher, 1948). However, it has been pointed out, quite correctly, that most validation studies were based on concurrent measurement of LPC, leader–member relations, and group performance scores, and that leader–member relations measures and even LPC scores might well be affected by the group's performance. We shall discuss this point shortly.

In addition, of course, a number of studies have failed to support the Contingency Model. Most frequently cited have been two laboratory experiments

TABLE III

SUMMARY OF LPC GROUP PERFORMANCE CORRELATIONS OF STUDIES EXTENDING THE CONTINGENCY HYPOTHESIS[a]

Study and date	Favorable			Intermediate			Unfavorable	
O'Brien (1969)	−.08			.77[b]				−.13
Anderson (1966)	−.50		.21		−.22			.12
Lawrence and Lorsch (1967)[b]	−.50	−.10	−.13	.66				
Nealey and Blood (1968)	−.22			.79[b]				
Nealey and Owen (1970)	−.50[b]							
Fiedler and Barron (1967)[c]								
Task I	−.42	−.56	−.32	.67	−.08	−.01	−.53	−.72
Task II	−.71	−.59	.69	.41	−.15	−.20	−.47	−.61
Median		−.37		.20				−.30

Note: The location of the correlation coefficient in the table indicates degree of judged favorableness of leadership situation. The farther to the left, the more favorable the situation.

[a] From Fiedler, 1971b. Copyright 1971 by the American Psychological Association. Reprinted permission.

[b] Study not conducted by writer or his associates.

[c] In Fiedler (1967).

by Graen, Orris, and Alvares (1971). However, the Graen *et al.* experiments are, themselves, methodologically faulty, as has been pointed out in the literature (e.g., Fiedler, 1971a; Chemers & Skrzypek, 1972). Specifically, all experimental manipulations in the Graen *et al.* studies were weak. Some groups with supposedly high position power had position power scores below the mean and vice versa. Likewise, statistical tests showed that the classification of leaders as belonging in the high or the low LPC groups was in a number of cases incorrect.[4]

A methodologically sound validation study was conducted by Chemers and Skrzypek (1972) at the U.S. Military Academy. This field experiment utilized 128 cadets from two cadet training companies. In order to assure that neither the LPC score nor the leader–member relations measure would be influenced by the group's performance, LPC as well as sociometric preference measures were obtained 3 weeks prior to the study. High- and low-LPC leaders were selected from those whose scores fell at least 1 standard deviation above or below the mean of the LPC distribution. Groups with good or poor leader–member relations were assembled by bringing together men who chose one another as coworkers or who expressed dislike for one another.

Each group performed one structured and one unstructured task in counterbalanced order. The structured task consisted of drawing the plan for a barracks building to scale from a set of specifications; the unstructured task required the group to design a program to facilitate an interest in world politics among enlisted men assigned overseas. Furthermore, groups were randomly assigned to a high or to a low position power condition. In the former, the leader had the responsibility to evaluate the performance of each group member and assign a score which would become a part of the cadet's permanent service record. In the low position power condition, the leader was instructed to act as chairman, and the group was told that the leader had no real power to reward or punish group members.

In summary, leader LPC and leader–member relations were experimentally determined *in advance,* and task structure and leader position power were strongly manipulated, yielding the full eight-celled situational favorableness dimension of the Contingency Model.

Leader LPC and group effectiveness scores were correlated for each octant of the situational control dimension. The dash–dot line on Fig. 4 plots the

[4]A laboratory experiment by Vecchio (1977) also failed to confirm the Contingency Model. Although the author claims that he conducted a very rigorous test of the model, groups with supposedly good leader–member relations were assembled "so that leaders were assigned to supervise two favorable ranked classmates and one unfavorably ranked classmate (Favorable Group Atmosphere) or two unfavorably ranked classmates (Unfavorable Group Atmosphere)." In other words, each of the groups was deliberately designed to have at least one group member with whom the leader did not wish to work. Unless this study was designed for some other purpose, I am at a complete loss to understand the rationale for this curious procedure which deliberately weakens the manipulation of the single most important component of the situational favorableness dimension.

resultant correlations against the predicted curve. As Table II shows, the rank-order correlation of the two sets of correlation coefficients was .86 ($p < .02$). The interaction of LPC, leader acceptance, and task structure was also highly significant ($F = 6.19, p < .025$) and accounted for about 28% of the group performance variability (Shiflett, 1973), and thus strongly supports the model.

In addition, a number of subsequent laboratory and field studies (e.g., Rice & Chemers, 1975; Sashkin, 1972) provide further evidence supporting the predictive ability of the Contingency Model. Three carefully designed experiments were conducted by Hardy (1971, 1975) and Hardy, Sack, and Harpine (1973) in which LPC scores also were obtained 1 or 2 weeks prior to the study. In two of these studies (Hardy, 1975; Hardy et al., 1973) leader–member relations were experimentally manipulated by assigning subjects to groups on the basis of preassessed sociometric scores. The 1971 Hardy study used 56 4-person groups of college students to test cells 1–4, Hardy et al. used 56 groups of high school students to test cells with weak position power, namely, 2, 4, 6, and 8, and the 1975 Hardy study tested 39 groups of elementary school students from the fourth grade in cells 5–8 of the model.

As in most laboratory tests, the results obtained for octant 2 did not support the prediction. The results for all other seven octants were significant in the predicted direction. Table IV summarizes the findings.

On the whole, there is now little question about the basic validity of the Contingency Model. The evidence is very clear that low-LPC leaders perform better than high-LPC leaders in situations in which they have very high or relatively low control and influence, and high-LPC leaders perform better in

TABLE IV

SUMMARY OF VALIDATION EXPERIMENTS CONDUCTED BY HARDY AND HIS ASSOCIATES

	Contingency model octant							
Group	1	2	3	4	5	6	7	8
56 3-man group of college students (Hardy, 1971)	L > H[a]	H < L	L > H[a]	H > L[a]	—	—	—	—
56 Groups of high school students (Hardy et al., 1973)	—	H < L	—	H > L[b]	—	H > L[b]	—	L >
39 Elementary school groups (Hardy, 1975)	—	—	—	—	H > L[a]	H > L[a]	H > L[a]	L >

Abbreviations: H = High LPC leader; L = Low LPC leader.
[a] F-test significant in predicted direction $p < .05$.
[b] F-test significant in predicted direction $p < .01$.
[c] F-test significant in predicted direction $p < 10$.

situations in which their control is moderate. These findings are quite strong for octants 1, 4, 5, and 8, in which correlations account for substantial portions of the variance, that is, about 36%, 16%, 5%, and 12% respectively. Octant 3 appears to account for about 8% of the variance, while the variance accounted for by octants 2, 6, and 7 is negligible. Whether further refinements in scaling the situational control dimension and improvements in the LPC score will result in substantial increases in the accuracy of these predictions remains to be seen. The unreliability of the typical group performance criteria and of the various personality and situational measures in leadership are likely to remain serious limitations in our efforts to add to the precision of predicting leadership performance. It must also be remembered, however, that the Contingency Model does not take into account a number of other important factors. Among these are the leader's and the group's abilities, motivation, the leader's and member's sex, and the relation of the leader and the group to key persons at higher levels of the organization. Further research will be needed to integrate these other factors into a more general theory of leadership.

IV. Dynamics of the Leadership Process

A viable leadership theory must be able to explain leadership as an integral part of a continuously changing organizational process. Frequent shifts in management, personnel turnover, new assignments, and turbulence in the political and economic environment are part of organizational life. But in addition, the leader himself changes. While personality attributes remain reasonably constant over the space of a few months or even a few years, the way in which a leader approaches the job may undergo considerable change as he or she learns by experience or by training how to cope more confidently with job related problems. Since these organizational factors as well as the leader's own development affect situational control, the effectiveness with which the leader performs the job will also vary.

The dynamic nature of this process is most easily visualized in the schematic drawing of the Contingency Model, shown in Fig. 5. Situational control is again indicated on the horizontal axis while the vertical axis of the figure indicates leadership effectiveness. The solid and the broken lines trace the predicted performance of the relationship- and of the task-motivated leader, respectively.

As this schematic drawing suggests, the effectiveness of the leader will change as his motivational structure changes or as situational control and influence change. As we will show in a later section, the LPC score remains fairly constant over time. Our major concern is, therefore, with changes in situational control. These principally take place as leaders acquire experience and training or as they are given new assignments, and as personnel turnover among their

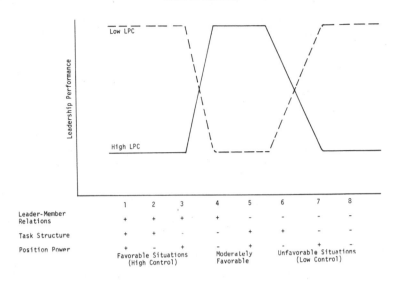

Fig. 5. Schematic representation of the Contingency Model relationship between leader LPC scores and task performance in different conditions of leader situational control. From Fiedler, 1977a. Reprinted by permission of W. H. Winston & Sons.

subordinates or superiors require them to develop new patterns of interpersonal relations with these important others in the work environment.

The effects which changes in situational control will have on the leader's performance can readily be seen on Fig. 5. For example, let us assume a situation in which the leader's control is initially in the very low zone (i.e., at the far right of Fig. 5). Here, the task-motivated leader's performance should be better than that of the relationship-motivated leader. As the leader gains in ability to cope with the situation, or as the situation becomes more predictable, the leader will increase his situational control. (This can be visualized as a movement toward the moderate-control zone in the middle of the graph.) We should then find that the performance of the task-motivated leader decreases, while that of the relationship-motivated leader increases, as situational control shifts from low to moderate. With a still further increase in situational control to the high-control zone, the performance of the relationship-motivated leader will again decrease, while that of the task-motivated leader will increase.

The changes in the leader's situation which mainly affect his or her control and influence are operationally defined by the Contingency Model as changes in the leader–member relationship, task structure, and position power. However, situational control can also be interpreted in terms of the leader's certainty about the outcomes and consequences of his or her behavior and decisions, as has been shown by Nebeker (1975), Mai-Dalton (1975), and Beach, Mitchell, and Beach (1978). Having group support, knowing exactly what is to be done and how it is to be done, and having the power to reward and punish subordinates as a means of assuring compliance provides the leader with a high degree of confidence that his directions will be carried out and that they will have predictable consequences. There is, therefore, little need to be insecure and anxious about the outcome. Any environmental condition which introduces instability and uncertainty will reduce situational control and increase the leader's anxiety about the outcome. This is likely to cause the leader to take some compensatory action in order to regain control and to reduce the uncertainty about the outcomes and the attendant anxiety. This change in leader behavior will bring about an increase or decrease in leadership performance depending on how well the particular leader behavior happens to match the requirements of the situation.

A. LEADERSHIP EXPERIENCE

One factor which almost inevitably changes situational control comes with the experience which leaders gain on the job (e.g., Bons & Fiedler, 1976). Tasks tend to become more routine, leaders get to know their subordinates, and in most instances they are able to handle them better as time goes on. Likewise, with time on the job, the leader will learn the boss's standards and expectations.

As the Contingency Model predicts, leadership experience may increase situational control but it does not generally increase leadership performance. While some managers or supervisors get better with time on the job, others tend to get worse. Everyone knows of some young and inexperienced leaders who have outperformed every veteran in sight. History provides such examples as Joan of Arc who was only 17 years old when she defeated her much more experienced opponents at the Battle of Orleans, and William Pitt who was only 24 at the time he became one of England's most distinguished prime ministers.

A review of various empirical studies on leader experience and performance (Fiedler, 1970) summarized the findings on 13 different organizations. These included military units and *ad hoc* teams, industrial and business organizations, meat markets, and voluntary organizations. The median correlation between the leader's years of experience and rated performance was $-.12$. One of the studies compared the leadership performance of 48 Belgian Navy petty officers with an average of 9.8 years of experience and the performance of 48 new recruits without any formal leadership experience. The groups of leaders were matched on leader and group member intelligence and leadership style. The teams worked on four simulated military tasks developed in cooperation with responsible Navy officers. Yet, the performance of experienced and inexperienced leaders was almost identical on all four of these tasks.

A replication compared leadership effectiveness on experimental tasks for one group of captains and majors with 5–17 years of experience and 4 years of military college and for a group of new recruits who had just completed their basic training course. Here again, the average performance of groups led by inexperienced trainees was about as high as the average performance of groups led by the experienced and trained officers. Moreover, the officers with relatively more training and experience performed no better than did the officers with relatively little experience. And studies of post office supervisors, business managers, foremen, and police sergeants also showed no consistent relationship between years of leadership experience and leadership effectiveness (Fiedler, 1972a).

As Fig. 5 shows, the Contingency Model predicts that leadership experience will have different effects on the performance of relationship- and task-motivated leaders. A number of investigations have supported this hypothesis. One example comes from a study of infantry squads (Fiedler, Bons, & Hastings, 1975a). These basic infantry units consist of 8–11 enlisted men. A group of 28 sergeants, who served as squad leaders, was evaluated at the time the units were formed and when the organization was, therefore, still in a state of flux. These same sergeants were again evaluated by the same superiors after they had had 5 months of experience in working with their units. While these sergeants judged the situation as providing moderate situational control at the first time of evaluation, they judged their situational control to be relatively high at the time of the second evaluation.

Figure 6 shows that the prediction based on the Contingency Model was supported. The relationship-motivated leaders performed relatively well while the situation was still uncertain and relatively unstructured. However, the task-motivated leaders performed relatively better 5 months later when the situation had become more stabilized and their control had presumably moved into the high zone.

A similar finding was obtained in a study of general managers of 32 consumer cooperatives (Godfrey, Fiedler, & Hall, 1959). This federation consisted of small companies, each typically serving one county of the State of Illinois. The federation maintained excellent records of company performance which were used as criteria for bonuses as well as for subsequent promotion of managers to more desirable jobs. The major criteria were the percent of net income to total sales and the percent of overhead costs to total sales. An analysis of various economic indicators showed that the economy of the county had relatively little influence on the performance of the organization, since a company in a booming economy also tended to have more competitors. The leadership situation was judged as high in control for experienced managers but only of moderate control for the less experienced general managers.

The group was first divided into task- and relationship-motivated managers and then further subdivided into an experienced and a relatively inexperienced group. As Fig. 7 shows, the relationship-motivated managers who were inexperienced performed better than those who were experienced. In contrast, task-

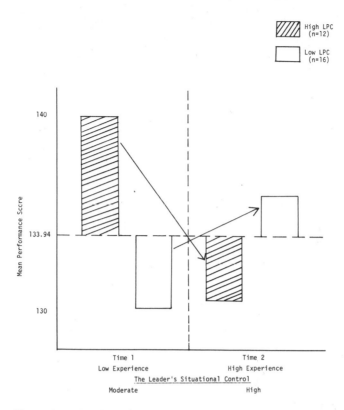

Fig. 6. Change in performance of high- and low-LPC leaders as a function of increased experience. Interaction significant. Adapted from Fiedler *et al.* (1975a).

motivated managers who were experienced performed better than those with relatively low experience.

If the situation is in the low-control zone for the inexperienced leader, we would, of course, expect that the increasing experience will move the leader into the moderate-control zone. Hence, the inexperienced leader should perform well if he or she is task-motivated, while the experienced leader should perform relatively well if he or she is relationship-motivated.

This can be inferred from a study which McNamara (1968) conducted with Canadian elementary and secondary school principals. The performance evaluation of elementary principals was based on superintendents' ratings, while that of secondary principals was based on the average achievement test scores of ninth- and eleventh-grade students on a province-wide test.

In general, experienced elementary school principals enjoy relatively high control in their leadership situation. Their schools are small and they can easily

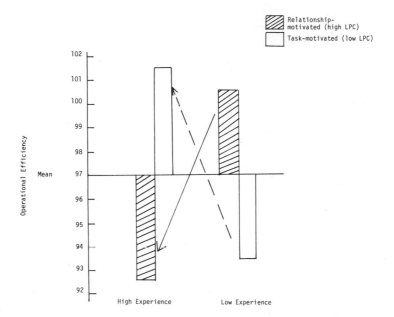

Fig. 7.   Effect of experience on the performance of high- and low-LPC managers. From Fiedler, 1972a, reprinted by permission.

get to know their staff members. Their tasks tend to be structured since policies and curricula are determined by the school district. Moreover, elementary school students present relatively few disciplinary problems. Thus, the situation gives the experienced principal a great deal of control; in contrast, the inexperienced principal, who still has to learn the ropes, will have only a moderate degree of situational control.

The secondary schools were complex organizations, employing 30–40 teachers who, in turn, reported to various department heads. Moreover, the task of high school principals is relatively unstructured since it requires them to develop policies, interact with various civic and governmental agencies, and maintain discipline over teenage students who are notoriously difficult to deal with. We would estimate, therefore, that the inexperienced principals have low situational control. The experienced principals would have moderate situational control. We thus have the following conditions:

High control: Experienced elementary school principals
Moderate control: Inexperienced elementary and experienced
secondary school principals
Low control: Inexperienced secondary school principals

McNamara divided the principals into those with little experienced on the job (less than 2 years) and those who were "established" (more than 3 years). The resulting average performance scores for elementary and for secondary school principals with high and low LPC scores are shown on Figs. 8A and B. As the Contingency Model predicts, secondary school principals who were task-motivated performed best if they were inexperienced, that is, in low-control situations; relationship-motivated principals performed best if they were experienced, placing them in moderate-control situations. The performance of experienced and inexperienced elementary school principals followed the same pattern as that seen for general managers in the study of cooperatives or the study of infantry sergeants, in which experienced leaders were rated as having high situational control. Similar findings, also on college teachers have been reported by Hardy and Bohren (1975). In brief, the data indicate that a dynamic interpretation of the Contingency Model permits us to explain as well as to predict the effects of leadership experience on task performance.

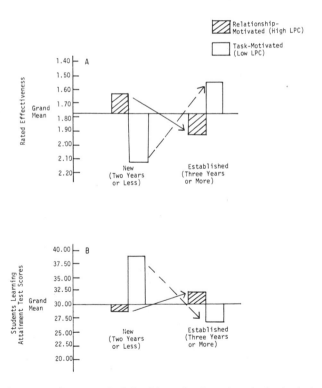

Fig. 8.   Average performance of relationship- and task-motivated school principals with relatively low and high levels of experience. A. Elementary school principals. B. Secondary school principals. Interaction significant. From Fiedler, 1972a, reprinted by permission.

B. SELECTION AND ROTATION

Figures 6, 7, and 8 also have important implications for leadership selection and rotation. At the time of selection most leaders are, of course, inexperienced. As is evident from our data, the performance of task- and relationship-motivated leaders changes in different directions as they gain in experience and training. Selection is, therefore, not the one-time problem of putting square pegs into square holes and round pegs into round holes. Rather, we have to make our selection in the knowledge that the shape of the pegs and the holes changes over time. In selecting leaders we must obviously decide whether we want optimum performance immediately or whether we can afford to wait until the leader's experience and training have made the situation optimal for the particular type of personality the individual brings to the job.

The problem is illustrated schematically in Fig. 9, which shows the expected performance curves of relationship- and task-motivated (high- and low-LPC) leaders who begin their management jobs in situations in which they have very low control (points A and A'), or in moderate-control situations (points B and B'). That is, the performance of the relationship-motivated leader will gradually increase as he moves from the low- to the moderate-control zone (point A to point B). The organization must then either wait until the relationship-motivated leader's control and influence increase with experience, or else it must provide such aids to increasing the leader's control as giving him a harmonious

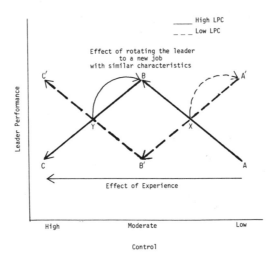

Fig. 9.   Schematic illustration indicating the points in time at which task- and relationship-motivated leaders should be rotated to different jobs. Curved arrows indicate one possible rotation strategy.

group or intensive leadership and task training. This same strategy will also apply to the task-motivated leader whose situational control at the time of his selection is moderate but expected to increase to a high-control situation with time and experience (that is, from point B' to point C' on the graph).

If the organization opts for immediate performance, it will, of course, choose the task-motivated leader for the situation which is, at the time of selection, low in control (point A'); it will select the relationship-motivated leader for the moderate-control situation. We must then expect that the performance of these leaders will gradually decrease as their experience provides them with increasing control and influence. The ideal strategy will, therefore call for rotating or transferring these leaders to a different situation at points X and Y. In other words, the task-motivated leader who reaches point X should be reassigned to a position which provides him either high or relatively low situational control, while the relationship-motivated leader who reaches point Y should be reassigned to another position corresponding to point B. How much time will be required before points X and Y are reached and require reassignment will depend, of course, on the complexity of the task, the nature of the group, and the intellectual resources of the leader, as well as the availability of training. An organization may well consider giving a task-motivated leader in situation A', or a relationship-motivated leader in situation B, a "difficult" group of subordinates, or a more "challenging" task. There may even be reason for discouraging leaders in these situations from obtaining task training. As we shall see, this counterintuitive recommendation is in part supported by several studies described below.

C. LEADERSHIP TRAINING

The effects of leadership training programs are often difficult to identify since the specific procedures and approaches differ widely from one program to another. The results of leadership training have been generally disappointing, however. For example, Campbell, Dunnette, Lawler, and Weick (1970, p. 325) summarize the literature to that time by saying,

> Thus, with regard to the bulk of the literature on training effects, it remains to be demonstrated whether the changes in the criteria used to measure training effects have any importance for the organization's goals. . . . it *must* be demonstrated that "what is learned" in a training program contributes to making an individual a better manager.

Stogdill's survey of the literature reported in his massive *Handbook of Leadership* (Stogdill, 1974, p. 199) led him to a similar conclusion.

It seems possible, however, that many leadership training programs may well be effective in changing behavior or increasing the leaders' situational control without affecting average performance. That is, the overall effects of increasing the situational control of high- and of low-LPC leaders may simply cancel each other out by making some leaders more and others less effective. This is well-illustrated by an ingenious experiment conducted by Chemers, Rice, Sundstrom, and Butler (1975) at the University of Utah. In this study, ROTC cadets were given the LPC scales, and those whose scores fell into the upper and the lower third of the distribution were assigned to leadership positions of 4-man teams. The other ROTC cadets, along with students from a psychology class, served as group members. The group's task consisted of deciphering simple coded messages, that is, cryptograms. The number of letters, correctly identified within a given time, constituted the criterion of performance. The groups were randomly divided so that half of the high- and half of the low-LPC leaders received training in decoding. This training consisted of teaching the leaders a number of simple rules by which these tasks can be accomplished (e.g., the most frequent letters and words in the English language is "e"). This training procedure had the effect of structuring the task since the leaders now were given a specific "best" procedure to follow, as well as guidelines which indicated whether they were on the right track.

As it happened, the group atmosphere was rated as quite low by leaders (in large part because there was considerable ill feeling between the ROTC and psychology students, and because the ROTC cadets felt that they were on the spot). None of the leaders had high position power. Thus, given poor leader–member relations, low position power, and an unstructured task, the situation for untrained leaders fell into the low situational control zone (octant 8), while the trained leaders also had poor leader–member relations and low position power but a structured task. Their leadership situation, therefore, provided correspondingly greater control (i.e., approximately octant 6).

Figure 10 shows the results of this study. In the untrained condition the task-motivated (low-LPC) leaders performed better than did the relationship-motivated leaders. However, in the trained condition the relationship-motivated leaders were more effective. Most importantly, however, the task-motivated leaders *with training* had less effective groups than did the task-motivated leaders *without training*. In other words, the interaction was highly significant. Thus, we can infer that the training given to task-motivated leaders actually *decreased* their effectiveness, as the Contingency Model would predict. In a personal communication, Chemers pointed out that the low-LPC leaders with training had irritated their group members by their expertise and their disdain for group member contributions, and that the resulting arguments seemingly led to poor performance.

Various contaminating factors make it difficult to replicate these results in field studies. For example, managers with many years of experience in an organization are likely to have had more training than managers who are new, and many organizations send their managers to training courses as a reward for good

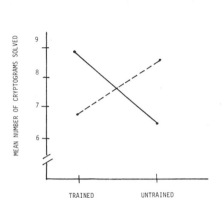

Fig. 10. Comparison of task performance by high- and low-LPC leaders with and without task training. From Chemers *et al.* (1975).

performance or as a sign of esteem rather than as a means for remedying poor performance.

It should also be noted that some training programs deliberately or unwittingly decrease leader control and influence. Training in participative management obviously requires the leader to relinquish some of his power over the decision-making process. Some programs strongly impress leaders with the complexity and difficulty of the job and thus decrease the leaders' confidence that they have much control over their subordinates or the task. Thus, in one of our unpublished analyses of Army personnel, noncommissioned officers with relatively more training tended to perceive their tasks as somewhat more complex and their position power as lower than was the case for those with relatively little training.

Data have been collected in several field studies which measured the amount of training in terms of weeks of attendance in various leadership courses and performance in terms of superiors' evaluations. While these predictor and criterion measures leave much to be desired, the results have generally been in the expected direction. For example, in one study of police patrol sergeants, situational control was judged to be moderate for experienced and trained sergeants and low for inexperienced sergeants. Here the correlation between amount of training and performance was significantly positive ($.84$, $n = 7$, $p < .01$) for relationship-motivated sergeants, but slightly negative ($-.14$, $n = 8$) for task-motivated sergeants (Fiedler, 1972a).

The effects of training are obviously complex. We need to understand how different approaches to task training and human relations training affect the leader's actual and perceived situational control, and we need to consider whether training might also affect the leader's personality or motivational structure. As the final section of this chapter will show, the Contingency Model has led to the development of a training program which teaches the leader to change the situation to fit his or her personality rather than attempting to change leader personality or behavior to fit the situation.

D. ORGANIZATIONAL TURBULENCE

Turbulent and unstable conditions in an organization result in uncertainty and thus lower the leader's situational control (Bons & Fiedler, 1976). These decreases in situational control might arise from any number of reasons. The most common of these are "shake-ups" in the organizational hierarchy, the reassignment of leaders to different units or jobs, or shifts of the organization's position in response to new economic or political demand (e.g., new product lines, new competitors, new legislative constraints).

The effects of certain organizational changes on the leader's performance were recently investigated in a longitudinal study of an infantry division (Bons & Fiedler, 1976) in which 135 Army squad leaders were tested and evaluated shortly after the units were formed and again 5–8 months later.

The organizational change was defined as occurring if a squad leader was given new subordinates, new bosses, or a new job. (Note that this was a different group from that described in Fig. 5.) A military setting for a study of this type is particularly appropriate, since personnel and job changes in military units are quite frequent during the first year of an organization's existence and, therefore, permit the investigator to follow personnel through an entire assignment cycle.

The typical squad leader is a regular Army sergeant with 5–6 years of service. He commands a group of 8–10 enlisted men and he reports to two superiors, namely a second lieutenant who is the platoon leader, and a senior noncommissioned officer who is the platoon sergeant. In the present study, the performance of the squad leaders was evaluated by both of these superiors. The performance scale consisted of eight factored items relevant to task performance and eight items relevant to "personnel performance," specifically morale, discipline, and job satisfaction. In addition, as we shall discuss in more detail later on, the leader's behavior was also rated by his subordinates on a variety of scales including the Consideration and Structuring items of Stogdill's (1963) Leader Behavior Description Questionnaire XII and rewarding and punitive behavior.

Inexperienced squad leaders, as a group, generally described their situation at the first testing session as providing low situational control. Situational control increased to the moderate level for those squad leaders whose organizational environment remained stable, that is, who remained with their squad throughout the entire 6- to 8-month period and served under the same platoon leader and platoon sergeant throughout that time. The experienced squad leaders, with more than 5 or 6 years of Army service, rated themselves as having moderate situational control at first and relatively high control at the termination of the training period, provided their situation remained stable. Since the changes in subordinate units, or in assignment to a different superior, were an old story for experienced leaders but were much more unsettling for inexperienced leaders, we shall here deal with the latter group.

The Contingency Model enables us to make the following predictions: (a) in the stable condition, the inexperienced leaders will move from the low into the moderate-control zone and relationship motivated leaders should perform better than task-motivated leaders; (b) in the condition of organizational turbulence, which decreases the situational control of the leader from moderate to low control (or confines him to the low-control situation), the task-motivated leader should perform better than the relationship-motivated leader. In other words, a decrease in situational control should increase the effectiveness of the low-LPC leader but decrease that of the high-LPC leader.

The results supported these hypotheses. The data points in Fig. 11 show performance at time 2, when performance for time 1 and leader intelligence are statistically controlled by covariance analysis. In effect, the graph permits us to infer that the performance of the low-LPC leader increased somewhat in the turbulent condition between time 1 and time 2, while that of the high-LPC leader markedly decreased. In the stable condition, the performance of the high LPC

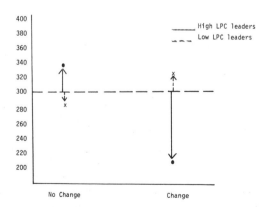

Fig. 11.   Task performance at time 2 by inexperienced high- and low-LPC leaders in stable and unstable organizational conditions with time 1 performance and leader intelligence controlled by covariance analysis. Midline indicates estimated performance at time 1.

leader increased while that of the low-LPC leader remained relatively unchanged.

To summarize this discussion, the importance of these findings is threefold.
First and foremost, our work suggests that the Contingency Model provides a
framework for explaining the dynamic nature of the leadership process. Second,
the data contradict theories of leadership which implicitly or explicitly hold that
one particular managerial style determines good leadership performance.
Likewise, our results contradict the assumption underlying many leadership
training programs which seek to increase leadership performance by increasing
the leader's control and influence. Rather, our data show that an increase in the
leader's situational control and influence will have a differential effect on the
performance of relationship- and task-motivated leaders. Likewise, a decrease in
situational control may improve performance by making the task seem more
challenging and exciting. In large part, the Contingency Model thus helps to
explain why leadership experience and leadership training have usually failed to
increase leadership performance across the board, and why managerial selection
and rotation generally have yielded mixed results.

V. Meaning of Situational Control and LPC

As the preceding sections have shown, the performance of a group or
organization depends to a considerable part on the proper match of the leader's
personality attributes (measured by LPC) and the degree to which the situation
provides him or her with control and influence. We shall here consider these two
main elements of the theory in greater detail.

A. SITUATIONAL CONTROL

An operational definition of situational control or favorableness has been
presented in the earlier part of this chapter in terms of leader–member relations,
task structure, and position power. The situational control dimension can be
conceptually defined as the degree to which the situation enables leaders to
determine the outcome of their decisions and actions. A high degree of control
will therefore make the leader feel less anxious and more certain that the task will
be successfully completed.

A number of studies support this interpretation. First, the reported tension
and anxiety of leaders is significantly higher in situations in which leader–
member relations are poor, the task is relatively unstructured, and position power
is low (Fiedler, 1966, 1967). Second, Nebeker (1975) showed that high situational control can be interpreted as low decision uncertainty. He constructed
scale which asked subjects to indicate the probability that such behaviors a

criticizing poor work, supervising, instructing, and dealing with subordinates will have the intended results. These managers were also asked to indicate how much control and influence they thought they had over the productivity and morale of their work group, using a continuous measure of situational control (see page 67).

In a study of 43 naval aviation maintenance shop supervisors, Nebeker found a correlation of $-.56$ ($p < .01$) between situational control and decision uncertainty, and a correlation of $-.30$ ($p < .05$) between perceived control and decision uncertainty. In a second study of 49 public works managers, the correlation between situational control and decision uncertainty was $-.25$ ($p < .05$) and between situational control and self-perceived control and influence .55 ($p < .01$).

The scaled situational control or favorableness dimension is a theoretically weighted combination of three scales. The question now arises whether the theoretical weights (giving four times as much weight to leader–member relations and twice as much to task structure as to position power) reflect an optimal combination of these three factors. Nebeker compared

a multiple regression solution, where the components of situational favorability are used to predict decision uncertainty, with the zero-order coefficients obtained by the theoretical combination.[3] In both studies, the actual coefficients obtained were equivalent for either method [$r = .56$ vs. $R = .58$ in one study, and $r = .40$ vs. $R = .39$ in the other].

On the basis of these findings Nebeker concluded,

It is impressive that the zero-order coefficients account for just as much of the variance as do the multiple regression coefficients. Such a comparison actually favors the theoretical combination, since the multiple regression solution is a "best fit" and can, therefore, capitalize on error variance. It appears that Fiedler's theoretical combination of the component variables of situational favorability is about as close to optimal in predicting uncertainty as we could possibly expect. [Nebeker, 1975, p. 292]

A subsequent study by Mai-Dalton (1975) found an almost identical relationship ($R = .54$) between rated decision uncertainty and the situational control subscales.

Still another experiment by Beach et al. (1978, in press) asked students to estimate the probability of success and the situational favorableness of a series of hypothetical leadership situations. The experiment presented these leadership situations as having either good or poor leader–member relations, high or low task structure, and high or low position power, using a $2 \times 2 \times 2$ factorial design. The two measures estimated probability of success and situational favorableness, correlated .89 ($p < .0001$), suggesting that these are essentially identical concepts. A multiple correlation was then computed with situational favorableness or control as the criterion and the three situational control subscales as predictors.

The Beta weights obtained by Hoffman's (1960) method were quite similar to those predicted by the Contingency Model, that is, .45 for leader–member relations, .33 for task structure, and .11 for position power, roughly in the proportion of 4:3:1.

These findings have important implications for integrating the Contingency Model with the work of other decision theorists (e.g., MacCrimmon & Taylor, 1976; Schroder, Driver, & Streufert, 1967). This can be seen by examining the "information searching behavior" of high- and low-LPC persons under conditions of high and of low uncertainty. For example, a study by Mai-Dalton (1975) asked subjects to complete an In-Basket Test which requires responses to letters, memoranda, or messages addressed to the leader within a given period of time. In moderate-control situations in which high-LPC leaders tend to be most effective, these individuals were also most likely to ask for additional information, while low-LPC persons manifested most information searching behavior in high-control situations.

A strong argument also can be made for considering such variables as mechanistic versus organic climates (Burns & Stalker, 1961), environmental uncertainty (Lawrence & Lorsch, 1967), and organizational climate (House & Rizzo, 1971) as special cases of situational control. A mechanistic climate is defined as one in which the organization is stable and therefore predictable, while an organic climate is more ambiguous and fluid and thus less predictable. Csoka (1975) conducted a study of Army dining hall stewards in 52 Army mess halls. He predicted that the high-LPC leaders would perform better in an organic climate while low-LPC leaders would excel in a mechanistic climate. Organizational performance was rated on standardized scales by company commanders and by food service officers who evaluated the quality of the meals as well as the attractiveness and sanitation of the service.

As predicted by the Contingency Model, task-motivated (low-LPC) leaders performed better in dining halls rated as having a relatively mechanistic climate ($-.51$, $n = 17$, $p < .05$), while relationship-motivated (high-LPC) leaders performed better in the dining halls rated as having an organic climate ($+.57$, $n = 17$, $p < .05$). (Leader LPC and group performance for all of 52 dining halls correlated $-.08$.) In an effort to approximate the Contingency Model situational control dimensions still further, Csoka categorized the groups as high or low on leader–member relations, as having a mechanistic or organic climate (to substitute for high or low task structure), and as having a high position power in all groups. The resulting correlations shown in Table V again support the predictions. The Csoka study thus provides an important bridge between the Contingency Model and other theories by demonstrating that a mechanistic or organic organizational climate is neither conducive nor detrimental to performance. Rather, it affects the leader's control and influence, and thus determines in part whether high- or low-LPC leaders will be more effective under the given conditions.

TABLE V

CORRELATIONS BETWEEN LPC AND PERFORMANCE
RATINGS IN EACH OCTANT REORDERED ON A
MECHANISTIC–ORGANIC CONTINUUM

Octant 1	Octant 6	Octant 3	Octant 5
$-.66^a$	$-.80^b$	$-.69^b$	$.80^a$
$n = 14$	$n = 20$	$n = 11$	$n = 7$

[a] $p < .05$.
[b] $p < .005$.

B. LPC SCORE

LPC has generally been seen as the weakest part of the Contingency Model. The measure has been difficult to interpret, and a number of questions remain, even after more than 25 years of continuous research. This section briefly discusses some methodological issues related to LPC, and the interpretation of the score.

1. Reliability and Stability of LPC

The internal consistency of the LPC score has never been in question. A recent review by Rice (1978) reports a mean split-half reliability from various reported studies of .88. Some investigators have found separate interpersonal and task factors in previous scales (e.g., Fox, Hill, & Guertin, 1973; Yukl, 1970) but the task factor has been relatively unimportant in most of these analyses. A new 18-item scale shown on page 61 of this chapter has been designed to minimize task factor items and has somewhat higher internal reliability than did the previously reported scales.

The more critical problem is the retest reliability or stability of the LPC score, since it determines whether the measure can serve as a predictor of leadership. The stability of the score also has bearing on whether LPC measures a transitory attitude, as has been claimed by Fishbein, Landy, and Hatch (1969b); and Stinson and Tracy (1974), or a more stable personality attribute.

The inference that the LPC score must have some stability over time is supported by such investigations as Chemers and Skrzypek (1972), Fiedler et al. (1969), and Hardy and his associates (1973; Hardy, 1971, 1975; Hardy & Bohren, 1975), since all of these obtained the leader's LPC scores several weeks prior to the study. If LPC measured a transitory attitude, it is unlikely that significant results in the hypothesized direction could have been obtained.

The question of stability has now been extensively investigated by Rice (1978) whose survey of the literature on LPC uncovered 23 retest correlations. The retest reliabilities in these studies ranged from .01 to .91 with a median of .67 and a mean of .64 (SD = .36). A correlation between the length of the test–retest interval and the magnitude of the stability coefficient was $-.30$ ($n = 23$, n.s.). Since the interval between testing ranged from a few days to 2½ years, these findings indicate that the magnitude of the stability of LPC is not primarily a function of time. Bons (1974) obtained a retest reliability for a group of higher level Army leaders over a 5-month period of .72 ($n = 45$, $p < .001$) and Prothero and Fiedler (1974) obtained a retest correlation of .67 ($n = 18$, $p < .01$) for faculty members of a school of nursing over a 16- to 24-month period. There is evidence that a very unsatisfactory work experience in a laboratory experiment can change the LPC score temporarily, and that a major life change, e.g., a stressful combat assignment may affect LPC (Bons, Bass, & Komorita, 1970). On the other hand, to place the median retest correlation for LPC of .67 in some perspective, it should be noted by way of comparison that the test–retest correlation of the Minnesota Multiphasic Inventory (MMPI) over a period of 1 week was .60, and the median stability coefficient of the Hartshorne and May honesty scales over 6 months was .50 (Sax, 1974). Mehrens and Lehmann (1969) reported the stability of the California Psychological Inventory for 13,000 subjects over a 1-year period as .65 for males and .68 for females. Thus the stability of LPC clearly falls within the acceptable range for established personality attribute measures. The variance of retest reliabilities appears to be high. It should be pointed out, however, that the lowest correlations of .01 came from participants in a civil service executive development workshop, and the next lowest correlations of .23 came from a group of undergraduates participating in an 8-week business game. In both of these cases, the training program may well have created demand characteristics or even implicit instructions as to the "proper" attitude one should adapt toward poor co-workers (Rice, 1978). It is, in any event, difficult to compare the variance of retest correlations of LPC with the variance of other social psychological measures since it is rare to find even one or two stability estimates reported (Robinson & Shaver, 1973).

2. Meaning of LPC

There has been considerable controversy about the precise interpretation of LPC. It has been described as a measure of an attitude (Fishbein, Landy, & Hatch, 1969b), of cognitive complexity (Mitchell, 1970), of work orientation (Rice, 1975), and of a motivational hierarchy or goal structure (Fiedler, 1972b). There is very little question, however, that individuals who perceive their LPCs in very negative and perjorative terms (low LPC) are basically more concerned with the task than with their interpersonal relations; those who perceive their LPCs in a more positive and differentiated manner (high LPC) are basically more concerned with interpersonal relations than with task accomplishment.

The main problem of defining the exact meaning of the LPC score stems from two sources. First, LPC does not consistently correlate with any of the usual personality tests. While this is good insofar as it tells us that we are measuring a unique trait or attribute, it also precludes the usual construct validation procedure of defining one test score in terms of other tests or personality measures. A second source of difficulty in defining LPC derives from the fact that high- and low-LPC persons tend to behave differently in situations in which their control is high and in which their control is low. We shall return to this second problem after reviewing the "main effects" attributable to high and low LPC scores.

At the simplest level, the LPC score can be seen as measuring an attitude of the leader toward the person with whom he or she finds it most difficult to work, that is, someone who is extremely frustrating when a leader tries to get a job done (Fishbein et al., 1969b). Different people get frustrated for different reasons. Someone who cares passionately about getting a job done will react with a great deal of acrimony and resentment when someone poses a threat to job accomplishment. On the other hand, someone to whom the task is of lesser importance will react in a more moderate and detached manner toward a poor co-worker. He will be less emphatic in his condemnation and perhaps less infuriated by the person who does not do his share. The extremely negative ratings by the low-LPC leader suggest, therefore, that the poor work relationship is of such overriding importance to the leader that it completely distorts and colors his perception of the poor co-worker's other personality attributes. A high-LPC leader seems to look at the poor co-worker first as an individual, as someone who could still be valued for other characteristics rather than just for his contribution to the job.[5]

In addition, there are also qualitative differences in the way in which people with high and with low LPC scores perceive those with whom they cannot work. Fishbein et al. found that high-LPC persons tend to describe their LPCs as bull-headed, bossy, dogmatic people who avoid work, are know-it-alls, and thus threaten smooth interpersonal relations in a work group. Low-LPC persons tend to see their LPCs as unintelligent, unreliable, self-centered, and lazy—in other words as poor team players who are detrimental to getting the job done.

The relatively greater concern for interpersonal relations by high-LPC leaders, and for task performance by low-LPC leaders, is also shown by Borden's (1976) recent study which correlated the degree to which leaders perceived their job as valuable and the way they perceived their interpersonal relations with superiors and with subordinates. Borden noted that the leader's boss as a rule not only defines the task, but that his evaluation of the leader also defines the effectiveness with which the task has been accomplished. A good relationship

---

[5]There is some evidence of a middle-LPC group which differs in behavior and attitudes from both high- and low-LPC persons. These individuals, who comprise about 7–10% above and below the population mean of 60, either have a "mixed" motivation pattern or else a distinctly different leadership approach. They seem less concerned about the opinions and attitudes of others and less dependent on superiors' and subordinates' evaluations, as well as less desirous of accepting a leadership position (Bass, Fiedler, & Krueger, 1964; Mai-Dalton, 1975). Further research is needed to describe this group in a more adequate manner.

with the boss has a number of advantages for a leader who is concerned about his job. It enables him to communicate more freely with the person who assigns and evaluates task performance and, consequently, also to obtain better guidance on how the task is to be done. According to Borden's hypothesis, the low-LPC leader's evaluation of the job will correlate with the degree to which he has a good relationship with his boss. In contrast, a good relationship with subordinates implies that the leader can rely on his group for emotional support and satisfaction of interpersonal needs. The value which the job has for the high-LPC leader should correlate with the leader's perceptions of leader–subordinate relations. This relationship will not hold for low-LPC leaders. As Table VI shows, the results of analysis for a sample of platoon sergeants and a sample of platoon leaders generally support these hypotheses.

In a similar vein, Hansson and Fiedler (1973) found evidence that high-LPC persons tend to be more concerned with being in harmony with their interpersonal environment than are low-LPC persons. High-LPC employees of a park department expressed greater interest in continued employment the more they agreed with management on policies, goals, and departmental purposes (.30, .47,* and .39,* $ns = 24; p* = < .05$). In contrast, the corresponding correlations obtained for low-LPC employees were low and insignificant ($-.12, .01$, and .09; $ns = 19$), indicating that the feeling of solidarity and identification with the organization is more important to high- than to low-LPC persons.

The same conclusion emerged from an unpublished analysis of men in 32

TABLE VI

CORRELATIONS BETWEEN LEADER–SUBORDINATE RELATIONS
AND THE DEGREE TO WHICH THE LEADER
CONSIDERS HIS JOB TO BE VALUABLE

Leader	Leader–superior relations		Leader–subordinate relations	
	High LPC	Low LPC	High LPC	Low LPC
Squad leaders	.12	.30[a]	.35[b]	.24
(sample 1)	(56)	(64)	(56)	(61)
Squad leaders	33[b]	38[b]	40[c]	.25
(sample 2)	(66)	(50)	(66)	(50)
Platoon sergeants	.22	.66[c]	.74[c]	.23
(sample 3)	(29)	(34)	(19)	(29)
Platoon leaders	.30	.64[c]	.60[b]	.23
(sample 4)	(25)	(29)	(15)	(17)

Number of cases is indicated in parentheses.
[a] $p < .05$.
[b] $p < .01$.
[c] $p < .001$.

infantry squads. In each of these squads, one high- and one low-LPC man was asked to describe himself and his squad leader on identical scale items. (As previous research has shown, individuals feel closer to a person they perceive as similar to themselves than to someone they perceive to be different, e.g., Fiedler, Warrington, & Blaisdell, 1952; Secord, Backman, & Eachus, 1964.) Each of these men also indicated how much he (a) enjoyed being a member of his squad; (b) was interested in making a career of the Army, and (c) was satisfied and contented with military life. Feeling close to the squad leader (perceiving him as similar) was significantly correlated with satisfaction with military life for high-LPC squad members (.54, .31, .45, respectively), but not for low-LPC squad members (.09, − .11, − .05, respectively). Thus, the high LPC person associates a good relationship with his boss (in this case, his squad leader) with a feeling of wanting to belong to the organization; the low LPC person associates a good relationship with his boss with a feeling that his job is satisfying and valuable.

Chemers and Skrzypek (1972) found that high-LPC leaders generally made significantly more social emotional comments, while low-LPC leaders generally displayed considerably more task-relevant behavior in various task situations in their West Point study. Nebeker and Hansson (1972) found high-LPC persons to be significantly more optimistic about human nature and positive in their attitudes toward others than were low-LPC persons, and hence more likely to seek close interpersonal relations with others. The evidence from these and similar studies is, therefore, quite consistent in showing that high-LPC persons are more concerned and affected by interpersonal relations while low-LPC persons are more concerned with task performance.

3. LPC and the Person–Situation Interaction

The interpretation of the LPC score is complicated by the frequent finding that the behavior of high- and low-LPC leaders is strongly affected by the control and influence which the situation provides. In low-control situations and under stress, high-LPC leaders generally attend to interpersonal relations while low-LPC leaders attend to the task. However, in situations in which the leader enjoys high control and influence, the high-LPC leader's behavior is seen as more task relevant and less considerate while the low-LPC leader is seen as less concerned with the task and as more considerate. In other words, not only the individual's leadership performance but also his leadership behavior is affected by the interaction of personality attributes reflected by LPC and situational control.

This is shown in a number of empirical studies. For example, Meuwese and Fiedler (1965) compared the behavior of Reserve Officer Training Corps cadets under relatively stress-free and relatively stressful conditions. Each group, consisting of 3 men, performed two creative tasks (i.e., developing a new pay system for the ROTC and inventing a fable about the Army for school children). In both of these conditions the highest ranking cadet was appointed to be the leader. In the low-stress condition the sessions were quite informal, the students were told to come in civilian clothes, and were assured that their performance would not affect their Army career. In the high-stress condition, the men came in uniform and they addressed each other by rank. An Army officer with the rank of major, lieutenant colonel, or colonel, who was unknown to the cadets, sat across the table from the group and continually evaluated their performance. Subsequent postsession ratings indicated that this last condition had been quite stressful.

As Fig. 12 shows, in the low-stress condition, low-LPC leaders were rated as democratic and promoting group participation while high-LPC leaders were seen as showing more concern with the task, that is, as frequently proposing new ideas and as integrating the ideas of others. In the high-stress condition, however, the low-LPC leader tended to behave in a task-relevant manner while the high-LPC leaders behaved more frequently in a democratic, participative manner which showed concern with interpersonal relations (Fiedler, 1967, pp. 191–192).

Similar results have been obtained in a study of group creativity by Fiedler

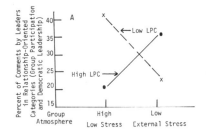

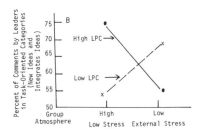

Fig. 12.   The effect of leader motivation (LPC) and situational stress on interpersonal, social–emotional, and job-relevant leader behavior. A. Relationship-oriented categories. B. Task-oriented categories. From Meuwese and Fiedler (1965).

et al. (1961), an experiment on Air Force instructor behaviors in stressful and nonstressful situations (Ayer, 1968), and in a study of school principals by Hawley (1969).

These complex findings can be explained by considering the high and the low LPC score as indicating a different motivational or goal hierarchy. High-LPC persons are seen as giving highest priority in work situations to having close and emotionally supportive interpersonal relations with subordinates. Low-LPC persons, on the other hand, give highest priority to task accomplishment which provides them with tangible evidence of their competence. (Intelligent and experienced persons may, of course, seek to attain these goals in a somewhat different manner than will dull and inexperienced persons.)

Maslow (1954) has pointed out that satisfied needs cease to motivate. In other words, assured that they will attain their primary goal, individuals will then seek to achieve the goals which are next in priority. In groups which provide high situational control the leaders have this assurance: High-LPC leaders have the support of their subordinates; low-LPC leaders know that the task will be completed (Beach *et al.,* 1975). Under these high-control conditions, the relationship-motivated leader can then turn his attention to other aspects of his situation, for example, seeking the approbation of such important others as the boss or faculty member who serves as experimenter, as well as gaining more complete control of the group. As one astute observer noted, in a high-control situation, the relationship-motivated leader acts like an "underemployed professional mother," that is, in an overly controlling, managing, and demanding manner. The low-LPC leader who knows the task will get done can sit back, relax, and behave in a generally considerate and pleasant manner.

Several studies can be interpreted as providing direct support for the motivational hierarchy hypothesis. Larson and Rowland (1973) worked with a group of highway department managers in an executive development seminar. In the course of this program, high- and low-LPC managers were asked to complete an In-Basket Test which requires the individual to respond to various letters, memoranda, requests, and messages which he supposedly finds on his desk. Larson and Rowland randomly assigned the managers in their study to one of two conditions. In a nonthreatening, low-stress condition, the managers were told that the procedure was experimental and was administered so that their opinion about its usefulness could be obtained. In the high-stress condition, the managers were urged to do their best since the test was "a well-known predictor of administrative ability." The effectiveness of the stress manipulation was verified by means of palmar sweat measures.

The responses to In-Basket items were rated as primarily showing concern with the task or concern with interpersonal relations. As predicted, the high-LPC managers gave more task-relevant responses in the low-stress condition and more relationship-oriented responses in the high-stress condition. The reverse was the case for low-LPC managers who gave more relationship-oriented statements in the low-stress condition and more task-relevant statements in the high-stress condition.

Similar results were obtained in a laboratory experiment by Green, Nebeker, and Boni (1976) in which 26 high-LPC and 26 low-LPC persons played the part of a committee chairperson in a role-played and prerecorded committee meeting. Each of the subjects listened to the tape-recorded committee session which was interrupted at seven different times to permit the "committee chairman" to "say just what you would say if you were actually there." He was to respond to disagreements among committee members, requests for more information, the need to deal with difficult committee members, etc. The leaders were given either relatively high- or low-position power, and the prerecorded meetings were designed to be either harmonious and cooperative or torn by conflict and disharmony.

Ratings of tape-recorded responses showed that the "chairmen" with high LPC were somewhat less considerate than were those with low LPC in the high-control condition. In the condition which involved low situational control, high-LPC chairmen were significantly more considerate and concerned with interpersonal relations while low-LPC chairmen were significantly more task oriented.

4. Changes in Situational Control and Their Effects on the Behavior of High- and Low-LPC Persons

The dynamic nature of the relationship between situational control and leader behavior becomes apparent in a number of studies. In one particularly important experiment of this type by Sample and Wilson (1965), members of a large introductory psychology class were divided into small groups under high- and low-LPC leaders with the instruction to plan, run, and report an experiment with a laboratory rat. Unknown to the students, an observer was assigned to each group to record the same leader's behavior for each of these three phases, using Bales' (1951) interaction process analysis system. The three subtasks could be scaled in terms of the leader's situational control. Planning, the least structured task, gave the leader low control. Reporting ranked next, then running the experiment which gave the leader relatively high situational control since the task at that point was very highly structured.

Figure 13 presents the results of this study. The vertical axes of the graphs show the leader's task-relevant behavior and socioemotional behavior; the horizontal axes show the three phases in order of high, medium, and low task structure, respectively, that is, running, reporting, and planning. As can be seen, the low-LPC leaders made more positive social–emotional comments and fewer task-relevant statements in the running phase than did high-LPC leaders. However, in the planning phase in which the leader's situational control was low,

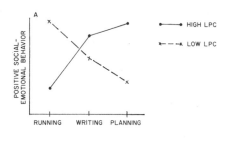

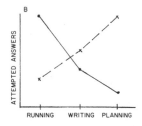

Fig. 13A and B   Changes in social–emotional and task relevant behavior by relationship and task-motivated leaders in different phases of the same group task. Data from Sample and Wilson (1965). Reprinted from Fiedler, 1971c with permission.

low-LPC leaders showed concern with the task and high-LPC leaders made more socioemotional comments.

The dynamic interaction between leader LPC and situational control becomes especially clear in an experiment involving human relations training for leaders. If the motivational hierarchy interpretation of LPC is correct, training which increases leader–group relations will increase the leader's situational control. With greater situational control (a shift to the left on Fig. 13) high-LPC leaders should become *less* considerate and *less* concerned with their interpersonal relations while task-motivated leaders would become more concerned with interpersonal relations and, hence, more considerate. An experiment was conducted in Iran by Chemers (1969) which used 48 Americans living in Iran who served as leaders and 96 Iranians who volunteered to serve as group members. The Americans were split into high- and low-LPC groups. Half of each group was given a control training on the physical geography of Iran and the other half received culture assimilator training designed to increase the ability of Americans to get along with Iranians and to interact with them in a more effective manner. [The effectiveness of this culture training program has been reported in a number of studies (see Mitchell, Dossett, Fiedler, & Triandis, 1972).]

At the conclusion of three tasks, the Iranian group members rated the

American leader, the leader's consideration behavior, and the group climate. The mean ratings, converted to z-scores, are shown on Table VII. As can be seen, all interactions were significant in the predicted direction: The low-LPC leaders who received training were seen as more considerate (Fig. 14), the group climate was rated as better, and leaders were rated highly. The high-LPC leaders who had received the identical training were less esteemed, were rated as less considerate, and the group climate was seen as less pleasant. No differences were found between high- and low-LPC leaders in the control condition. We may thus infer that the training increased the leader's situational control and that this increased situational control had a beneficial effect on the interpersonal behavior of low-LPC leaders but a detrimental effect on that of high-LPC leaders.

Similar changes in leader behavior also occur in real-life conditions when factors in the organizational environment increase or decrease the leader's situational control. This is shown in the previously mentioned study of infantry squad leaders (Bons & Fiedler, 1976). As will be recalled, leaders were assigned to new squads shortly after formation of the units. They were tested and evaluated at that time and again some 5–8 months later. In the intervening period, some of the squad leaders remained in a stable environment in which they worked with the same superiors and the same group of subordinates and, therefore, increased their situational control as they gained experience on the job. Other squad leaders had to adjust to new bosses and to new subordinates. We expect, of course, that a turbulent environment decreases the leader's situational control. In the latter situation, the high-LPC leaders should seek closer interpersonal ties, while the low-LPC leaders should seek greater control over the group in order to accomplish the task.

Control in a military organization is primarily exercised by offering rewards or by implicit or explicit threat of punishment to assure compliance in the per-

TABLE VII

INTERACTION OF TRAINING AND LEADERSHIP STYLE ON
SEVERAL MEASURES OF INTERPERSONAL RELATIONS[a]

Scale Member ratings of:	Culture		Geography		F	p
	High LPC	Low LPC	High LPC	Low LPC		
Group atmosphere	−.354	.118	.091	−.029	5.00	.05
Leader's consideration behavior	−.366	.342	.033	−.216	11.00	.01
Evaluation of leader	−.403	.205	.037	−.001	6.73	.025
Climate: liking for situation	−.421	.231	.002	.017	6.27	.025

[a] Standardized (z) scores.
[b] From Chemers (1969).

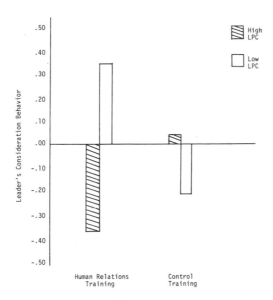

Fig. 14. Subordinates' behavior ratings of high- and low-LPC leaders with human relations training and with control training. From Chemers (1969).

formance of the task. Rewarding behavior clearly is more conducive to the development of good interpersonal relations than is punitive behavior. We would expect, therefore, that these two types of behavior will be used differently by high- and by low-LPC leaders as their situational control changes. Figure 15 shows the subordinates' ratings of their squad leader's rewarding behavior. The points on the graph indicate the rated behavior at time 2, with behavior ratings and leader intelligence statistically controlled by covariance analysis. The dashed midline on the graph indicates the mean behavior score at time 1, that is, the presumed ratings leaders obtained at the first rating period.

At the left side of the graph we find that the leaders' rewarding behavior in a stable leadership environment did not change noticeably between time 1 and time 2. However, in the unstable condition, in which the leader changed jobs, high-LPC squad leaders became dramatically more rewarding in their interactions with subordinates, while low-LPC leaders became drastically less rewarding, that is, less concerned with good interpersonal relations.

Figure 16 shows the results of a similar analysis for threatened or actual punitive behaviors (official punishment or court-martial). The analysis compared leaders who were or who were not given a new squad in the time intervening between the first and the second evaluation and testing periods.

As can be seen, all leaders tended to become more punitive by time 2, and there was no difference in the behavior of relationship-motivated leaders in the

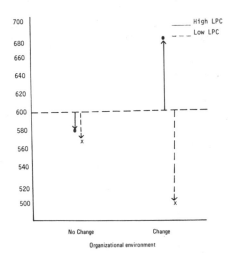

Fig. 15. Rewarding behavior of high- and low-LPC leaders at time 2 in stable and unstable organizational conditions, with leader intelligence and behavior scores at time 1 controlled by covariance and analysis. Midline indicates mean scores at time 1.

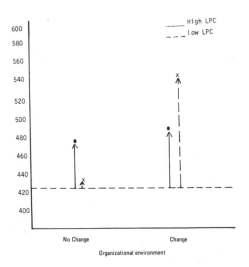

Fig. 16. Administrative–punitive behavior of high- and low-LPC leaders at time 2 in stable and unstable organizational conditions, with leader intelligence and behavior scores at time 1 controlled by covariance analysis. Midline indicates mean scores at time 1.

stable and in the unstable leadership condition. However, task-motivated leaders became significantly more punitive in the unstable condition in which their situational control decreased, presumably because they felt a need for more control over group members in order to accomplish the task.

C. LEADER BEHAVIOR AND ORGANIZATIONAL PERFORMANCE

In light of the foregoing discussion, let us now attempt to explain effective leadership performance in behavioral terms for the typical case.

In *high-control* situations, high-LPC leaders are seen as inconsiderate and more concerned with the task than with their interpersonal relations. Low-LPC leaders are rated as relatively unconcerned with the task, but considerate, pleasant, and relaxed in their interactions with group members. Recall here that a high-control situation implies that the leader has the group's support as well as a highly structured task and high position power. Under these conditions, the group knows what the task involves and wants to perform it. A group of motivated and knowledgeable subordinates obviously requires no more than minimal guidance from the leader.

The low-LPC leader in a high-control situation provides minimal guidance. If the motivational hierarchy hypothesis of LPC is correct, the low-LPC leader behaves in this fashion because his primary goal of task accomplishment is being satisfied, he trusts his group, and he can now focus on his secondary goal of good interpersonal relations. The high-LPC leader, whose primary goal of securing group support is satisfied, now turns to the task. He is generally described in such situations as directive, managing, autocratic, and structuring. He provides strong leadership where none is needed. In fact, his behavior may very well interfere with task accomplishment: His overcontrolling behavior may be resented by group members who are already doing their best on the job. In short, the high-LPC leader's behavior may be maladaptive in high-control situations.

In *moderate-control* situations, in which high-LPC leaders generally perform best, low-LPC leaders become increasingly concerned with the task. They are described as relatively more task-oriented, structuring, and controlling, and as less considerate and less concerned with interpersonal relations. High-LPC leaders, on the other hand, are generally rated as considerate and interpersonally oriented.

To understand the full significance of these behavior patterns on subordinate performance, we must recall the nature of the two moderate-control situations. One of these (octant 4) is usually characterized by tasks which involve free expression of members' opinions, attitudes, and information. These are tasks which require tact and sensitivity on the part of the leader. Examples are policy and decision-making committees, research and development teams, and organizations in which the leader plays a coordinating rather than a controlling role.

These situations frequently require the leader to reconcile conflicting viewpoints, to negotiate between subgroups, and to encourage and support new ideas. The second moderate-control situation involves work units in which the leader has high task structure and position power, but relatively poor relations with the group (octant 5). Again, the leader must be tactful and sensitive under these conditions. While he may know exactly what to do, and while he may have the legitimate power to enforce his decisions, prudence and concern for productivity demand that he behave with circumspection lest the group turn against him or engage in subtle sabotage. The high-LPC leader, who attends to the interpersonal problems in his group, is likely to succeed here. The low-LPC leader, who withdraws from interpersonal relations and focuses on the task to the neglect of group members, is likely to find an unwilling and uncooperative work team.

In the *low-control* situation, which is characterized by poor leader–member relations, low task structure, low position power, and/or high stress, the low-LPC leaders tend to perform well.

The high-LPC leader tends to become anxious in this situation and seeks emotional support. He is relatively nondirective, nonstructuring, and he pays less attention to the task. In conditions of *very high* stress, high-LPC leaders may withdraw almost completely from the leadership role, as indicated by the way their subordinates tend to describe them, namely as nondirective, nonstructuring, nonsupportive, and inconsiderate. It is then not surprising that the task performance of high-LPC leaders is poor in low-control situations.

Low-LPC leaders, on the other hand, are described as directive, structuring, and concerned with the task, but inconsiderate and unconcerned with their relations with subordinates. In other words, the low-LPC leader is likely to be effective because he is firmly committed to the task regardless of the consequences which this might have on his relations with subordinates. If they do not perform well, he will not hesitate to reprimand or punish them or to discard them. This pattern of behavior is well-illustrated by company troubleshooters and "start-up men" who are sent to new or ailing offices and plants, or to organizations which are in a state of crisis. These individuals enjoy the challenge of a new job and they perform well under stress, but they rarely remain highly effective after the organization has again settled into a comfortable routine. Under these circumstances, which are likely to provide moderate situational control, the organization is likely to call on a manager who has the ability to keep people working together in harmony and who has the knack for keeping the organization running smoothly, namely, a high-LPC leader.

D. WHAT DOES LPC "REALLY" MEASURE?

Let us now briefly recapitulate what we know about LPC. First, and perhaps foremost, LPC is an internally consistent measure which is relatively stable over time. It thus appears to be a personality attribute which is transsituational in nature.

It is, no doubt, discouraging that there should still be questions about the interpretation of this score after more than 25 years of continuous research. However, this is a problem which LPC shares with many other social–psychological measures including, for example, cognitive complexity, locus of control, or the K Scale of the MMPI. In fact, as recent controversies show, there is even doubt that we know, after all these years, what intelligence tests "really" measure. Admittedly, LPC poses a more difficult problem.

As has been said earlier, it may be argued whether LPC is an orientation toward work, an attitude, a cognitive complexity measure, or an index of a motivational hierarchy. However, there is general consensus among those who have worked with this measure that a high LPC score identifies a person whose major concern and first priority is the development and maintenance of good interpersonal relations; a low LPC score identifies a person whose major concern and priority is the accomplishment of the task or, perhaps in a more general sense, to obtain tangible evidence of his or her own competence. These concerns are especially apparent in conditions of low situational control, high stress, and high uncertainty. There is consistent but less compelling evidence that the opposite types of behaviors occur in situations which provide the leader with a high degree of control and certainty. These findings favor a motivational hierarchy interpretation, although other interpretations, consistent with these findings, are also tenable. Whatever the precise and final interpretation of the LPC score might turn out to be, there is very little question that it measures a personality attribute which has very important consequences for organizational behavior.

VI. A New Approach to Leadership Training[6]

One acid test of a dynamic leadership theory is its ability to increase the leader's effectiveness and the organization's performance. Our ability to control a process is, of course, a strong indication that we understand it. The Contingency Model suggests that we can improve leadership performance by changing the match between the leader's personality and his or her situational control

[6]This effect may have broader implications for relating leadership theory and personality theory. A possible bridge between personality and leadership theories becomes apparent when we recall (a) that leader uncertainty and anxiety tend to be high when situational control and influence are low, and (b) that high- and low-LPC persons attempt to cope with anxiety and uncertainty in a different manner. There is also growing evidence that the intelligence of the leader complexly interacts with the LPC score and the situation in affecting behavior. Since intelligent people generally have more resources for dealing with anxiety and uncertainty, this finding is not surprising. The exact role which intelligence plays in these interactions is now under investigation.

and influence. Increasing leadership performance implies then either changing the leader's personality attributes which are reflected by LPC or else changing the leader's situational control. The latter obviously presents the easier task, particularly since organizational changes as well as leadership experience and training imply almost constant changes in the leader's situational control. One method of dealing with the problem of maintaining the right match between the leader's personality and the control and influence the situation provides is to teach the leader to modify the situation to match his personality. A training program to accomplish this purpose has recently been devised.

A. GENERAL DESCRIPTION OF THE PROGRAM

The training program, called Leader Match (Fiedler *et al.*, 1976), is presented in the form of a self-administered workbook, which can also be augmented by appropriate lecture–discussions and films. Completing the manual takes from 4 to 8 hours.

Each chapter of the workbook consists of a short explanation of the various basic concepts of the Contingency Model. The explanations are followed by several short problems, case studies, or leadership episodes (probes) for which the trainee selects the best answer. The trainee is then given immediate feedback on the response. An incorrect response requires review of the chapter and trying the probe again in order to assure that the material is completely understood. The manual also contains two review sections and several short tests to identify problem areas which need additional review.

The first part of the manual requires trainees to complete the LPC scale which identifies and interprets their motivational structure. The next four chapters are devoted to teaching trainees how to measure their situational control, that is, leader–member relations, task structure, and position power, and to determine the degree to which the trainee's current leadership job and personality are appropriately matched.[7]

In the final chapters trainees learn to modify factors in their situation in order to obtain the appropriate match between their personality and situational control and to apply the program to the leadership situations of their subordinates in leadership positions.

B. VALIDATION STUDIES

Nine validation studies of Leader Match have now been completed. Four of these were conducted in civilian organizations and five in military settings. The

---

[7]The trainees' ability to measure situational control accurately, in an absolute sense, is, of course, less important for this purpose than teaching them to focus on the relevant factors in the leadership situation and how to modify these as needed.

latter are of particular importance, since a large number of leaders perform identical tasks and, therefore, can be compared under more controlled conditions.

1. Civilian Organizations

The subjects for the four civilian studies consisted of: (a) volunteers of a public health agency, (b) middle managers of a county government, (c) police sergeants, and (d) public works supervisors and managers (Fiedler, Mahar, & Schmidt, 1975). In each study those eligible for training were randomly assigned to either the trained or the control condition; 2–4 months after training a performance evaluation was obtained from at least two of the subject's supervisors.

In all four studies, trained leaders were rated as performing better than untrained leaders, with 80% of the performance items in the predicted direction and 33% significantly so. However, because of serious attrition problems, and the possibility that the attrition may have reflected poor motivation on the part of some trainees, the results of these studies had to be interpreted with considerable caution, and studies under more controlled conditions were essential.

2. Military Organizations

Two tests were made with naval personnel, namely 52 junior officers and chief petty officers from eight naval air squadrons, and 20 officers and petty officers from a naval destroyer (Leister, Borden, Fiedler, 1977). One half of the officers and petty officers were randomly assigned to a training group which received the Leader Match program, while the other half were assigned to the control group. The subjects in both groups completed several questionnaires. The trainees then participated in two 4-hour supervised training sessions during which they read the manual, viewed a 28-minute film, "Leadership: Style or Circumstance" (CRM Productions, 1974), and participated in a short discussion.

Performance ratings were completed prior to training for each subject by three of his or her immediate supervisors. Ratings were again obtained 6 months later from at least two of the *same* supervisors. It was thus possible to determine the degree to which a particular leader's performance had increased or decreased subsequent to training. The specific method involved conversion of pre- and post-training performance scores to standardized scores and comparing the mean change in performance scores of trained and control groups. This method of using change scores is considered appropriate for a study of this nature (Overall & Woodward, 1975).

The results indicated that the performance of the trained group had increased significantly over the 6-month period when compared with the control group on task performance items as well as on personal performance items ($p <$ .001 and .002, respectively) (See Fig. 17). This means that the increase in

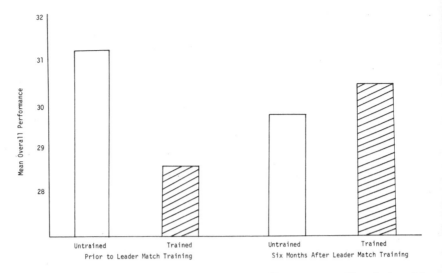

Fig. 17. Comparison of performance ratings of Navy officers and petty officers in the training and control conditions before and after Leader Match training.

performance occurred in the interpersonal relations area, morale, and discipline, as well as in assigned tasks. Moreover, a separate analysis of the naval air station and destroyer samples indicated almost identical findings.

Two studies were conducted independently by investigators at West Point using Army personnel (Csoka & Bons, 1978). The first of these dealt with trainees who were scheduled to serve as acting platoon leaders in various battalions throughout the United States during the summer months. One-third of 114 trainees were randomly selected for Leader Match training, while the others served as controls. At the end of the assignment, the acting platoon leaders were rated by superior officers who had no information about the study. Leaders trained with Leader Match received significantly higher ratings in their unit than did those in the control group (see Fig. 18). The second study involved cadets who served as the leaders of 53 training platoons, with one half of these young men randomly chosen to receive Leader Match training. At the end of the semester, all platoon leaders were evaluated by their superior officers. As shown in Table VIII, the platoon leaders with training were significantly more often considered to be the best in their company than those without training. Interviews indicated that trained leaders had been able to modify their situational control as recommended by the training manual.

A ninth study has just been completed on 18 university and college ROTC programs in which Leader Match was used in 9 randomly selected schools while the other 9 schools served as controls. At the end of the training, cadets from

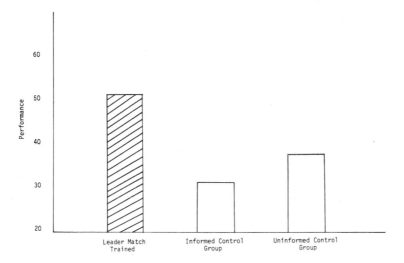

Fig. 18. Performance ratings given to acting platoon leaders who had received Leader Match training and who had been assigned to the control conditions. From Csoka and Bons (1978).

these 18 schools along with cadets from other schools in the ROTC regional command, were assigned at random to platoons at an advanced ROTC summer training camp, with no more than two cadets from each school in the same platoon. Cadets were randomly assigned to four or five leadership positions while at camp, and their leadership performance was evaluated by an officer and a noncommissioned officer as well as by means of peer group ratings. The average performance ratings of cadets from the schools with Leader Match training was significantly higher than performance of control school cadets on all measures, with training accounting for 28% of the variance in officer and NCO

TABLE VIII
PERFORMANCE RANKS IN COMPANY FOR PLATOON
LEADERS WITH OR WITHOUT LEADER MATCH TRAINING[a]

	Rank order in company		
	Best	Second best	Poorest
Trained	14[b]	4	8
Untrained	7	9	11

[a] From Csoka and Bons (1978).
[b] Chi Square 5.35, $p < .05$.

ratings and 15% and 23% in peer group ratings on combat and administrative leadership, respectively (Fiedler & Mahar, 1977, unpublished).

VII. Conclusion

The Contingency Model provides a conceptual framework which enables us to explain the effects of such change-inducing conditions as organizational turbulence, leadership experience, training, and job rotation. The integrating concept in the dynamic interpretation of this theory is the leader's situational control and influence which, as it changes, brings about a corresponding change in the leader's behavior and performance. Further support of the theory is provided by studies which show that the concepts of this theory can be applied to a leadership training program which teaches the leader to match situational control to his or her personality.

The Contingency Model has a number of shortcomings which need to be remedied as new research data become available. Specifically, we need a conceptually cleaner definition and a better metric of the situational control dimension, and we need to continue research on personality and behavioral correlates of LPC, as well as on the effect of this variable on interpersonal encounters outside the leadership context. Further research also is called for to determine the role which such other leader attributes as intelligence, sex cognitive complexity, and task ability play in determining organizational performance and the role which subordinates play in the leadership process (Fiedler & Leister, 1977).

Above all, we need to seek concepts which integrate different leadership theories of proven worth. The interpretation of the situational control dimension as a correlate of uncertainty and anxiety is a promising development in this direction. Leadership, and the authority relationship of which it is a part, is a central and important phenomenon in our everyday life. It plays a powerful role in the governance of our institutions and our society, and it makes obvious the critical need for understanding, developing, and improving the leadership resources at our disposal.

REFERENCES

Anderson, L. R. Leader behavior, member attitudes, and task performance of intercultural discussion groups. *Journal of Social Psychology,* 1966, **69,** 305–319.

Ashour, A. S. The Contingency Model of Leadership Effectiveness: An evaluation. *Organizational Behavior and Human Performance,* 1973, **9,** 339–355.

Ayer, J. G. Effects of success and failure of interpersonal and task performance upon leader perception and behavior. Unpublished master's thesis, University of Illinois, 1968.

Bales, R. F. *Interaction process analysis.* Cambridge, Mass.: Addison-Wesley, 1951.

Bass, A. R., Fiedler, F. E., & Kreuger, S. *Personality correlates of assumed similarity (ASo) and related scores.* Urbana, Illinois: Group Effectiveness Research Laboratory, University of Illinois, 1964.

Beach, B. H., Mitchell, T. R., & Beach, L. R. *Components of situational favorableness and probability of success.* Tech. Rep. 75-66. Seattle: University of Washington, Organizational Research Group, 1975.

Bons, P. M. The effect of changes in leadership environment on the behavior of relationship and task-motivated leaders. Unpublished doctoral dissertation, University of Washington, 1974.

Bons, P. M., Bass, A. R., & Komorita, S. S. Changes in leadership style as a function of military experience and type of command. *Personnel Psychology,* 1970, **23,** 551–568.

Bons, P. M., & Fiedler, F. E. Changes in organizational leadership and the behavior of relationship- and task-motivated leaders. *Administrative Science Quarterly,* 1976, **21,** 433–472.

Borden, D. F. The effects of leadership style on leader-supervisor and leader-subordinate interpersonal relations. Unpublished master's thesis, University of Washington, 1976.

Burns, T., & Stalker, G. M. *The management of innovation.* London: Tavistock, 1961.

Campbell, J. P., Dunnette, M. D., Lawler, E. E., & Weick, K. E. *Managerial behavior, performance, and effectiveness.* New York: McGraw-Hill, 1970.

Chemers, M. M. Cultural training as a means for improving situational favorableness. *Human Relations,* 1969, **22,** 531–546.

Chemers, M. M., Rice, R. W., Sundstrom, E., & Butler, W. Leader esteem for the least preferred co-worker score, training, and effectiveness: An experimental examination. *Journal of Personality and Social Psychology,* 1975, **31,** 401–409.

Chemers, M. M., & Skrzypek, G. J. An experimental test of the Contingency Model of leadership effectiveness. *Journal of Personality and Social Psychology,* 1972, **24,** 172–177.

CRM Productions. *Leadership: Style or circumstance.* Los Angeles, 1974. (Film)

Csoka, L. S. Organic and mechanistic organizational climates and the Contingency Model. *Journal of Applied Psychology,* 1975, **60,** 273–277.

Csoka, L. S., & Bons, P. M. Manipulating the situation to fit the leader's style—Two validation studies of Leader Match. *Journal of Applied Psychology,* 1978, in press.

Fiedler, F. E. A contingency model of leadership effectiveness. In L. Berkowitz (Ed.), *Advances in experimental social psychology.* Vol. 1. New York: Academic Press, 1964. Pp. 149–190.

Fiedler, F. E. The effect of leadership and cultural heterogeneity on group performance: A test of the contingency model. *Journal of Experimental Social Psychology,* 1966, **2,** 237–264.

Fiedler, F. E. *A theory of leadership effectiveness.* New York: McGraw-Hill, 1967.

Fiedler, F. E. Leadership experience and leader performance—Another hypothesis shot to hell. *Organizational Behavior and Human Performance,* 1970, **5,** 1–14.

Fiedler, F. E. Note on the methodology of the Graen, Orris, and Alvarez studies testing the Contingency Model. *Journal of Applied Psychology,* 1971, **55,** 202–204. (a)

Fiedler, F. E. Validation and extension of the Contingency Model of Leadership Effectiveness: A review of empirical findings. *Psychological Bulletin,* 1971, **76,** 128–148. (b)

Fiedler, F. E. Personality, motivational systems, and behavior of high and low LPC persons. *Human Relations,* 1971, **25,** 391–412. (c)

Fiedler, F. E. Leadership experience and leadership training—Some new answers to an old problem. *Administrative Science Quarterly,* 1972, **17,** 453–470. (a)

Fiedler, F. E. Personality, motivational systems, and behavior of high and low LPC persons. *Human Relations,* 1972, **25,** 391–412. (b)

Fiedler, F. E. The contingency model—A reply to Ashour. *Organizational Behavior and Human Performance,* 1973, **9,** 356–368.

Fiedler, F. E. Situational Control and a dynamic theory of leadership. In B. King, F. E. Fiedler, & S. Streufert (Eds.), *Managerial Control and Organizational Democracy.* Washington, D.C.: W. H. Winston & Sons, 1977. (a)

Fiedler, F. E. What triggers the person-situation interaction in leadership. In D. Magnusson & N. S. Endler (Eds.), *Personality at the Crossroads: Current Issues in Interactional Psychology.* Hillsdale, N.J.: Lawrence Erlbaum Assoc., Inc., 1977. Pp. 154–163. (b)

Fiedler, F. E., Bons, P. M., & Hastings. L. The utilization of leadership resources. In W. T.

Singleton & P. Spurgeon (Eds.), *Measurement of human resources*. London: Taylor & Francis, 1975. Pp. 233–244. (a)

Fiedler, F. E., & Chemers, M. M. *Leadership and effective management*. Glenview, Ill.: Scott, Foresman, 1974.

Fiedler, F. E., Chemers, M. M., & Mahar, L. *Improving leadership effectiveness: The Leader Match Concept*. New York: Wiley, 1976.

Fiedler, F. E., & Leister, A. F. Leader intelligence and task performance: A test of a multiple screen model. *Organizational Behavior and Human Performance*, 1977, **20**, 1–14.

Fiedler, F. E., Mahar, L., & Schmidt, D. *Four validation studies of contingency model training*. Tech. Rep. 75-70. Seattle: University of Washington, Organizational Research, 1975. (b)

Fiedler, F. E., Meuwese, W., & Oonk, S. An exploratory study of group creativity in laboratory tasks. *Acta Psychologica*, 1961, **18**, 100–119.

Fiedler, F. E., O'Brien, G. E., & Ilgen, D. R. The effect of leadership style upon the performance and adjustment of volunteer teams operating in a stressful foreign environment. *Human Relations*, 1969, **22**, 503–514.

Fiedler, F. E., Warrington, W. B., & Blaisdell, F. J. Unconscious attitudes as correlates of sociometric choice in a social group. *Journal of Abnormal and Social Psychology*, 1952, **47**, 790–796.

Fishbein, M., Landy, E., & Hatch, G. A consideration of two assumptions underlying Fiedler's Contingency Model for prediction of leadership effectiveness. *American Journal of Psychology*, 1969, **82**, 457–473. (a)

Fishbein, M., Landy, E., & Hatch, G. Some determinants of an individual's esteem for the least preferred co-worker: An attitudinal analysis. *Human Relations*, 1969, **22**, 173–188. (b)

Fox, W. M., Hill, W. A., & Guertin, W. H. Dimensional analysis of the least preferred co-worker scales. *Journal of Applied Psychology*, 1973, **57**, 192–194.

Godfrey, E., Fiedler, F. E., & Hall, D. M. *Boards, management, and company success*. Danville, Ill.: Interstate Press, 1959.

Graen, G. B., Alvares, D., Orris, J. B., & Martella. J. A. The contingency model of leadership effectiveness: Antecedent and evidential results. *Psychological Bulletin*, 1970, **74**, 285–296.

Graen, G. B., Orris, J. B., & Alvares, K. M. Contingency Model of Leadership Effectiveness: Some experimental results. *Journal of Applied Psychology*, 1971, **55**, 196–201.

Green, S., Nebeker, D., & Boni, A. Personality and situational effects on leader behavior. *Academy of Management Journal*, 1976, **19**, 184–194.

Hansson, R. O., & Fiedler, F. E. Perceived similarity, personality, and attraction to large organizations. *Journal of Applied Social Psychology*, 1973, **3**, 258–266.

Hardy, R. C. Effect of leadership style on the performance of small classroom groups: A test of the Contingency Model. *Journal of Personality and Social Psychology*, 1971, **19**, 367–374.

Hardy, R. C. A test of poor leader–member relations cells of the contingency model on elementary school children. *Child Development*, 1975, **45**, 958–964.

Hardy, R. C., & Bohren, J. F. The effect of experience on teacher effectiveness: A test of the contingency model. *Journal of Psychology*, 1975, **89**, 159–163.

Hardy, R. C., Sack, S., & Harpine, F. An experimental test of the contingency model on small classroom groups. *Journal of Psychology*, 1973, **85**, 3–16.

Hawley, D. E. A study of the relationship between the leader behavior and attitudes of elementary school principals. Unpublished master's (M.Ed.) thesis, University of Saskatchewan, 1969.

Hill, W. The Validation and extension of Fiedler's theory of leadership effectiveness. *Academy of Management Journal*, March 1969, 33–47.

Hoffman, P. A. A paramorphic representation of clinical judgment. *Psychological Bulletin*, 1960, **57**, 116–131.

House, R. J., & Rizzo, J. R. Toward the measurement of organizational practices: A scale development and validation. *Experimental Publication System (Washington, D.C.)*, 1971, **12**, Ms. No. 481-1.

Hunt, J. G. Fiedler's leadership contingency model: An empirical test in three organizations. *Organizational Behavior and Human Performance,* 1967, **2,** 290–308.

Larson, L. L., & Rowland, K. Leadership style, stress, and behavior in task performance. *Organizational Behavior and Human Performance,* 1973, **9,** 407–421.

Lawrence, P. R., & Lorsch, J. W. *Organization and environment: Managing differentiation and integration.* Cambridge, Mass.: Harvard University Press, 1967.

Leister, A. F., Borden, D., & Fiedler, F. E. The effect of contingency model leadership training on the performance of Navy leaders. *Academy of Management Journal,* 1977, **20,** 464–470.

MacCrimmon, K. R., & Taylor, R. N. Decision making and problem solving. In M. D. Dunnette (Ed.), *Handbook of industrial and organizational psychology.* Chicago: Rand McNally, 1976.

Mai-Dalton, R. *The influence of training and position power on leader behavior.* Tech. Rep. 75-72. Seattle: University of Washington, Organizational Research, 1975.

Maslow, A. H. *Motivation and personality.* Chicago: Harper, 1954.

McNamara, V. D. Leadership, staff, and school effectiveness. Unpublished doctoral dissertation, University of Alberta, 1968.

Mehrens, W. A., & Lehmann, I. J. *Standardized tests in education.* New York: Holt, 1969.

Meuwese, W., & Fiedler, F. E. *Leadership and group creativity under varying conditions of stress.* Urbana: University of Illinois, Group Effectiveness Research Laboratory, 1965.

Mitchell, T. R. Leader complexity and leadership style. *Journal of Personality and Social Psychology,* 1970, **16,** 166–174.

Mitchell, T. R., Biglan, A., Oncken, G., & Fiedler, F. E. The Contingency Model: Criticisms and suggestions. *Academy of Management Journal,* September 1970, **13,** 253–268.

Mitchell, T. R., Dossett, D. L., Fiedler, F. E., & Triandis, H. C. Culture training: Validation evidence for the culture assimilator. *International Journal of Psychology,* 1972, **7,** 97–104.

Nealey, S. M., & Blood, M. R. Leadership performance of nursing supervisors at two organizational levels. *Journal of Applied Psychology,* 1968, **52,** 414–422.

Nealey, S. M., & Owen, T. W. A multitrait-multimethod analysis of predictors and criteria of nursing performance. *Organizational Behavior and Human Performance,* 1970, **5,** 348–365.

Nebeker, D. M. Situational favorability and environmental uncertainty: An integrative study. *Administrative Science Quarterly,* 1975, **20,** 281–294.

Nebeker, D. M., & Hansson, R. O. *Confidence in human nature and leader style.* Tech. Rep. 72-37. Seattle: University of Washington, Organizational Research, May 1972.

O'Brien, G. E. Group structure and the measurement of potential leader influence. *Australian Journal of Psychology,* 1969, **21,** 277–289.

Overall, J. E., & Woodward, J. A. Unreliability of difference scores: A paradox for measurement of change. *Psychological Bulletin,* 1975, **82,** 85–86.

Prothero, J., & Fiedler, F. E. *The effect of situational change on individual behavior and performance: An extension of the contingency model.* Tech. Rep. 74-59. Seattle: University of Washington, Organizational Research, 1974.

Rice, R. W. The esteem for least preferred co-worker (LPC) scores: What does it measure? Unpublished doctoral dissertation, University of Utah, 1975.

Rice, R. W. Psychometric properties of the esteem for least preferred co-worker (LPC) scale. *Academy of Management Review,* 1978, **3,** No. 1, 106–118.

Rice, R. W., & Chemers, M. M. Predicting the emergence of leaders using Fiedler's Contingency Model of Leadership Effectiveness. *Journal of Applied Psychology,* 1973, **57,** 281–287.

Rice, R. W., & Chemers, M. M. Personality and situational determinants of leader behavior. *Journal of Applied Psychology,* 1975, **60,** 20–27.

Robinson, J. P., & Shaver, P. R. *Measures of social psychological attitudes.* Ann Arbor, Mich.: University of Michigan, Institute for Social Research, 1973.

Sample, J. A., & Wilson, T. R. Leader behavior, group productivity, and rating of least preferred co-worker. *Journal of Personality and Social Psychology,* 1965, **1,** 266–270.

Sashkin, M. Leadership style and group decision effectiveness: Correlational and behavioral tests of Fiedler's Contingency Model. *Organizational Behavior and Human Performance,* 1972, **8,** 347–362.

Sax, G. *Principles of education measurement and evaluation.* Belmont, Calif.: Wadsworth, 1974.

Schneier, C. E. The contingency model of leadership: An extension to emergent leadership and leader's sex. *Organizational Behavior and Human Performance,* 1978, **21,** 220–239.

Schroder, H. M., Driver, M. J., & Streufert, S. *Human information processing.* New York: Holt, 1967.

Secord, P. F., Backman, C. W., & Eachus, H. T. Effects of imbalance in the self-concept on the perception of persons. *Journal of Abnormal and Social Psychology,* 1964, **68,** 442–446.

Shaw, M. E. *Scaling group tasks: A method of dimensional analysis.* Tech. Rep. No. 1. Gainesville: University of Florida, 1963.

Shiflett, S. C. The contingency model of leadership effectiveness: Some implications of its statistical and methodological properties. *Behavioral Science,* 1973, **18,** 429–440.

Shiflett, S. C., & Nealey, S. M. The effects of changing leader power: A test of situational engineering. *Organizational Behavior and Human Performance,* 1972, **7,** 371–382.

Shima, H. The relationship between the leader's modes of interpersonal cognition and the performance of the group. *Japanese Psychological Research,* 1968, **10,** 13–30.

Stinson, J. E., & Tracy, L. Some disturbing characteristics of the LPC score. *Personnel Psychology,* 1974, **24,** 477–485.

Stogdill, R. M. *Manual for the Leader Behavior Description Questionnaire—Form XII: An experimental revision.* Columbus: Ohio State University, 1963.

Stogdill, R. M. *Handbook of leadership.* New York: Free Press, 1974.

Taylor, D. An investigation of the relative stabilities of some prominent measures of leadership. Unpublished master's thesis, University of Washington, 1975.

Tumes, J. The Contingency Theory of Leadership: A behavioral investigation. Paper presented at the meeting of the Eastern Academy of Mangement, Boston, May 1972.

Vecchio, R. P. An empirical examination of the validity of Fiedler's model of leadership effectiveness. *Organizational Behavior and Human Performance,* 1977, **19,** 180–206.

Yukl, G. Leader LPC scores: Attitude dimensions and behavioral correlates. *Journal of Social Psychology,* 1970, **80,** 207–212.

AN ATTRIBUTIONAL THEORY OF CHOICE

Andy Kukla

UNIVERSITY OF TORONTO
TORONTO, CANADA

I. Introduction

Molar behavior is traditionally characterized by the two parameters of *intensity* (the vigor with which a person exerts himself toward his chosen goal) and *direction* (which among the available goals he chooses to work toward). In an earlier paper (Kukla, 1972b), an analysis of behavioral intensity was presented in terms of a theoretical framework which integrated concepts drawn from both decision theory (Edwards, 1954, 1961) and attribution theory (Heider, 1958; Kelley, 1967, 1973). In this chapter, the same framework is used to elucidate the complementary phenomenon of behavioral direction or choice.

In Section II, the theory of choice is formulated in its most general form.

113

The later sections, however, explore the consequences of this theory only within the special domain of achievement-related activities. Nevertheless, the more general statement is necessary to demonstrate the logical continuity between the decision-theoretical and the present attributional treatment of choice, as well as to provide a foundation from which analyses of other activities can eventually be formulated.

Each of the three major sections of the chapter introduces a new fundamental assumption. In Section II we adopt the decision-theoretical principle of expected-utility maximization, but embed it within an attributional conceptual scheme. In Section III it is assumed that, for the case of achievement-related tasks, the utilities of success and failure are functions of the ability one demonstrates by his performance. Finally, in Section IV, the personality disposition of resultant achievement motivation is identified with a general tendency to view oneself as high in ability. The first of these three assumptions is the common ground upon which, discounting differences in vocabulary, almost all precise cognitive theories of motivation meet (Feather, 1959). The second assumption is entirely new, while the third has already been introduced in the earlier theory of intensity (Kukla, 1972b).

II.   The Choice Principle

A.   DECISION THEORY

According to decision theory, whether a person undertakes a task X from among a larger set of alternatives depends on two properties of the possible *outcomes* $(x_1, x_2, \ldots , x_n)$ of X: the subjective likelihood of their occurrence should X be chosen, and their attractiveness or unattractiveness to the actor. The former are the *subjective probabilities* of the outcomes $(P_{x_1}, P_{x_2}, \ldots , P_{x_n})$; the latter are their *utilities* $(U_{x_1}, U_{x_2}, \ldots , U_{x_n})$. The tendency for the actor to choose X is asserted to be a function of the *subjectively expected utility* of X (SEU_X), which is defined as:

$$SEU_x = \sum_{i=1}^{n} (P_{xi})(U_{xi}) \tag{1}$$

Thus the choice of X becomes more likely to the extent that the outcomes of X are more attractive, or that the probabilities of the more attractive outcomes increase at the expense of the probabilities of the less attractive outcomes (it is usually assumed that the subjective probabilities of all the outcomes sum to unity).

For the most part, only tasks which have exactly two possible outcomes will be discussed below. This makes for greater ease of presentation without affecting the substance of the analysis, which remains essentially the same in the n-outcome case. When, in the two-outcome case, the utility of one outcome is greater than the utility of the other, it will be convenient to call the first *success* (s) and the second *failure* (f). Thus the *SEU*s of the tasks to be discussed can be represented by

$$SEU = U_s P_s + U_f P_f \qquad (2)$$

where $P_s + P_f = 1$.

B.   ATTRIBUTION THEORY

1.   *"Can" and "Try"*

In classical decision theory, the concepts of subjective probability and utility provide the only resources for representing a person's cognitive state at the moment of choice. But, as the work of attribution theorists has made abundantly clear, people entertain many ideas about actions in addition to the likelihood and attractiveness of their outcomes. It is to be expected, then, that a full account of the relationship between cognition and motivation will require an extension of the language of decision theory so that some of these attributional cognitions can also be taken into account.

Fortunately, the relationship between the concepts of decision theory and those of attribution theory is quite direct. For example, Heider (1958) claims that whether or not a particular outcome is achieved is thought to depend jointly on a "can" factor and a "try" factor: "If a person can do something and he tries to do it, then he will do it" (p. 86). In this statement, the concepts "can," "try," and "do" are used dichotomously, that is, as though one either could or could not do something, etc. But when this didactic simplification is removed and the concepts used as continuous variables, it is evident that what is being offered is an analysis of the determinants of subjective probability: The greater the degree to which one can do something, and the harder one tries to do it, the likelier it is that it will get done. That is,

$$P_s = f(K, E) \qquad (3)$$

where f is an increasing function, K is the degree to which one believes he can produce the successful outcome (the symbol C is reserved for a different use), and E is the amount of effort one intends to expend toward success. In this way, a portion of Heider's "naive analysis of action" is directly tied to a decision-theoretical concept. The result, from the point of view of decision theory, is a wider conceptual scheme which can hope to do more justice to the complexities of the relationship between thought and action.

2. Ability and Difficulty

Heider also maintains that the degree to which one believes someone "can" do something is accounted for in part by the perceived properties of the external situation and in part by the perceived properties of the actor. The former is identified with the *difficulty* of achieving the goal, the latter with the *ability* to achieve it. Thus,

$$K = f(A, F) \tag{4}$$

where f is again an increasing function, A is perceived ability, and F is perceived facility, the inverse of difficulty.

According to Kelley (1967, 1973), such an apportionment of a characteristic (can) into personal (ability) and situational (facility) components is based in large part on an interpersonal comparison. If a relationship exists between most persons in some reference group and an object, the relationship tends to be attributed to properties of the object. But if the relationship exists between relatively few people and the object, it is more often attributed to properties of the person. Thus, if most people like a particular film, it will be said that it is a good film, while the exceptional judgments will be explained in terms of the idiosyncratic taste of those who dislike it. In the case of the "can" relationship between persons and tasks, this analysis suggests that if most people are thought to be equally capable of succeeding at a task, this capacity with be attributed to properties of the task. Depending on whether the capacity is great or small, it will be concluded that the task is either easy or difficult. If, however, some person's capacity is thought to be very different from most others', this exceptional degree of efficacy will be attributed to him. Depending on whether his capacity exceeds or is less than that of most others, it will be concluded that he has either high or low ability.

Recent data appear to verify Kelley's analysis, both in the general case (Feldman, Higgins, Karlovac & Ruble, 1976; Goethals, 1972; Hansen & Lowe, 1976) and in the specific case of ability versus difficulty attributions (Frieze & Weiner, 1971; Weiner & Kukla, 1970). But both Kelley and Heider have suggested that factors other than interpersonal comparison also play a role in determining personal versus situational attributions. This question of the antecedents of certain attributional beliefs is typical of the issues dealt with by attribution theorists. In this chapter, however, the concern will be with the motivational consequences of having the attributional beliefs one happens to hold, regardless of where they came from.

3. Luck

In addition to effort, ability, and difficulty, Heider also conceives that one's outcomes are thought to be influenced by uncontrolled fluctuations in environmental conditions, or *luck*. Weiner, Frieze, Kukla, Reed, Rest, and Rosenbaum (1971) conclude that Heider's naive analysis of action can be summarized thus:

> Future expectations of success and failure are based upon the assumed level of ability in relation to perceived task difficulty . . . as well as an estimation of intended effort and anticipated luck. [p. 96]

More succinctly,

$$P_s = f(A, F, E, L) \qquad (5)$$

Weiner *et al.* point out that these four attributional variables can be comprised within the two basic dimensions of *internality–externality* (whether the property resides in the person or in the environment) and *stability–variability* (whether the property can be expected to persist over a period of time). Ability describes a stable, internal characteristic; difficulty is a stable property of the external environment; effort is internal and variable; and finally, luck is external and variable.

For the remainder of the chapter, we shall restrict our attention to activities whose outcomes are conceived to be unaffected by luck. This restriction to skill tasks, like the previous restriction to two-outcome tasks, is adopted in order to avoid the conceptual complexities which arise in attempting to treat the fully general case. But this second limitation is considerably more severe, since it is not clear whether the subsequent arguments and derivations could all be carried out if luck were not eliminated from the analysis. Of course, it is unlikely that any task is ever conceived to be totally free from the influence of chance. Thus the following theoretical apparatus is appropriate to the extent that the perceived role of chance is minimal. Like all treatments of idealized phenomena (e.g., the ideal gas laws in chemistry), its justification can come only from the demonstration that the real phenomena are similar enough to the ideal cases for the theory to have predictive success.

III. Achievement Situations

A. ACHIEVEMENT-RELATED UTILITY AND DEMONSTRATED ABILITY

None of the foregoing elaborations of the P_s concept has yet had any effect on the principle of *SEU* maximization. Indeed, there are many circumstances in which it makes no motivational difference whether the value of P_s is arrived at through one set of attributional values or another. For example, if a hungry person is concerned solely with obtaining food, it will be of no consequence whether a particular course of action leads to a high probability of success because he has high ability for getting food in this way, or because it is an easy way to get food. In such cases, where action is unaffected by the values of the attributional variables, the present theory is equivalent to classical decision theory. But there are also situations in which people are motivated not only to realize a particular external state of affairs, but to realize it *in a particular fashion*. For example, a person may want not only to have many friends, but also to feel that the friendships he acquires are due to the exercise of his own efforts (E) rather than to chance (L), or the inherent friendliness of others (F), or his own intrinsic charm (A). On the other hand another person may prefer that people become his friends for any reason *other* than his own efforts. In these cases, *the utilities of the outcomes are themselves affected by the values of the attributional variables*. Whenever such a situation obtains, the resulting behavioral choices can be explicated only within the broader attributional scheme.

Among the situations in which utilities vary with the values of the attributional variables, the most frequently investigated has been the class of *achievement-related activities*. An achievement-related task is one for which no extrinsic rewards or punishments are expected and where, by definition, the only source of utility is the satisfaction of success itself or the dissatisfaction of failure. The large number of published investigations of achievement-related behavior affords a promising testing ground for a new theoretical analysis.

It is assumed here that the utilities of success and failure at an achievement-related task are both functions of the amount of ability one would demonstrate by that success or failure. That is, a person is attracted to an achievement task to the extent that he believes success would entail the conclusion that he has high ability; conversely, he is repulsed by the task to the extent that he believes that failure demonstrates he has low ability. More exactly still, *the utility of success* (U_s) *is proportional to the least amount of ability necessary to account for succeeding; and the negative utility of failure* $(-U_f)$ *is inversely proportional to the greatest amount of ability which is commensurate with failing*.

Now the amount of ability which is entailed by a success or a failure depends entirely upon what information is preestablished about the attributional variables. For example, if nothing is known about them, then either success or failure is commensurate with *any* degree of ability. Success demonstrates nothing about one's ability, since the task could have been extremely easy. Similarly, failure could have been due to extreme difficulty. Thus the least amount of ability consistent with such a success verges on zero, and the greatest amount of ability consistent with such a failure is maximally high. In this case, our hypothesis suggests that one would anticipate neither achievement-related pleasure at success $(U_s = 0)$ nor displeasure at failure $(U_f = 0)$. Thus $SEU = 0$ for all tasks of this nature, and an actor should exhibit no preferences among them.

The opposite extreme occurs when the actor's ability for the task is a given; that is, the actor knows, and he knows that anyone who cares to inform himself can find out, that his ability for the task has such and such a value. In this instance, where the level of ability is in effect stipulated, there can be no difference between the ability one believes he possesses and the ability one believes he demonstrates. Our hypothesis then leads to the prediction of a simple main effect of stipulated ability: The higher the ability one is understood to have for a particular task, the more attractive is success at that task and the less aversive is failure. This result has been reported in two studies by Nicholls (1975, 1976). On the other hand, there is a body of apparently contrary data which will be discussed in the next section.

In the studies by Nicholls, the subjects were asked how they felt about success or failure *given* that they obtained them with high or low ability. Thus there was no question of their demonstrating an ability level different from the stipulated one. But such a situation is unusual in comparison with everyday evaluations, or even with the kinds of evaluations subjects in most choice studies are likely to engage in. Ordinarily, the level of ability is not clearly established between an actor and other interested parties (e.g., a subject and an experimenter) either before or after a performance. Thus the actor cannot simply select the task for which he will be known to have the highest ability. But neither does task selection occur in an attributional vacuum. Typically, some items of information which have a bearing on demonstrated ability are well-established. The actor's aim in the achievement situation will be to select, on the basis of this information, the task with which he stands the best chance of demonstrating the highest possible ability level. The task so selected will evidently depend on the nature of the information available.

B.   WEINER ON UTILITY

Weiner (1972, 1974), also working within an attributional framework, has offered a different hypothesis concerning the source of achievement-related utility. He suggests that it is the *effort* variable which determines the attractiveness or aversiveness of one's achievement outcomes: Successes are deemed to be attractive to the extent that they are obtained with high effort, while failures are aversive to the extent that they are permitted to happen as a result of low effort. Weiner cites a number of experiments in support of this conclusion (Cook, 1970; Eswara, 1972; Lanzetta & Hannah, 1969; Leventhal & Michaels, 1971; Rest, Nierenberg, Weiner, & Heckhausen, 1973; Weiner, Heckhausen, Meyer, & Cook, 1972; Weiner & Kukla, 1970; Zander, Fuller, & Armstrong, 1972). Most of these studies follow a paradigm established by Weiner and Kukla (1970), in which subjects are asked to evaluate several outcomes stipulated to have been obtained with several values of the attributional variables. Thus a subject might be asked how attractive he finds success at a task at which he has low ability but expends much effort, etc. Since the value of ability is stipulated in these questions, we should expect the same results as in the Nicholls studies. But, according to Weiner (1972), the overall result of these studies is that "perceived effort is the most important determinant of affective responses to success and failure" (p. 378).

Now quite apart from the experimental evidence, Weiner's hypothesis has a paradoxical implication. For if achievement evaluation is determined by effort in the way he suggests, it follows that a person is in all circumstances best off. expending as much effort as possible: If he succeeds this results in the most attractive possible success, and if he fails it results in the least aversive possible failure. It is clear, however, that people do not always work as hard as they can at all achievement tasks. Yet the only way to avoid this claim is either to deny the validity of Weiner's hypothesis, or to give up the principle of expected-utility maximization (a step which Weiner contemplates, cf. Meyer, Folkes, & Weiner, 1976, p. 421). If we are to avoid the drastic second alternative, we must provide an alternative interpretation of Weiner's data which also accounts for the discrepancy between these data and Nicholls'.

Significantly, there is a procedural difference between most of the Weiner studies and the two by Nicholls. In the former, the attractiveness or aversiveness of the achievement outcome is usually operationalized as the degree of reward or punishment administered either to oneself or to another person. For example, in one of the original experiments by Weiner and Kukla (1970), subjects were asked to assume that a grade-school student in their classroom achieved, for example, a success with high ability and low effort, and that their task was to reward or punish him with some number of gold or red stars, respectively. Weiner (1972, 1974) interprets the finding that success with high effort was more rewarded than success with low effort as indicating that effort determines the attractiveness of success. But it is not self-evident that such reinforcing behavior is a valid index of attractiveness, even if the subjects were reinforcing themselves rather than someone else. Alternatively, the subjects may be rewarding effort and punishing its lack because this is the only practical way to influence performance. That is, they may reason that there is no point in administering rewards and punishments on the basis of ability or task difficulty, since there is nothing the recipient of the rewards or punishments can do about these quantities. And one may reward effort on this basis even if there is no relationship between effort and achievement-related affect.

Still another possibility is that the rewards and punishments are meted out on moral grounds. There is after all a sense of moral obligation associated with a student's performance at an exam. We tend to think that people *ought* to work hard at academic tasks, whether they like it or not. And we also tend to think that the fulfillment of a moral obligation *deserves* to be rewarded and its nonfulfillment punished. But this kind of moral evaluation is not equivalent to the achievement evaluation under discussion. To be sure, both concerns may be present at the same time: A person may try to save a drowning man both because he feels a moral obligation to do so and because he anticipates the pleasure of a successful performance. But it is unlikely that concerns with morality play much of a role when we do crossword puzzles. Thus, it may be that the relationship between effort and reinforcing behavior found in the Weiner studies is due to the fact that concerns with moral evaluation were aroused. This would account for the data without supposing that effort determined achievement evaluation.

Only two of the experiments cited by Weiner did not use reinforcement behavior as an index of achievement-related affect (Weiner & Kukla, 1970, Experiment 3; Zander et al., 1972). In both these cases, the subjects were asked how much "pride" or "shame" they would feel given various outcomes. But "pride" and "shame" are terms drawn from the vocabulary of moral evaluation. Since, in both experiments, hypothetical tasks of an unspecified nature were being evaluated, it is easy to imagine that requests for judgments about pride and shame led the subjects to suppose that these tasks had a moral dimension. Thus these data also may be explained by postulating that effort determines moral, but not achievement evaluation.

This *post hoc* explanation acquires a measure of plausibility when we note the alternative procedure followed by Nicholls. In the first of his studies, Nicholls (1975) asked his subjects how *pleased* they would be if they succeeded with high ability but no effort, and if they succeeded with low ability but high effort. Contrary to all the studies cited by Weiner, Nicholls found that the high ability success led to more "pleasure" than the high effort success. The only available interpretation of this discrepancy is that "pleasure," unlike "pride," does not evoke the apparatus of moral evaluation, and is thus a purer measure of achievement-related affect. Nicholls' (1976) second study also supports this interpretation. When subjects were asked whether they would prefer to be a person who succeeded with high ability and low effort or one who succeeded with low ability and high effort, most subjects indicated a preference for the former. But when they were asked which of these two conditions would give them the greater "pride or pleasure," thus again bringing in thoughts about morality, the usual findings of the Weiner studies were obtained: Subjects said that they would feel greater "pride or pleasure" with high effort than with high ability. Corresponding effects were found with failure, that is,

> ... students indicated that shame over failure would be occasioned by the very circumstances (high ability and low effort) they would prefer when presented with a choice. [Nicholls, 1976, p. 310]

The resolution of this paradox suggested here is that asking the students about pride and shame evoked a moral evaluation, the determinants of which are quite different from the achievement evaluation evoked when they were asked a morally neutral question about their personal preferences.

In sum, it is suggested that effort determines utility, not in the domain of achievement situations, but rather in situations where there is a felt moral obligation to do something. Weiner and Peter (1973) have presented evidence showing that effort determines the evaluation of an explicitly moral situation in just this way. They also note the parallelism between these results and the corresponding results on achievement evaluation. But from the perspective taken here, this parallelism is due to the fact that moral concerns were inadvertently tapped in the achievement studies. When the possibility of a moral interpretation is minimized (as in Nicholls' studies), we find that stipulated ability, rather than stipulated effort, is the major determinant of how one reacts to success and failure *per se*.

C. UTILITY IN ORDINARY CIRCUMSTANCES

Recall the hypothesis concerning achievement-related utility: U_s is proportional to the least amount of ability necessary to account for succeeding, and $-U_f$ is inversely proportional to the greatest amount of ability which is commensurate with failing. The consequences of this hypothesis in certain degenerate cases (e.g., when the actor's level of ability is stipulated) have already been discussed. In this section, we consider its implications for the type of experimental arrangements which have usually obtained in achievement studies.

In most achievement studies, subjects have been led to believe that the difficulty levels of the tasks are well-established. Indeed, it is often arranged that the only way subjects can indicate their choice is by specifying the level of difficulty they wish to attempt. On the other hand, their ability level is typically left unspecified. In such circumstances, the least amount of ability entailed by success evidently depends on the stipulated difficulty of the task. For, by the properties of the ability and difficulty concepts described above (Section II, B, 2), success at a difficult task means that one can do what most people cannot do, that is, that one *must* have high ability. But success at an easy task means only that one can do what most other people can also do, which is consistent with having either high or low ability. Thus such a success proves only that the actor has at least the low ability level. If the utility of success is a function of demonstrated ability, it follows that U_s *is an increasing function of task difficulty* (or, as we prefer to say, a decreasing function of facility). Assuming that facility, F, is permitted to range from zero (no one can succeed) to unity (everyone can succeed), this relationship is provisionally captured by the formal statement that:

$$U_s = 1 - F \qquad (6)$$

Similar considerations lead to the further assumption that

$$U_f = -F \qquad (7$$

For if one fails at a very easy task, it means that he cannot do what most others can do, that is, that he must have low ability. But failure at a very difficult task is compatible with having either high or low ability, so that such a failure proves only that the actor has no more than the relatively high level. By our hypothesis, such a failure would not be very aversive, since it does not force one to concede much about his lack of ability. Thus, $-U_f$ is seen to be a direct function of task facility.

Equations (6) and (7) represent the determinants of achievement-related utility in most ordinary circumstances (extraordinary circumstances will be discussed in Section IV, D). These equations invite comparison with their counterparts in Atkinson's theory of achievement motivation (Atkinson, 1957, 1964; Atkinson & Feather, 1966; Atkinson & Raynor, 1974). Atkinson claims that achievement-related utility is determined by P_s, the subjective probability of success, according to the formulas:

$$U_s = 1 - P_s \qquad (8)$$

and

$$U_f = -P_s \qquad (9)$$

Evidently, Atkinson's assumption is that P_s plays precisely the same role in achievement situations as is here ascribed to F. Furthermore, Atkinson and his colleagues frequently use the terms P_s and "perceived difficulty" interchangeably, so that both Atkinson's and the present theory make the same *verbal* claims about utility. But in the attributional theory, P_s and perceived difficulty are distinct concepts, the latter being only one of several determinants of the former (cf. Eq. [5]). The essential difference between Eqs. (6–7) and Eqs. (8–9) is succinctly expressed in a passage by the Sufi master Meher Baba, who takes the side of the attributional theory. According to Baba (1971),

> ... success and failure are generally measured, appreciated or suffered more in relation to what has been achieved in the same field by others, than in relation to a target which has been hit or missed. [p. 79]

Another difference between the two theories is that Atkinson adopts Eqs. (8–9) as fundamental postulates in his theory, whereas Eqs. (6–7) are derived from the more basic assumption that the source of utility is demonstrated ability.

Atkinson and his colleagues have cited numerous studies which either directly support Eqs. (8–9) or, more usually, indirectly support them by verifying various behavioral predictions from the theory in which they are embedded. But a large proportion of these studies have ostensibly manipulated P_s by providing the subjects with group performance norms. As we have seen (Section II, B, 2), this is precisely the type of information which is likely to affect F more strongly than any of the other attributional variables. As a result, these data can as well be interpreted as confirming Eqs. (6–7). This is not to say, however, that the two sets of equations do not generate divergent predictions. Suppose, for example, that a person is led to believe that almost no one can succeed at a task (low F) but that he personally has a very good chance at success (high P_s). Atkinson's equations would predict that success at such a task would not be very attractive; according to the attributional theory, however, such a success would be highly attractive.

Evidence specifically favoring Eqs. (6–7) over Eqs. (8–9) comes from a study by Karabenick (1972). In this experiment, subjects found success to be somewhat attractive and failure somewhat aversive even when they reported that $P_s = 1$ and $P_s = 0$, respectively. The present theory can explain these results under the reasonable assumptions that $F < 1$ (not everyone was expected to succeed) in the first case and $F > 0$ (not everyone was expected to fail) in the second case. But Atkinson's theory would predict indifference to success and failure in these circumstances.

The dependence of the difficulty–utility relationship on a logically prior link between difficulty and demonstrated ability receives strong support from a study by Nicholls (1977). Here, 5- and 7-year-old children assessed the relative attractiveness of success at tasks characterized as easy, moderate, or difficult. Only the 7-year-olds consistently indicated that success at the difficult task would be most rewarding. This suggests that the cognitive link between difficulty and utility is not yet well-established among 5-year-olds. Depending on how the concept of ''difficulty'' is interpreted (whether as F or as P_s), these results can be seen as compatible with either Atkinson's or the present theory. But other data from the same study provide evidence for the crucial role of demonstrated ability. A clear majority of the older, but not of the younger children, selected the difficult task as the one which would require the most ability. Further, when the data were analyzed for indications of asynchronous development, there proved to be a tendency for the difficulty–ability link to become established before the difficulty–utility link. This is precisely what would be expected on the basis of the demonstrated ability hypothesis: The younger children did not yet value success at the difficult task because they did not yet realize that such a success demonstrates the possession of high ability.

D. CHOICE IN ORDINARY CIRCUMSTANCES

Substituting Eqs. (6–7) in the expression for *SEU* (Eq. [2]) yields:

$$SEU = P_s (1 - F) + P_f(-F) \tag{10}$$

Since $P_s + P_f = 1$, this equation is equivalent to:

$$SEU = P_s - F \tag{11}$$

That is, the tendency to select an achievement task should depend on the difference between its subjective probability of success and its perceived facility.

Equation (11) entails that the relationship between perceived facility and SEU is as depicted in Fig. 1. This figure has three distinct regions, set apart by the vertical lines. The region at the left comprises those tasks which are perceived as so difficult that the actor has no expectation whatever of succeeding at them, so that $P_s = 0$. Within this region, Eq. (11) has the form

$$SEU = -F \tag{12}$$

that is, all the members of this region of very difficult tasks have a negative SEU, but this SEU tends to become less negative as the tasks become increasingly more difficult. Psychologically, this is because the selection of any of these tasks is

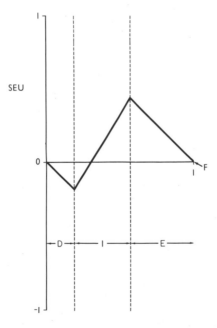

Fig. 1. Theoretical relationship between subjectively expected utility (SEU) and the perceived facility (F) of achievement tasks, showing the domains of easy (E), intermediate (I), and difficult (D) tasks.

expected to result in the proof of some degree of incompetence; but the more difficult the task, the less the degree of incompetence thus demonstrated.

The region at the right of the figure comprises those tasks which are perceived as so easy that the actor has no expectation whatever of failing at them, so that $P_s = 1$. In this region, Eq. (11) has the form

$$SEU = 1 - F \tag{13}$$

Thus all the members of this region of easy tasks have a positive SEU, and SEU tends to become less positive as the tasks become increasingly easier. This is because the selection of any of these tasks is expected to result surely in the proof of some degree of competence; but the easier the task, the less the degree of competence demonstrated.

In the middle region of the figure are those intermediate tasks at which neither success nor failure is thought to be assured. Without detailed parametric information concerning the way in which F and P_S covary, it is impossible to predict just what shape the SEU function will have here. But, even though local irregularities may exist, it is clear that the overall direction of the function must be upward from the negative-SEU difficult tasks in the left-hand region to the positive-SEU easy tasks in the right-hand region. As the gap between the two extreme regions is traversed, there must presumably be some point in the intermediate region where $SEU = 0$. In Fig. 1, the generally upward direction of the curve is provisionally depicted as a linear function. But nothing in the ensuing analysis depends on this linearity.

Validating evidence for the derivations in this section will be presented after the personality variable of resultant achievement motivation is incorporated into the analysis.

IV.   Resultant Achievement Motivation

A.   THE CONCEPT OF RESULTANT ACHIEVEMENT MOTIVATION

1.   Atkinson's Theory

In Atkinson's achievement theory, it is assumed that achievement-related choices are determined not only by situational factors (the P_s of the tasks), but also by the personality disposition of *resultant achievement motivation*. According to Atkinson, this personality variable influences choice by systematically altering the utilities of success and failure. Strictly speaking, Eqs. (8–9) represent only the situational contribution to utility, which Atkinson calls the *incentive values* of success and failure. Taking into account both situational and personal factors leads to the more complete statements:

$$U_s = M_s (1 - P_s) \tag{14}$$

and

$$U_f = M_f (-P_s) \tag{15}$$

where $(1 - P_s)$ and $(-P_s)$ are, as before, the hypothesized incentive values of success and failure, and M_s and M_f are the "motive to succeed" and the "motive to avoid failure," respectively. A subject's level of resultant achievement motivation is identified with the quantity $(M_s - M_f)$. Evidently, a high resultant achiever, for whom M_s is large and M_f is small, is a person who derives a great deal of pleasure from success but relatively little displeasure from failure. A low resultant achiever, on the other hand, for whom M_s is small and M_f is large, anticipates little pleasure from success and much displeasure from failure.

Substituting Eqs. (14–15) into the formula for SEU (Eq. [2]), and recalling that $P_s + P_f = 1$, we arrive at:

$$SEU = M_s (1 - P_s)(P_s) + M_f (-P_s)(1 - P_s) \tag{16}$$

This formula can in turn be simplified to:

$$SEU = (M_s - M_f)(P_s)(1 - P_s) \tag{17}$$

The form of Eq. (17) highlights the fact that, in Atkinson's model, the direction of achievement-related behavior is fully determined by the P_s of the task and the subject's level of resultant achievement motivation $(M_s - M_f)$.

The resulting theoretical differences between high and low resultant achievers is depicted in Fig. 2. Whenever $M_s > M_f$, SEU is an inverted-U function of perceived difficulty (which Atkinson identifies with P_s) lying wholly above zero; and whenever $M_f > M_s$, SEU is a noninverted-U function of perceived difficulty lying wholly below zero. As would be expected from this conception, subjects who score high on standard tests of resultant achievement motivation differ systematically from low scores in their choices of achievement tasks (Atkinson, 1964; Atkinson & Feather, 1966; Atkinson & Raynor, 1974). The extent to which the data support the theoretically derived relations in Fig. 2 will be discussed below (Section IV, C).

2. Resultant Achievement Motivation and Perceived Ability

Recently, an alternative interpretation of what is measured by resultant achievement motivation tests has been presented by Kukla (1972b) and Meyer (1973b). Working independently, both Kukla and Meyer have suggested that the essential difference between the high- and low-motive groups lies in the degree

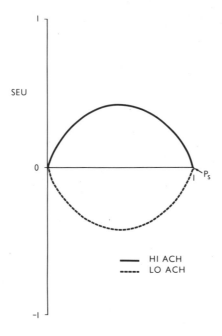

Fig. 2. Theoretical relationships between subjectively expected utility *(SEU)* and the subjective probability of success (P_s) at achievement tasks for subjects high and low in resultant achievement motivation (HI ACH) (LO ACH), according to Atkinson's (1964) theory.

of *ability* which they tend to ascribe to themselves. According to this view, people who score high on standard tests of resultant achievement motivation are those who have a generalized tendency to see themselves as highly capable individuals, while low scorers tend to think of themselves as having little ability for most tasks. Thus, in contrast to Atkinson's conception of resultant achievement motivation as an *affective* disposition, Kukla and Meyer take it to be a *cognitive* (specifically, an attributional) disposition.

The evidence seems to favor Kukla's and Meyer's view. The difference in affective reaction to success and failure postulated by Atkinson has been reported only once, in a study by Litwin (1966); and Litwin's index of affect was the amount of reward deemed appropriate for success, a measure whose suitability was questioned in Section III, B. Other attempts to verify the relationship between resultant achievement motivation and affect have proven inconclusive (Brown, 1963; Feather, 1967; Karabenick, 1972; Morgan, 1964). In comparison, a number of studies have found that high resultant achievers claimed a higher degree of ability for a variety of tasks than did low resultant achievers (Kukla, 1972a; Meyer, 1970; Weiner & Potepan, 1970). Furthermore, it has long been known that the high-motive group generally has a greater probability of success than the low-motive group (Atkinson, Bastian, Earl, & Litwin, 1960; Brody, 1963; Feather, 1965; McClelland, Atkinson, Clark, & Lowell, 1953; Pottharst, 1955). From the viewpoint of Atkinson's theory, this fact has been treated as an extratheoretical difference between the motive groups which complicates theoretical deductions. But a difference in P_s is to be expected from the present viewpoint, since P_s is an increasing function of A (Eq. [5]). Hallermann (1975, Experiment 5) has recently confirmed that subjects high in perceived ability have a higher P_s than those low in perceived ability.

Contrary to Kukla's and Meyer's hypothesis, however, are the results of Touhey and Villemez (1975) and Heckhausen (1975) who failed to find the predicted perceived ability difference between the motive groups. Possibly these negative findings can be accounted for by the presence of special task characteristics whose effects overwhelmed those of the subjects' cognitive dispositions. Of course, the same can be said of the data contrary to Atkinson's view, the only difference being that Atkinson would have to invoke this *post hoc* explanation rather more often. In any case, such a saving argument could not be made on behalf of either theory if the data pertained directly to subjects' affective reactions or perceived abilities for tasks in general, rather than for this or that specific experimental task. Surprisingly, this kind of evidence does not exist for Atkinson's conception, that is, no one has yet asked high and low resultant achievers how they *generally* feel about success or failure. But there is corresponding evidence for the attributional conception of resultant achievement motivation. For example, Coopersmith (1967) has reported a correlation between "self-esteem" and anxiety of $-.67$. Clearly, the self-esteem variable is conceptually similar to a general tendency to ascribe high ability to oneself; and tests of anxiety are routinely used to measure the M_f component of resultant achievement motivation (Atkinson, 1964).

A more direct link between resultant achievement motivation and the general tendency to have a high opinion of one's abilities has been established in a recent study by Kukla (1977). In this experiment, subjects were asked to estimate how much ability and how much luck they had at both intellectual and artistic tasks. As expected from the attributional conception, subjects high in resultant achievement motivation gave a greater estimation of both their intellectual and their artistic abilities than did low resultant achievers. In isolation, this finding could also be explained by supposing that the motive groups, for reasons unrelated to perceived ability, differed in how successful they had been in the past, and that the greater perceived ability of the high-motive group was a reflection of this performance difference. But by the same token, the high-motive subjects should then also have perceived themselves as luckier in their endeavors. Yet there was no difference between the motive groups in perceived luck for either intellectual or artistic tasks. Given these results, the only way to maintain that the reported ability difference was due to a difference in success rates would be to postulate that ability estimates increase more rapidly than luck estimates with increasing success. But such a tendency could definitely be ruled out in this experiment. For although these subjects saw themselves as more successful in intellectual than in artistic pursuits, the difference between intellectual luck and artistic luck was as large as that between intellectual ability and artistic ability. That is, there was a significant main effect due to tasks (intellectual/artistic) but no interaction between tasks and attributes (ability/luck). This contrasted sharply with the effects of motive level (high/low) where the interaction with attributes was significant, but not the main effect. This pattern of results provides strong evidence for the view that high resultant achievers have *essentially* (rather than incidentally, as an effect of differential success rates) a greater tendency to ascribe high ability to themselves as compared with low resultant achievers.

3. Affective Versus Cognitive Dispositions

The issue between Atkinson's and the attributional theory's conceptions of resultant achievement motivation can be placed in a broader context. Presumably, resultant achievement motivation must, of logical necessity, refer to the strength of the tendency to engage in achievement tasks. In the language of decision theory, such a behavioral tendency corresponds to the concept of *SEU*. But there are two sorts of reasons why one person may assign higher *SEU*s than another person to some class of activities: (a) he may assign higher utilities to the outcomes of these activities, or (b) he may assign higher subjective probabilities to the more desirable outcomes and lower subjective probabilities to the less desirable outcomes. These alternatives apply to any motivational differences. For example, if one person is higher than another in affiliative tendencies, it could be either because he values friendship more or because he is more confident of making friends. In the realm of resultant achievement motivation, alternative (a) corresponds to Atkinson's conception of high- and low-motive subjects; alternative (b) is the one adopted here.

No doubt there are individual differences along both the above dimensions. The point at issue, however, is which of these factors allows for an explanation of the various known differences between the motive groups. The data seem to indicate that high- and low-motive groups, as constituted by traditional measures of resultant achievement motivation, do differ in their perceived abilities and hence also in their subjective probabilities, but that they do not differ in their affective reactions to success and failure. Also, it was shown in the earlier analysis of intensity (Kukla, 1972b) that the ability difference alone was sufficient to account for many of the known data concerning high and low resultant achievers' performance intensities. Indeed, several new hypotheses about intensity were derived from the ability difference which have since received confirmation (Hallermann, 1975; Kukla, 1974; Latta, 1976; Meyer, 1973a). On this basis, it seems appropriate in this chapter to explore the extent to which the ability difference can also account for the data on choice. This procedure does not reflect a programmatic preference for alternative (b) over alternative (a). It may be that future research will establish data which are best explained by assuming that high and low resultant achievers, or some other identifiable groups, assign divergent utilities to success and failure even when they share identical attributional cognitions. If so, this assumption could be incorporated into the present theory without altering its basic structure.

B. RESULTANT ACHIEVEMENT MOTIVATION AND CHOICE

1. Resultant Achievement Motivation and SEU

Let H and L represent subjects who are relatively high and low in resultant achievement motivation, respectively. Now both H and L will generate S-shaped curves like the one in Fig. 1. For both of them there will exist (a) a region of very easy tasks where $P_s = 1$ and so $SEU = 1 - F$; (b) a region of less easy tasks where $0 < P_s < 1$ and $SEU = P_s - F$, over which SEU gradually decreases with further decrements of F; and (c) a region of very difficult tasks where $P_s = 0$ and $SEU = -F$. The essential difference between H and L, however, is that H tends to assign a greater value to A (perceived ability) than L does. But, by Eq. (5), it then followed that H also assigns a greater P_s to tasks of a given difficulty. This has the effect of altering Hs SEU curve, as compared to Ls, in the manner shown in Fig. 3. First, the region of very easy tasks will continue longer for H, since he will still be assigning values of $P_s = 1$ to tasks at which L already conceives he may fail. Second, over the interval of tasks where $0 < P_s < 1$ and $SEU = P_s - F$, SEU will be greater for H than for L because his P_S will be greater. And finally, the region of very difficult tasks will begin sooner for L, since H will still have some nonzero probability of success at the point where L has already given up all hope of succeeding.

Figure 3 shows that, for any level of perceived facility, the SEU of an achievement task for H is always greater than or equal to its SEU for L. That is, high resultant achievers have a greater overall tendency to engage in achievement tasks than do low resultant achievers. This explains why, given a choice between an achievement task and an unspecified alternative, high-motive subjects are more likely than low-motive subjects to select the achievement task (Atkinson, 1953). It also accounts for the fact that Hs exceed Ls in their choice of an achievement task when the difficulty of that task is unspecified and the alternative is an activity unrelated to achievement strivings (Weiner & Rosenbaum, 1965). These are minimal properties of the motive concept. Their experimental confirmation does not so much constitute empirical support for the theory as it validates the motive measures employed in the studies. But the fact that the present analysis results in the proper conclusions here does provide a check on

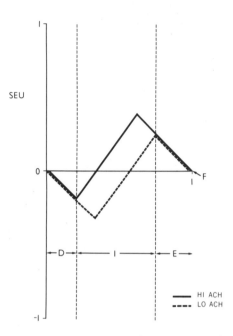

Fig. 3. Theoretical relationships between subjectively expected utility (*SEU*) and the perceived facility (*F*) of achievement tasks for subjects high and low in resultant achievement motivation, showing the domains of easy (*E*), intermediate (*I*), and difficult (*D*) tasks.

the formal adequacy of the theoretical apparatus. The same conclusions are also derivable from Atkinson's theory, although on very different grounds (see Fig. 2).

Some more substantive results of the analysis are presented below. In this discussion, we continue to use *H* and *L* as abbreviations for high and low resultant achievers. Also, *E* will represent those easy tasks at which both *H* and *L* fully expect to succeed; *D* will be the difficult tasks at which they both expect to fail; and *I* will stand for tasks to which at least one of them assigns an intermediate probability of success. The domains of *E, D,* and *I* are displayed in Fig. 3.

2. HI > LI

It is clear from Fig. 3 that high-motive subjects assign a greater *SEU* to tasks of intermediate perceived difficulty than do low-motive subjects. Thus, given the opportunity to select their own difficulty levels, *H*s should select *I* tasks more often than *L*s. This greater preference for intermediate tasks is a well-replicated result (Atkinson *et al.*, 1960; Atkinson & Litwin, 1960; Litwin, 1966; McClelland, 1958; Raynor & Smith, 1966; Weiner, 1965). It is often considered to be the best evidence for Atkinson's theory, from which it is also derivable. But here this datum is derived without Atkinson's assumption that the motive groups differ in their capacities to enjoy success or dislike failure. The difference in perceived ability is itself sufficient to generate such behavior.

3.   E > D

Figure 3 also shows that all subjects, whether high or low in resultant achievement motivation, should prefer a very easy task to a very difficult one. None of the achievement studies just cited in support of $HI > LI$ have analyzed their data in a form appropriate for testing this hypothesis; nor have any of them been suitably designed to permit such a test. No doubt this is because Atkinson's theory, which these studies set out to validate, makes no prediction for an E versus D comparison.

The main methodological problem, in relation to the present hypothesis, is that the subjects in the above choice studies have been permitted to choose their tasks from among a large number of available difficulty levels. Thus there is no way to know whether the number of tasks perceived as easy is the same as the number of tasks perceived as difficult. But unless this condition is satisfied, it is not possible to ascertain whether easy or difficult tasks were on the whole more attractive. For suppose, to construct an extreme example, that of a large number of difficulty levels available, only one is perceived as difficult while 10 are perceived as easy. Suppose also that 80% of the subjects prefer an easy task over a difficult one. Such a state of affairs is entirely compatible with the present hypothesis. But if the 10 easy tasks are all nearly equal in attractiveness, each one may be selected by about 8% of the subjects, as compared with a 20% choice of the single difficult task. Thus, even though the difficult task is less attractive than any of the 10 easy ones, it could be chosen by more subjects than any one of the easy tasks. This split-voting problem arises whenever comparisons are made between, rather than within, task difficulty levels. In principle, the problem could be resolved by summing all the choices of easy tasks and comparing that with the sum of the choices of difficult tasks. But this presupposes an entirely precise knowledge of the range of tasks which count as easy or difficult in the present sense. No study yet conducted has had the resources for establishing such information.

However, the split-voting problem is circumvented whenever subjects are presented with a choice set which contains tasks at exactly one easy level and exactly one difficult level of F. In that case, the proportion of choices of easy versus difficult tasks can be directly compared. This condition is satisfied in studies by Trope and Brickman (1975), Trope (1975), and Moulton (1965). In all these studies, subjects were required to choose among tasks which were described, both verbally and numerically, as difficult, intermediate, or easy; and it was specified that all the difficult tasks were equally difficult, as were all the intermediate tasks and all the easy tasks (in Moulton's study, there was only one task at each of the three levels). In both studies by Trope, easy tasks were selected significantly more often than difficult ones; and in Trope's (1975) second experiment, where the subjects' levels of resultant achievement motivation was also assessed, the same preference for easy over difficult tasks was found to characterize both high- and low-motive groups. In Moulton's study, on the other hand, the easy task was selected only marginally more often than the difficult task by the L group, and actually less often by Hs.

The $E > D$ hypothesis can also be tested by a between-subjects design, offering one group a choice between a difficult achievement task and an alternative activity, and the other group a choice between an easy achievement task and the same alternative. This procedure was followed in an experiment by Weiner and Rosenbaum (1965) and in two by Weiner (1970). In all three cases, the easy task was clearly selected more often than the difficult task by both Hs and Ls.

The question naturally arises whether the "easy" and "difficult" tasks employed in these studies did indeed qualify as easy and difficult in the present sense, that is, as tasks for which success is seen as either certain or hopeless. This seems a reasonable assumption in some cases. For example, in one of Weiner's (1970) studies, the easy and difficult tasks were said to have been succeeded at by 95% and 5% of previous subjects; and furthermore the subjects were manipulated into experiencing a success every time they selected an easy task and a failure every time they chose a difficult one. In other studies cited here, however, it seems far less likely that these extreme conditions were satisfied. But these data are nevertheless relevant to the present hypothesis, for Fig. 3 shows that tasks toward the easy end of the facility continuum, even if they are not strictly "easy," must generally have a higher SEU than tasks toward the difficult end.

The most explicit test of the hypothesis is found in a study by Kukla (1975). Here, subjects were required to express their preference between a single easy task and a single difficult task, under the express assumption that success had a probability of one for the former and zero for the latter. Both Hs and Ls stated that they would rather work at the trivially easy task rather than at the impossibly difficult one.

In sum, the hypothesis that $E > D$ receives support from six of seven methodologically appropriate experiments.

4. $E > EE$ *and* $DD > D$

Figure 3 also leads to the novel hypothesis that, of two impossibly difficult ($P_s = 0$) tasks, the more difficult one (DD) will be preferred to the somewhat less difficult (D) one by both H and L. That is, if one is certainly going to fail, one prefers to fail at the most difficult task available. According to the attributional theory, this is because the more difficult the failed task is, the greater is the upper limit of ability compatible with that failure.

Conversely, of two trivially easy ($P_s = 1$) tasks, both H and L should prefer the somewhat less easy (E) one to the easier (EE) one. For the less easy the task succeeded at, the greater is the lower limit of ability demonstrated by that success.

The study by Kukla (1975) cited above provides evidence for both these hypotheses. In this experiment, both high- and low-motive subjects reported a preference for the more difficult of two impossibly difficult tasks and for the less easy of two trivially easy tasks.

The choices involved here are, to be sure, artificial in the sense that they are rarely encountered in everyday life. But theoretical refinement often comes about through the investigation of extreme boundary conditions, where it is likeliest that competing and otherwise similar theoretical formulations will make widely divergent predictions.

C. COMPARISONS WITH ATKINSON'S THEORY

The differences between Atkinson's and the present theory can be summarized as follows. Both theories adopt the principle of *SEU* maximization, and both assert that achievement-related utilities are functions of "perceived difficulty"; but only Atkinson equates the difficulty concept with P_s. Furthermore, the relationship between utility and difficulty is a basic postulate in Atkinson's theory, whereas the present theory derives it from a more fundamental relation between utility and demonstrated ability. Finally, Atkinson conceives of resultant achievement motivation as an affective tendency, while the attributional theory equates it with perceived ability.

Atkinson's assumptions, we have seen, lead to the theoretical curves of Fig. 2. Thus it follows from Atkinson's analysis, as from the present one, that Hs should exhibit a greater preference for intermediate tasks than Ls. But it is only in Atkinson's theory that an "intermediate" task means a task of intermediate *subjective probability*. According to the present analysis, choice differences between Hs and Ls exist precisely because these subjects assign different probabilities to tasks of the same perceived difficulty. Indeed, the attributional theory suggests that if the subjective probabilities of Hs and Ls were equalized, there would be no remaining differences in task preference between them. This is because $SEU = F - P_s$ for subjects of any motive level, and there is no reason to believe that Hs and Ls differ in their perceptions of F, as opposed to P_s. The evidence on this point is inconclusive. When subjective probabilities were directly assessed (instead of inferred from manipulations which more likely affect perceived difficulty), Hamilton (1974) did but Schneider (1973) did not find the traditional differences in task selection ($HI > LI$) between the motive groups.

Atkinson's theory also entails that the point of greatest difference between Hs and Ls, the point at which Hs are maximally attracted and Ls maximally repulsed, occurs when $P_s = .5$. But this highly specific prediction has always failed to receive experimental confirmation (Hamilton, 1974; Heckhausen, 1968; Litwin, 1966; Schneider, 1973). No comparable specification of parametric values is attempted by the attributional theory. But an ordinal prediction concerning maximal and minimal points of preference can be derived. Figure 3 reveals that the most preferred difficulty level for Hs is more difficult than the most preferred level for Ls. Similarly, the least preferred difficulty level for Hs is also more difficult than the least preferred level for Ls. These hypotheses await adequate testing.

In further contrast to the attributional theory, Atkinson's theory does not predict a general preference for easy versus difficult tasks. As Fig. 2 shows, all tasks for which $P_s = 0$ or $P_s = 1$ should be equally attractive to subjects of all motive levels. Thus the data to the contrary, especially Kukla's (1975) study employing tasks whose probabilities were explicitly zero or one, disconfirm Atkinson's views. The same is true of the fact that subjects preferred the more difficult of two zero-P_s tasks and the less easy of two tasks whose $P_s = 1$ (Kukla, 1975). Again, Atkinson's theory requires that all such tasks have the same SEU, and so also that there be no systematic preferences among them.

Atkinson's theory also generates the predictions that $HI > (HE, HD)$ and $(LE, LD) > LI$; that is, high-motive subjects should prefer intermediate tasks to either easy or difficult ones, while low-motive subjects should prefer either easy or difficult tasks to intermediate ones. The attributional theory makes no predictions for these comparisons: Fig. 3 shows that a given intermediate task may or may not have a greater SEU than a given easy or difficult task for either H or L. Of the seven experiments discussed previously as appropriate for a comparison between difficulty levels, five also assessed resultant achievement motivation and employed an intermediate task (Moulton, 1965; Trope, 1975; Weiner, 1970, Experiments I and II; Weiner & Rosenbaum, 1965). Atkinson's hypothesis that $HI > HD$ was confirmed in all five experiments. But $HI > HE$ was reported only twice (Moulton, 1965; Weiner, 1970, Experiment II) as compared with three disconfirming findings of $HE > HI$. $LE > LI$ was confirmed in all the studies except Moulton's. But none of the studies found that $LD > LI$. In sum, of the 20 relevant outcomes in these studies (four outcomes in each of five experiments), 11 were in accordance with Atkinson's predictions and 9 were in the opposite direction. The unanimously disconfirmed hypothesis that $LD > LI$ could be explained by supposing, as achievement theorists sometimes do (e.g., Atkinson & Litwin, 1960), that the L group was still rather high in resultant achievement motivation since the lowest resultant achievers tend to be underrepresented among college students. Thus these subjects also preferred intermediate tasks over difficult ones. But by the same token they should then also have preferred intermediate tasks over easy ones. Yet in four of the five studies, the L group preferred both intermediate tasks to difficult ones and easy tasks to intermediate ones. This pattern of results is incompatible with achievement theory under any assumed level of motivation among the subjects.

D. CHOICE IN EXTRAORDINARY CIRCUMSTANCES

It is evident that the equations $U_s = 1 - F$ and $U_s = -F$ are indispensible for generating the predictions made in Section IV, B. But the derivation of these equations in Section III, C was said to be valid only under certain normal conditions, in which the perceived difficulty of the task determines the amount of ability demonstrated by success or failure. In other circumstances, this normal link between difficulty and demonstrated ability will not hold; that is, the amount of ability which can be inferred from success or failure may be unaffected by the difficulty of the task succeeded or failed at. In such cases, the present theory must predict that none of the previously discussed effects of F will be found: Easy, intermediate, and difficult tasks will not have systematically different utilities, and neither high nor low resultant achievers will exhibit any systematic task difficulty preferences. This consequence of the theory makes sense out of a number of previously disparate findings.

1. Skill Versus Chance Conditions

Feather (1967) investigated the attractiveness of success and repulsiveness of failure (U_s and U_f) in relation to whether the task was thought to be determined by one's own skill or by chance factors outside of one's personal control. Clearly the demonstrated ability hypothesis entails an effect of difficulty only in the skill condition. For if a task is conceived to be influenced by chance alone, then success or failure has no bearing on how much ability one has. Feather's results confirm this expectation. Attractiveness estimates were found generally to increase with increasing difficulty ($U_s = 1 - F$), but to do so less rapidly in the chance than in the skill condition; that is, the effect of difficulty on U_s was systematically diminished by a chance orientation. Similarly, repulsiveness-of-failure estimates were higher with decreasing difficulty ($U_f = -F$) but increased less rapidly in the chance than in the skill condition. In sum, the task's difficulty level made less of a difference, both in relation to the attractiveness of success and the repulsiveness of failure, when chance rather than skill was thought to be the main outcome determinant.

On the basis of these data, Feather suggests that Atkinson's equations, $U_s = 1 - P_s$ and $U_f = -P_s$, be amended to:

$$U_s = C(1 - P_s) \tag{18}$$

and

$$U_f = -CP_s \tag{19}$$

where C, the degree of "perceived internal control," represents the extent to which skill rather than chance is seen as the determinant of one's outcomes. For Feather, then, the effects on utility of perceived control and of perceived difficulty (which, like Atkinson, he equates with P_s) are two independent facts. But in the attributional theory both effects are derivable from the same fundamental assumption that utility is a function of demonstrated ability.

2. Internals Versus Externals

Wolk and DuCette (1973) assessed subjects' preferences for tasks of intermediate difficulty as a function of resultant achievement motivation and the personality dimension of internality–externality (Rotter, 1966). The latter is defined as the disposition to believe that what happens to one is due to his own skill or lack of skill (internality), as opposed to factors outside of personal control (externality). Thus internals should habitually differ from externals in the same way as subjects given a skill orientation differ from those given a chance orientation. In particular, externals should have a diminished tendency to consider the difficulty of the task succeeded or failed at as diagnostic of their ability. As a result, they should find such successes and failures to be matters of relative indifference, and so should show less pronounced patterns of preferred choices. From this it also follows that the differences in choice behavior between high and low resultant achievers should be diminished among externals as compared with internals. This last consequence receives clear support from Wolk and DuCette's data. In two studies, the correlations between resultant achievement motivation and a measure of intermediate-task preference were $+.53$ and $+.44$ among internals, and $-.07$ and $+.10$ among externals. As Wolk and DuCette point out, these data can also be explained by Feather's hypothesis (Eqs. [18–19]), since internals by definition have a higher level of C, perceived internal control.

3. Salience Versus Irrelevance of Effort

In Experiment 3 of Kukla's (1972a) study, some of the subjects were told that performance at the experimental task would be influenced both by their level of ability and by how much effort they exerted (AE condition). Other subjects were told that only ability determined performance, and that they would get essentially the same result whether or not they tried hard (A condition). The AE condition is an "ordinary" one in the sense that the demonstrated ability hypothesis entails the usual effects of perceived difficulty. In fact, the different degrees of attractiveness possessed by tasks of various difficulty levels are specifically due to the uncertainty concerning the extent to which a given outcome reflects ability or effort expenditure. For suppose, as is the case in the A condition, that a subject believes his performance reflects only his ability. Then, since demonstrated ability is the determinant of utility, and since his ability can be directly read off from his performance (there being no question of the unknown contribution of effort), it should not matter to the subject whether that reading is based on a good performance at an easy task or a bad performance at a difficult task. The same level of ability being demonstrated in either case, the subject should be indifferent to the difficulty level of the task. Thus the prediction is that the usual effects of F should be found in the AE condition, but that they should be attenuated in the A condition.

Kukla's data exactly parallel those of Wolk and DuCette. In condition AE, high resultant achievers as usual selected more intermediate tasks than did low resultant achievers. But the high- and low-motive groups' choices did not differ at all in condition A. Unlike the results of Feather and those of Wolk and DuCette, these findings cannot be explained by Feather's hypothesis, since both conditions in Kukla's study are equally "skill" rather than "chance" orientations to the task. There is, of course, a crucial distinction as to the type of determination by skill involved in each of these conditions. But it is not a distinction which is dealt with by Feather's analysis.

4. High Versus Low Diagnosticity

Weiner et al. (1971) have suggested that the effects of task difficulty on achievement-related choice are due to high and low resultant achievers' information-seeking propensities. They argue that the selection of tasks of intermediate difficulty maximizes information about one's own ability (one learns relatively little about ability by succeeding at very easy tasks or failing at very difficult ones). Furthermore, it is assumed that high resultant achievers are motivated to obtain such information, whereas low resultant achievers are motivated to avoid it. This is offered as an alternative interpretation of Atkinson's hypotheses that high resultant achievers prefer intermediate tasks to either difficult or easy ones, and that low resultant achievers prefer either easy or difficult tasks to intermediate ones ($HI > (HE, HD)$ and $(LE, LD) > LI$; see Section IV, C). However, as we have seen, the data do not well support these hypotheses.

The failure of the second of these hypotheses, $(LE, LD) > LI$, is explicitly noted in a more recent paper (Meyer et al., 1976), and the information-seeking hypothesis is accordingly modified. According to Meyer et al., all subjects, regardless of their level of resultant achievement motivation, attempt to maximize ability-relevant information. This view does indeed circumvent the problem faced by the previous formulation. But it would also seem to entail that there exist no differences between the motive groups' task preferences. That this is an intended consequence of Meyer et al.'s view is indicated by the fact that these authors report an experiment in which high and low resultant achievers did not differ in their preference for intermediate tasks, a finding which, it is said, "contradicts Atkinson's model of motivation but does support an attributional conception" (Meyer et al., 1976, p. 420). But a single null result of this kind cannot stand against the massive evidence that, even though low resultant achievers may not actually prefer easy or difficult tasks to intermediate ones, their choice of intermediate tasks is nevertheless reduced as compared with high resultant achievers (Section IV, B, 2).

In addition, Trope and Brickman (1975) have pointed out that the relationship between difficulty and information value postulated by Weiner *et al.* and Meyer *et al.* is not universally valid. Information value depends also on the extent to which the performances of high- and low-ability people are separated on the task. For example, compare a task *A* at which the most able person has a .51 probability of succeeding and the least able a .49 probability of succeeding, with a task *B* at which the most able has a .99 probability and the least able a .89 probability of success. Evidently, *A* is an intermediate and *B* an easy task. But one would obtain more information about his ability from his outcomes at tasks like *B*. Trope and Brickman report an experiment in which the variables of task difficulty and information value, or "diagnosticity," were independently manipulated. The results showed that subjects preferred high-diagnostic over low-diagnostic tasks independently of their difficulty. This finding, which cannot be explained by Atkinson's theory, is compatible with Meyer *et al.*'s general suggestion about information value. But data from the same study also showed an effect of task difficulty which was independent of diagnosticity. Contrary to both Atkinson's views and those expressed by Meyer *et al.*, easy tasks were preferred to difficult ones.

Trope (1975) subsequently reported a replication of his first study, with the addition of a measure of resultant achievement motivation. The results here showed that the high-motive group preferred high- over low-diagnostic tasks to a significantly greater extent than the low-motive group. Indeed, when differences in the perception of diagnosticity were statistically controlled, low resultant achievers actually chose low-diagnostic tasks more often than high-diagnostic tasks. This seems to return us to Weiner *et al.*'s (1971) original hypothesis that high resultant achievers seek out but low resultant achievers avoid ability-relevant information, but without the presumed link between diagnosticity and difficulty which generated the unsupported prediction that $(LE, LD) > LI$. Still unexplained, however, is Trope's replication of the finding that easy tasks were preferred to difficult ones independently of their information value.

These results can all be explained by the demonstrated ability hypothesis of the present theory. Instead of assuming that people are motivated to obtain as much (or as little) valid information about their ability as they can, we must suppose that they wish to appear to have as much ability as possible. Then, to the extent that they expect to succeed, they will want to select high-diagnostic tasks, since that will maximize the display of their ability. But to the extent that they expect to fail, they will prefer low-diagnostic tasks, since that will minimize the disclosure of their lack of ability. Finally, recall that high resultant achievers, being higher in perceived ability, generally have greater expectations of success than low resultant achievers. It follows that high resultant achievers will exhibit a greater preference for high-diagnostic tasks than low resultant achievers, which is what Trope reports. As for the additional preference for easy over difficult tasks, its derivation from the demonstrated ability hypothesis was discussed in Section IV, B, 3. Essentially, people choose a likely success at an easy task over a likely failure at a difficult task because, even though the information values of both tasks may be equally small, the former demonstrates a modicum of ability and so has a slight positive value, whereas the latter demonstrates a modicum of inability and so has a slight negative value.

The relationship between high versus low diagnosticity conditions is in a crucial respect similar to that between internals versus externals, or skill versus chance conditions, or effort-salient versus effort-irrelevant conditions, or indeed 7-year-olds versus 5-year-olds (cf. Section III, C). In all cases, the ordinary effects of task difficulty on achievement-related activities occur only with the first member of each pair. And in all cases, the absence of ordinary difficulty effects with the second member of each pair can be attributed to the breakdown of the usual connection between difficulty and demonstrated ability.

REFERENCES

Atkinson, J. W. The achievement motive and recall of interrupted and completed tasks. *Journal of Experimental Psychology*, 1953, **46**, 381–390.

Atkinson, J. W. Motivational determinants of risk-taking behavior. *Psychological Review*, 1957, **64**, 359–372.

Atkinson, J. W. *An introduction to motivation*. Princeton, N.J.: Van Nostrand, 1964.

Atkinson, J. W., Bastian, J. R., Earl, R. W., & Litwin, G. H. The achievement motive, goal setting, and probability preferences. *Journal of Abnormal and Social Psychology*, 1960, **60**, 27–36.

Atkinson, J. W., & Feather, N. T. (Eds.) *A theory of achievement motivation*. New York: Wiley, 1966.

Atkinson, J. W., & Litwin, G. H. Achievement motive and test anxiety conceived as motive to approach success and motive to avoid failure. *Journal of Abnormal and Social Psychology*, 1960, **60**, 52–63.

Atkinson, J. W., & Raynor, J. O. (Eds.) *Motivation and achievement*. Washington, D.C.: Winston, 1974.

Baba, M. *Beams from Meher Baba on the spiritual panorama*. New York: Harper, 1971.

Brody, N. *N* achievement, test anxiety, and subjective probability of success in risk taking behavior. *Journal of Abnormal and Social Psychology*, 1963, **66**, 413–418.

Brown, M. Factors determining expectancy of success and reaction to success and failure. Unpublished manuscript, University of Michigan, 1963.

Cook, R. E. Relation of achievement motivation and attribution to self-reinforcement. Unpublished doctoral dissertation, University of California, Los Angeles, 1970.

Coopersmith, S. *The antecedents of self-esteem*. San Francisco: Freeman, 1967.

Edwards, W. The theory of decision making. *Psychological Bulletin*, 1954, **51**, 380–417.

Edwards, W. Behavioral decision theory. *Annual Review of Psychology*, 1961, **12**, 473–498.

Eswara, H. S. Administration of reward and punishment in relation to ability, effort, and performance. *Journal of Social Psychology,* 1972, **87,** 139–140.

Feather, N. T. Subjective probability and decision under uncertainty. *Psychological Review,* 1959, **66,** 150–164.

Feather, N. T. The relationship of expectations of success to need achievement and test anxiety. *Journal of Personality and Social Psychology,* 1965, **1,** 118–126.

Feather, N. T. Valence of outcome and expectation of success in relation to task difficulty and perceived locus of control. *Journal of Personality and Social Psychology,* 1967, **7,** 372–386.

Feldman, N. S., Higgins, E. T., Karlovac, M., & Ruble, D. N. Use of consensus information in causal attributions as a function of temporal presentation and availability of direct information. *Journal of Personality and Social Psychology,* 1976, **34,** 694–698.

Frieze, I., & Weiner, B. Cue utilization and attributional judgements for success and failure. *Journal of Personality,* 1971, **39,** 591–605.

Goethals, G. R. Consensus and modality in the attribution process: The role of similarity and information. *Journal of Personality and Social Psychology,* 1972, **21,** 84–92.

Hallermann, B. Untersuchungen zur Anstrengungskalkulation. Unpublished doctoral dissertation, Ruhr Universität, Bochum, Germany, 1975.

Hamilton, J. O. Motivation and risk-taking behavior: A test of Atkinson's theory. *Journal of Personality and Social Psychology,* 1974, **29,** 856–864.

Hansen, R. D., & Lowe, C. A. Distinctiveness and consensus: The influence of behavioral information on actors' and observers' attributions. *Journal of Personality and Social Psychology,* 1976, **34,** 425–433.

Heckhausen, H. Achievement motive research: Current problems and some contributions towards a general theory of motivation. In D. Levine (Ed.), *Nebraska Symposium on Motivation.* Vol. 16. Lincoln: University of Nebraska Press, 1968. Pp. 103–174.

Heckhausen, H. Perceived ability, achievement motive and information choice: A study by Meyer reanalyzed and supplemented. Unpublished manuscript, Ruhr Universität, Bochum, Germany, 1975.

Heider, F. *The psychology of interpersonal relations.* New York: Wiley, 1958.

Karabenick, S. A. Valence of success and failure as a function of achievement motives and locus of control. *Journal of Personality and Social Psychology,* 1972, **21,** 101–110.

Kelley, H. H. Attribution theory in social psychology. In D. Levine (Ed.), *Nebraska Symposium on Motivation.* Vol. 15. Lincoln: University of Nebraska Press, 1967. Pp. 192–240.

Kelley, H. H. The process of causal attribution. *American Psychologist,* 1973, **28,** 107–128.

Kukla, A. Attributional determinants of achievement-related behavior. *Journal of Personality and Social Psychology,* 1972, **21,** 166–174. (a)

Kukla, A. Foundations of an attributional theory of performance. *Psychological Review,* 1972, **79,** 454–470. (b)

Kukla, A. Performance as a function of resultant achievement motivation (perceived ability) and perceived difficulty. *Journal Research in Personality,* 1974, **7,** 374–383.

Kukla, A. Preferences among impossibly difficult and trivially easy tasks: A revision of Atkinson's theory of choice. *Journal of Personality and Social Psychology,* 1975, **32,** 338–345.

Kukla, A. Self-perception of ability and resultant achievement motivation. Unpublished manuscript, University of Toronto, 1977.

Lanzetta, J. T., & Hannah, T. E. Reinforcing behavior of "naive" trainers. *Journal of Personality and Social Psychology,* 1969, **11,** 245–252.

Latta, R. M. Differential tests of two cognitive theories of performance: Weiner versus Kukla. *Journal of Personality and Social Psychology,* 1976, **34,** 295–304.

Leventhal, G. S., & Michaels, J. W. Locus of cause and equity motivation as determinants of reward allocation. *Journal of Personality and Social Psychology,* 1971, **17,** 229–235.

Litwin, G. H. Achievement motivation, expectancy of success, and risk-taking behavior. In J. W.

Atkinson & N. T. Feather (Eds.), *A theory of achievement motivation*. New York: Wiley, 1966.

McClelland, D. C. Risk taking in children high and low in need for achievement. In J. W. Atkinson (Ed.), *Motives in fantasy, action, and society*. Princeton, N.J.: Van Nostrand, 1958.

McClelland, D. C., Atkinson, J. W., Clark, R. W., & Lowell, E. L. *The achievement motive*. New York: Appleton, 1953.

Meyer, W.-U. Selbstverantwortlichkeit und Leistungsmotivation. Unpublished doctoral dissertation, Ruhr Universität, Bochum, Germany, 1970.

Meyer, W.-U. Anstrengungsintention in Abhängigkeit von Begabungseinschätzungen und Aufgabenschwierigkeit. *Archiv für Psychologie*. 1973, **125**, 245–262. (a)

Meyer, W.-U. *Leistungsmotiv und Ursachenerklärung von Erfolg und Misserfolg*. Stuttgart: Klett, 1973. (b)

Meyer, W.-U., Folkes, V., & Weiner, B. The perceived informational value and affective consequences of choice behavior and intermediate task selection. *Journal of Research in Personality*, 1976, **10**, 410–423.

Morgan, J. N. The achievement motive and economic behavior. *Economic Development and Cultural Change*, 1964, **12**, 243–267.

Moulton, R. W. Effects of success and failure on level of aspiration as related to achievement motives. *Journal of Personality and Social Psychology*, 1965, **1**, 399–406.

Nicholls, J. G. Causal attributions and other achievement-related cognitions: Effects of task outcome, attainment value, and sex. *Journal of Personality and Social Psychology*, 1975, **31**, 379–381.

Nicholls, J. G. Effort is virtuous, but it's better to have ability: Evaluative responses to perceptions of effort and ability. *Journal of Research in Personality*, 1976, **10**, 306–315.

Nicholls, J. G. Children's responses to task difficulty cues: An aspect of the development of achievement motivation. Unpublished manuscript, Victoria University, Wellingon, New Zealand, 1977.

Pottharst, B. C. The achievement motive and level of aspiration after experimentally induced success and failure. Unpublished doctoral dissertation, University of Michigan, 1955.

Raynor, J. O., & Smith, C. P. Achievement-related motives and risk-taking in games of skill and chance. *Journal of Personality*, 1966, **34**, 176–198.

Rest, S., Nierenberg, R., Weiner, B., & Heckhausen, H. Further evidence concerning the effects of perceptions of effort and ability on achievement evaluation. *Journal of Personality and Social Psychology*, 1973, **28**, 187–191.

Rotter, J. B. Generalized expectancies for internal versus external control of reinforcement. *Psychological Monographs*, 1966, **80**(No. 1, Whole No. 609).

Schneider, K. *Motivation unter Erfolgsrisiko*. Göttingen: Hogrefe, 1973.

Touhey, J. C., & Villemez, W. J. Need achievement and risk-taking preference: A clarification. *Journal of Personality and Social Psychology*, 1975, **30**, 713–719.

Trope, Y. Seeking information about one's own ability as a determinant of choice among tasks. *Journal of Personality and Social Psychology*, 1975, **32**, 1004–1013.

Trope, Y., & Brickman, P. Difficulty and diagnosticity as determinants of choice among tasks. *Journal of Personality and Social Psychology*, 1975, **31**, 918–925.

Weiner, B. The effects of unsatisfied achievement motivation on persistence and subsequent performance. *Journal of Personality*, 1965, **33**, 428–442.

Weiner, B. New conceptions in the study of achievement motivation. In B. Maher (Ed.), *Progress in experimental personality research*. Vol. 5. New York: Academic Press, 1970. Pp. 67–109.

Weiner, B. *Theories of motivation: From mechanism to cognition*. Chicago: Markham, 1972.

Weiner, B. (Ed.) *Achievement motivation and attribution theory*. Morristown, N.J.: General Learning Press, 1974.

Weiner, B., Frieze, I., Kukla, A., Reed, L., Rest, S., & Rosenbaum, R. M. Perceiving the causes of success and failure. In E. E. Jones, D. Kanouse, H. H. Kelley, R. E. Nisbett, S. Valins, & B.

Weiner (Eds.), *Attribution: Perceiving the causes of behavior*. New York: General Learning Press, 1971.

Weiner, B., Heckhausen, H., Meyer, W.-U., & Cook, R. E. Causal ascriptions and achievement behavior: A conceptual analysis of effort and reanalysis of locus of control. *Journal of Personality and Social Psychology,* 1972, **21**, 239–248.

Weiner, B., & Kukla, A. An attributional analysis of achievement motivation. *Journal of Personality and Social Psychology,* 1970, **15**, 1–20.

Weiner, B., & Peter, N. A cognitive-developmental analysis of achievement and moral judgments. *Developmental Psychology,* 1973, **9**, 290–309.

Weiner, B., & Potepan, P. A. Personality characteristics and affective reactions towards exams of superior and failing college students. *Journal of Educational Psychology,* 1970, **61**, 144–151.

Weiner, B., & Rosenbaum, R. M. Determinants of choice between achievement and nonachievement-related activities. *Journal of Experimental Research in Personality,* 1965, **1**, 114–121.

Wolk, S., & DuCette, J. The moderating effect of locus of control in relation to achievement-motivation variables. *Journal of Personality,* 1973, **41**, 59–70.

Zander, A., Fuller, R., & Armstrong, W. Attributed pride or shame in group and self. *Journal of Personality and Social Psychology,* 1972, **23**, 346–352.

GROUP-INDUCED POLARIZATION OF ATTITUDES AND BEHAVIOR[1]

Helmut Lamm

PÄDAGOGISCHE HOCHSCHULE
KÖLN, WEST GERMANY

and

David G. Myers

HOPE COLLEGE
HOLLAND, MICHIGAN

I. Introduction

Research on the effects of social interaction in small groups, a central concern of social psychology back in Kurt Lewin's day, took a backseat during

[1]The authors are listed alphabetically since they made approximately equal contributions, Lamm being primarily responsible for Sections II, A and III, B and Myers for Sections II, B and III, C and D, all other portions being a joint effort. The writing of this chapter and the authors' work reported in it were supported by grants from the Deutsche Forschungsgemeinschaft (to Lamm, Sonderforschungsbereich 24, Universität Mannheim) and the National Science Foundation (to Myers). We are grateful to Robert S. Baron, Martin Kaplan, Charlan Nemeth, and Dean G. Pruitt for their helpful comments on earlier drafts.

145

most of the past 25 years while social psychologists concentrated on the intrapersonal dynamics of attitude change and other social cognition. Recently there has been a renewed interest in the interplay between psychological and social processes, particularly in the small group and its effects on attitudes, decisions, and other responses.

The most striking example is the several hundred research studies on group-induced shifts in attitudes and behavior, especially on the *group polarization* phenomenon (née "risky shift"). Following Moscovici and Zavalloni (1969), investigators have used "group polarization" to signify group-produced enhancement of a prevailing individual tendency. This phenomenon was first noted in research with Choice Dilemma items[2] where it was observed that items which elicit relatively risky initial tendencies generally elicit shift further toward the risky extreme after discussion (the so-called "risky shift"), and items which elicit relatively cautious initial tendencies are likely to elicit postdiscussion responses which are even more cautious.

Previous reviews of these findings have mirrored the state of the literature. The first round of reviews analyzed evidence for the existence of a risky shift phenomenon and possible explanations of it (R. D. Clark, 1971; Dion, Baron, & Miller, 1970; Kogan & Wallach, 1967; Pruitt, 1971a, 1971b; Vinokur, 1971). Some of these reviews hinted that "risky shift" might be a misnomer, since the phenomenon was possibly one instance of a more pervasive group influence phenomenon that had no intrinsic connection with risk-taking. Subsequent research confirmed these speculations, so a second-level review (Myers & Lamm, 1976) focused on the generality of the *group polarization* effect across a variety of laboratory tasks. By the time that review was written in the summer of 1974, the generality of the phenomenon was well-established. In fact, seldom in the history of social psychology has a nonobvious phenomenon been so firmly grounded in data from across a variety of cultures and dependent measures. The cross-national authorship of this chapter is indicative of the cross-national character of this literature. This phenomenon is not likely to become an historical curiosity which fails to generalize across time and people. We concluded, therefore, that the reality of the group polarization effect was more certain than its explanation, although much progress had been made in winnowing unfruitful theories and in refining explanations which were congenial with the facts.

Our present chapter will differ from these previous reviews in its focus on the most recent empirical and theoretical advances and in its consideration of

---

[2]The Choice Dilemmas represent ficticious everyday life situations in which a protagonist is faced with the choice between a risky course of action (e.g., buying stocks; undergoing surgery) and a cautious alternative (e.g., investing in blue chips; remaining in the present ailing state of health). This is the decision task on which the "risky shift" was discovered. The subject must respond by indicating the minimum odds of success—that is, the highest risk of failure—at which he or she would still recommend that the riskier of the two given actions be chosen.

whether the laboratory-based polarization phenomenon is also evidenced in real-world situations. By centering our scrutiny of group interaction effects upon the group polarization phenomenon we hope to progress toward a better general understanding of group influence processes. This understanding should specify the limits of group polarization and give us insight into other effects of social interaction.

Before commencing our overview of recent empirical findings we would like to sharpen the concept of group polarization with four observations. First, remember that group polarization refers to a strengthening of the dominant tendency, *not* to increased cleavage and diversity *within* a group.

Second, it denotes an exaggeration of the initial mean tendency derived from data *averaged over groups*. (This includes between-subjects designs where baseline choices made alone are compared with choices made by other people following group discussion of group decision.) "Group polarization" does *not* suggest that, despite ceiling and regression effects, a particular group that is initially quite extreme will shift even further toward the extreme than a more moderate group from the same population. It says, rather, that the *average* group score tends to be amplified by discussion.

Note, third, that the polarization hypothesis is a more precise prediction than group *extremization*, which denotes movement away from neutrality regardless of direction. Thus if a jury moved from a predeliberation opinion of "probably guilty" to a verdict of "definitely *not* guilty" their shift would be an instance of extremization but not of polarization.

Finally, group polarization can occur without individual group members becoming more polarized. This could easily happen if a sharply split group of people converged on a decision which was slightly more polar than their initial average.

II. Effects of Group Discussion

A. OVERVIEW OF RECENT EMPIRICAL RESEARCH

Our review of research will give closest attention to research reported since the cluster of earlier reviews in 1970 and 1971. In particular we will concentrate on studies appearing since 1974 when our own previous review was written. A variety of decision tasks—nonevaluative judgments, attitudes, legal decisions, risk-taking, ethical choices, etc.—have been the subject of recent research. Although our organization of studies into such areas is somewhat arbitrary, it may be helpful in ascertaining whether group polarization occurs across various dependent measures or whether group effects vary with the decision task. Studies concerned with applied settings will be discussed in Section II, B.

1. Social and Political Attitudes

a. Studies Finding Group Polarization. A number of attitude studies indicate that the group polarization phenomenon generalizes beyond the Choice Dilemmas (Myers & Lamm, 1976). These studies have included attitudes concerning De Gaulle and Americans (Moscovici & Zavalloni, 1969), one's college and a rival college (Doise, 1969), "issues raised by the events of May 1968" (Paicheler & Bouchet, 1973), diverse social issues (Gouge & Fraser, 1972), and racial attitudes (Myers & Bishop, 1970).

Two more recent studies (Paicheler, 1976a, 1976b) found polarization of attitudes toward women's emancipation. Groups of French students held initially favorable attitudes toward women's liberation (in one experiment an average of 1.10 over 10 items, on a −3 to +3 scale), and discussion moved them toward more favorable attitudes (about 1.80).

Stephenson and Brotherton (1975) provide a nice field demonstration of group polarization. Mining supervisors indicated on a 7-point scale whether they thought that a given statement described the ideal mining supervisor. Two types of groups were assembled: homogeneous ones, in which all agreed or all disagreed with the given statement, and heterogeneous ones, in which half of the group was located on one side and half on the other side. Homogeneous groups manifested polarization after discussion whereas heterogeneous ones did not.

b. Studies with mixed evidence on group polarization. In other studies there was asymmetry in shift, rather than a polarization of whatever attitude tendency was initially dominant.

Myers and Bach (1974) observed polarization toward greater pacifism in groups of "doves," but depolarization (i.e., also shift toward greater pacifism) in "hawks." (They attribute the latter shift to the existence of an external norm of pacifism.) Myers (1975) observed polarization toward even more feminist attitudes by groups whose members already held prediscussion, profeminist attitudes, but no shift by antifeminist groups. Although this resulted in a net increase in intergroup polarization, as predicted, the asymmetry in shift is again possibly explained by the existence of an external, liberal norm. Cvetkovich and Baumgardner (1973) found group polarization on punitive/nonpunitive attitudes toward civil disobedience. Furthermore, they found a shift toward more nonpunitive attitudes even for those mixed groups where no initial "nonpunitive" dominance was evident (initial average of .01 on a scale of −3 to +3). In addition, they found no polarization for groups whose initial attitude was on the punitive side (.91). Estimates obtained from subjects indicated that the shifts obtained were in the direction of what group members perceived to be the dominant (nonpunitive) reference-group position ("external norm").

Some puzzling findings on the effects of group discussion-to-consensus come from a recent study by Kerr, Davis, Meek, and Rissman (1975). Using a scale from 1 (bad) to 7 (good), they found no shift toward the other side of the scale in attitude toward the New Left (3.84–4.29), and a decrease in favorability of attitudes toward Frenchmen (4.41–4.06) and toward Nixon (3.45–3.23).

In summary, it seems that in these attitude studies where group polarization is not evident in every condition, shift occurs in the direction of what participants believed to be the position held by their respective reference group. In all cases, this external norm has represented the progressive or liberal side of the continuum.

2. Judgments

There is some evidence that group discussion can polarize judgments of *fact*. However, the phenomenon is more reliably confirmed with tasks requiring more *subjective* evaluation, a recent example being the polarization of ratings concerning the importance of values (life goals) (Billig & Cochrane, 1976).

3. Interpersonal Impressions

Several experiments gave subjects the task of evaluating, on a global good–bad dimension, a person described by certain cues. By and large these investigations confirmed that discussion tends to strengthen initial impressions (Myers & Lamm, 1976, p. 608).

4. Evaluations of Given Courses of Action

Some experiments had participants indicate their preferences regarding imaginary courses of action. For example, Myers and Bishop (1971) devised imaginary decision situations in which a protagonist faced two alternative courses of action, one of which was favored by most subjects in the experiment. These prediscussion preferences were generally polarized by subsequent group discussion. In other studies the three possible Choice Dilemma outcomes (risky action–successful, risky action–not successful, cautious action) were rated as to their desirability/undesirability. The results provide further evidence for group polarization: Outcomes found initially to be (un)desirable were rated as even more (un)desirable after group discussion (e.g., Vinokur, 1971).

5. Risk-Taking

a. *Hypothetical life-decision situations (Choice Dilemmas).* There are scores of studies using Kogan and Wallach's (1967) Choice Dilemmas (see footnote 2) as a risk-taking instrument. Several investigators have constructed items with different content (e.g., consumer products that might or might not prove satisfactory) but with the same format as the Kogan–Wallach Choice Dilemmas. Some researchers have used a rating scale (degree of preference for the risky vs. the cautious course of action). By and large, risky shift is obtained on items which elicit risky individual responses and cautious shift is obtained on items which elicit cautious individual responses.

Research by Burnstein and Vinokur (e.g., Vinokur, 1971) suggests that the risk-shifting items are those where the risky action is perceived as optimal (i.e., where its "subjective expected utility"—as measured through ratings of the likelihood and desirability of its possible outcomes—is greater than that of the nonrisky action), and that the caution-shift items are those where the nonrisky action is perceived as optimal. Similarly, Marquis and Reitz (1969) and Davis, Kerr, Sussman, and Rissman (1974) found shift toward risk on monetary bets with positive expected utility and shift toward caution on bets with negative expected utility. This is generally in line with the group polarization hypothesis in that cautious shift occurs on items for which individual responses favor the cautious side of the risk–caution scale, and risky shift occurs when there is an individual preference for the risky side.

b. Gambling behavior   Several types of gambling or betting tasks have been used to investigate the effects of group interaction on risk-taking. We will consider here only research where the riskier alternatives did not have higher expected value than the less risky options.

In one group of studies, subjects had to choose among different probabilities of winning, lower probabilities being associated with greater payoff. In these studies, the various betting items differ by the magnitude of the stake, but the expected value of the two choices is equal. In general, individual risk-taking is high and risky shift ensues when the stake is relatively small, and individual and shift responses are cautious with a large stake (e.g., Lamm & Ochsmann, 1972; Zaleska, 1974). Initial risk levels and risky shift were also smaller with actual money than with play money (Lamm & Ochsmann, 1972). These and other gambling studies indicate that the direction of group-induced shift generally varies in accord with the effect of the experimental parameters on individual betting tendencies; group discussion amplifies situational effects, just as the group polarization hypothesis predicts.

Blascovich and his associates performed a series of studies involving "blackjack," a casino game in which, on any particular trial, either the player or the house—whichever has the winning cards—obtains the stakes. Thus, the outcome alternatives are either to lose the stake one has put up, or to win twice its value. The size of the stake put up constitutes the measure of risk-taking. These studies provided for 20 trials to be played individually, then 20 trials to be played by groups (discussion with decision). Individuals in a control condition did not change in risk-taking over a second set of 20 trials, but groups did move toward higher risk (Blascovich, Ginsburg, & Howe, 1975). However, this was also found when the group context provided mere coaction without discussion (Blascovich, Ginsburg, & Veach, 1975).

Knox and Safford (1976) found greater caution in race track bets by groups than by individuals, confirming the results of McCauley, Stitt, Woods, and Lipton (1973). These instances of group caution appear to be further demonstrations of group polarization, since the median individual bets tended to be already toward the cautious end of the range of possible bets. But, as McCauley *et al.* (1973) point out, we cannot be sure whether this initial tendency corresponded to subjective perceptions of cautious bets.

c.   *Other risk situations.*   Malamuth and Feshbach (1972) found groups more likely than individuals to place risky station-to-station telephone calls rather than person-to-person calls despite the fact that the latter alternative was the rational choice (with the higher expected monetary outcome).

Finally, there are four field studies giving college students a choice among various examination or course-grading schedules. Three of these found that participants in groups chose safer alternatives than individuals deciding for themselves. In two of these studies the initial individual preferences are reported and, as we might expect, they were predominantly on the cautious side of the distribution of alternatives. A fourth, more recent, study (Yinon, Shoham, & Lewis, 1974) found a difference only when the students were role playing with no real stakes. But another study of real risk-taking found no difference in real versus hypothetical choice of dates or of course-grading systems (Spector, Cohen, & Penner, 1976).

It appears, then, that most of these various demonstrations of risky and of cautious shifts can be summarized as instances of group polarization.

6.   *Prosocial Behavior*

Schroeder (1973) found that group interaction strengthened initial prosocial advice regarding donations of time and money. This is confirmed by other studies using questionnaire measures which report that prosocial values are amplified by group discussion (e.g., Muehleman, Bruker, & Ingram, 1976).

In contrast, Baron, Roper, and Baron (1974) found that groups were less charitable than individuals when it came to actually donating their own money. While it is not known whether initial choices were also subjectively stingy (which would make this another instance of polarization), this experiment does connect with some other experiments on group selfishness which we will shortly consider. Further work by Baron (Baron & Sanders, 1975) indicated that when individuals made decisions in groups (under majority rule) they were less likely to vote for altruistic actions that would cost them time or embarrassment than were individuals deciding alone.

7.   *Antisocial Behavior*

Although many real-world examples of intense aggression in group contexts

come readily to mind, there has been little systematic inquiry concerning th
effects of group interaction on aggression and other antisocial behaviors. Som
studies of deindividuation (e.g., Diener, Fraser, Beaman, & Kelem, 1976) indi
cate that higher levels of antisocial behavior are exhibited in group contexts tha
when individuals are alone. But these studies did not involve any discussio
among group members; each person acted individually although in a grou
context. Three recent experiments investigating the effect of group interaction o
aggression are, therefore, of interest.

Yinon, Jaffe, and Feshbach (1975) had individuals and 3-person group
administer a learning task. Feedback for incorrect answers was to be given eith
by a flashing light or by one of ten levels of electric shock. Since expecte
monetary payoff for both the subjects and the supposed victim was zero if shoc
was never used, but payoff increased with shock level, most individuals chose i
use some shock. As the investigators predicted from responsibility diffusio
theory, groups administered even higher shock levels than did individuals.

Mathes and Kahn (1975) gave individuals and 3-person groups oppo
tunities to punish by administering monetary fines. If the subjects had bee
previously insulted and fined by the learner they were more likely to behav
aggressively, especially during the last half of the trials. During these trials tl
communicating groups assessed slightly higher fines, suggesting again that ind
vidual tendencies are amplified by the group.

In both of these studies aggression benefited the victim as well as tl
aggressor. In contrast, Wolosin, Sherman, and Mynatt (1975) gave individu
and group decision-makers an explicit choice between self-sacrificial altruis
and aggressive selfishness. Groups delivered more than twice the number
shocks—on 74% of the trials as compared with 34% of the trials by individu
subjects.

It is interesting that these three studies, which were conducted indepe
dently and published almost simultaneously, all compared the aggressiveness
individuals and 3-person groups, all reported higher levels of aggression in t
groups, and all resurrected as a possible explanation the concept of diffusion
responsibility (which was one of the first suggested explanations of risky shif
We will return to these findings in our later theoretical discussion.

8. Interparty Conflict

a. Negotiation. Several studies have investigated the effects of intragro
discussion on aspirations or demand levels concerning an upcoming negotiatic
Discussion generally led to a tougher negotiation stance (higher aspirations
higher opening bids).

Rabbie and Visser (1972) found that discussion-to-consensus led to higl
aspirations in a tariff-negotiation simulation when subjects were given a stro

bargaining position. Louche (1975a), using a very similar procedure and the same negotiation task, had subjects discuss and decide unanimously on their intended initial demand and found increased demands following discussion. In a subsequent study Louche (1975b) compared the intended initial demands made by individuals preparing negotiations in isolation, by coacting individuals, and by interacting individuals. More extreme initial demands were made by interacting groups than by isolated individuals (with coacting individuals intermediate). Also, in the interacting and coacting conditions the two parties' opening positions were further apart from each other, as compared with the individual condition. This last finding is quite similar to the findings that intragroup discussion leads toward greater attitude cleavage between separated homogeneous groups. A recent study by Holmes, Ellis, and Rosenbaum (1976) also found an extremization of demands through intragroup discussion preparatory to negotiations in a tariff conflict.

The group-induced extremity in the above studies might be partly due to in-group feeling created by assembling several subjects espousing the same side of an issue. In fact, all the cited studies except Holmes et al. (1976) either preselected subjects according to their attitudes concerning labor/management or had them choose the side they preferred. This was not the case in Lamm and Sauer (1974) Pairs of subjects were to negotiate the distribution of some money between themselves. First, however, they discussed their intended initial demands with other individuals whom they were not competing against. This discussion produced a significant shift toward even higher demands; this shift did not occur in a coaction control condition where subjects individually reconsidered their initial demands. The same pattern of results was obtained in an additional experiment (Lamm, unpublished observations) where subjects in the group condition were told that they would negotiate as one party against the other party.

    b.   Other conflict situations.   In a study using the Prisoner's Dilemma game, Rabbie and Visser (1976) had either individuals or groups (dyads or triads) confront each other. The intragroup discussion concerned items of a questionnaire which measured goal orientations (e.g., toward cooperation or toward competition). This was administered after the first and the last trials of the game. In several experiments it was found that subjects in dyads manifested more defensive orientations (e.g., "lose as little as possible") than did subjects playing individually. In addition, groups faced with a competitive counterpart were more likely than individuals to make the competitive (defensive) choice.

Myers and Bach (1976) also used a Prisoner's Dilemma format to compare individuals and groups. Discussion on any trial concerned the alternative to be chosen (the price level in a simulated gas price war). No differences between groups and individuals were found, all choices being highly competitive. But in postexperimental ratings individuals tended to perceive their own actions as more justified than their opponents' actions and groups were even more inclined toward this self-justification.

9. Conclusion

This overview of recent experimental research on the effects of group interaction is generally consistent with the group polarization hypothesis. When individuals exhibit a dominant initial tendency this inclination is usually amplified by subsequent group discussion. We have, however, noted several exceptions and these, too, deserve explanation within any comprehensive theory of group influence. First, however, we will consider the extent to which these experimental findings connect with observed group influences in real-world situations.

B.   GROUP POLARIZATION IN THE "REAL WORLD"

With the phenomenon and its external validity on a variety of measures now established, the literature has the potential to evolve into a more mature stage—experimentation and naturalistic observations which relate the laboratory phenomenon to group influences in the real world. Although it is too early to judge how extensive or productive this state will be, we hope, by offering some rudimentary observations, to stimulate more laboratory research directed to application and more field research. Is group polarization a hothouse laboratory phenomenon or does it also occur in situations with self-evident import, such as when groups make business, political, or legal decisions? And are there any useful practical applications which may be derived from the principles developed in the laboratory?

Simultaneous with these new extensions must be further refinements in theoretical explanation. There is a two-way street between theory development and the empirical extensions. On the one hand, theoretical advances occur when a variety of observations are integrated into a broad perspective and linked with other research and theory. Extensions of the phenomenon stimulate theory development since the theories must be capable of accounting for the empirical findings. This was evident when risk-specific explanations of the risky shift phenomenon dissipated with evidence that the group effect was, in fact, not specific to risk measures. At the same time, the development of a more adequate understanding of the dynamics of the phenomenon is a prerequisite for specifying the real-world situations in which it will occur. Thus we will later give close attention to the most recent developments in theoretical explanation of group polarization and other group effects.

Research connecting group polarization with important real-world phenomena may be classified in two areas: *experiments*—in the lab or in the field—which investigate possible implications of group polarization for socially relevant attitudes, decisions, and actions; and *naturalistic observations* of apparent group polarization dynamics, often by investigators unaware of the experimental literature.

1. Experiments

Recent experiments have attempted to extend the polarization phenomenon to business management and marketing concerns (Deets & Hoyt, 1970; D. L. Johnson & Andrews, 1971; Peterson & Fulcher, 1971; Rabbie & Visser, 1972; Reingen, 1973, 1974, 1975, 1976; Semin & Glendon, 1973; Woodside, 1972, 1974; Woodside & DeLozier, 1975), to casino and racetrack gambling (Blascovich, Ginsburg, & Howe, 1976; Knox & Safford, 1976; McCauley *et al.*, 1973), to prison and mental health settings (Myers, Schreiber, & Viel, 1974b; Siegel & Zajonc, 1967), and to the effects of group conversation on student evaluations of faculty (Andrews & Johnson, 1971; D. L. Johnson, 1972; Krapf, 1972; Myers, 1975; Shrewsberry & Johnson, 1972).

Most of these investigations confirmed a group polarization effect; some did not. Some were conducted by experimental social psychologists who had previously conducted laboratory research on group influence; increasing numbers of studies are being conducted by people from other fields who wish to explore possible extensions of social psychological findings into their own subject matter. A noteworthy example of this trend are a set of new studies exploring group-induced polarization of political attitudes and decisions (Blascovich, 1976; Kirkpatrick, 1975; Kirkpatrick, Bernick, Thomson, & Rycroft, 1975; Kirkpatrick, Davis, & Robertson, 1976; Kirkpatrick & Robertson, 1976; Lewin & Kane, 1975; Moscovici and Zavalloni, 1969; Myers & Bach, 1974). One fascinating experiment [reported separately by Minix (1976) and Semmell (1976)] engaged groups of army officers, ROTC cadets, or university students in discussion of hypothetical but credible international military crises, each of which involved some threat to the United States. Instead of the usual 10-point numerical scale, the respondents chose one of ten response options, ranging from bilateral negotiations to use of nuclear force. On each of the six cases the student groups were somewhat more inclined to recommend diplomatic alternatives than were the army officers, and on each case these student versus officer differences were further polarized by deliberation within their own groups. Regardless of whether the discussion proceeded to consensus or to a majority vote the officer groups generally came to recommend even more forceful initiatives while the students moved slightly toward even less forceful responses. The ROTC cadets were intermediate in both initial and shift scores. These results closely parallel our earlier observations of increased intergroup polarization following discussion within separate groups of high- or low-prejudice people (Myers & Bishop, 1970) or within groups having traditional or liberal attitudes regarding women's roles

(Myers, 1975). They also underscore Sidney Verba's contention that face-to-face groups

> are the locus of most political decision-making, they are important transmission points in political communications, and they exercise a major influence on the political beliefs and attitudes of their members. [1961, p. 2]

In a study of social psychological processes in crowd behavior (N. R. Johnson, Stemler, & Hunter, 1977), laboratory subjects read hypothetical situations "presenting dilemmas of choice for incipient crowds" (e.g., a crowd of blacks gathering after "police brutality") and were presented with seven different actions varying in their extremity (from doing nothing to violence). Discussion prompted more extreme actions, just as in the experiment noted above. N. R. Johnson et al. (1977) suggest that "further experimental research of this nature . . . might lead to better grounded theories of collective behavior" (pp. 186–187).

   a. Jury decisions.   Among the various arenas of experimental extensions we have chosen to take a closer look at one which seems of special interest to social psychologists and which has been the subject of several very recent reports: group discussion effects on the judgments of simulated jurors. The judgments of jurors and of juries have been the subject of considerable recent scrutiny (witness excellent reviews of the current literature by Davis, Bray, & Holt, 1978; Kaplan, 1975). A small subset of these studies examines the jury as a small group. Among the questions which small group researchers may ask of the jury is, do decisions following jury deliberation differ in any predictable way from the average predeliberation opinion of individual jury members? If group polarization is at work then we may expect to find that the initial inclinations of jurors will be amplified by their subsequent deliberation.

   Since actual juries may not be directly observed while deliberating, investigators have used simulations of the jury process. While this procedure enables experimental control, it is obviously several steps removed from the courtroom—in the composition of the subjects engaged, in the complexity of the case material, and in the artificiality of the experiment in contrast to the drama and the responsibility which a real juror confronts. At best, these experiments are therefore only suggestive of group processes which may operate in courtrooms.

   Several studies reveal a clear polarization effect in mock juries. Myers and Kaplan (1976) and Kaplan and Miller (1976) had jurors discuss traffic cases in which defendants were made to appear guilty or not guilty. After discussing low-guilt cases subjects became more definite in their judgments of innocence and more lenient in recommended punishment. After discussing the more incriminating cases, the jurors polarized toward harsher judgments of guilt and punishment.

Hans and Doob (1976) engaged a heterogeneous sample of adult Canadians in individual or group judgment of a burglary case in which the jurors were informed or not informed of the defendant's prior conviction record. Group discussion magnified the effect of this independent variable. As Hans and Doob conclude,

> What is most striking about the overall pattern of results obtained is that what is apparently a *weak* manipulation (one prior conviction) in the individual verdict condition proves to be a *strong* manipulation in the group verdict condition. [p. 243]

Davis, Kerr, Stasser, Meek, and Holt (cited in Davis *et al.*, 1978) found that individual jurors given a harsh criterion of reasonable doubt gave a significantly higher number of guilty judgments than did individuals given a milder criterion, and that this difference was even larger in the corresponding group decision conditions.

Kaplan (1978) contrived discussions of a manslaughter case by note-passing. This produced a polarization of opinions even when the information received from others contained the same number of guilt- and innocence-supporting arguments the subject had just cited. That is, although the information each subject received was no more extreme than what she/he already possessed, this information was sufficient to intensify responses.

Rumsey (1975) had individuals and 4-member mock juries assign penalties for crimes. Penalties were more severe for important crimes than unimportant crimes and discussion exaggerated this difference. However, penalties were also more severe when the crime was intentional rather than unintentional and discussion did not exaggerate this difference.

Two other studies reveal hints of a group polarization effect by manipulating group composition rather than the case stimuli. Vidmar (1972) composed groups of jurors high or low in dogmatism. The high-dogmatism juries shifted toward harsher sentences following discussion and low-dogmatism groups shifted toward more lenient sentences, but this was despite the fact that the high- and low-dogmatism juries did not differ in their predeliberation judgments. Laughlin and Izzett (1973) observed that groups composed of subjects which were attitudinally similar to the defendant shifted toward greater leniency following group discussion, whereas subjects who were attitudinally dissimilar did not shift.

Practical applications of jury composition have been attempted in a couple of celebrated cases by social scientists who provide the defense with survey-based profiles of jurors likely to be sympathetic to the defendant (Schulman, Shaver, Colman, Emrich, & Christie, 1973). A seeming assumption here is that a small edge in jury composition may be magnified into a substantial later advantage to the defense.

Other jury studies seem on the surface less congenial to the group polarization principle. Izzett and Leginski (1974) observed that an initial tendency for unattractive defendants to receive harsher sentences than attractive defendants was *reduced* rather than magnified by discussion.

There appears to be a general trend toward greater leniency after discussion (Davis, Kerr, Atkin, Holt, & Meek, 1975; Davis, Kerr, Stasser, Meek, & Holt, 1976; Foss & Foss, 1973; Gleason & Harris, 1976; Laughlin & Izzett, 1973; Rumsey, 1975, 1976; Rumsey & Castore, 1974; Rumsey, Laughlin, & Castore, 1974; Wahram, 1977; although not Heimbach, 1970). In some of these experiments it is difficult to know whether this represents group polarization or not. It appears, however, that leniency is, in general, the socially valued tendency. Silzer and Clark (1978) report that most of their 420 subjects perceive themselves as more lenient than a typical jury would be, and that 86% would rather free a guilty person than convict someone who is innocent. This confirms the earlier conclusion of Kalven and Zeisel (1966) that the paramount value underlying jury decisions is "innocent until proven guilty." So once again, the external norm as well as the prediscussion tendency helps predict shift.

Some evidence from actual courtrooms is available. Kalven and Zeisel (1966) reported that the initial majority was predictive of the jury decision in 90% of 225 trials, a tendency confirmed in experimental studies by Davis and colleagues and by Nash (1973).

Walker and Main (1973) compared civil liberties decisions by individual federal district court judges with similar decisions by 3-judge panels. The group judgments differed substantially from the individual judgments: 65% libertarian by groups versus 30% by individuals. (This is contrary to the group polarization hypothesis, which would predict that the trend toward nonlibertarian judgments observed in the individual condition would be even stronger in the group condition.) A subset of these decisions also involved rulings of the constitutionality of statutes. Main and Walker (1973) observed that these constitutionality decisions were also more libertarian in the group condition (65% vs. 45%). We will have more to say later about this anamolous finding that the trend of individual decisions was reversed by the group condition. Walker and Main (1973) speculated that the preexisting private values of the judges were actually prolibertarian but their individual decisions were compromised in the face of antilibertarian public pressure. Presumably these private values were released and reinforced in the professional group context.

2. *Naturalistic Observations of Social Polarization*

If group polarization is something more than a laboratory creation of social psychologists, then we may expect that instances of it will already have been observed and noted by social scientists who are unfamiliar with the experimental literature. Before we offer several examples a word of caution is in order. While these observations carry the force of naturally occurring reality, it is difficult to disentangle causes, correlates, and effects. The most that can be said is that these interesting observations are consistent with the experimental literature.

   b.   Student change during college.   A number of investigations of student development have revealed an "accentuation phenomenon." As Feldman and Newcomb (1969) expressed it:

> Initial differences among students in different colleges and in different curricula are accentuated or amplified as students progress through college. Instances of this same phenomenon also occur with respect to initial differences among students entering different types of residences [p. 209].

For example, the tendency for fraternity members to be more conservative and prejudiced than independents tends to be larger among seniors than among freshmen and sophomores.

   Chickering and McCormick (1973) concluded from their decade of research on student development at various colleges that if the students who enroll at a particular college have a predominantly practical–vocational outlook they will emerge even more that way. Colleges which attract more intellectually oriented or nonconformist students will further strengthen these tendencies in their students. Another more recent study provides the same conclusion:

> In short, the qualities students bring to college generally tend to persist and become accentuated as a result of their college education [Wilson, Gabb, Dienst, Wood, & Bavry, 1975, p. 123].

Other data by Astin and Panos (1969) and B. R. Clark, Heist, McConnell, Trow, and Yonge (1972) confirm the same point.

   It is, to be sure, not entirely clear what produces this accentuation phenomenon. Students are not only attracted to and interacting with similar others, they are also taking classes and concentrating their attention on activities which are compatible with their inclinations. It seems, nonetheless, reasonable to expect that, as Feldman and Newcomb (1969) surmise, the accentuation phenomenon occurs partly because "the reciprocal influences of members of one another reinforce and strengthen extant orientations" (p. 223).

   c.   Social conflict.   The possibility that intragroup discussion might enhance intergroup polarization was suggested by an experiment (Myers & Bishop,

1970) which composed homogeneous groups of relatively high-, medium-, or low-prejudice persons. Discussion with similar others significantly increased the attitude gap between the high- and low-prejudice groups.

Some field observations are consistent with these laboratory findings. Coleman (1957) concluded from his analyses of opinion polarization during community conflict that

> group discussion . . . is such an important phenomenon in community controversies that in the case studies examined most descriptions of behavior during the intense part of the controversy were descriptions of discussion and of attempts to persuade or reinforce opinion [p. 18].

Homogeneous grouping was an apparent source of community polarization and the occurrence of social conflict further heightened

> the proliferation of associations among those who feel one way, and the attenuation of association between those who feel differently. One's statements meet more and more with a positive response; one is more and more free to express the full intensity of his feeling [p. 14].

This dynamic can be seen at work in the well-known Robbers Cave experiment (Sherif, 1966) in which the competition and intragroup dynamics moved the rival groups to extreme antagonism and perceptions of one another, and in the Stanford Prison Experiment (Zimbardo, 1975) in which the aggressive reactions of guards appeared to feed on one another in spiraling escalation.

Intragroup interaction may magnify conflict partly because, as we noted earlier, the tendency of individuals to justify their own behavior when in conflict is intensified by discussion—people in groups are even more inclined toward self-justification (Myers & Bach, 1974) and are likely to make higher demands for themselves (Lamm & Sauer, 1974). This phenomenon of group-enhanced self-justification is part of the "groupthink" process which Janis (1972) has proposed to help explain political decision fiascoes, such as the escalation of the Vietnam War.

Gang delinquency provides yet another example. Enduring gangs reportedly differ sharply from one another but develop homogeneous within-group attitudes. Cartwright (1975) concludes that this occurs as a result of group processes such as "interstimulation" among gang members and "a process of summation, or progressive urging on of members from one deed to another" (p. 7).

Riley and Pettigrew's (1976) findings of attitude polarization in naturalistic situations may also reflect a group polarization effect. The racial attitudes of white Texans were measured by surveys before and after two dramatic events: the desegregation of schools in Little Rock, Arkansas, in 1957, and the assassination of Martin Luther King and subsequent civil disorders in 1968. The preevent attitudes of various demographic groups differed as one might expect: Lower-class people were more segregationist than middle class, East Texans more than West Texans, old people more than young, etc. What effect would dramatic events likely have on these intergroup attitude differences? Recall the experimental observations that intragroup discussion can polarize intergroup differences; prediscussion differences between army officers and students (Semmel, 1976) and between high- and low-prejudice groups (Myers & Bishop, 1970), for example, were amplified by intragroup discussion. Riley and Pettigrew's field observations parallel these experimental studies. Group opinion differences were generally heightened by the dramatic event; the initial opinion tendency of each demographic group tended to polarize following the dramatic event. Riley and Pettigrew labeled this the ''counterceiling effect'' to stress that

> this effect occurs when the greatest change, either positive or negative, occurs for demographic types with the least range to exhibit chance. . . . Were the basic change scores corrected for ceiling and floor effects, the apparent effect . . . would be considerably more striking [pp. 1006–1007].

The surveys conducted before and after the King assassination ascertained attitudes regarding interracial contact in a dozen different realms, ranging from formal contacts in public places to intimate contacts, such as living together as roommates. This enabled a comparison of attitude shift (before vs. after the event) within each demographic group. Recall that the group polarization effect was first defined by item differences. Individual Choice Dilemma items differ from one another in (a) mean initial response and (b) mean shift, and (a) and (b) are very highly correlated; items which elicit relatively risky initial tendencies elicit shift further toward the risky extreme after discussion. Once again, Riley and Pettigrew's observations parallel the laboratory findings. Attitudes toward formal interracial contacts were initially most positive and also had the largest favorability shift. In fact, the rank-order correlation across the 12 interracial situations between preevent means and the amount of attitude change shortly after the assassination was +.965.

Although we cannot be certain what produced these attitude polarizations, it seems likely that dramatic events stimulate discussion. When the event is subject to multiple interpretations, intragroup discussion apparently intensifies the dominant local viewpoint. In the absence of dramatic events and their accompanying intragroup discussion, social influences that are common to all groups (e.g., the national media) may reduce attitude polarization.

The recent experiments on group aggression described earlier are germane to our understanding of the social origins of antisocial behavior. Recall that each of these experiments (Mathes & Kahn, 1975; Wolosin et al., 1975; Yinon et al.,

1975) reported higher levels of aggression in 3-person groups than in individuals. These studies all resurrected the idea of responsibility diffusion, which is assumed to mediate decreased bystander intervention in the presence of others. Muehleman *et al.* (1976) make the interesting observation that helping behavior is most likely to be inhibited in group situations where appearing cool and unfoolish is a more dominant response to the situation than is helping. When an emergency situation is unambiguous and the helping response is therefore more predominant, the presence of others may *increase* helping.[3]

Freedman (1975) offers a similar theory about the effects of social density. Crowding, he suggests,

> *serves to intensify the individual's typical reactions to the situation.* If he ordinarily would find the circumstances pleasant, would enjoy having people around him, would think of the other people as friends, would in a word have a positive reaction to the other people, he will have a more positive reaction under conditions of high density. On the other hand, if ordinarily he would dislike the other people, find it unpleasant having them around, feel aggressive toward them, and in general have a negative reaction to the presence of the other people, he will have a more negative reaction under conditions of high density. And if for some reason he would ordinarily be indifferent to the presence of other people, increasing the density will have little effect one way or the other [p. 91].

Although this sounds like a social facilitation effect, Freedman concludes—as have most theorists regarding group polarization—that the density-intensity effect is not an arousal phenomenon. Freedman (1975) believes it rather occurs because "high density makes other people a more important stimulus and thereby intensifies the typical reaction to them" (p. 105). This jives with Moscovici and Lecuyer's (1972) finding that less group polarization occurred when people sat in a straight line with reduced face-to-face contact than when they talked face-to-face—which surely made the other people more salient stimuli.

d. Group counseling. If the group polarization principle helps explain what some observers feel are negative effects of group interaction (not only conflict, but also the emergence of radical movements and the debilitating effects of group interaction in closed environments such as penal and mental institutions), then it may also help us understand group effects which are widely felt to be beneficial. Malamuth (1975) had groups discuss what advice they would give to real human beings whom they met and who were believed to be facing life

---

[3]Similarly, Diener, Westford, Dineen, and Fraser (1973) observed that a group context (without interaction) inhibited aggression, possibly because of participants' concern over peer opinion. Similar evidence was obtained by Diener (1976). An important task for the future is to investigate the effects of group interaction in conjunction with the effects of mere group presence, especially in the areas of prosocial and antisocial behavior.

dilemmas similar to some of those in the Choice Dilemmas questionnaire. Malamuth's (1975) peer counseling experiment, which was an analog to actual peer counseling programs, indicated that "such group counseling experiences result in a more extreme advice than that given by individuals" (p. 53).

Toch (1965) describes additional examples of the power of mutual assistance in small self-help groups. Social interaction in Alcoholics Anonymous and Synanon groups strengthens the members' commitment to shared goals. Members of TOPS (Take Off Pounds Sensibly) sing their weekly pledge:

The more we get together
Together, together—
The more we get together,
The slimmer we'll be.
For your loss is my loss;
And my loss is your loss;
The more we get together
The slimmer we'll be.

    e. Religious fellowship. Another apparent example of group polarization in natural settings is provided by various religious social support systems. Heightened religious identity is usually achieved by a substantial amount of interaction among members of the religious body and a certain amount of insulation from the surrounding society. As Thomas Kempis advised, "a devout communing on spiritual things sometimes greatly helps the health of the soul, especially when men of one mind and spirit in God meet and speak and commune together." Emile Durkheim theorized that "dynamic density" (the extent of intragroup communication) determines the intensity of religious commitment. Some sociologists of religion (e.g., Hoge, 1974) suggest that this may be one reason why the increasing individualism and social mobility of the modern age is associated with decreased religious commitment.

Perhaps American culture's most striking example of intense religious identity emerging from separation with similar others is provided by the Amish, who live, go to school, work, and worship only among themselves. In earlier eras small interacting groups contributed significantly to the dynamic of the early Christian church and, during the 18th century, to John Wesley's Methodist movement. According to a Wesley biographer (Schmidt, 1972), the mutual edification and commitment which occurred in these "classes" and "bands," as they were called, was the chief feature of the movement's structure. Close scrutiny of religious social support systems in *When Prophecy Fails* confirms the power of the small group to amplify the religious impulse (Festinger, Riecken, & Schachter, 1956; see also related observations by Batson, 1975; Hardyck & Braden, 1962).

In summary, there are multiple indications that the group polarization phenomenon uncovered in laboratory experiments is indeed manifest in significant real-world situations as well.

III. Theoretical Explanation of Group Polarization and of Other Group Effects

These various demonstrations of group polarization—in the laboratory and in the field—motivate our search for an understanding of the phenomenon. Can we identify the dynamics of group influence which are at work? Might a satisfactory theoretical understanding of the phenomenon point to new research and application in areas which seem, on the surface, unrelated to group polarization?

The various reviews of 1970–1971 scrutinized a host of theories devised to explain the risky shift. Several viable candidates survived these reviews and will be described and evaluated here: *social decision rules* (schemes for combining individual positions into a group product), *informational influence* (cognitive learning resulting from the emission and reception of cogent arguments concerning the decisional issues), and *social comparison* effects resulting from mere exposure to others' positions. We will also consider *responsibility dynamics,* since the concept of responsibility diffusion, though largely discarded as an explanation of risky shift and group polarization, seems now to be useful for explaining some of the group effects summarized above—such as when groups behave more selfishly than individuals even when, contrary to the polarization hypothesis, this reverses the prevailing tendency among individuals.

These possibilities for group influence are not mutually exclusive. They may feed on one another or each may operate during different phases of the decision-making process, and the concepts themselves are somewhat overlapping (e.g., responsibility diffusion may be supported by available arguments). Yet, each of these theoretical perspectives has generated its own interesting research on group process. Thus each has been of value, even if the other theories could incorporate its predictions.

A. APPLICATION OF SOCIAL DECISION RULES BY GROUP MEMBERS

1. Introduction

One possibility is that the change in positions occurs because group members follow some rule for combining their individual preferences into a group decision (or into an implicit group decision in situations where no consensus is formally required).

A group decision rule (or "social decision scheme") represents a widely accepted norm, applicable in certain group situations, that specifies the weight that the various individual positions should carry in determining the final, group product. No change in individual preferences needs to be assumed. A "pure" social decision explanation of polarization is based only on the distribution of positions favored by individual decision participants. Of course, elements of other explanations can be integrated with the "pure" theory of social decision rules as when Kerr *et al.* (1975) assigned greater weights to positions congruent with the external reference-group norm.

There are a number of possible rules (Davis, 1973), but the simplest and most familiar is majority rule. On a two-choice issue it predicts that the group choice would be the alternative espoused by the majority of members. When there are more than two alternatives, more complex decision rules are also possible. For example the position favored by a *plurality* (i.e., by more members than is the case with any other position) might tend to become the group choice.

The role of decision rules—(*a*) as a sufficient condition and (*b*) as a necessary condition—in choice shift can be tested (*a*) by constructing the decision situation such that decision rules could operate but other plausible factors (e.g., social comparison or relevant arguments) are not engaged, or (*b*) by engaging other factors in a situation where decision rules could not plausibly operate, and noting whether shift occurs.

2. Evidence for the Operation of Decision Rules

Many studies have been concerned with the possibility that skewness in initial responses predicts shift toward the mode of the distribution. Skewness suggests a plurality or even a majority around the hump of the distribution which might pressure minority persons out in the tail of the distribution to move toward the mode, thus creating an apparent polarization in the group average. Skewness will, in fact, often exist when the initial average response departs from neutrality, so a majority or plurality rule explanation of group polarization is quite plausible.

It is something of a surprise, then, that decision schemes which depend on skewness have been so clearly contradicted. Among the findings which we earlier enumerated (Myers & Lamm, 1976) are these: (*a*) both positively and negatively skewed distributions have produced risky shift; (*b*) polarization of the group median (which is, by definition, part of the majority) has been demonstrated numerous times, although the magnitude is often less than shifts in the group mean; (*c*) group shifts have occurred with dyads, where obviously no skewness can exist; (*d*) group shift can occur without group convergence, that is, without the emergence of any implicit group product; and (*e*) group shift sometimes runs counter to the initial majority, as when discussion moves participants to become more pacifistic, aggressive, self-serving, or lenient despite the fact that as individuals they did not behave this way. Of course, these latter findings run counter to group polarization itself and pose a problem for other theories as well.

However, not all group decision schemes are rooted in skewness. Indeed, it is both the strength and the weakness of the social decision scheme approach that there are many possible mathematical schemes for combining individual judgments into a group product, each of which may be applicable under certain conditions, with certain tasks, etc. This has caused Graesser (1975) to suggest that the social decision scheme approach may not be falsifiable, since even if predictions from several particular schemes are rejected one may always argue that the correct scheme has not yet been identified. Of course, some philosophers of science argue that nonfalsifiability is a characteristic of all theory, but that nonfalsifiable theories can nonetheless provide useful ways of organizing experience.

If some mathematical combination of individual preferences *is* found to describe a particular distribution of group products quite well the question then becomes, are groups in fact applying this decision rule or might it only be a seeming by-product of some other group process? For example, if majorities rule in a particular situation, is this because of the decision scheme or because majorities emit more persuasive argumentation?

There is evidence that discussion does produce genuine internal preference changes, not just social decision scheme effects on overt responding (see, e.g., Burnstein, Miller, Vinokur, Katz, & Crowley, 1971). Thus it is fortunate that social decision scheme theorists are beginning to focus their considerable mathematical and methodological competency on the internal psychological dynamics of groups. If a given social psychological explanation is translatable into a social decision scheme it certainly should be so translated, because this permits a rigorous operational test of the explanation. It might also be useful to ask subjects directly about their preferences for particular rules in different types of decision situations and to ask participants after group interaction whether they sensed any implicit decision rule.

B. RESPONSIBILITY DYNAMICS

1. Responsibility Diffusion

Despite the decline of responsibility diffusion as an explanation of risky shift, the concept appears plausible and fruitful in certain situations. Thus it has figured prominently in theorizing about why people are often less inclined to help when other bystanders are present (Latané & Darley, 1970).[4]

In decisions involving cost to an outside person it seems plausible to assume that group participants might come to feel less responsible when others are sharing accountability for that decision. Unlike decision rules and informational

---

[4] One recent study (Misavage & Richardson, 1974) indicates that *interaction* among bystanders increases the speed of helping presumably by a process of "focusing of responsibility." It appears worth the effort to pursue the idea that participation in discussion reduces one's sense of anonymity.

influence theories, the responsibility-diffusion mechanism might therefore be able to explain and predict shifts toward more self-serving decisions which (a) constitute depolarization, (b) take place in decision groups without discussion, and (c) occur independently of the distribution of initial preferences within the group.

There are a few well-done studies involving a costly decision for someone else, and they all suggest a responsibility-diffusion interpretation. Yinon *et al.* (1975) attribute their finding of greater risky aggression by groups to the presumed lesser personal responsibility experienced in groups. However, no measure of self-attribution of responsibility was obtained. Wolosin *et al.* (1975) used shock coupled with monetary gain for the decision-makers and explained their findings of more shocks administered by groups to a lesser sense of personal responsibility in groups. The responsibility self-ratings ("did you feel personally responsible for the shocks . . .") showed a marginal trend toward less felt responsibility in the group condition.[5]

Mathes and Kahn (1975) had subjects administer monetary punishments for incorrect learning responses. Responsibility diffusion was invoked to explain the higher fine levels chosen by groups on later trials. These authors found that subjects did feel less responsible when they had fined the victim in groups.

Mynatt and Sherman (1975) used a false-feedback procedure so that the outcomes were the same in the group and the individual conditions. They found differences only when there were negative outcomes (the "advisee" lost money as a consequence of subjects' "wrong" decisions on a problem-solving task). This finding suggests that the responsibility-diffusion hypothesis is applicable only in the case of decisions that are costly to an outside party.

While the above studies rightly focused on decisions that brought definite costs to an outside party, it should be noted that the responsibility-diffusion mechanism is applicable also in risk-taking situations where the choice of a risky alternative involves the *possibility* of a costly outcome for the target person. The methodological problem here, in explaining any risky shifts, is to separate other processes facilitating risky shift (social comparisons, for example) from responsibility diffusion. This could be done by appropriate choice of risk-taking tasks—i.e., where risky positions do not indicate skill or other desirable characteristics—and by obtaining sufficient phenomenological data from the subjects. Self-reported responsibility dynamics might indicate whether subjects contemplate their possible guilt and accountability *during* the decision-making process or whether, as Blascovich has suggested (personal communication), differences

---

[5]Note that here each subject, even in the group condition, had to actively press the "shock" button. (Generally—in a merely verbal joint group decision—a reluctant member can passively accept the emerging consensus by not perceiving himself or herself as responsible.) This may provide an explanation for the nonsignificant findings on responsibility self-ratings in this study.

between group and individual settings reflect *post hoc* attributions (justification of antisocial behavior).

Further, it should be noted that in the studies invoking responsibility diffusion, the alternatives which were more costly for the victim were those that provided more gain for the decision-makers (money, revenge, better learning by the victim). This suggests that responsibility diffusion, serving as a justifying mechanism, comes into play when conditions like selfish gain or angry arousal predispose subjects toward such behavior.

In summary, it seems that in situations involving costs to an outside party and gain to the decision-maker responsibility diffusion may provoke more self-serving action by groups. Perhaps this is why theologian Reinhold Niebuhr (1932, p. xii) was struck by the "inferiority of the morality of groups," which he ascribed to

> the revelation of a collective egosim, compounded of the egoistic impulses of individuals, which achieve a more vivid expression and a more cumulative effect when they are united in a common impulse than when they express themselves separately and discreetly.

In view of the empirical evidence and the social relevance of group egoistic and antisocial behavior, responsibility diffusion deserves further research, especially research which carries the concept beyond the status of an after-the-fact conjectural explanation of observed results.

2. *Responsibility "Infusion"*

As Baron and his associates (e.g., Baron *et al.*, 1974) have pointed out, the making of a joint group decision renders these members dependent on one another. Thus even while it possibly reduces felt responsibility toward outsiders, the joint decision may also *increase* a sense of responsibility toward fellow members. This "responsibility infusion" norm prescribes abstaining from acts that would negatively affect other group members' welfare. If, for example, helping an outside person necessitates a sacrifice, then intragroup responsibility dictates that no decision be proposed that would commit the other group members to a course of action that would be costly for them. This is Baron *et al.*'s (1974) proposed explanation of "stingy shift," and it is supported by secondary analyses performed by those authors (initially generous members, who decreased their pledge in their recommendation for group decision returned to their earlier levels in postgroup, private, decisions).

Baron and Sanders (1975) invoke responsibility infusion toward the ingroup and responsibility diffusion toward outsiders for their finding of less compliance with a favor requested by the experimenter when individuals decided on this request by majority vote than when they decided for themselves alone. Participants were less altruistic toward the experimenter when they knew that their decision could bind others.

Baron and his colleagues have thus provided evidence for a mechanism that can be expected to operate in group arrangements creating interdependence among members. Responsibility infusion predicts a group-induced shift toward less self-sacrificing behavior. It has also been invoked by Wolosin *et al.* (1975) as an alternative interpretation of their finding of group-induced preference for egotistic decisions.

Responsibility infusion can also be expected to reduce chosen risk levels in situations involving the possibility of actual negative outcomes (e.g., monetary losses), thus counteracting other processes that would entail shifts toward higher risk levels. It could therefore help explain the repeated finding of no shift, or cautious shift, on betting items with relatively large monetary stakes. The relevance of this mechanism is also illustrated when considering work groups which decide on their piece-rate. Casual observation suggests that members with greater capacity will frequently accept lower levels of output (and thus smaller gains for themselves) out of concern for their less capable fellow members.

A socially relevant direction for research is pitting the two normative orientations—responsibility toward an outside party and responsibility toward group members—against each other and uncovering the conditions under which responsibility diffusion and responsibility infusion can be minimized. Both imply social or interpersonal passivity and less willingness to help someone outside the group. Egotistical within-group processes are legion. Social psychologists should, therefore, investigate conditions and ways to counter these self-serving processes to the benefit of the outsiders in need of help.

We conclude, then, that while responsibility dynamics have not proven terribly fruitful as an explanation of group polarization, they may facilitate our understanding of certain other group interaction effects. Now we turn to two explanations of group polarization which have proven fruitful.

C. INFORMATIONAL INFLUENCE

Among the assorted explanations for group polarization, informational influence is the most strongly and consistently supported. Arguments which emerge during discussion predominantly favor the generally preferred alternative. Since it is unlikely that any given person will have already considered all these arguments or found them all salient, some of the discussion arguments are likely to be persuasive. By this view, group influence resides in the substance of what other people have to say, not merely in exposure to their positions. We will summarize quickly most of the evidence relevant to an information-processing explanation (see Myers & Lamm, 1976, for details and documentation), giving closer scrutiny to recent advances in it.

A number of experiments attempted to disentangle the argument-exchange component of group discussion from exposure to others' positions in order to see if one of these components—exposure to others' arguments or to their positions—is necessary and sufficient for changed responses. These experiments clearly indicated that when, by various clever methods, subjects are exposed to relevant arguments but gain no information about others' positions, they nonetheless evidence the expected shift. In thus seems clear that arguments have a persuasive impact above and beyond any impression they convey about the positions of the persons who spoke them.

Another clever demonstration of the impact of informational variables comes from a recent study by Kaplan and Miller (1976). Simulated jury members were provided with tape-recorded arguments. In some juries all group members heard the arguments (through headphones) in the *same order;* in other juries each group member heard the arguments in a *different order*. Since recency effects made the later arguments more salient, the different-order condition diversified the distribution of remembered facts among jury members. This resulted in an enhanced group polarization effect in the different-order condition, since each group member had more information to gain from the discussion.

In addition to these experimental manipulations of the availability of arguments, other research has content-analyzed the arguments generated by individuals and groups. A look inside the "black box" of discussion revealed that the initial average response to an item predicts very well the trend of prediscussion and discussion arguments which in turn provide an excellent prediction of the mean shift on the item. Since the discussion content evidently mediates the relationship between the initial mean and the mean shift we may expect that if, in a given discussion, the spoken arguments depart from the initial responses it will be the arguments and not the initial response mean which will predict the direction of group shift (Myers & Bach, 1974).

Meticulous analyses of the presumed informational influence mechanisms, principally by Vinokur and Burnstein (1974, 1978), have established that response shifts are a function of the *direction* (pro–con), *cogency,* and *novelty* of each argument which the subject receives. Vinokur and Burnstein constructed a mathematical model of informational influence which has been successful even in predicting variation among group shifts *within items*. Since the prediscussion response means for particular groups do not predict variation among group shifts on a given item, this confirms that the discussion content—its direction, cogency, and novelty—is the crucial determinant of group shift, not the group's initial average. We shall elaborate on this in the following.

There presumably exists a pool of persuasive arguments for each item. A group that is quite polarized on a particular item before discussion is likely already in possession of most arguments which polarize a group. A less extreme group has more to gain from the sharing of arguments. This explains why a given group's initial response mean predicts so poorly how that group is going to shift relative to other groups.

But why then does the initial *item* mean predict so well the general trend o group shifts on that item? We have just noted that the prediscussion response trend predicts the preponderance of discussion arguments which, in turn, predicts the trend in group shifts. Still, we may inquire, why do the spoken arguments polarize opinion when they merely reflect what the average subject already possesses? For example, if on a Choice Dilemma item three-fourths of the individually considered arguments favor risk and, therefore, three-fourths of the subsequent discussed arguments favor risk, and thus the risk-to-caution ratio is unchanged by the discussion, why does the group become more risky?

Three reasons may be proposed. First, as Vinokur and Burnstein have demonstrated in their several studies, arguments which are consistent with the dominant tendency are perceived as more persuasive than opposite arguments; hence they apparently carry heavier weight. Anderson and Graesser (1976) have also recently observed that information of relatively extreme valence tends to be assigned greater weight than more neutral information.

Second, the spoken arguments do not, in fact, always mirror the distribution of individually considered arguments. People are more polar and decisive in discussion than when they individually list relevant arguments. For example, one recent study (Judd, 1975) observed that while 65% of written arguments favored the dominant alternative, the discussed arguments were even more imbalanced—79% favoring the preferred alternative (see also Bishop & Myers, 1974; Ebbesen & Bowers, 1974). This is consistent with evidence (Crawford, 1974; Manis, Cornell, & Moore, 1974) indicating that the social context can induce people to tailor their communications and with Janis's (1972) speculation that members of political decision-making groups will

show interest in facts and opinions that support their initially preferred policy and take up time in their meetings to discuss them, but they tend to ignore facts and opinions that do not support their initially preferred policy [p. 10].

When working alone the subjects are responding only to the materials; when engaged in discussion they are responding to other people as well.

A third reason why discussion may polarize opinion, even if it only adds information having the same direction and cogency as existing information, is suggested by the set-size effect in studies of impression formation. Increasing the number of nonneutral trait adjectives describing a person results in more extreme evaluative judgments. It is therefore fortunate that students of information integration (Anderson & Graesser, 1976; Kaplan, 1978) are now applying their considerable theoretical and methodological sophistication to informational influence in group discussion. By experimentally constructing information, rather than depending on naturally occurring differences in arguments, these studies provide impressive new evidence for informational influence.

In Kaplan's (1978) experiments, subjects read transcripts of an attempted manslaughter trial and then noted down five facts that they considered relevant for the verdict, each on a separate card. These cards were supposedly passed to jurors in other rooms while the subject received five cards from the other jurors, one from each juror. In the first experiment, half the subjects received facts in the same proportion as they had emitted. Thus if a subject cited four incriminating facts and one vindicating fact, she/he received five new facts in the same four-to-one ratio. Although proportionally similar to the subject's own information, this was sufficient to polarize judgments—making them harsher in a highly incriminating case and more lenient in a nonincriminating case.

A second experiment set normative influence against informational influence by informing the subjects of others' supposed judgments, which were always consistent with the dominant tendency of the case. If the facts provided were, however, opposed to the direction of others' verdicts, it was still the facts and not the exposure to others' supposed verdicts which determined response shift. That is, subjects who received facts in the *opposite* proportion to what they emitted (but from jurors who subscribed to the subjects' positions) shifted in the direction toward which the new information was pointing, as in the first experiment. This study is an improvement on previous ones which confounded the arguments with information about others' positions. (These experiments also demonstrate how information integration theory can handle depolarization or averaging effects as well as group polarization.)

A *third* experiment gave subjects five facts that were either redundant of one another or nonredundant and which supposedly originated either from five different jurors or all from one juror. The number of sources had no effect, but stronger shifts occurred with the more informative, nonredundant fact sets. These results can all be accommodated within information integration theory by assuming that a person's first response is a composite of a neutral initial impression (before reading the item) and the value of the information provided on the item. Individuals therefore enter discussion with a judgment which reflects the prevalent tendency of the information, but not as polar as the information would imply.

> Subsequent discussion, provided it is proportionally similar in value to the original information base, increases the information integrated by the individual, offsetting the more neutral initial impression and thereby polarizing the postdiscussion response [Kaplan, 1978].

Anderson and Graesser (1976) provide an explicit test of the extent to which information integration models fit observed attitudes following group discussion. Unlike the approach of Bishop and Myers (1974) and Vinokur and Burnstein (1974, 1978), described above, information integration theory provides an umbrella which can incorporate a variety of plausible factors, including source effects and bare assertions without substantive content. To control the subjects' information resources each group member was primed with a different piece of information (two paragraphs of predetermined favorability about given nineteenth-century presidents). The subject next *shared* this information with other group members and then openly *discussed* the presidents with the other group members. Although the shared information was, on the average, of the same degree of favorability as the initial information, this was nevertheless sufficient to polarize initial tendencies. If, for example, the members of a dyad or triad possessed moderately positive information, additional moderately positive information amplified their positive attitude. (This parallels the set-size effect in the impression-formation literature; people rather than pieces of paper were used as carriers of new information.) To provide a test of an averaging model of information integration, subjects were asked to estimate the weight (importance) and scale value (favorability) of their own paragraphs and of the paragraph summaries presented by the other participants. Note that in contrast to the molecular analyses of Vinokur and Burnstein, this molar analysis asks subjects to estimate the gross impact of a communication, including any persuasive effects not captured by merely summing the cogency of each bit of argument. Goodness-of-fit tests revealed that the information-integration model gave an excellent account of the subjects' final attitudes regarding each president. These strengths of the information-integration model are somewhat offset, however, by the fact that the molar units (the paragraphs) which the subjects judged were close to the total stimulus (the president). That is, the composite of subjects' judgments of what their attitude would be if based only on each paragraph predicted well their actual attitude based on all the paragraphs. Although the more molecular approaches suffer problems which the information-integration analysis remedies, they do at least provide parameter estimates which are made more independently of the measured attitude. Thus both approaches have made important contributions to our understanding of informational influence in group discussion.

While these various findings constitute compelling evidence of informational influence in group discussion, a final set of findings indicates that group discussion does something psychologically more interesting than merely permit information exchange. Passive receipt of arguments outside of an *interactive* context, or listening to discussions without participating in them, generally results in less shift than when people are actively engaged. This may result, at least in part, merely from increased attention to arguments in the interactive context. But it may also be that, stimulated by the discussion, people generate and share new ideas not previously considered by group members. Private thought can also induce a small attitude polarization (see Tesser, 1975; Tesser & Conlee, 1975). Indeed, this may have been the basis for the occasional but seldom replicated finding that private study can produce risky shift.[6]

[6]Suspecting that pretest commitments may have inhibited response change in these failures to replicate the familiarization effect, Myers (unpublished observations) attempted to demonstrate a polarizing effect of private rehearsal without (vs. with) a pretest measure. No significant effect of private study and thought occurred in either condition.

The work of attitude researchers is germane here, for it appears that passive comprehension of arguments is not a sufficient condition for internalization of attitude change. As Greenwald (1968) has demonstrated, passive learning about the target of an attitude is not sufficient to change the attitude; the subject must actively reformulate, or rehearse, the information in order for an internalization of attitude change to result. (This observation parallels the thinking of theorists like Jerome Bruner and Jean Piaget, who have concluded that children's intellectual development takes place more by self-generated activities, such as active play, than by being passive while taught.) It seems quite reasonable to presume that the social confrontation inherent in debate and discussion motivates covert rehearsal, as when people quietly think about their next contribution.

Arguments that are openly expressed may be additionally important as a public verbal commitment toward whatever alternative is defended. Since these spoken arguments tend to favor the socially preferred choice more predominantly than to privately processed arguments, the self-attribution and dissonance-reduction dynamics that accompany such overt expression will likely contribute to attitude intensification. Although these and other possible mechanisms of group influence have not yet been fully explored, it nonetheless seems reasonable to presume that informational influence in group discussion involves group *dynamics* as well as a pooling of individually processed information. These group dynamics might be incorporated within the information-integration perspective by studying how they affect such factors as the distribution and weighting of pieces of information.

D. SOCIAL COMPARISONS

There is little doubt that the substantive information which is communicated and rehearsed in group discussion is an important source of group polarization. But in addition to this information processing, are there also social–emotional processes at work? Might social comparisons, motivated by a concern for perceiving and presenting oneself favorably, contribute to the amplification of dominant response tendencies? Several variations on social comparison theory suggest that mere exposure to others' preferences is a sufficient condition for shift. In general, this bag of theories (itemized by Pruitt, 1971a, 1971b) proposes that people modify their responses when they discover that others share their inclinations more than they would have supposed. This is presumed to prompt change either because the group norm is discovered to be more in the preferred direction than previously imagined or because people are released to more strongly act out their secret preferences after observing someone who embodies their ideal more strongly than they do.

1. Recent Theoretical Developments

Very recently, two research teams (Baron, Sanders, & Baron, 1975; Jellison

& Arkin, 1977) have offered creative adaptations of Festinger's (1954) theory of social comparison to account for recent findings. Jellison and Arkin (1977) take social comparison theory in a behaviorist direction by emphasizing the external rewards elicited by socially presenting oneself as basically similar yet somewhat distinctive in the socially approved direction. Taking off from Festinger's assumption of "a unidirectional drive upward in the case of abilities which is largely absent in opinions" (producing a competitivelike drive to see oneself as relatively high in ability, but a pressure toward uniformity in opinions), Jellison and Arkin (1977) suggest that people try to present themselves as relatively high in ability because external rewards, including the secondary rewards of social approval, are associated with high ability. The earlier research of Jellison and his associates supported the main assumption of their social-comparison-of-abilities theory by demonstrating that, on risk tasks involving skill, high risk-taking is associated with attributions of high ability. Risky shifts previously observed on skill tasks might therefore have occurred because moving to higher risk is a way of presenting oneself as high in ability. But what about nonrisk tasks? Jellison and Davis (1973) have demonstrated that greater extremity on the generally preferred side of an opinion issue can also be positively correlated with attributed ability. This extension of the theory to explain the general polarization effect requires that "polarization does not take place when extreme judgments on a task do not reflect ability...." (Jellison & Arkin, 1977). Thus a virtue of this theory is that it clearly suggests how it might be disconfirmed.

Whereas Jellison and Arkin (1977) modify Festinger's (1954) theory of social comparison by stressing external rewards and punishments, and excluding internal forces such as the cognitive need to define social reality and evaluate oneself relative to it, Baron et al. (1975) modify the Festinger theory by eradicating the dichotomy between the dynamics of ability comparison and of opinion comparison. People evaluate their opinions and traits, Baron et al. (1975) presume, much as Festinger supposed they evaluate their abilities. Differing amounts of many different types of personal attributes have differential social desirability and, as with abilities, one is evaluated in terms of how much of the attribute she/he possesses. Thus Baron et al. (1975) reconceptualize Festinger's distinction between ability and opinion comparison as *rank-order evaluation* and *accuracy evaluation*. People engaged in rank-order evaluation are concerned about their position relative to comparison others[7] on dimensions which have positive or negative social desirability (e.g., ability, honesty, prejudice). Accuracy evaluation occurs on dimensions which do not differ in social value, such that the premium is placed on being right, not on perceiving oneself as different from the group. Thus, if on a day when rain seemed imminent, a team of weathermen

---

[7] Another recent formulation of social comparison theory emphasizes that the social comparison mechanisms which contribute to polarization will be fully engaged only when the comparison others are known to be socially comparable to oneself (Goethals & Zanna, 1977).

gathered at their morning staff meeting to agree on the chances of rain, they would *not* be expected to polarize toward estimating a higher probability of rain than reflected in their individual judgments. As Baron *et al.* (1975) point out, this modification of social comparison theory is not entirely novel, for other investigators (e.g., Wheeler, 1966a) have already demonstrated that the upward comparison drive extends to desirable traits beyond ability.

Baron and Roper (1976) supported this social comparison theory by demonstrating that polarization of judgments on an autokinetic conformity task occurred only if value was experimentally placed upon relatively extreme judgments. When people believed that larger estimates of movement indicated intelligence and ability, they made larger judgments in front of others than in private. When deviation was not an indicator of intellectual promise an averaging effect occurred. Since in this experiment the desirable extreme was associated with high ability, the results can be interpreted as supporting both the Jellison–Arkin and the Baron–Sanders–Baron versions of social comparison theory. Contrasting these theories requires a simple task which engages a clear social preference but which is unrelated to ability. Such an experiment will be reported later.

First, however, we quickly review the earlier findings relevant to social comparison theories (once again, see Myers & Lamm, 1976, for details and documentation). These results form the building blocks of the social comparison explanation and any complete explanation of group polarization will need to accommodate them.

2. The Foundational Assumption

The foundational assumption of social comparison theories is that people are motivated to see and to present themselves as better embodiments of socially desired abilities, traits, and attitudes than are most other members of their groups. This assumption is well-supported by various types of evidence. First, people tend to suppose that their own responses are closer to their internal ideals than is the group norm (operationally speaking, the average peer is guessed to have responded more neutrally than oneself). This seems to be a widespread phenomenon. For example, most businessmen perceive themselves to be more ethical than the average businessman (Baumhart, 1968), and most people perceive their own views as less prejudiced than the norm of their community (Lenihan, 1965). An exhaustive series of investigations with adolescent and adult French people confirms the same strong and consistent tendency: People tend to perceive themselves as superior to the average member of their groups (Codol, 1976). These perceptions are, of course, distorted; the average person is not better than the average person. (This tendency toward inflated relative self-perception is surely a source of much human discontent. When an employer awards merit raises and half of the employees receive less than the median increase, perceptions of injustice are likely to be widespread since few will perceive themselves as less competent than their average peer.)

Social comparison explanations presume that discussion exposes people to others' positions, causing them to adjust their own responses in order to maintain their favorable self-perception. There is a body of evidence which indicates that subjects do, indeed, realistically revise their estimates of the group norm after discussion. This even happens if arguments are exchanged but explicit mention of responses (positions) is prohibited, indicating that under normal circumstances arguments may serve to implicitly convey information about others' positions in addition to their direct persuasive impact.

Furthermore, it has been reliably demonstrated that people who deviate from one's own position in the idealized direction are more highly regarded than people who do not, or who deviate an equal amount in the other direction. A parallel finding exists in the attitude literature (Eisinger & Mills, 1968): We perceive extremists on our side of an issue as more sincere and competent than moderates.

While these findings are all well-established, their theoretical significance is still somewhat ambiguous. Just as social comparison theorists have noted that spoken arguments convey implicit cues about others' positions and may serve to rationalize shifts once people are motivated to change, so also have informational theorists reminded us that there are plausible informational influence explanations of the mere-exposure phenomena described above. Burnstein, Vinokur, and Pichevin (1974), for example, show that people who adopt extreme choices are presumed to possess cogent arguments and are perhaps, therefore, admired for their ability. Furthermore, the fact that subjects are much less confident about their estimates of others' choices than about the correctness of their own choices suggests that the tendency to perceive others as more neutral than oneself may simply reflect ignorance about others' choices. If you really do not know how other people feel, is it not reasonable to check a response near the middle of the scale?

In sum, the group polarization literature provides well-documented confirmation of hypotheses derived from the assumption that people are motivated to see and present themselves in a favorable light, relative to others. But the results are somewhat ambiguous because it is possible to construct a scenario which explains these findings without reference to normative social pressures or a desire to engage in rank-order evaluation.

It is therefore fortunate that support for the social comparison assumption has recently emerged from some independent lines of research. Schlenker (1975) has shown that people present themselves with a positive bias, unless public exposure is forthcoming that would debunk positive self-presentation. Fromkin (1970, 1972) provides evidence that people want to perceive themselves as somewhat different from others. Although a considerable body of research on conformity and reactions to being markedly deviant indicates that people are discomfited by being substantially different from others, it now appears that people also find it unpleasant to sense that they are undistinctive. Fromkin demonstrates that people feel better when they understand themselves to be unique and they will act in ways which will create a sense of individuality.

These conclusions are reinforced by Lemaine's (1974) analysis of the contribution to one's identity of differentiating oneself from others. McGuire and Padawer-Singer's (1976) observation that self-concept is defined by differences from comparison others further strengthens the point. When simply asked to describe themselves, sixth-grade children were more likely to spontaneously mention their distinctive attributes. Foreign-born children were the most likely to mention their birthplace, redheads their hair color, and so forth. These contemporary research findings will come as no surprise to personality theorists. As Fromkin notes, Fromm (1941), Horney (1937), and Maslow (1962) long ago proposed that people have a "need for separate identity" or "need for uniqueness." Situations which diminish one's sense of individuality purportedly revive the threat of "ego diffusion" (Erikson, 1959), an uncomfortable state of confused self-concept. These assorted observations lend strength to social comparison theory's assumption that people *are* motivated to see themselves as basically similar to others, yet different—in the right direction and to the right extent.

3. Perceived Differences and Shift

Given this diverse support for the foundational assumption of social comparison theory, the next question is whether this social motivation does, in fact, contribute to the observed effects of group discussion. This question has been pursued in two ways. The first has been to inquire whether the perceived difference between oneself and others correlates with an individual's shift score on a specific item. The expectation here is that people who most perceive themselves as outshining their peers will suffer most disconfirmation of their perceived relative positions and so should be most stimulated to shift when informed of the actual group norm. But, to the contrary, there is no such correlation between perceived deviation from the norm and subsequent shift, even when one's own initial choices are held statistically constant. This is a troubling finding for social comparison theory, although Baron et al. (1975) suggest that this low correlation may occur because even those who don't actually feel different beforehand may wish to present themselves as strong embodiments of the ideal once they get in the group context. They suggested, as we have (Myers & Lamm, 1976), that the extent to which people feel that their present positions underplay their ideals may be a more crucial element of social comparison dynamics. This conclusion is supported by Lamm's findings that groups composed of individuals with high self-ideal discrepancy on the issues discussed evidenced more shift than did groups with low self-ideal discrepancy (Lamm, Schaude, & Trommsdorff, 1971), but there was no difference in shift among groups of subjects who strongly underestimated peer positions and those who did not underestimate peer positions (Lamm, Trommsdorff, & Rost-Schaude, 1972).

Moreover, there are now several independent observations of group-induced shift *toward* the perceived group average (Baron *et al.*, 1974; Myers *et al.*, 1974; Vidmar, 1974). (Remember that most risky shift studies have found a shift away from the perceived group norm and toward more extreme risk.) In some of these studies it seems reasonable to presume that the subjects' ideal may in fact have been in the same direction as the perceived norm, but that a social constraint—surveillance by an experimenter who represented a conflicting norm—compromised the initial choices. In Freudian terms, the subjects may have compromised between two ideals: a secret id preference and a superego ideal. The observation of one or more peer group members espousing a permissive or aggressive response might then have released the average participant from the "superego" dictate. This conjecture finds support in the attitude research of Cialdini, Levy, Herman, and Evenbeck (1973). Subjects were observed to moderate their attitude position—to compromise their internal ideal by moving toward the scale neutral point—prior to an anticipated discussion. We presume that had Cialdini *et al.*'s (1973) subjects actually then engaged in discussion they might have been liberated to realize their internal ideals.

This enhancement of private preferences may help explain those anomalous findings in which, contrary to group polarization, groups shift *away* from the initial average tendency (e.g., Walker & Main, 1973; Wolosin *et al.*, 1975; and jury studies showing a leniency shift). Perhaps, for example, individual participants in the Wolosin *et al.* (1975) study were hesitant to indulge their secret self-serving inclinations only so long as they were deciding individually. Observing someone else promote the self-serving action may have freed other subjects to express their impulses—meaning also that more new information would be learned and rehearsed in support of the emerging norm than for the initially favored choice. This interpretation is close to the responsibility-diffusion interpretation of these results.

4. *Exposure to Others' Choices*

The most direct evidence bearing upon a social comparison explanation of group shifts comes from those studies which provide the assumed necessary and sufficient conditions for shift—mere exposure to others' responses. One set of studies manipulated exposure to others' responses by providing fake norms. As these studies have shown, subjects move toward such norms, but this simply indicates that conformity effects can be demonstrated on Choice Dilemma items as with numerous other measures. Of greater interest is whether the effect of normative pressure is increased by making the fake norm consistent with one's ideal (vs. making it equally deviant from one's position in the direction opposite of one's ideal). Here the evidence is mixed, although data seem to be accumulating in support of the proposition that arguments or social pressures that are consistent with one's ideals generate more response change than pressures away from one's position (Baron, Monson, & Baron, 1973; R. D. Clark, Crockett, & Archer, 1971; Ebbesen & Bowers, 1974; Paicheler, 1976a, 1977; Silzer & Clark, 1978).

A final set of studies has examined social comparison effects by exposing people to information about the actual initial choices of other people *without* any discussion or exposure to others' arguments, much as happens when people read the outcome of an opinion poll. Myers has recently conducted a series of such experiments which we will now review.

In one experiment (Myers, Bach, & Schreiber, 1974) subjects in a control condition simply indicated their positions on some Choice Dilemma problems. Subjects in a second condition were exposed to the distribution of these responses prior to making their own decisions. These subjects responded with more polarized attitudes (i.e., more extreme positions on the generally favored side) than did the control group. In other words, observation of others' responses stimulated a *deviation* from the observed norm—the opposite of conformity to the average.

Since this experiment, unlike previous experiments, used a between-groups design, we reasoned that the stronger social comparison effect observed in this study might have been due to the repeated measures designs of previous experiments which required subjects to first bind themselves to a pretest choice. It takes only a quick recall of some classic conformity studies (e.g., Asch, 1956) to realize that this was an excellent procedure for inhibiting response change. Consequently a follow-up study (Myers, unpublished observations) used a similar procedure except that half of those who observed others' choices did so after first making a pretest commitment and half did so without pretest. Attitude materials requested subjects to evaluate hypothetical positive or negative college professors (Myers, 1975). Although the social comparison effect was small, only those who had not made a pretest commitment evidenced significantly more polarized responses than the control distribution which had been observed.

Our subsequent experiments further explored the attitudinal effects of mere exposure to others' attitude responses. Their purpose was, first, to ascertain whether the phenomenon would generalize across a variety of methods and materials and, second, to explore some psychological dynamics which might mediate the phenomenon.

One experiment (Myers, 1977) compared two versions of social comparison theory. One version (Levinger & Schneider, 1969) presumes that exposure to the group norm, or average, is sufficient to stimulate a more polarized response, because people want to keep a step ahead of the average. The other (Pruitt, 1971a, 1971b) postulates that the key is not discovery of the peer group average, but rather observation of a group member who models the person's ideal in a relatively extreme form. This supposedly *releases* people from the constraints of the assumed group norm, liberating them to act out their private inclinations, just as "trigger persons" can release latent impulses in a crowd situation.

These two explanations of attitude polarization were experimentally contrasted by showing some people a complete percentage distribution of others' opinions (therefore exposing them to some extreme models), while others learned only of the group average (norm). Two types of stimulus materials were used—jury problems (Myers & Kaplan, 1976) and Choice Dilemma items. To control for any time or subject differences between the pretest condition and the subsequent experimental conditions the experimental groups were exposed, in balanced fashion, to the pretest responses on some items but not on others, making each subject his or her own control. As Table I indicates, we observed with both item sets that responses were significantly more polarized ($p < .01$) on items where subjects had observed others' responses than on items where they had not. Contrary to release theory, exposure merely to the average other response was sufficient to polarize responses. Those exposed to the full distribution of others' choices were not significantly more polarized than those who merely witnessed the group norm.

A follow-up experiment (Myers, 1977) used a between-groups comparison to examine the exposure effect (instead of the more sensitive within-subjects design) and it asked an additional question of empirical interest: What if we took the relatively polarized responses of those who had observed others' choices and exposed a third group to these? Would additional polarization occur with a second iteration of the exposure treatment?

TABLE I
MEAN CHOICE-DILEMMA RESPONSE, BY CONDITION

Condition	N	No exposure			Exposure		
		Risky items	Cautious items	Polarization	Risky items	Cautious items	Polarization
Pretest	67	4.34	7.62	3.28	—	—	—
Average exposure	52	4.45	7.80	3.35	4.04	7.92	3.88
Percent exposure	52	4.27	7.55	3.28	3.79	7.98	4.19

Note: Responses could range from the risky extreme, which advised the proposed course of action even if its chance of success was only 1 (in 10), to the cautious extreme of 10 (in 10).

TABLE II
MEAN JURY ITEM RESPONSE, BY CONDITION

| Condition | N | No exposure | | | Exposure | | |
		Low guilt	High guilt	Polari- zation	Low guilt	High guilt	Polari- zation
Pretest	67	35.43	70.75	35.32	—	—	—
Average exposure	52	36.54	71.83	35.29	27.12	72.79	45.67
Percent exposure	52	40.19	74.71	34.52	31.15	78.37	47.21

Note: Response could range from judgments of no guilt (0) to high guilt (100).

The dependent variable in this experiment was, again, a polarization score, defined as the mean gap between responses to four cautious and four risky Choice Dilemma items. In the first stage of the experiment 30 pretest subjects completed each item individually. In a second stage 30 more subjects were shown the exact distribution of responses by the 30 subjects preceding them in the pretest condition while 30 control subjects answered without feedback, just as did the pretest subjects. In the third stage of the experiment, two more groups were given the same treatments, except that those in the exposure condition were shown the responses of the preceding 30 people in their own condition.

The entire experiment was run by a computer as the subject sat at a high-speed terminal. This not only eliminated any possibility of experimenter effects but, more importantly, enabled the instant tabulation of responses and their presentation to subsequent subjects with precisely controlled format. As can be seen in Table III, responses in the two exposure conditions were significantly more polarized than in the control conditions ($p < .001$). The second iteration of feedback did not, however, significantly exaggerate the polarization effect.

We also correlated the initial response mean for each of the eight items with the polarization effect which each item elicited (second stage minus first stage). As you might expect, this correlation was substantial (.87), indicating that risky shift was greatest on the initially riskiest items. But skewness was also highly correlated with both initial and shift scores ($r = .95$ and .82, respectively). Perhaps, therefore, the polarization effect is merely the result of conformity to the observed mode or median, thus eliminating the tail of an otherwise skewed distribution. Two other findings suggest that this is not the case. First, the relationship between skewness and shift was totally eliminated when the initial response average was partialed out ($r = .11$), but the relationship between initial average and shift was left substantially intact ($r = .54$) when skewness was partialed out. Second, exposure to others' responses did not decrease variability among responses. This indicates that no implicit group decision was emerging.

Is this reliable comparison effect merely a hothouse laboratory phenomenon or might it also be observed in a natural setting? Our next experiment (Myers, Wojcicki, & Aardema, 1978) asked whether exposure to others' attitudes in a real-world setting could polarize initial attitude tendencies. Evidence from previous studies indicates there is no powerful bandwagon effect resulting from the publication of election polls (Klapper, 1964), but these studies generally present poll results from the general public, rather than from a significant social reference group. We expected that a small bandwagon effect might be obtained if exposure to the opinions of significant others informed people that their preferences were shared more strongly than they were aware. Our second purpose was, much as in one of the preceding experiments, to contrast release theory with the assumption that correctly perceiving the group norm (average) is sufficient to produce shift. Participants were 269 members of a local church who participated in an opinion polling survey designed in cooperation with the church leadership. Approximately one-third participated in a pretest condition by simply indicating their opinions regarding selected issues on a 7-point scale. These people also guessed how the average member would respond to each item. As can be seen in Fig. 1, they did, as expected, perceive themselves more strongly in the preferred direction than the average other member ($p < .001$). Remaining members were randomly divided into three conditions prior to completing the questionnaire some 3 weeks later. *Control* participants completed the items without information about others' responses. Participants in the *average exposure* condition were shown results from the first stage of the survey in the form of the average response to each item, while people in the *percentage exposure* condition were shown the complete distribution of responses. This treatment was introduced with an appropriate explanation and no one objected or later mentioned it when given a chance to comment upon the survey.

As Fig. 1 suggests, those exposed merely to the average pretest opinion were intermediate between the control and percentage exposure conditions. In this experiment it appeared that exposure to the group norm and to extreme models had small additive effects. An additional finding evaluated the presumption that if attitude comparison is strengthening the initially dominant point of view, then items for which there is clearly a socially preferred tendency should elicit greater polarization than items initially near the neutral point. This supposition was confirmed by correlational analysis.

Although this experiment indicates that a bandwagon effect can occur as a result of publishing the results of a local opinion poll, this effect may be limited to situations where a range of responses is offered, enabling people to differentiate themselves from the "average man" by moving a step ahead. In limited two-choice situations, such as in a presidential election, the need to differentiate oneself from the norm is not likely to result in a bandwagon effect

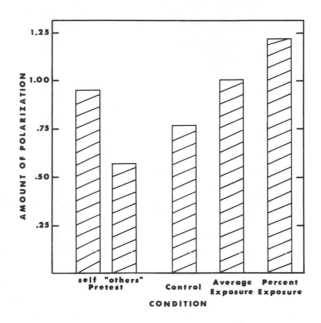

Fig. 1. Opinion polling experiment: Amount of attitude polarization, by condition (score indicates extent to which dominant viewpoint is favored on a -3 to $+3$ scale).

following the publication of polls, or so we suppose. These speculations will be a subject of future research.

Each of the comparison effects reported to this point might plausibly be interpreted (as by Burnstein & Vinokur, 1975) as resulting from stimulation to think up arguments which others might have had to justify their choices. Thus what appears at first glance to be a social comparison effect might in reality be an information-processing effect. Our latest experiment (Myers, 1977) examined this by using a simple judgment task which could not plausibly engage a set of rationally considered arguments. Under such conditions an informational influence explanation would predict no comparison effect. Recall also that contrasting the Jellison–Arkin and Baron–Sanders–Baron versions of social comparison theory required a simple task which would engage clear social preferences without involving perceived ability. According to the Jellison–Arkin position, polarization should occur only when an opinion issue involves a matter of fact, not "when there is no correct position on the issue because it is strictly a matter of judgment."

In this experiment pairs of high school seniors were asked to judge the attractiveness of 20 persons pictured on slides, half of them being attractive and half of them unattractive. The procedure was simple: Person A viewed the first slide on a slide viewer and announced his or her rating to the experimenter, using a 100-point scale. Person B heard this judgment prior to viewing the slide and also giving a rating. On the second slide person B viewed first and rated and then passed the viewer to person A, and so forth. If this simple exposure is sufficient to polarize responses, then we may expect that the second person judging the slide will tend to give more positive ratings to the attractive slides than did the first person and more negative ratings on the unattractive slides. As Table III indicates, this expectation was strongly confirmed ($\chi^2(2) = 24.7$, $p < .0001$). The second respondent was seven times as likely to give a different response as to conform to the first response and when doing so was almost twice as likely to deviate in the dominant direction—to go the first person one better—as to deviate in the contrary direction. Analysis of variance confirmed that the mean polarization effect, though small, was highly significant ($p < .001$). We cannot imagine how any type of group decision theory could be stretched to explain this simple finding, but this comment is not to insist that a theory must explain all phenomena in order for it to be useful for explaining certain other phenomena.

What have these experiments established? First, they indicate that comparison-induced polarization occurs using a variety of methodologies and stimuli. The phenomenon appears to be reliable and generalizable, although subtle. Second, some theoretical explanations for the phenomenon appear incapable of handling the results. It is difficult to conceive how all the findings could be adequately explained by implicit group decision mechanisms, by the processing of persuasive rational arguments, by the releasing effects of observing extreme models, or by the social comparison of abilities.

These findings, taken in combination with the personality research on individuation noted earlier, appear to provide strong evidence for the presumption that people want to differentiate themselves from others, to a small extent and in the right direction. By ''one-upping'' the self-presentations of others, people can see and present themselves as basically similar, yet desirably distinctive. This

TABLE III
FREQUENCY OF SECOND JUDGMENTS EXCEEDING,
MATCHING, OR MODERATING FIRST JUDGMENTS

Stimuli	Second judgment compared with first		
	More positive	Same	More negative
Attractive	99	26	75
Unattractive	52	29	119

conclusion provides a needed complement to social psychology's historic emphasis on conformity and the discomforting effects of marked deviance.

Notice, finally, how far we have strayed from the initial concern with risk-taking. What began as the risky shift phenomenon was transformed into research on polarization and other group influences. Our attempts to explain polarization then led us down several paths, including investigations of self-perception, self-presentation, and attitude comparison. These unanticipated discoveries and new directions typify the course of much scientific investigation.

IV. Conclusions

Having focused our chapter on the effects of group interaction and on the theoretical explanation of these effects, we conclude by briefly taking stock in each of these areas.

Anderson and Graesser (1976) have suggested a useful distinction between the attitude-formation and consensus-formation stages of the emergence of a group decision. (Communication theorists have further differentiated the stages of a group discussion, but this two-part distinction seems sufficient for the present.) Thus the social and informational dynamics which we have just discussed seem applicable to the attitude-formation stage. Social decision schemes and responsibility-diffusion dynamics seem germane to the consensus stage during which emergent attitudes are combined into a group product.

We have suggested how the dynamics of informational influence and social comparison usually polarize the dominant initial leanings of group members, and also why these dynamics sometimes move choices *away* from the action tendencies of individual respondents. Although the informational influence of relevant arguments has been experimentally separated from social comparison effects, we must remember that in natural situations there is no neat dichotomy. These processes will operate jointly and feed on one another. Arguments convey information about one's position. The desire to present oneself favorably motivates people to emit persuasive arguments in the presumed socially desirable direction. Indeed, the extent to which the social and information aspects of group discussion are interwoven is symptomized by the difficulty which experimenters have had in achieving a clean separation of the two. These two dynamics in combination help us understand why the effect of group interaction is likely to be a polarization effect when the initial sample average leans toward one side of the issue and when responses close to that pole are socially valued.

Sometimes discussions are carried forward to the point where a consensus emerges, either as a natural product of the discussion or as a result of an explicit requirement as in jury decision-making. This opens the door for the application of decision rules and the introduction of responsibility dynamics, as well as possibly intensifying the persuasive argumentation. Although both decision schemes and responsibility dynamics seem linked to the consensus formation stage, it is difficult to completely separate them from the attitude formation stage since they may ride piggyback on the content of the discussion.

Existing research has seldom made this distinction between the attitude formation and consensus formation stages of group decision-making. As Anderson and Graesser (1976) admonish, the distinction seems worth making in future research by focusing attention on individual choices if attitude change is being studied and on the group product if decision schemes are being studied.

Has the original risky shift literature repeated the history of some of social psychology's other literatures? Sometimes the discovery of an intriguing phenomenon stimulates a barrage of experiments which reveal that the phenomenon is more complex than first thought, at which point interest wanes as researchers move on, leaving a mess behind. Fortunately, this appears not to have happened with the risky shift. The discovery of risky shift ultimately led to a new and broader conception of the phenomenon which seems operative in real-world situations where group interaction affects people's welfare. The theories devised to explain these group effects have generated new predictions relevant to our understanding of attitude change and of the social comparison process. Future study of group interaction seems, therefore, to have the potential of developing a creative synthesis between theory and its social usefulness, thus making this an area which fulfills Kurt Lewin's vision for social psychology.

REFERENCES

Anderson, N. H., & Graesser, C. C. An information integration analysis of attitude change in group discussion. *Journal of Personality and Social Psychology,* 1976, **34,** 210–222.

Andrews, I. R., & Johnson, D. L. Small group polarization of judgements. *Psychonomic Science,* 1971, **24,** 191–192.

Asch, S. E. Studies of independence and conformity: A minority of one against a unanimous majority. *Psychological Monographs,* 1956, **7**(9, Whole No. 416).

Astin, A. W., & Panos, R. J. *The educational and vocational development of college students.* Washington, D.C.: American Council on Education, 1969.

Baron, R. S., Monson, T. C., & Baron, P. H. Conformity pressure as a determinant of risk taking: Replication and extension. *Journal of Personality and Social Psychology,* 1973, **28,** 406–413.

Baron, R. S., & Roper, G. Reaffirmation of social comparison views of choice shifts: Averaging and extremity effects in an autokinetic situation. *Journal of Personality and Social Psychology,* 1976, **33,** 521–530.

Baron, R. S., Roper, G., & Baron, P. H. Group discussion and the stingy shift. *Journal of Personality and Social Psychology,* 1974, **30,** 538–545.

Baron, R. S., & Sanders, G. Group decision as a technique for obtaining compliance: Some added considerations concerning how altruism leads to callousness. *Journal of Applied Social Psychology,* 1975, **5,** 281–295.

Baron, R. S., Sanders, G. S., & Baron, P. H. Social comparison reconceptualized: Implications for choice shifts, averaging effects, and social facilitation. Unpublished manuscript, University of Iowa, 1975.

Batson, C. D. Rational processing or rationalization? The effect of disconfirming information on a stated religious belief. *Journal of Personality and Social Psychology,* 1975, **32,** 176–184.

Baumhart, R. *An honest profit.* New York: Holt, 1968.

Billig, M., & Cochrane, R. Judgments of values and group polarization: Tests of the value-for-risk hypothesis. *European Journal of Social Psychology,* 1976, **6,** 495–501.

Bishop, G. D., & Myers, D. G. Informational influence in group discussion. *Organizational Behavior and Human Performance,* 1974, **12,** 92–104.

Blascovich, J. Technological innovation adoption: An experiment in bureaucratic decision making. Paper presented at the meeting of the Midwest Political Science Association, 1976.

Blascovich, J., Ginsburg, G. P., & Howe, R. C. Blackjack and the risky shift. II: Monetary stakes. *Journal of Experimental Social Psychology,* 1975, **11,** 224–232.

Blascovich, J., Ginsburg, G. P., & Howe, R. C. Blackjack: Choice shifts in the field. Unpublished manuscript, University of Wisconsin, Milwaukee, 1976.

Blascovich, J., Ginsburg, G. P., & Veach, T. L. A pluralistic explanation of choice shifts on the risk dimension. *Journal of Personality and Social Psychology,* 1975, **31,** 422–429.

Burnstein, E., Miller, H., Vinokur, A., Katz, S., & Crowley, J. Risky shift is eminently rational. *Journal of Personality and Social Psychology,* 1971, **20,** 462–471.

Burnstein, E., & Vinokur, A. What a person thinks upon learning he has chosen differently from others: Nice evidence for the persuasive-arguments explanation of choice shifts. *Journal of Experimental Social Psychology,* 1975, **11,** 412–426.

Burnstein, E., Vinokur, A., & Pichevin, M. F. What do differences between own, admired, and attributed choices have to do with group induced shifts in choice? *Journal of Experimental Social Psychology,* 1974, **10,** 428–443.

Cartwright, D. S. The nature of gangs. In D. S. Cartwright, B. Tomson, & H. Schwartz (Eds.), *Gang delinquency.* Monterey, Calif.: Brooks/Cole, 1975. Pp. 1–22.

Chickering, A. W., & McCormick, J. Personality development and the college experience. *Research in Higher Education,* 1973, No. 1, 62–64.

Cialdini, R. B., Levy, A., Herman, C. P., & Evenbeck, S. Attitudinal politics: The strategy of moderation. *Journal of Personality and Social Psychology,* 1973, **25,** 100–108.

Clark, B. R., Heist, P., McConnell, T. R., Trow, M. A., & Yonge, G. *Students and colleges: Interaction and change.* Berkeley: University of California, Center for Research and Development in Higher Education, 1972.

Clark, R. D., III. Group-induced shift toward risk: A critical appraisal. *Psychological Bulletin,* 1971, **76,** 251–270.

Clark, R. D., III, Crockett, W. H., & Archer, R. L. Risk-as-value hypothesis: The relation between perception of self, others, and the risky shift. *Journal of Personality and Social Psychology,* 1971, **20,** 425–429.

Codol, J. P. On the so-called "superior conformity of the self" behavior: Twenty experimental investigations. *European Journal of Social Psychology,* 1976, **5,** 457–501.

Coleman, J. S. *Community conflict.* New York: Free Press, 1957.

Crawford, T. J. Sermons on racial tolerance and the parish neighborhood context. *Journal of Applied Social Psychology,* 1974, **4,** 1–23.

Cvetkovich, G., & Baumgardner, S. R. Attitude polarization: The relative influence of discussion group structure and reference group norms. *Journal of Personality and Social Psychology,* 1973, **26,** 159–165.

Davis, J. H. Group decision and social interaction: A theory of social decision schemes. *Psychological Review,* 1973, **80,** 97–125.

Davis, J. H., Bray, R. M., & Holt, R. W. The empirical study of social decision processes in juries. In J. Tapp & F. Levine (Eds.), *Law, justice and the individual in society: Psychological and legal issues.* New York: Holt, 1978, in press.

Davis, J. H., Kerr, N. L., Atkin, E. S., Holt, R., & Meek, D. The decision processes of six and twelve person mock juries assigned unanimous and two-thirds majority rules. *Journal of Personality and Social Psychology,* 1975, **32,** 1–14.

Davis, J. H., Kerr, N. L., Stasser, G., Meek, D., & Holt, R. Victim consequences, sentence severity, and decision processes in mock juries. Unpublished manuscript, University of Illinois, 1976.

Davis, J. H., Kerr, N. L., Sussman, M., & Rissman, A. K. Social decision schemes under risk. *Journal of Personality and Social Psychology,* 1974, **30,** 248–271.

Deets, M. K., & Hoyt, G. C. Variance preferences and variance shifts in group investment decisions. *Organizational Behavior and Human Performance,* 1970, **5,** 378–386.

Diener, E. Effects of prior destructive behavior, anonymity, and group presence on deindividuation. *Journal of Personality and Social Psychology,* 1976, **33,** 497–507.

Diener, E., Fraser, S. C., Beaman, A. L., & Kelem, R. T. Effects of deindividuation variables on stealing among Halloween trick-or-treaters. *Journal of Personality and Social Psychology,* 1976, **33,** 178–183.

Diener, E., Westford, K. L., Dineen, J., & Fraser, S. C. Beat the pacifist: The deindividuating effects of anonymity and group presence. *Proceedings of the 81st Annual Convention of the American Psychological Association,* 1973, pp. 221–222.

Dion, K. L., Baron, R. S., & Miller, N. Why do groups make riskier decisions than individuals? In L. Berkowitz (Ed.), *Advances in experimental social psychology.* Vol. 5. New York: Academic Press, 1970.

Doise, W. Intergroup relations and polarization of individual and collective judgments. *Journal of Personality and Social Psychology,* 1969, **12,** 136–143.

Doise, W. An apparent exception to the extremization of collective judgments. *European Journal of Social Psychology,* 1971, **1,** 511–518.

Ebbesen, E. B., & Bowers, R. J. Proportion of risky to conservative arguments in a group discussion and choice shift. *Journal of Personality and Social Psychology,* 1974, **29,** 316–327.

Eisinger, R., & Mills, J. Perception of the sincerity and competence of a communicator as a function of the extremity of his position. *Journal of Experimental Social Psychology,* 1968, **4,** 224–232.

Erikson, E. H. Identity and the life cycle. *Psychological Issues,* 1959, **1,** 1–171.

Feldman, K. A., & Newcomb, T. M. *The impact of college on students.* San Francisco: Jossey-Bass, 1969.

Festinger, L. A theory of social comparison processes. *Human Relations,* 1954, **7,** 117–140.

Festinger, L., Riecken, H. W., & Schachter, S. *When prophecy fails.* Minneapolis: University of Minnesota Press, 1956.

Foss, R. D., & Foss, N. E. Effects of irrelevant variables and group discussion on stimulated jury decisions. Paper presented at the meeting of the Western Psychological Association, April 1973.

Freedman, J. L. *Crowding and behavior.* New York: Viking, 1975.

Fromkin, H. L. Effects of experimentally aroused feelings of undistinctiveness upon valuation of scarce and novel experiences. *Journal of Personality and Social Psychology,* 1970, **16,** 521–529.

Fromkin, H. L. Feelings of interpersonal undistinctiveness: An unpleasant affective state. *Journal of Experimental Research in Personality,* 1972, **6,** 178–185.

Fromm, E. *Escape from freedom.* New York: Farrah & Rinehart, 1941.

Gleason, J. M., & Harris, V. A. Group discussion and defendant's socio-economic status as determinants of judgments by simulated jurors. *Journal of Applied Social Psychology,* 1976, **6,** 186–191.

Goethals, G. R., & Zanna, M. P. The role of social comparison and persuasion in choice shifts. Unpublished manuscript, Williams College, 1977.

Gouge, C., & Fraser, C. A. A further demonstration of group polarization, *European Journal of Social Psychology,* 1972, **2,** 95–97.

Graesser, C. C. A social averaging theorem for group decision making. Thesis proposal, University of California, San Diego, 1975.

Greenwald, A. G. Cognitive learning, cognitive response to persuasion, and attitude change. In A. G. Greenwald, T. C. Brock, & T. M. Ostrom (Eds.), *Psychological foundations of attitudes.* New York: Academic Press, 1968.

Hans, V. P., & Doob, A. N. S.12 of the Canada Evidence Act and the deliberations of simulated juries. *Criminal Law Quarterly,* 1976, **18,** 235–253.

Hardyck, J. A., & Braden, M. Prophecy fails again: A report of a failure to replicate. *Journal of Abnormal and Social Psychology,* 1962, **65,** 136–141.

Heimbach, J. T. Social psychology in the jury room: The effects of evidence, confession, and group interaction in sentencing. Paper presented at the meeting of the Midwestern Psychological Association, X X, May 1970.

Hoge, D. R. *Commitment on campus: Changes in religion and values over five decades.* Philadelphia: Westminster Press, 1974.

Holmes, J. G., Ellis, R. J., & Rosenbaum, D. Outgroup threat and ingroup cohesion as sources of ethnocentrism and polarization. Unpublished manuscript, University of Waterloo, 1976.

Horney, K. *The neurotic personality of our time.* New York: Norton, 1937.

Izzett, R. R., & Leginski, W. Group discussion and the influence of defendant characteristics in a simulated jury setting. *Journal of Social Psychology,* 1974, **93,** 271–280.

Janis, I. L. *Victims of groupthink.* Boston: Houston, 1972.

Jellison, J. M., & Arkin, R. M. Social comparison of abilities: A self-presentational approach to decision making in groups. In J. M. Suls & R. L. Miller (Eds.), *Social comparison processes.* New York: Halsted Press, 1977. Pp. 235-257.

Jellison, J. M., & Davis, D. Relationships between perceived ability and attitude extremity. *Journal of Personality and Social Psychology,* 1973, **27,** 430–436.

Johnson, D. L. Small group polarization of ratings in student evaluation of faculty. Paper presented at the meeting of the Southeastern Psychological Association, April 1972.

Johnson, D. L., & Andrews, I. R. The risky-shift hypothesis tested with consumer products as stimuli. *Journal of Personality and Social Psychology,* 1971, **20,** 382–385.

Johnson, N. R., Stemler, J. G., & Hunter, D. Crowd behavior as "risky shift": A laboratory experiment. *Sociometry,* 1977, **40,** 183–187.

Judd, B., Jr. Information effects in group shift. Unpublished master's thesis, University of Texas at Arlington, 1975.

Kalven, H. G., Jr., & Zeisel, H. *The American jury.* Boston: Little, Brown, 1966.

Kaplan, M. F. Information integration in social judgment: Interaction of judge and informational components. In M. F. Kaplan & S. Schwartz (Eds.), *Human judgment and decision processes.* New York: Academic Press, 1975.

Kaplan, M. F. Group discussion effects in a modified jury decision paradigm: Informational influences. *Journal of Applied Social Psychology,* 1978, in press.

Kaplan, M. F., & Miller, C. E. Juror judgment and discussion: Effect of variety of shared information on amount of polarization. Paper presented at the meeting of the Psychonomic Society, St. Louis, 1976.

Kerr, N. L., Davis, J. H., Meek, D., & Rissman, A. K. Group position as a function of member attitudes: Choice shift effects from the perspective of social decision scheme theory. *Journal of Personality and Social Psychology,* 1975, **31,** 574–593.

Kirkpatrick, S. A. Problems of risk-taking in bureaucracies. Paper presented at the annual meeting of the International Studies Association, Washington, D.C., 1975.

Kirkpatrick, S. A., Bernick, E. L., Thomson, R. J., & Rycroft, R. W. Risks in political decision-making: An experimental analysis of choice shifts. *Experimental Study of Politics*, 1975, **4**, 55–92.

Kirkpatrick, S. A., Davis, D. F., & Robertson, R. D. The process of political decision-making in groups. *American Behavioral Scientist*, 1976, **20**, 33–64.

Kirkpatrick, S. A., & Robertson, R. D. Choice shifts in political decision-making: An experimental test of value theory. Paper presented at the meeting of the Midwest Political Science Association, 1976.

Klapper, J. T. *Bandwagon: A review of the literature*. New York: Office of Social Research, Columbia Broadcasting System, 1964.

Knox, R. E., & Safford, R. K. Group caution at the race track. *Journal of Experimental Social Psychology*, 1976, **12**, 317–324.

Kogan, N., & Wallach, M. A. Risk-taking as a function of the situation, the person, and the group. In T. M. Newcomb (Ed.), *New directions in psychology*. Vol. 3. New York: Holt, 1967.

Krapf, G. Polarization of responses in student evaluation of teachers as a function of group discussion. Unpublished master's thesis, Radford College, 1972.

Lamm, H., & Ochsmann, R. Factors limiting the generality of the risky-shift phenomenon. *European Journal of Social Psychology*, 1972, **2**, 99–102.

Lamm, H., & Sauer, C. Discussion-induced shift toward higher demands in negotiation. *European Journal of Social Psychology*, 1974, **4**, 85–88.

Lamm, H., Schaude, E., & Trommsdorff, G. Risky shift as a function of group members' value of risk and need for approval. *Journal of Personality and Social Psychology*, 1971, **20**, 430–435.

Lamm, H., Trommsdorff, G., & Rost-Schaude, E. Self-image, perception of peers' risk acceptance and risky shift. *European Journal of Social Psychology*, 1972, **2**, 255–272.

Latané, B., & Darley, J. M. *The unresponsive bystander: Why doesn't he help?* New York: Appleton, 1970.

Laughlin, E. R., & Izzett, R. R. Juror-defendant attitude similarity and choice shift in the jury trial. Paper presented at the meeting of the Midwestern Psychological Association, May 1973.

Lemaine, G. Social differentiation and social originality. *European Journal of Social Psychology*, 1974, **4**, 17–52.

Lenihan, K. J. Perceived climates as a barrier to housing desegregation. Unpublished manuscript, Columbia University, Bureau of Applied Social Research, 1965.

Levinger, G., & Schneider, D. J. Test of the "risk is a value" hypothesis. *Journal of Personality and Social Psychology*, 1969, **11**, 165–169.

Lewin, M. A., & Kane, M. Impeachment of Nixon and the risky shift. *International Journal of Group Tensions*, 1975, **5**, 171–176.

Louche, C. Les effets de la catégorisation sociale et de l'interaction collective dans la préparation et le déroulement d'une négociation inter-groupe. *Bulletin de Psychologie*, 1975, **28**, 941–947. (a)

Louche, C. La préparation d'une négociation en groupe et ses effets sur le comportement des négociateurs et leurs représentations. *Bulletin de Psychologie*, 1975, **28**, 113–117. (b)

Madaras, G. R., & Bem, D. J. Risk and conservatism in group decision-making. *Journal of Experimental Social Psychology*, 1968, **4**, 350–365.

Main, E. G., & Walker, T. G. Choice shifts and extreme behavior: Judicial review of the federal courts. *Journal of Social Psychology*, 1973, **91**, 215–222.

Malamuth, N. M. A systematic analysis of the relationship between group shifts and characteristics of the choice dilemmas questionnaire. Unpublished doctoral dissertation, University of California at Los Angeles, 1975.

Malamuth, N. M., & Feshbach, S. Risky shift in a naturalistic setting. *Journal of Personality*, 1972, **40**, 38–49.

Manis, M., Cornell, S. D., & Moore, J. C. Transmission of attitude-relevant information through a communication chain. *Journal of Personality and Social Psychology*, 1974, **30**, 81–94.

Marquis, D. G., & Reitz, H. J. Effect of uncertainty on risk taking in individual and group decisions. *Behavioral Science*, 1969, **14**, 281–288.

Maslow, A. H. *Toward a psychology of being*. New York: Van Nostrand, 1962.

Mathes, E. W., & Kahn, A. Diffusion of responsibility and extreme behavior. *Journal of Personality and Social Psychology*, 1975, **31**, 881–886.

McCauley, C., Stitt, C. L., Woods, K., & Lipton, D. Group shift to caution at the race track. *Journal of Experimental Social Psychology*, 1973, **9**, 80–86.

McGuire, W. J., & Padawer-Singer, A. Trait salience in the spontaneous self-concept. *Journal of Personality and Social Psychology*, 1976, **33**, 743–754.

Minix, D. A. The role of the small group in foreign policy decision making: A potential pathology in crisis decisions? Paper presented to the meeting of the Southern Political Science Association, 1976.

Misavage, R., & Richardson, J. T. The focusing of responsibility: An alternative hypothesis in help-demanding situations. *European Journal of Social Psychology*, 1974, **4**, 5–15.

Moscovici, S., & Lecuyer, R. Studies in group decision I: Social space, patterns of communication and group consensus. *European Journal of Social Psychology*, 1972, **2**, 221–244.

Moscovici, S., & Zavalloni, M. The group as a polarizer of attitudes. *Journal of Personality and Social Psychology*, 1969, **12**, 125–135.

Muehleman, J. T., Bruker, C., & Ingram, C. M. The generosity shift. *Journal of Personality and Social Psychology*, 1976, **34**, 344–351.

Myers, D. G. Discussion-induced attitude polarization. *Human Relations*, 1975, **28**, 699–714.

Myers, D. G. The polarizing effects of social comparison. Unpublished manuscript, Hope College, 1977.

Myers, D. G., & Bach, P. J. Discussion effects on militarism–pacifism: A test of the group polarization hypothesis. *Journal of Personality and Social Psychology*, 1974, **30**, 741–747.

Myers, D. G., & Bach, P. J. Group discussion effects on conflict behavior and self-justification. *Psychological Reports*, 1976, **38**, 135–140.

Myers, D. G., Bach, P. J., & Schreiber, F. B. Normative and informational effects of group interaction. *Sociometry*, 1974, **37**, 275–286.

Myers, D. G., & Bishop, G. D. Discussion effects on racial attitudes. *Science*, 1970, **169**, 778–789.

Myers, D. G., & Bishop, G. D. Enhancement of dominant attitudes in group discussion. *Journal of Personality and Social Psychology*, 1971, **20**, 386-391.

Myers, D. G., & Kaplan, M. F. Group-induced polarization in simulated juries. *Personality and Social Psychology Bulletin*, 1976, **2**, 63–66.

Myers, D. G., & Lamm, H. The group polarization phenomenon. *Psychological Bulletin*, 1976, **83**, 602–627.

Myers, D. G., Schreiber, F. B., & Viel, D. J. Effects of discussion on opinions concerning illegal behavior. *Journal of Social Psychology*, 1974, **92**, 77–84.

Myers, D. G., Wojcicki, S. A., & Aardema. B. Attitude comparison: Is there ever a bandwagon effect? *Journal of Applied Social Psychology*, 1978, in press.

Mynatt, C., & Sherman, S. J. Responsibility attribution in groups and individuals: A direct test of the diffusion of responsibility hypothesis. *Journal of Personality and Social Psychology*, 1975, **32**, 1111–1118.

Nash, M. Unanimity in criminal jury verdicts. *Journal of Forensic Psychology*, 1973, **5**, 5–13.

Niebuhr, R. *Moral man and immoral society*. New York: Scribner's, 1932.

Paicheler, G. Norms and attitude change I: Polarization and styles of behaviour. *European Journal of Social Psychology*, 1976, **6**, 405–427. (a)

Paicheler, G. Norms and attitude change III: Homogeneous and heterogeneous groups. Unpublished manuscript, École Pratique des Hautes Études, 1976. (b)

Paicheler, G. Norms and attitude change II: The phenomenon of bipolarization. *European Journal of Social Psychology*, 1977, **7**, 5–14.

Paicheler, G., & Bouchet, J. Attitude polarization, familiarization, and group process. *European Journal of Social Psychology*, 1973, **3**, 83–90.

Peterson, R. A., & Fulcher, D. G. Risky shift in marketing decision making: A nonconfirmation. *Psychological Reports*, 1971, **29**, 1135–1138.

Pruitt, D. G. Choice shifts in group discussion: An introductory review. *Journal of Personality and Social Psychology*, 1971, **20**, 339–360. (a)

Pruitt, D. G. Conclusions: Toward an understanding of choice shifts in group discussion. *Journal of Personality and Social Psychology*, 1971, **20**, 495–510. (b)

Rabbie, J. M., & Visser, L. Bargaining strength and group polarization in inter-group polarization. *European Journal of Social Psychology*, 1972, **2**, 401–416.

Rabbie, J. M., & Visser, L. Competitive and defensive orientations in interpersonal and intergroup conflict. Unpublished manuscript, University of Utrecht, 1976.

Reingen, P. H. Risk taking by individuals and in informal groups with the use of industrial product purchasing situations as stimuli. *Journal of Psychology*, 1973, **85**, 339–345.

Reingen, P. H. Phenomena of shifts along a risk dimension tested with established groups. *Journal of Social Psychology*, 1974, **94**, 295–296.

Reingen, P. H. Risky shift or confused subjects? Unpublished manuscript, Iona College, 1975.

Reingen, P. H. Effect of group discussion on honesty–dishonesty in business situations: A test of the cultural value hypothesis. Unpublished manuscript, Iona College, 1976.

Rettig, S. Group discussion and predicted ethical risk taking. *Journal of Personality and Social Psychology*, 1966, **3**, 629–633.

Riley, R. T., & Pettigrew, T. F. Dramatic events and attitude change. *Journal of Personality and Social Psychology*, 1976, **34**, 1004–1015.

Rumsey, M. G. Post-discussion penalty shifts and the polarization hypothesis. Unpublished doctoral dissertation, University of Indiana, 1975.

Rumsey, M. G. Effects of defendant background and remorse on sentencing judgments. *Journal of Applied Social Psychology*, 1976, **6**, 64–68.

Rumsey, M. G., & Castore, C. H. The effect of defendant's character and group discussion on individual sentencing judgments. Paper presented at the meeting of the Midwestern Psychological Association, May 1974.

Rumsey, M. G., Laughlin, E. R., & Castore, C. H. Group discussion, sentence judgments and the leniency shift. Unpublished manuscript, Purdue University, 1974.

Sanders, G. S., & Baron, R. S. Is social comparison irrelevant for producing choice shifts? *Journal of Experimental Social Psychology*, 1977, **13**, 303–314.

Schlenker, B. R. Self-presentation: Managing the impression of consistency when reality interferes with self-enhancement. *Journal of Personality and Social Psychology*, 1975, **32**, 1030–1037.

Schmidt, M. [*John Wesley: A theological autobiography*] (N. P. Goldhawk, trans.). Vol. 2. X X: Abdingdon, 1972.

Schroeder, H. E. The risky shift as a general choice shift. *Journal of Personality and Social Psychology*, 1973, **27**, 297–300.

Schulman, J., Shaver, P., Colman, R., Emrich, R., & Christie, R. Recipe for a jury. *Psychology Today*, 1973, **6**(12), 37–44, 77–84.

Semin, G. R., & Glendon, A. I. Polarization and the established group. *British Journal of Social and Clinical Psychology*, 1973, **12**, 113–121.

Semmel, A. K. Group dynamics and the foreign policy process: The choice-shift phenomenon. Paper presented at the meeting of the Southern Political Science Association, 1976.

Sherif, M. *In common predicament: Social psychology of intergroup conflict and cooperation.* Boston: Houghton, 1966.

Shrewsberry, R. D., & Johnson, D. L. A comparison of group and individual responses on an impression formation task. *Paper presented at the meeting of the Southeastern Psychological Association, April 1972.*

Siegel, S., & Zajonc, R. B. Group risk taking in professional decisions. *Sociometry,* 1967, **30,** 339–349.

Silzer, R. F., & Clark, R. D., III. The effects of proportion, strength and value orientation of arguments on decision making. *European Journal of Social Psychology,* 1978, in press.

Spector, P. E., Cohen, S. L., & Penner, L. A. The effects of real vs. hypothetical risk on group choice-shifts. *Personality and Social Psychology Bulletin,* 1976, **2,** 290–293.

Stephenson, G. M., & Brotherton, C. J. Social progression and polarization: A study of discussion and negotiation in groups of mining supervisors. *British Journal of Social and Clinical Psychology,* 1975, **14,** 241–252.

Tesser, A. Toward a theory of self-generated attitude change. Unpublished manuscript, University of Georgia, 1975.

Tesser, A., & Conlee, M. S. Some effects of time and thought on attitude polarization. *Journal of Personality and Social Psychology,* 1975, **31,** 262–270.

Toch, R. *The social psychology of social movements.* Indianapolis: Bobbs-Merrill, 1965.

Trommsdorff, G. Gruppeneinflüsse auf Zukunftsbeurteilungen. Meisenheim/Glan: Hain, 1978, in press.

Verba, S. *Small groups and political behavior.* Princeton, N.J.: Princeton Unversity Press, 1961.

Vidmar, N. Group-induced shifts in simulated jury decisions. Paper presented at the meeting of the Midwestern Psychological Association, May 1972.

Vidmar, N. Effects of group discussion on category width judgments. *Journal of Personality and Social Psychology,* 1974, **29,** 187–195.

Vinokur, A. A review and theoretical analysis of the effects of group processes upon individual and group decisions involving risk. *Psychological Bulletin,* 1971, **76,** 231–250.

Vinokur, A., & Burnstein, E. The effects of partially shared persuasive arguments on group induced shifts: A group problem solving approach. *Journal of Personality and Social Psychology,* 1974, **29,** 305–315.

Vinokur, A., & Burnstein, E. Novel argumentation and attitude change: The case of polarization following discussion. *European Journal of Social Psychology,* 1978, in press.

Wahram, R. Status, deviance, sanctions, and group discussion. *Small Group Behavior,* 1977, **8,** 147–168.

Walker, T. G., & Main, E. C. Choice-shifts in political decision making: Federal judges and civil liberties cases. *Journal of Applied Social Psychology,* 1973, **2,** 39–48.

Wheeler, L. Motivation as a determinant of upward comparison. *Journal of Experimental Social Psychology,* 1966, Suppl. 1, 27–31. (a)

Wheeler, L. Toward a theory of behavioral contagion. *Psychological Review,* 1966, **73,** 179–192. (b)

Wilson, R. C., Gabb, J. G., Dienst, E. R., Wood, L., & Bavry, J. L. *College professors and their impact on students.* New York: Wiley, 1975.

Wolosin, R. J., Sherman, S. J., & Mynatt, C. R. When self-interest and altruism conflict. *Journal of Personality and Social Psychology,* 1975, **32,** 752–760.

Woodside, A. G. Informal group influence on risk taking. *Journal of Marketing Research,* 1972, **9,** 223–225.

Woodside, A. G. Is there a generalized risky shift phenomenon in consumer behavior? *Journal of Marketing Research,* 1974, **17,** 225–226.

Woodside, A. G., & DeLozier, M. W. Effects of word of mouth advertising on consumer risk taking. Unpublished manuscript, University of South Carolina, 1975.

Yinon, Y., Jaffe, Y., & Feshbach, S. Risky aggression in individuals and groups. *Journal of Personality and Social Psychology*, 1975, **31**, 808–815.

Yinon, Y., Shoham, I., & Lewis, T. Risky-shift in a real vs. role-played situation. *Journal of Social Psychology*, 1974, **93**, 137–138.

Zaleska, M. The effects of discussion on group and individual choices among bets. *European Journal of Social Psychology*, 1974, **4**, 229–250.

Zimbardo, P. G. Transforming experimental research into advocacy for social change. In M. Deutsch & H. A. Hornstein (Eds.), *Applying social psychology: Implications for research, practice, and training*. Hillsdale, N.J.: Lawrence Erlbaum Associates, 1975.

ADVANCES IN EXPERIMENTAL SOCIAL PSYCHOLOGY, VOL. 11

CROWDING: DETERMINANTS AND EFFECTS[1]

Janet E. Stockdale

LONDON SCHOOL OF ECONOMICS AND POLITICAL
SCIENCE
LONDON, ENGLAND

[1]Preparation of this paper was facilitated by a Social Science Research Council Grant. I wish to express my thanks to Peter Gresham, Peter Kelvin, John Schopler, and to my colleagues Beryl Geber and Philip Sealy for their invaluable comments during the preparation of this paper.

I. Concept of Crowding

A. BASIC PROBLEMS

Does crowding have behavioral and physiological consequences inimical to the social and physical well-being of the individual and society? Answers to this question have been sought in various settings using diverse research techniques. The question takes too much for granted. Is there a consensual definition of crowding? Is there a monotonic relation between the level of crowding and negative behavioral effects?

A popular belief is that crowding is synonymous with density. Also the concept of density has been grasped with enthusiasm by demographers, urban planners, politicians, sociologists, and social psychologists grateful for the quantitative power it offers in the analysis of a variety of spatially determined behaviors and their theoretical and practical implications. Density offers an apparently highly valid operationalization of crowding, but extensive work has demonstrated the inadequacy of density as a precondition for negative behavioral and affective changes in humans. Although research with animals in both laboratory and natural settings implicated population density as the prime determinant of certain pathological behaviors (e.g., Calhoun, 1962a, 1962b; Marsden, 1972; Southwick, 1967), comparable effects do not emerge generally either in experimental studies of human behavior (e.g., Freedman, Klevansky, & Ehrlich, 1971; Ross, Layton, Erickson, & Schopler, 1973) or demographic studies of the relations between indices of population density and social pathology (e.g., Freedman, Heshka, & Levy, 1975). The failure to confirm the density model has necessitated a reappraisal of the concept of ''crowding'' and its defining conditions.

Density is emotionally neutral, while ''crowding'' usually has a strong negative affective connotation. If crowding is defined solely in terms of population density this leads to a paradoxical situation. A state that is implicitly negative generates no negative effects. One way out of this paradox is to retain the density definition of crowding but to reject the negative behavioral connotation and to argue that crowding does not have detrimental effects on the social and physical well-being of humans and their task performance (Freedman, 1975).

An alternative approach is to search for a more adequate conceptualization of crowding. For the concept of ''crowding'' to be scientifically valuable, it must be defined in a way which is precise enough to make it a useful variable within theory and research yet also makes sense in terms of the connotations of ''crowding'' as used in everyday language—connotations which reflect justifiable public concern rather than scientific curiosity. As soon as one invokes variables other than density to define crowding as an independent or predictor variable, it becomes necessary to reject the view that a dense world is a crowded world, both in an objective sense and in the subjective view of a participant.

One must distinguish crowding—a perceived and subjective state—from conditions which normally give rise to that state (see Stokols, 1972a; Rapoport, 1975). Psychologically, crowding must be *perceived crowding*—an experience of individuals—just as freedom is always perceived freedom. Recognition that crowding is in the eye of the beholder means that crowding cannot be objectively measured in terms of density. This has important implications.

Analyses of crowding must proceed in two stages. First there is the development of an adequate concept of crowding (this demands identification of both the essential stimulus components and the psychological processes which are initiated by such stimuli and which engender subjective crowding); second the examination of the effects which are a consequence of crowding (whether the subjective state of crowding is detrimental to the well-being of the individual or group must be determined empirically).

I shall begin by examining the deficiencies of the density model by reference to animal studies and field and laboratory studies of humans. I shall then outline the major developments in analyses of crowding before presenting a conceptual framework in which crowding is defined as a subjective state with multiple predeterminants and potential effects. This I shall use to evaluate crowding research and to determine what progress has been made toward an adequate conceptualization of crowding and an understanding of its effects. However, this review makes no attempt to be exhaustive. The density of the research findings is likely to produce feelings of crowding in the reader.

B. DENSITY MODEL

1. Animal Studies

Early studies of crowding reflect the simplistic approach to crowding. Implicit in this approach is the assumption that manipulation of density is the one precondition for crowding. High density is seen not only as the nominal stimulus but also the functional stimulus for crowding. However, this failure to distinguish "density" from the psychological stimulus conditions active in the production of "crowding" has led to conceptual and methodological abiguity. It has stultified the development of research into the determinants and effects of crowding.

The conceptualization of crowding in terms of high population density derives initially from studies of animal populations in laboratory and natural settings. It is tempting to draw a general conclusion from animal studies that high population density, and therefore crowding, produces detrimental behavioral and physiological changes. When conditions deny the opportunity for emigration, the normal response to increased population density (Calhoun, 1963a), then high density typically will be associated with changes in behavior, patterns of reproduction, and mortality. Calhoun (1962a, 1962b) observed that when colonies of Norway rats were allowed to breed naturally with adequate food and water in a fixed physical space, there was severe disruption of sexual and maternal behavior, and of eating and social behavior. Changes in sexual behavior and inadequate maternal care led to a breakdown in the reproductive cycle, a decrease in frequency of successful pregnancy, and an increase in infant mortality. This resulted in a slowing of population growth, and population density asymptoted and sometimes declined. Asymptotic density is typically far below that which experimenters calculate is maximal for the space supplied, though above the optimum. Calhoun's studies acted as the model for many subsequent laboratory studies of animal populations. Changes in population growth and behavioral concomitants have been confirmed by Marsden (1972), Southwick (1955, 1967), and Snyder (1968) in laboratory settings and in natural settings by Deevey (1960) and Christian (e.g., Christian, Flyger, & Davis, 1960).

However, there are many variables that contribute to the effects observed among animals under high density conditions and it is difficult to attribute these effects solely to density. Laboratory populations offer the advantage of ease of manipulation and measurement of density, but high densities in the laboratory would never be duplicated in the wild since confinement eliminates movement which could ameliorate population pressure. Furthermore in most animal studies an increase in density is achieved through an increase in population. Availability of space is confounded with the number of animals with whom a given animal is in perceptual or social contact, and attributions of crowding to density alone are of dubious validity.

A feature of Calhoun's initial experiments, in which the most severe instances of behavioral pathology and their consequences were observed, was the emergence of "a behavioral sink," typified by pathological togetherness, but this should not be adopted as characteristic of high density. This phenomenon appears to be primarily dependent on feeding arrangements and linear arrangement of interconnecting pens, which encourage animals to congregate for feeding. Using octagonal enclosures subdivided into central and peripheral sections, Kessler (1966) was successful in breeding a physically healthy population of mice to "standing room only" conditions.

The importance of other variables is illustrated by reference to observations of aggressive behavior. Changes in the level and type of aggression appear to be related to the ability of animals to maintain normal dispersion patterns and social structure when confined at densities far exceeding those in the wild (cf. Calhoun, 1952, 1963b). Different species and strains exhibit different patterns of aggressive behavior dependent upon their environmental conditions. When artificially grouped, their responses may depend on whether the species is solitary, semisolitary, or communal (Eisenberg, 1967).

Many of the animal studies identify patterns of deviant behavior within a population and demonstrate that population pressures affect certain individuals more than others with the receipt and production of aggression often reflecting the group's hierarchy (cf. Crew & Mirskaia, 1931; Calhoun, 1962a, 1963a; Clarke, 1955; Marsden, 1972).

These behavioral studies indicate that across a spectrum of species, effects are associated with increases in either population density or population size. However, these effects are strongly influenced by environment, including behavioral setting, and by both subgroup differences and individual characteristics, such as genetic endowment, age, sex, prior experiences, and the social organization of the population. As Freedman (1973) points out, perhaps all we are left with is the conclusion that in enclosed colonies very large populations lead to social and eventually physical anomalies.

The difficulty of demonstrating unequivocal influence of high density is accentuated by the existence of complex interrelations between behavioral and physiological variables (cf. Brain, 1972; Christian, 1959, 1963; Christian & Davis, 1964; Christian, Lloyd, & Davis, 1965; Thiessen & Rodgers, 1961). Most workers in this area see physiological changes and atypical behavior patterns as directly attributable to high population density (thus environmental stress), which places abnormal limitations on activities such as food allocation and sex. The social stress theory originally saw exhaustion of the adrenopituitary system as a prime determinant of population decline (Christian, 1950), but Christian et al. (1965) emphasize that social pressure arising from high density influences both behavior and endocrine function and that behavioral changes are major determinants of reduced population growth. Many elements of the social stress theory are incorporated in the theory proposed by Wynne-Edwards (1962, 1965) who argued that a variety of behavioral conventions such as dominance, subordination, hierarchies, and territoriality evolve and act to regulate population. Such conventions convey information about population size.

Calhoun (1962b) suggests that behavioral breakdown under conditions of high density appears to be due to "social pressure generated by population." This could be interpreted in terms of an excessive level of stimulus input or behavioral interference. These stimulus conditions, although often correlated with population density, are dependent on other factors such as physical surroundings, availability of resources, individual and group characteristics, social structure and, in particular, group size. Evidence points toward group size (and consequent social interaction level) as more salient than available space. An increase in group size alone or in combination with spatial limitation may entail changes in spatially related processes such as territoriality and social spacing. These contribute more to an understanding of stimuli that engender crowding and its effects than density (cf. Goeckner, Greenough, & Mead, 1973; Snyder, 1968; Vine, 1973).

The dangers inherent in generalizing from research on nonhumans to humans are obvious (Lloyd, 1975). It is naive to expect manipulations of density, a badly defined variable with numerous complex interrelations, to have equivalent effects in man and other species. Within limits man is adaptable (Dubos, 1970) and his genetic programming and learning capacity mean he is unlikely to display stereotyped responses to stressors; the flexibility of individual and interpersonal behavior provides mechanisms for mitigating the impact of these stimuli. Such considerations introduce limitations in the use of animal studies to suggest probable consequences of crowding among humans, but these studies focus attention on the methodological problems which must be overcome in studies of human crowding.

2. Urban and Housing Density

Indices of population density—the ratio of some defined quantity of space to the number of units occupying it—apparently offer insight into crowdedness. Biderman, Louria, and Bacchus (1963) report the amount of space available in a variety of settings. These vary from reported incidents in the slave trade (1.1 square feet), through a World War II basement shelter in London (4.0 square feet), to the minimum prison cell recommended by the American Prison Association (38.5 square feet). Although population density appears to be a precisely defined variable, different indices reflect different aspects of an individual's environment (cf. Carey, 1972; Day & Day, 1973; Webb, 1975). A major distinction has been made between areal density (e.g., people per square kilometer) and dwelling density, i.e., number of individuals per living space within dwellings, but other indices include number of people per room, number of families per dwelling, number of apartments per building, and number of living units per neighborhood (cf. Booth, 1975; Galle, Gove, & McPherson, 1972; Webb, 1975).

Early demographic studies generally agreed in showing a relation between a gross measure of density and various indices of social, physical, and mental breakdown but they took little account of potentially important variables such as economic and educational levels and ethnic characteristics which tend to be highly correlated with population density (cf. Green, 1939; Landis & Page, 1938; Pollock & Furbush, 1921; Shaw & McKay, 1942; Schmid, 1955; Schmitt, 1957). Although the majority of later studies have employed multivariate procedures (e.g., Schmitt, 1966; Winsborough, 1965), some basic difficulties remain in the use of partial correlation and multiple regression techniques and their interpretation (cf. Freedman et al., 1971; Levy & Herzog, 1974; Roncek, 1975). In his detailed methodological critique of the evidence relating density and crime, Roncek argues that a primary defect of many studies is excessive aggregation of data which creates problems in approximating to individual relationships between density and pathology, utilizing ecological correlations derived from such data. As the degree of aggregation increases, the magnitude of the correlations increases and the poorer they are as indicators of relationships existing at the level of the individual (Booth, Welch, & Johnson, 1976). Furthermore, unknown variables may contribute to the observed relations, and although some models permit tentative statements about direction of causation, the correlational approach precludes an unambiguous inference. With more sophisticated methodological and statistical controls, the typical finding is that density has little or no independent effect on the incidence of social pathology (cf. Baldassare, 1975; Gillis, 1974; Pressman & Carol, 1971). One study which demonstrated a relation between measures of density and social pathology was that carried out by Galle *et al.* (1972). The major data analysis consisted of correlating four measures of density (reflecting both "structural" factors and "interpersonal press"), one index of social class and one of ethnicity with five measures of social pathology. Density was related to each of the pathologies, and in each case a significant relation between the components of density and the pathologies remained when class and ethnicity were used as controls.

Further analysis supported the view that rather than a spurious relation existing between density and pathology, density acts as a mediating variable, partially interpreting the way social structure variables related to the pathologies. The techniques used by Galle *et al.* have not been accepted without qualification (e.g., Freedman *et al.*, 1975; Roncek, 1975), and their conclusions have been closely reexamined by McPherson (1975) using additional data on the same population. Using an alternative model, permitting the estimation of both simultaneous and lag effects over a period of 10 years, McPherson showed that when controls are introduced for the stability and the previous effects of the independent variables, density appeared to have a negligible effect on pathology. Thus the assumptions about causal lags in the cross-sectional model (Galle) and the panel model (McPherson) lead to opposite conclusions. The difficulty of knowing whether the assumptions of either of the two models are met precludes a definitive conclusion. McPherson, however, suggests that the effect of density *as measured* is probably minimal. He suggests that the combination of finer grained measurements, shorter lagged observational periods, multiple waves of measurements, and direct measures of potentially contributing variables would reveal a small but quantifiable overcrowding effect.

One potential determinant of social pathology in urban areas is living alone (cf. Galle *et al.*, 1972; McCarthy, Galle & Zimmern, 1975). This factor is highlighted in Webb and Collette's (1975) study of the relation between sociospatial characteristics of urban household environments and prescription rates for stress-alleviative drugs. In-dwelling density was found to be highly but negatively related to the prescription of such drugs, single-person households accounting for a substantial proportion of such prescriptions. Notwithstanding the difficulties associated with the stress measure, it could be argued that high in-dwelling density can operate to minimize the impact of potential environmental stressors. Levy and Herzog (1974) argue that "persons per room" reflects not only the negative irritant quality of the presence of others but also the benefits of family membership which may provide protection against stress. This suggests that isolation, rather than overcrowding, may be a more serious problem for modern urban society.

Despite the demographic evidence, the extensive belief in the deleterious effects of overcrowding has become almost a medical axiom. This belief derives partly from studies of housing conditions, in which overcrowding of interior space is usually seen as "bad" housing. Quasi-experimental studies should in principle provide an opportunity for exploring the potential causal relationships among variables examined using the correlational approach. While such studies offer the advantage of natural settings and the opportunity for detailed observation and measurement, they do not have the substantial number of subjects used in demographic studies. Housing and demographic studies encounter similar problems of control but housing studies, which compare two groups of occupants in different housing, contain the problem of nonrandom allocation of subjects.

One French study argued that habitable space per person in a dwelling unit had an important effect on tension among the occupants (Chombart de Lauwe & Chombart de Lauwe, 1959). The majority of studies, however, show high dwelling densities to have a negligible effect on emotional or physical health of adults (cf. Booth & Cowell, 1977; Mitchell, 1971). Housing design emerges as a more important correlate of pathological behaviors. Many occupants of high-rise apartments, rather than experiencing spatial constraint or too much interpersonal interaction, suffer from insufficient social contact (e.g., Fanning, 1967; Hird, 1967).

Types of housing must reflect the needs and values of people. A review of the social effects of "living off the ground" carried out by the Department of the Environment (1975) confirms that high-rise living poses a variety of problems to residents. Different people are affected in different ways. The failure of tall buildings (up to 20% of high-rise occupants are dissatisfied) is determined by the type of household. The most important determinants of peoples' reactions to their surroundings are the attributes and consequent needs of individuals or family units. Although high-rise dwellings are clearly unsuitable for families with small children, they can be popular with single people, adult households, and some of the elderly. As became clear in the animal studies, it is imperative to regard personal and group characteristics as major predeterminants of the individual's reactions to his environment. It is also important to recognize the contributions of culturally determined norms and expectations to crowding and their effects, especially in housing (cf. Draper, 1973; Munroe & Munroe, 1972). Future studies must also make a distinction between ethnicity and culture in assessing the role of the immediate environment in determining the level of crowding and crowding stress (Schmidt, Goldman, & Feimer, 1976). If subcultural groups perceive and use environmental information differently in the formulation of beliefs about crowding, then design efforts aimed at providing greater predictability, control, and behavioral freedom may not be universally appropriate.

Cassell (1971) argues that the notion that crowding exerts its deleterious effects solely through interpersonal spread of disease agents is no longer adequate to explain known phenomena. Rather, increased population density increases the importance of the social environment as a determinant of physiological response to stimuli, including potential disease. The impact of changes in the social environment will be mediated by the quality of the social interaction, the position of the individual within the group, and the adaptability of the group, with newcomers being at highest risk. This argument leads to the prediction that children should be more vulnerable to the effects of crowding than adults. Booth and Johnson (1975) examined the relation between measures of household and neighborhood crowding and child health and school performance, using a stratified multistage probability sample of Toronto families and controlling for contributing variables, such as socioeconomic status, ethnicity, etc. Crowded household conditions had little adverse effect on the physical and intellectual development of children. Parental health and socioeconomic status were more powerful predictors. Children living in congested households are slightly behind their age peers in school performance, are more frequently the object of school authority–parent contacts, and are shorter, weigh less, and are sicker than their uncrowded counterparts. Booth and Johnson suggest that the more limited control which the child can exert over his environment offers little opportunity to reduce the impact of crowded conditions.

The effects of crowding on overt aggression and insecurity among a group of Scottish children were studied by Murray (1974a, 1974b). Groups of children were selected on the basis of their scores on different indices of crowding. These indices reflected the number of persons per room, family size, house size, and density of family interaction. Murray emphasizes that although one must be cautious when arguing from indirect measures, the findings indicate that crowded children tend to be more aggressive, impulsive, and extroverted and, while boys tend to be more neurotic, girls tend to be less neurotic. Murray suggests that crowded households are typified by a high frequency of interpersonal encounters (Murray, 1973). Members of a crowded family experience a greater degree of mutual interference and inhibition and of agonistic encounters.

3. Small Group Laboratory Studies

In common with the majority of demographic and housing studies, early laboratory experiments fail to demonstrate any detrimental effect of density, either on task performance (Freedman et al., 1971) or on other affective reactions

(Ross *et al.*, 1973; Stokols, Rau, Pinner, & Schopler, 1973), although in many studies density interacted with the sex of the subject. Despite the implication that an accurate conceptualization of crowding and its effects will depend on factors other than spatial parameters, Freedman (1975) continues to define crowding in terms of objective density. While not quarreling with Freedman's conclusion that population density is not a primary determinant of individual and social pathology, the equation of crowding with physical density means that a substantial number of theoretical analyses and their implications are ignored. This is detrimental to an understanding of crowding and its effects.

Freedman's theoretical viewpoint is that density *does* affect human beings but that it serves to intensify an individual's typical reaction to the situation, so that the effect of density will depend upon whether the situation is initially pleasant or aversive. This view of density as a catalytic agent is attractive but it makes a number of questionable assumptions. For example, the theory appears to assume that individuals do have "typical" affective and behavioral reactions to situations. It also assumes that it is possible to identify these reactions as "good" or "bad" in a low-density situation to predict the intensification effect which should emerge under high density. Freedman does not appear to have considered either the problems of categorizing the initial reactions or the precise interaction effect that would be predicted.

These difficulties are evident if one attempts to apply the density-intensification interpretation to some of Freedman's earlier results. Freedman, Katz, and Kinder (cf. Freedman, Levy, Buchanan, & Price, 1972) examined the effect of room size on the number of competitive choices made by males and females in a variant of the "prisoner's dilemma" and showed a significant room size by sex interaction. While the percentage of competitive choices made by males was higher in the small (55.8%) than in the large (37.3%) room, the percentage of such choices made by females was higher in the large room (55.7%–45.7%). If one considers the reactions in the large room to represent "typical" reactions, then the scores suggest that males should be regarded as less competitive than females. According to Freedman's theory, an increase in density serves to intensify the "typical" reaction and so males should become less competitive and females more competitive with an increase in density. The data presented by Freedman demonstrate the opposite relationship. Clearly there are difficulties in defining the criteria for identifying the "typical" reaction but notwithstanding these difficulties, examination of Freedman's data suggests that he is willing to accept any interaction effect to support his hypothesis, even when the interaction appears to indicate a density-reduction rather than a density-intensification effect.

An important feature of those experiments which fail to show effects of spatial density on performance is that subjects were not permitted to move about in the physical space so the potential impact of reduced space was unlikely to be realized. Also, many of the tasks used did not demand any social interaction or create intragroup competition or the necessity for cooperation. So room size was irrelevant to the completion of the task. The free play situation used by Loo (1972) did permit the increased social pressures of encroaching stimulation and behavioral interference inherent in a high-density situation to act on the participants. The amount of space for free play was found to have a significant influence on a child's behavior and on the quality of his social relationships with others around him.

Another problem associated with manipulation of density is the recurrent confounding of density with numerosity. For example if the group size is held constant while the amount of space is varied, then this constitutes a change in *spatial* density. However, if the space is held constant and the group size is increased, then this reflects a change in *social* density (Loo, 1973; P. L. McGrew, 1970; W. C. McGrew, 1972). While the average amount of space per individual is comparable, the manipulations have different implications. Increases in group size mean increases in the number of others with whom an individual can or must interact. Thus may result in a decrease in the average amount of participation and personal satisfaction (see Kelley & Thibaut, 1969; Thomas & Fink, 1963). Increases in numbers also entail increases in perceptual and cognitive stimulation which may create problems of sensory overload. Furthermore, increase in group size, where other resources are held constant, will reduce not only space but other resources. This may result in increased competition with its attendant consequences such as decreased quality of interaction. Also the use of population densities only reflects the degree of physical proximity between individuals if they are evenly distributed over the available space; if not, a global measure of population density offers little insight into the individual's interaction distance.

4. Conclusions

Studies of population density undermine the density model of crowding. Consequently, there has been a reappraisal of the view that they are synonymous. This led to the view that while density is an objective measure of the presence of people relative to space available, crowding is a negative subjective experience determined by multiple factors. The essential problem, therefore, is the extent to which any measure of density can be regarded as a valid measure of crowding. The growing use of density measures which focus on interpersonal press such as persons per room emphasizes social determinants of crowding. However, if crowding is seen as a subjective state, can density ever reflect those aspects of the situation which induce crowding? It can be argued that density, however, measured, is still only an index of physical relationship. It offers no insight into the actual human experience of density, namely the rate, nature, and significance of the contact among individuals and the needs that are created, met, and frustrated (Day & Day, 1973).

An additional disadvantage of population density is that little is known about the meaning of different levels of density. The individual's reaction to a given level of population density will depend on individual and group charac- teristics. For example, the outcome may be different according to the age and sex of participants, the purpose of the interaction, and the degree of choice over being in that setting. Individual and group reactions will be further modified by economic factors which, *inter alia*, create the possibility of compensating for many potentially bad effects. For example, adequate economic resources may facilitate access to more or better space. Cultural factors also strongly influence attitudes toward physical proximity, use of space, and need for privacy.

The failure to find general rules for the effects of density in demographic and survey studies suggests that, rather than the number of people, the focus should be the number of social or cultural roles simultaneously enacted in a given physical space, namely activity overcrowding or "role overdensity." This view places great emphasis on the separation in time and space of members' activities as a way of minimizing the impact of a dwelling on the well-being of its resi- dents. Chapin (1961) proposes a "use-crowding" index which describes the situation in which a room designated for one function (e.g., living room) is also used for a different function (e.g., bedroom). While a numerical space measure assumes all families carry on more or less the same activities in the same ways, this index attempts to take account of both space and family needs simultane- ously.

Similar arguments may be applied to the laboratory studies of density. Density does indeed contribute to feelings of crowding and may influence levels of arousal (Aiello, Epstein, & Karlin, 1975), but these are not translated into behavior (cf. Freedman *et al.*, 1971). Again the use of typical indices of density contains flaws, including the failure to distinguish densities created by large groups from densities created by small interpersonal distances (Loo, 1973; Rapoport, 1975). Clearly each of these manipulations create different interper- sonal consequences. A manipulation in room size, holding group membership constant, results in a smaller average interpersonal distance and a necessity to solve coordination problems. In contrast a manipulation in group size in a fixed space, as well as creating smaller interpersonal distances, imposes additional sources of strain. Typically coordination problems are exacerbated, and there is increased scarcity of environmental resources which creates interference with individual and group goal attainment. This example illustrates the basic concep- tual difficulty inherent in the use of a density manipulation as an operationaliza- tion of crowding. It cannot be assumed that a situation characterized by high-population density necessarily contains those stimuli which engender crowding stress.

II. Analyses of Crowding

The identity of the stimuli which induce crowding vary widely according to the particular theoretical approach adopted. The two dominant theoretical viewpoints focus on the two man–environment interfaces: input and output. Input theories focus on the amount and rate of stimulation received by an individual and argue that stimulus overload is the prepotent determinant of crowding. In contrast, output theories focus on the set of behaviors available to an individual, as compared with those preferred by and demanded of him, and argue that perceived behavioral restriction or interference is the functional stimulus in the induction of crowding.

Input theories are a logical development from the antidensity view of urban life (G. Simmel, 1950; Wirth, 1938) which argues that urban residents by virtue of the size, density, and complexity of their physical and social environment experience excess stimulation. Many of us who live and work in cities may be aware of individual coping strategies designed to minimize the impact of congested transportation systems, noise, and unwanted social interaction (Milgram, 1970). The concept of overload has not been restricted to consideration of the problems of urban life; within the overload framework, the crucial stimuli for crowding have been variously defined as "unfamiliar or inappropriate social contacts" (Esser, 1972), "excessive stimulation from social sources" (Desor, 1972), "unwanted social interaction" (Baum & Valins, 1973), and "visual overexposure to others" (Kutner, 1973).

Output theories also see incongruity as basic to the induction of crowding, but they focus on the mismatch between behavioral needs and expectations and the behavioral options viable in the given spatial and social environment. The early definition of crowding in terms of population density contains an implicit output model, in that high population density is seen as leading to crowding through interference with the normal patterns of individual behavior and social interaction. This relationship was masked by the failure to draw a clear distinction between the parameters describing the physical environment and the functional stimuli, which define the individual's phenomenological environment and lead him to attribute his feelings of stress to crowding.

A prime example of the output approach to crowding is that of Proshansky, Ittleson, and Rivlin (1970) who see the essential characteristics of crowding as the restriction in the range of behavioral choices caused by the presence of others. They argue that the experience of crowding is only indirectly related to mere numbers or densities; the significant element is the lack of freedom of choice or action. Somewhat similar analyses are offered by Zlutnick and Altman (1972) who argue that crowding is a phenomenon of perceived interpersonal constraint, and by Esser (1972) who suggests that crowding may be the subjective experience of not being able to "have one's own way." The relation between the potential or actual behavioral interference generated by others and crowding stress has remained pivotal in more recent output analyses of crowding (cf. Schopler & Stockdale, 1977; Stokols, 1972b, 1976; Sundstrom, 1975b) which have focused on the environmental, personal, social, and cultural factors that will determine the extent of the behavioral interference and may modify its effects.

Crowding is defined by Stokols (1972b) as a subjective state in which one's demand for space exceeds the available supply. This experience arises from an interaction of physical, social, and personal variables which combine to sensitize the individual to the actual or potential constraints of limited space. Thus, crowding will be experienced only if the restrictive aspects of spatial limitation are perceived as salient and aversive. For example, spatial constraints may not be salient to the members of a group performing independent activities, but may have considerable impact on group members experiencing task coordination problems, or competitiveness, or antipathy within the group. The final stage in this sequential model of crowding (Sundstrom, 1975b) is the use of behavioral, cognitive, and perceptual strategies designed to reduce the level of crowding stress.

Stokols' (1976) formulation also assumes that feelings of crowding necessarily involve an increased salience of spatial concerns, but emphasizes that environmental control, through an augmentation of space, is critical in the reduction of actual or anticipated interference. In some cases the consequences of perceived lack of environmental control will be minimal but, if they are serious, the individual's physical or psychological security will seem as under more severe threat, and this increases the intensity and duration of crowding. Stokols (1976) makes a distinction between neutral crowding, in which violation of spatial expectations relates primarily to the physical dimensions of the environment, and personal crowding, in which the expectations concern not only the physical environment but also social factors which accentuate these restrictions and pose additional threats. This distinction is similar to that made by Stokols (1972b) between nonsocial crowding, where a person's supply of useable space is restricted at what he perceives to be an inadequate level by purely physical factors, and social crowding, in which the individual's awareness of spatial restriction is related directly to the presence of other persons, as well as to his relationship to them. Stokols also suggests that an individual's expectations for control over the environment vary according to whether the environment constitutes a primary or secondary setting for the individual. Primary settings are considered to be those in which an individual spends much of his time, relates to others on a personal basis, and engages in a wide range of personally important activities, whereas secondary settings are those in which one's encounters with others are relatively transitory, anonymous, and inconsequential. Stokols argues social interference will be potentially more disruptive and frustrating in primary settings, and consequently experiences of crowding will tend to be more intense and persistent in primary than in secondary settings.

Sundstrom (1975a, 1975b) sees crowding as an interpersonal process based on a sequence of events in which high-population density may facilitate aversive interpersonal events such as unwanted social inputs or intrusion and interruption of activities or interference, which may lead to stress, coping behaviors, and possible long-term consequences. For example, under high density, individuals may give inappropriate indicators of intimacy and the presence of others may be distracting or obstruct ongoing activities, especially if the activity involves movement from place to place or creates interference through competition for scarce resources.

Schopler and Stockdale's (1977) approach to crowding in terms of output interference explores the classes of variables capable of mediating the consequences of being in a crowded setting. Although some aspect of population density is typically connected with the experience of being crowded, it is not an accurate predictor of the amount of stress experienced in a setting. Schopler and Stockdale contend that the central source of stress for individuals in dense settings is the perception that their own goal attainment will (or could) be interfered with by the presence of others because it raises the costs of enacting behaviors. The magnitude of the interference is a function of the centrality of the vulnerable response sequences and the expected duration of the interference. In an attempt to reduce interference, individuals may rely on personal coping responses such as perceptual–cognitive filtering reactions (Milgram, 1970) or distancing others (Nesbitt & Steven, 1974), or initiate intragroup coordination to increase the predictability and synchronization of participants' responses.

According to this analysis the amount of interference experienced in a setting is the critical determinant of the degree of crowding stress, and the success of coping with interference problems is the mediator between stress and behavioral consequences. In contrast, both density and interference are assumed to contribute to the subjective experience of crowding. (Although in the majority of circumstances interference and density will be highly correlated, there are instances in low-density settings where interference from others can be the sole determinant of crowding and crowding stress.) The contribution made by interference to subjective crowding is determined by factors which accentuate the perceived difficulty of predicting and coordinating the behaviors of others. These will include the spatial arrangements in the setting, group size, the availability of resources, individual characteristics, the structure of the social relationships among participants in the setting, and the demands of the task to be performed. Tasks requiring complex behavioral responses or coordinated multistage solutions should induce more interference from others than simple, single-stage tasks. There are a number of studies within both the input and output frameworks which show the interaction of such variables in determining perceived crowding. Whether one focuses on the input or output stage of the interaction between man and his environment, it is clear that crowding is not context free but has multiple determining factors. The criterion for overload will depend on a host of factors; the experience of behavior interference is equally complex in its determinants.

III. Integrated Framework for Crowding Research

The current analysis of the etiology of crowding and its effects aims to provide a framework within which to examine theoretical and empirical approaches to crowding. Its major virtue resides in its taxonomic properties, which are invaluable in disentangling the data pertaining to crowding. Some of the conceptual distinctions and relational properties of the analysis are contained, explicitly or implicitly, in other models. The analysis also draws upon the ideas of Levi and Andersson (1975) concerning the relations between population, environment, and the quality of life.

Central to the analysis is the view that stress is generated by perceived lack of environmental control, where the environment is construed in terms of both stimulus input and behavioral output. The concept of perceived control is inherent in both input and output approaches to crowding. Input models imply that the individual has lost control over incoming stimuli and focus on the compensatory coping behaviors which may be viewed as attempts to regain control over environmental input. Similarly, the perceived constraints on behavioral freedom, emphasized by output theories of crowding, mean that the individual experiencing restriction is no longer in a position to exercise full control over his physical and social environment.

Within the present model, loss of control is seen as arising from two sources a discrepancy between preferred behavioral choices and those which are feasible in the particular behavior setting, and a discrepancy between optimal and actual informational input from physical and social sources. Both sources depend on the interactions of the individual with at least one other, or the output of others, even if they are not physically present. The idea that perceived cognitive control is critical determinant of the magnitude of stress responses is in line with a number of conceptions of the importance of individual environmental control (cf. Lazarus, 1966; Lefcourt, 1973; Mandler, 1964; Mandler & Watson, 1966; White, 1959). In the context of crowding there is evidence (Sherrod, 1974) that the provision of some means of perceived control ameliorates the postexposure deleterious effect of density on a measure of frustration tolerance. Furthermore, Rodin (1976) demonstrated that the opportunity to exercise choice and control is utilized differently by children from high- and low-density backgrounds, with children from larger households (i.e., high density) controlling the administration of available outcomes significantly less often than children from smaller households. Chronic high density fosters conditions in which both negative and positive events may be unpredictable and/or uncontrollable. Rodin argues that one of the consequences of such conditions may be a real or perceived inability to control the environment and regulate one's interactions. Individuals may learn that outcomes are not contingent on their responses and may no longer perform adaptively when such contingencies exist. This phenomenon of "learned helplessness" may entail cognitive and motivational deficits (Glass & Singer, 1972) and expectancies for lack of control and subsequent inertia (Wortman & Brehm, 1975).

The concept of control is also important in many analyses of privacy. Altman (1975) defines privacy as "selective control of access to oneself or to one's group." Altman makes privacy a key explanatory concept in his analysis of the etiology of crowding. He argues that it is only through inadequate control of social interactions, such that more than the desired density of interactions occur, that the subjective state of crowding arises. Altman emphasizes the "personal autonomy" function of privacy which is the theme of several other conceptualizations of privacy. He views privacy as essential for achieving self-identity—knowing where the self begins and ends, its capabilities and limitations (cf. Jourard, 1966; Schwartz, 1968). Privacy also serves to regulate relationships between persons or groups and the social world and serves a self-evaluation role providing an opportunity for social comparison. The interactional control facet of privacy implies control not only over the bidirectional information flow between oneself and others (cf. Jourard, 1966; N. J. Marshall, 1971; Weinstein, 1971; Westin, 1967) but also control over one's behavioral options (cf. A. Simmel, 1971; Van den Haag, 1971). This aspect of privacy is an important component of Kelvin's (1973) analysis which suggests that conditions of privacy may be regarded as the obverse of conditions under which the individual is subject to social power. Power is an attribute of a relationship between persons, and the nature of the relationship is causal in that the exercise of power by one individual modifies the probabilities of another's behavior (Kelvin, 1970). Kelvin argues that it is a necessary but not sufficient condition of privacy that the individual is free from the power or influence of others. He enjoys privacy to the extent that his behavior—beliefs, feelings, and actions—are not causally affected by others, but in contrast with isolation which is imposed, albeit indirectly, privacy is deliberately chosen and protected. Privacy is not therefore simply freedom of action due to the absence of intervention or constraint but freedom in a context of potential power.

In Altman's analysis of the relation between privacy and crowding the variety of privacy regulating mechanisms normally available to the individual plays a major integrative role. An individual or group is seen as having a desired level of privacy that is context dependent and includes expectations about what is good, acceptable, or appropriate (Goffman, 1959). This desired level of privacy derives from a combination of personal, interpersonal, and situational factors. According to Altman, privacy-regulating mechanisms, such as verbal and para-verbal communication, interpersonal spacing, territorial behavior, and cultural norms permit the individual to regulate social contacts and so achieve the desired degree of privacy.

Crowding is seen to arise solely from a failure of boundary control mechanisms that regulate privacy such that privacy goals are underachieved or can be achieved only at high cost. The condition of crowding is assumed to describe a subjective, motivational state of stress so that individuals who experience crowding stress are expected to engage in coping behaviors designed to restore the level of privacy. Therefore the consequences of crowding depend upon the success of these coping behaviors. The conceptualization of crowding in terms of a discrepancy between a desired and achieved goal is compatible with the current analysis and other equilibrium models (cf. Rapoport, 1975; Stokols, 1972b; Wohlwill, 1974). However, there are problems with the discrepancy model. In a cogent discussion of Altman's analysis of privacy, Willems and Campbell (1976) point out ambiguities in Altman's definitions of desired and achieved privacy. They question whether the discrepancy model offers sufficient predictive power. Furthermore, it is questionable whether a single goal—achievement of a desired level of privacy—operates in all situations in which crowding stress occurs. While in agreement with Altman about the importance of regulatory mechanisms in controlling social interaction and the role of coping mechanisms in mediating the consequences of crowding, I do not attribute such explanatory power to the concept of privacy in the etiology of crowding. By viewing the maintenance of privacy as central to all social interaction, Altman loses a valuable distinction between lack of privacy and crowding.

Both lack of privacy and crowding stress are engendered when the individual is deprived of control over environmental, and in particular, social interaction, but the two subjective states differ, primarily with respect to which facet of the individual is made vulnerable by loss of control. Perceived threat to self is the major feature that distinguishes the lack of privacy from crowding stress. The development of self-identity and the opportunity for self-evaluation are seen as major functions of privacy. Privacy is thus a matter of regulating interpersonal or group boundaries. When the self is perceived as under attack, either through enforced communication to others or from input from others, then the achieved level of privacy will be less than desired.

In my view, however, crowding stress is qualitatively different from the state in which the desired and attained levels of privacy are discrepant. Although crowding stress represents a perceived loss of control over the individual's environment, in terms of amount, rate, and appropriateness of stimulus input and the behavioral output options, the loss of control does not necessarily represent a threat to the integrity of the self. The threat is to the predictability of the interface between the individual and the environment and the lack of control is peripheral rather than central. Stokols (1976) argues that the intensity of the crowding experience is directly related to the severity of the threat to the individual's sense of security. Loss of privacy may be seen as an extension of this view, in that it represents an attack on the basic element of psychological security, the concept of self. Obviously there are situations in which perceived lack of control may involve both crowding stress and lack of privacy. The attribution of the perceived lack of control to crowding or to failure of privacy regulation will depend on the prepotent form of threat and the situational context.

Another potentially valuable way of conceptualizing the induction of perceived lack of control is in terms of the complexity of the social situation confronting individuals and their ability to process social complexity. Chandler, Koch, and Paget (1976) suggest that a sense of being crowded is the experiential consequence of operating in a social context governed by ordering and organizational principles which exceed one's cognitive resolving competence. High density or group size will engender the experience of crowding only if participants are unable to structure or organize attendant events in ways which are socially valid. Crowding, which is seen as a cognitive–affective reaction, can be understood only as a consequence of the interaction between the demands of the environment and the abilities of the individual. This interpretation has much in common with the current analysis of the role of inappropriate stimulus input and behavioral interference. Both of these variables may be viewed as imposing additional processing demands. The key concept may not be the richness of the sensory array but the complexity of the required response (cf. Evans & Eichelman, 1976).

The perceived level of stimulation and the complexity of the required response are dependent upon the characteristics of the group, such as size and structure, the sex, personality, and cognitive ability of the individual, which will themselves be influenced by genetic and earlier environmental factors, and a variety of other features. These include architectural design, resource availability, and task demands. The environmental context is the key to the relation between the stress engendered by perceived lack of control over the individual's immediate environment and subjective crowding. This analysis views crowding as the outcome of an attributional process in which the situational context permits the attribution of one's subjective state to the social or physical environment. Such attributions are labeled crowding. The preponent feature of the environment may be the presence of others or their output, or its physical features. The parameters of the objective physical setting are therefore important to the extent that they allow the participant in that setting to attribute their feelings to crowding, but they play no direct role in the induction of crowding stress. The perceived relative importance of social versus physical environmental stimuli may result in perceptions that are not merely quantitatively but qualitatively different. Thus under high-density conditions the cause of feeling crowded may be perceived as the physical setting, whereas under low density the cause may be perceived to be participants within the setting.

Attribution is also a feature of the model proposed by Worchel and Teddlie (1976) who suggest that the experience of crowding is a two-stage process requiring both a state of arousal, created by violation of personal space, and the attribution that the arousal is caused by other people in an individual's environment. Worchel's view holds that crowding is experienced as a stressful and negative emotion and the psychological effects are seen to be tenseness and discomfort, but if arousal is attributed to other sources, such as an exciting football game, an individual may not experience crowding even when his personal space is violated.

My view differs from Worchel and Teddlie in a number of ways. Crowding stress is seen to arise not merely from violation of personal space but from a mismatch between the individual's abilities and needs and the environmental demands and opportunities, which creates a perceived lack of environmental control. Violation of personal space is only one factor which affects perceived control and crowding stress and to exclude the myriad other factors—personal, social, cultural, and physical–environmental—is to neglect the multidimensional nature of crowding stress. Furthermore, it is not clear what Worchel and Teddlie mean by "arousal" and how this is related to crowding stress. Equally, it is recognized that there are difficulties inherent in using the concept of stress in explanations of spatial behavior (cf. Evans & Eichelman, 1976) and that it has different implications dependent upon the level of discourse. It will be a major task to link indices of stress—psychological and physiological, direct and inferred—to different behavior settings.

Worchel and Teddlie argue that the experience of crowding is not only a state of arousal but also the attribution that the arousal is caused by other people in an individual's environment. In the control–attribution framework offered here, a distinction is made between the experience of crowding stress and the verbal attribution of crowding. Crowding stress results from perceived lack of control over the environment. The state of stress experienced by the individual is labeled crowding if the behavioral setting allows the individual to attribute his subjective state to aspects of the social or physical environment. In the majority of situations attributions of crowding and indices of crowding stress will be congruent, but under certain circumstances there may be discrepancies. These may arise in two ways. Individuals may react to the perceived lack of control o their environment, yet not attribute their experience to their environmental context, and so do not report feeling crowded. This is likely to occur in those situations which are typically regarded as enjoyable and where the positive outcomes of the experience compensate for the experience of crowding stress. The alternative is that individuals may not manifest signs of crowding stress but do feel crowded. Examples of this are environments with high spatial density. In this case I would argue that past experience of such environments will induce expectation of perceived lack of control, through inappropriate stimulus input or behavioral interference. This expectation of crowding stress in an appropriate situational context may then result in a crowding attribution. There is ample evidence that individuals in high-density situations typically report feeling crowded although these feelings may not be reflected in indices of crowding stress. Future work must clarify the relation between indices of crowding stress and verbal attributions of crowding.

The analysis I am proposing copes with the context-dependent nature of crowding; one can feel crowded in both high- and low-density environments if the stimulus conditions created by those environments are inappropriate for the personal and sociocultural context. A similar point is made by Rapoport (1975) who argues that crowding and isolation or undercrowding (Loo, 1975) are two instances of an incongruence between the perceived density of the environment and norms or desired levels of interaction or information. The environment is seen as offering cues whereby people judge its nature, the potential for action which it offers, and the appropriate behavior. Such cues may be perceptual (e.g., many people visible), associational/symbolic (e.g., tall buildings), temporal (e.g., activities extending over 24 hours), physical/sociocultural (e.g., absence of defenses allowing control over interaction), or sociocultural (e.g., social heterogeneity). Cues imposing a higher information-processing demand lead to higher perceived density and their evaluation as unwanted, interfering, or uncontrollable leads to feelings of crowding. Furthermore, this analysis permits the extension of crowding to situations in which the inappropriate stimulus conditions antecedent to crowding are created by the perceived presence of others rather than by their actual presence. For example, an individual may report feeling crowded and attendant feelings of aggression, irritability and dislike for others when receiving excessive input via the telephone and mail and recurrent requests for personal action. Such a view emphasizes the role of time as an interacting environmental variable that will influence the action of psychosocial stimuli. Behavioral interference will be of little importance if one has unlimited time, but the introduction of time pressure will increase the impact of behavioral interference. Time is a resource and space is salient only in the context of time, in that there will be high perceived density only when there is an inappropriate stimulus input at a given time. The neglect of time is emphasized by Melbin

(1976) who suggests that people deal with time just as they do with space; they treat it as a scarce resource, put a price on attractive units of it, and compete for good temporal niches.

Crowding therefore must be viewed as multiply determined (Choi, Mirjafari, & Weaver, 1976), and the critical question is whether environmental, personal, and sociocultural properties, either singly or in combination, generate psychosocial stimuli which induce stress and evoke attributions of crowding. The consequences of crowding may be manifested in behavioral or physiological indicants of stress or in coping responses designed to reduce the impact of incongruity between individual (or group) abilities and needs and the environmental demands and opportunities, both explicit and implicit.

IV. Multidimensional Nature of Crowding

A. INTRODUCTION

Fundamental to crowding stress is perceived lack of choice and control arising from an incongruence between the needs and preferences of individuals or groups and the features of the environment. The environment has social and physical components and encompasses both stimulus dimensions—in particular the level of input from perceptual and social sources—and the behavioral implications of the physical and social context, which play a dual role. They not only foster feelings of uncontrollability and lack of choice but are necessary for attributions of crowding. This approach focuses attention on a range of potential determinants of lack of control and hence of crowding stress which may be reflected in changes in social behavior, perceptual reactions, and cognitive performance. An analysis of these determinants within this framework integrates a wealth of empirical evidence which has shown crowding and crowding stress to be multiply determined.

B. GROUP SIZE

The individual will perceive some degree of control (actual or potential) over his environment if he feels he has freedom of choice over the content and timing of his actions and the degree of perceived involvement of others. Conversely, lack of control will arise from actual or potential behavioral interference in which the presence of others is perceived as restricting, disrupting or blocking preferred or necessary actions. High social density is an obvious contender for the induction of behavioral interference in that an increase in group size (i.e., high social density) in a fixed physical space will increase interpersonal interaction and create increased difficulty in predicting and coordinating behavior of the group members.

Individuals in settings characterized by high social density typically display more negative affect (e.g., Griffith & Veitch, 1971), exhibit more asocial behavior (e.g., Ittleson, Proshansky, & Rivlin, 1970) and can suffer impaired perceptual and cognitive performance (Paulus, Annis, Seta, Schkade, & Matthews, 1976; Saegert, Mackintosh, & West, 1975).

Although S. Smith and Haythorn (1972) found that 2-man group subjects registered significantly higher anxiety states and generally reported more stress than those in 3-man groups, the presence of a third person when confined for 21 days may provide a welcome source of additional social stimulation. Other studies have shown an increase in negative reactions when a third person was added to dormitory rooms designed for two people. For example, Baron, Mandel, Adams, and Griffen (1976) showed that occupants of triple rooms not only expressed greater feelings of crowding, more negative interpersonal attitudes and experienced a more negative room ambience, but perceived less control over room activities. Furthermore, factor analyses suggest that crampedness, privacy and belief about control may have qualitatively different implications as a function of group size. Whereas for triples, privacy, control, interpersonal attitudes, and perceptions of crowding are located within the same phenomenal space, for doubles crampedness does not share the same phenomenal spaces as control and privacy. Crampedness appears to define restriction in space defined by physical characteristics (cf. Stokols, 1976), while the privacy factor emphasizes an avoidance of others and a concern for solitary activities (e.g., sleep and study). These differences are congruent with the current control–attribution model. Both doubles and triples are potentially vulnerable to perceived lack of control arising from behavioral interference, unwanted social interaction and privacy intrusion. Triples, however, experience a more complex social environment involving greater unpredictability of social contacts, diversity of personal characteristics, and increased difficulty in negotiating amount and use of space. This will lead triples to perceive crowding in terms of lack of control over their interaction with others, whereas doubles will be more likely to attribute perceived crowding to the characteristics of the physical surroundings.

If high social density, by virtue of the induction of perceived lack of environmental control, is a major factor in producing crowding stress, it is reasonable to expect an effect of social density in prison settings where individual control and outcome choice is minimal. Although the lack of freedom of behavioral choice and reduced control over interaction with others may merely accentuate potential crowding stress, there is the possibility that the prison culture, with values, roles, and traditions distinct from the general population, may change the response to crowding and limit the generality of some of the findings in prison settings.

There are clearly a number of methodological problems and ethical considerations associated with the use of prisons for crowding research (Veno & Peeke, 1974), but prisons do provide an excellent opportunity to separate the effects of social and spatial density (Paulus, McCain, & Cox, 1973) and the results are compatible with findings in other settings. Prison authorities typically take the view that crowding is reflected in physical density. But minimum space requirements, even if adhered to, may be achieved with different levels of social density (i.e., different group sizes) which may have very different implications for individuals. The degree of environmental control enjoyed by single-cell prisoners is likely to be greater than that available to men sharing dormitories. Paulus, Cox, McCain, and Chandler (1975) showed that inmates housed in dormitories typically displayed more negative affect and exhibited a lower tolerance for crowding than did single-cell inmates. Inmates housed in dormitories have also been found to have elevated blood pressure levels compared with inmates housed in single-occupancy cells (D'Atri, 1975).

The importance of group size over room size and density (space per person) in mediating crowding was also demonstrated by Nogami (1976) who investigated the separate effects of these variables on subjects responding interactively or coactively to perceptual and cognitive tasks. While performance measures were unaffected by group size, room size, or density, perceptions of crowding responded to both increases in group size and decreases in room size. Also, coacting individuals tended to feel more crowded than group members and males more crowded than females. Group size had a significant effect on moods and feelings with 10-person groups being generally angrier, less happy, more fearful, more lethargic, and more depressed than 4-person groups. A similar difference emerged between subjects working individually (coacting) and those working in a group (interacting). The most negative moods and feelings were reported by members of a large group working individually with a small area per person. It is likely that this combination of conditions induces the highest level of incongruity between behavioral preferences and options. For example, members of a large group with a small area per person are necessarily seated close to each other, which may entail restriction of movement. Furthermore, the coaction condition, in which subjects work individually and do not communicate with one other, precludes any possibility of seeking confirmation of the task solution or alleviating crowding stress through shared experience.

Results reported by McClelland and Auslander (1977) confirm the relative importance of social density over spatial density in determining perceptions of crowding. A group of 61 college students viewed 139 slides of public settings (restaurants, stores, etc.) and rated each slide on crowding and pleasantness. The slides varied, and were rated by experts, on 12 dimensions considered to be important in determining perceptions of crowding, such as number of people, amount of space, lighting, type of activity, and social factors. Stepwise multiple regression analysis revealed that crowding ratings can be predicted very well (r^2 = .68) with only number of people and their distribution in space (interpersonal distance). Space becomes an important predictor only after number of people is controlled and in fact has a positive zero-order correlation with crowding. Thus, social density is a better predictor of crowding than spatial density. Distribution of people in space makes a significant contribution independent of the two types of density. The primary physical determinant of perceived crowding in this study is thus the number of others within interaction distance. An individual will develop a set of expectations about what crowding is like, the costs of being crowded, and how to adapt with minimal cost on the basis of his past experience and his personal view of crowding. Such expectations should influence perceptions of a setting and interpersonal attraction and cause behavior designed to minimize the impact of anticipated crowding (Edney, 1972). This thesis was examined in an ingenious experiment by Baum and Greenberg (1975) in which subjects were told to expect a 4-person (no anticipation of crowding) or a 10-person (anticipation of crowding) group session of an unspecified nature and duration. These results indicated that anticipated crowding has both perceptual and behavioral effects. Subjects anticipating a 10-person group felt more crowded and more personal discomfort than those anticipating a 4-person group. They took easily defensible corner seat positions and showed less facial regard in response to a confederate than those anticipating the smaller group. Moreover, subjects who anticipated crowding perceived the room as smaller, stuffier, and less adequate and evaluated others less positively than those not anticipating crowding. Baum and Greenberg interpret the observed behavioral concomitants of anticipated crowding as strategies aimed at minimizing social encounters and maximizing control over social experience (Valins & Baum, 1973).

C.   GROUP MEMBERSHIP AND GROUP STRUCTURE

For a group of a given size, properties of the group such as structure may serve to alleviate the potential impact of social density. By providing a social structure which both maximizes the likelihood of smooth and successful interaction and minimizes the intrusion of unwanted interactions from outside the group, group membership can serve to reduce the experience of crowding (Baum, Harpin, & Valins, 1975). In contrast, the individual who is not a member of the group is less able to coordinate or synchronize interactions with others and feelings of exclusion may accentuate his perceived lack of environmental control. A multidimensional scaling analysis of similarity judgments of situations typically designated as crowded indicates that an important dimension in the perception of crowding is the extent to which the individual feels he does not belong to the group (Stockdale, Wittman, Jones & Greaves, 1977).

Concomitant disadvantages of social density may be mitigated if participants are able to devise a normative structure for guiding their interactions which will reimpose some degree of perceived environmental control. In line with this analysis Schopler, McCallum, and Rusbult (1977) argue that the addition of group structure will reduce subjective crowding, but only when interference is present. Their results confirmed that an imposed structure, which minimized discussion, lowered subjective crowding when 6-person groups met in a small room but not in a large room where interference from others is assumed to be minimal.

Baum and Koman (1976) predicted that, when stimulus features of the setting aroused perceptions of large numbers, subjects would respond not to differences in space availability but to the implications of high social density and that only under these conditions would the expectation of social structure moderate response to density. Subjects were told to expect a 5- or 10-person group session participating in a bargaining game in either a small room or large room. Half the subjects in each condition were told to expect a structured session in which a group leader would be appointed and rules would be supplied by the experimenter. Instructions to the remaining subjects contained no mention of social structure. Observational data and subjective ratings confirmed that not only did subjects who anticipated large groups report more perceived crowding than subjects anticipating small groups, but expectation of social structure, rather than varying amounts of space, influenced the intensity of response to high social density. Subjects who anticipated large unstructured group sessions took more isolated seats, reported more crowding and discomfort, and looked at others less frequently than subjects expecting large, structured group sessions. In contrast, the salient consequences of high spatial density were mediated by sex of subjects which did not interact with anticipated group size. Structure partially restores an individual's ability to control his environment and regulate his interaction with others. Baum and Koman therefore suggest that frequency and intensity of a large group interaction in a structured setting is not as stressful as social contact in large, unstructured groups.

Structural complexity of the social environment is seen as the major determinant of the experience of crowding by Chandler et al. (1976). They argue that social situations will be experienced as crowded to the extent that the collection of persons involved is perceived as evidencing no detectable organization or ordering principle. Although this argument applied to persons of all ages, it is assumed to be especially pertinent in the developmental study of children, in that the degree of "psychological congestion" experienced will be a function of the compatability between the complexity of their interpersonal environments and their level of cognitive development.

Chandler et al. held both room size and number of participants constant while varying the structural complexity of the social organization in which subjects participated and their own level of related cognitive developmental maturity. Children were required to arrange themselves by height in a room either with a flat floor, so that all participants began on an equal footing, or with a contoured floor, such that the height to which individuals rose depended not only on their stature, but also on the elevation of their position. The children (aged 5–4 to 9–7) were selected such that equal numbers of them were known to possess seriation skills alone, both seriation and unit measurement skills, or neither of these abilities. It was predicted that when asked to perform on a flat surface any child with a minimum of seriation skills would possess the requisite abilities necessary to understand their own place and that of others in a social group to be arranged by height. By contrast, the task of ordering one another by height in a contoured environment imposed additional organizational demands that are hypothesized to exceed the cognitive developmental capacities of all those who had not yet come to understand concepts of unit measurement. As predicted children who lacked the requisite cognitive skills for decoding the social situation were significantly more stressed and behaviorally disorganized than cognitively able children, and judged themselves to be dealing with a larger group in a smaller space than was actually the case.

D. TASK ACTIVITY

The extent to which individuals experience behavioral interference and overload will depend on the compatibility between expectations and goals and the physical and social environment. The normative levels of physical proximity and social interaction for a cocktail party are different from those for an airport lounge, and these are reflected in judgments of crowding (Desor, 1972). J. L. Cohen, Sladen, and Bennett (1975), again using a miniature room technique, found that where relatively high levels of proximity and interaction were expected, for example recreational settings and situations in which individuals are acquainted with each other, higher numbers of participants were acceptable. Also more people were acceptable in situations in which participants interact than in situations involving independent activity. However, all the interacting situations were positive (e.g., a party) and did not demand competition which, according to the behavioral interference view, might lead to the reverse finding through rivalry for access to limited resources and difficulty of coordinating interactions. Stokols et al. (1973) did find that group members felt more crowded and restricted when experimental tasks required them to compete than when they required mutual cooperation.

Cozby (1973) confirmed that social density preferences are influenced by whether the presence of others facilitates or inhibits individual goals. Clearly the aims of the individual attending a party where high social density is preferred, and studying for an examination for which low density is seen as more facilitatory, are substantially different. More people at a party will increase the likelihood of successful social interaction by providing a wide range of social interactions and minimizing the perceived social pressure to remain in a given social group (Stockdale & Zallik, 1976). In contrast the presence of others while studying is likely to create behavioral interference and distraction.

E. RESOURCE SCARCITY

Scarcity of resources constitutes a potentially potent source of behavioral interference, especially if the nature of the setting impedes minimization of the saliency of competition among group members for access to resources. Although studies by W. C. McGrew (1972) and Hutt and Vaizey (1966) report that an increase in social density is associated with changes in social interaction and aggressive behavior among children at play, neither of these studies varied the resources essential to play—the amount of toys. P. K. Smith and Connolly (1973) found that in general the amount of equipment provided had a more significant effect than the amount of space on most aspects of social behavior among preschool children. A reduction in the amount of equipment resulted in more parallel play, more visual and physical contact and an increase in aggressive and stress behaviors. Differences in resource availability may also contribute to differential behavior patterns associated with contrasting architectural designs (Valins & Baum, 1973).

The importance of resource scarcity as a determinant of subjective crowding has been demonstrated by Stockdale and Schopler (1976) who examined the effects of both resource scarcity and room size when group size was fixed. Two hundred and eight subjects were each informed that they and a group of fellow students had been successful in obtaining a 12-month lease on a converted four-story rooming house providing accommodation for 20 students in 10 simply furnished double rooms. Under the high spatial-density condition (36 square feet per person) the accommodation was described as smaller than the typical 2-person bed-sitting room, whereas under the low spatial-density manipulation (84 square feet per person) it was described as larger than the typical bed-sitting room. Scarcity of resources was manipulated by varying communal facilities for residents. Under the low scarcity condition there were an adequate number of bathrooms, kitchens, and tea/coffee-making facilities, there was a telephone on each floor, a study room providing ample study places for students wanting a quiet place to work, and an adequate television lounge. Under the high scarcity condition the shared facilities were insufficient for the 20 residents and subjects were informed that this resulted, for example, in frequent queues to use the bathrooms and kitchen and frequent difficulties in using the phone. Descriptions also contained background information about location of the rooming house and its neighborhood and this was identical in both cases. Subjects were told that the experimenters were interested in the ease with which people can imagine themselves to be in different situations. They were given a typewritten description of the accommodation and asked to try to put themselves into the situation described, to imagine what it would be like for them after a few weeks, and to complete a questionnaire which provided manipulation checks and assessed participant subjective feelings about the accommodation including crowding, privacy, comfort, behavioral interference, and affective reactions.

Perception of crowding was responsive to the manipulation of both physical density and resource scarcity. Subjects felt more crowded and more confined in the high- than in the low-density living conditions, and under conditions of high than low resource scarcity. The results also provided support for the hypothesized role of interference arising from high resource scarcity in producing feelings of crowding. The manipulation of resource scarcity significantly affected perceived interference. Subjects felt there would be greater interference with their everyday activities under conditions of high than under low resource scarcity, and the factor pattern confirmed the contribution of interference to general feelings of crowding. Furthermore, negative affective responses emerged with interference arising from high-resource scarcity but affective reactions were not responsive to density changes. This finding is congruent with an interpersonal view of crowding in which interference from others leads to feelings of crowding and of tension, worry and frustration.

Both experimental and field settings vary not only in the availability of environmental resources necessary for task completion or for personal goal attainment, but also with respect to the number of roles available to the participants. This is recognized in the theory of undermanning proposed by Barker (1960) who developed his ideas within a social ecological framework (cf. Barker, 1960, 1963, 1965, 1968; Barker & Wright, 1955). According to Barker's theory of manning, occupants of behavior settings, which are defined by both physical components and overt patterns of behavior, have an active interest in keeping the settings functioning, but the claim made by the setting upon its occupants varies with the numbers associated with it.

In their development of the degree of manning concept, Wicker, McGrath, and Armstrong (1972) suggest that as well as under and adequate manning, overmanning may exist with respect either to performer or nonperformer roles. Consistent with the theory, members of overmanned groups typically feel significantly less needed, less important, and less valuable to the group than those who participate in adequately manned groups (Hanson & Wicker, 1973). Wicker (1973) argues that a critical determinant of crowding and associated behavior is the degree of manning in a behavior setting, rather than the spatial limitations imposed on the occupants by physical parameters. In a study reported by Wicker (1974), the degree of manning was manipulated by varying the number of job assignments available in a 4-person "slot-car" task which involved running a miniature car round a circular racetrack. Again members of overmanned groups generally perceived themselves to be less important to the group, less influential in decision-making processes, and rated their situation as less pleasant than members of under or adequately manned groups. However, it appears from the pattern of group means that members of undermanned groups felt more crowded than members of overmanned groups. One reason for this finding may be that feelings of crowding were determined, not by spatial restrictions nor by an excess of people over task assignments, but by perceived sensory and interpersonal contact associated with high task demands.

F. ENVIRONMENTAL FEATURES

Properties of the physical environment are important determinants of crowding stress and perceived crowding to the extent that they contribute to perceived lack of control and enable the individual to attribute his feelings to the environment. This will occur if the physical environment increases inappropriate physical, perceptual, and social contact and behavioral interference. Equally, if the physical surroundings aid the individual in his attempts to control interaction with others and minimize constraints others impose on his behavior, this will reduce crowding and crowding stress. A number of architectural features (e.g., partitions and screens) can create feelings of perceptual and social separation, and therefore affect perceived crowding and overt behavior (cf. Baum, Riess, & O'Hara, 1974; Desor, 1972).

Baum and Davis (1976) found that color and visual complexity can also influence individuals' perceptions of room size and crowding. Dark-colored rooms were perceived as smaller, stuffier, and more crowded than light-colored rooms of the same size, and, within dark rooms, high complexity increased capacity and crowding thresholds when the activities were social, but led to perceptions of reduced spatial extent and room capacity for nonsocial activities. Baum and Davis suggest that whereas in the nonsocial setting high visual complexity may lead to excessive stimulation, it may enable individuals to screen themselves from the high stimulation levels associated with social interaction by diverting their attention from this potential source of stress. Similarly Worchel and Teddlie (1976) showed that the presence of pictures, designed to distract the individual from attributions of crowding, can reduce the experience of crowding in groups working at close interaction distances.

The design of residential environments is an important determinant of the way residents perceive their environment and respond to the potential disadvantages of high social density. A series of field studies by Valins and Baum (Baum & Valins, 1973; Valins & Baum, 1973) contrasted the responses of 34 students housed in double-occupancy rooms arranged along a corridor with those of residents of 4- or 5-person suites. The corridor and suite designs offered accommodation to comparable numbers of residents in equivalent amounts of space on each floor but, while in the corridor design each resident shared common areas (lounge and bathroom) with 33 others, in the suite design common areas were shared with only 3 or 5 others. Baum and Valins showed that in contrast with suite residents, corridor residents experienced more crowding, showed more avoidance of others and dislike of strangers, and had lower thresholds for perception of crowding. Baum and Valins argue that corridor design, with more residents sharing communal space, increased the number of unwanted interactions and reduced the control each resident can maintain over his social experience.

Although these studies suggest the efficacy of architectural features in buildings which will provide occupants with protection from overstimulation and behavioral interference, Stokols, Smith, and Prostor (1975) point out that there are certain methodological difficulties associated with much of the research. In an attempt to extend the generality of the findings, Stokols *et al.* utilized a field–experimental design in which individuals waiting in a Department of Motor Vehicles office were exposed to different levels of area partitioning. The results with respect to the effect of partitioning on perceived crowding failed to replicate the findings obtained in earlier laboratory experiments, with subjects in the maximally partitioned room feeling no less crowded than in the nonpartitioned situation. It remains to be determined whether previous results obtained using laboratory and scale-model techniques are artifactual. A plausible alternative explanation put forward by Stokols is that the exact nature of the relationship between design features and emotional reactions depends upon a number of situational circumstances. In public settings, such as this where the occupant's perception of control over the environment is minimal, the presence of partitions may further decrease control and create feelings of resentment and frustration.

G. INTERPERSONAL SPACING

Studies of crowding and proxemic behavior are complementary in that personal spacing is an acceptable technique of modulating interaction with others and minimizing behavioral constraint. Despite conflicting data and frequent lack of experimental control it does appear from personal space research that personal space is defined by situational factors, age, sex, cultural norms, and the degree of familiarity or interpersonal attitudes [see Evans and Howard (1973) and Altman (1975) for a review of personal-space research]. Examination of the spatial properties of larger social units such as groups and crowds indicate that a number of characteristics including group size and status (Knowles, 1973) and group activity (Knowles & Bassett, 1976) affect distancing of others from the group. Violation of an individual's personal space or a group's social space may lead to perceived lack of control and crowding stress, and different spacing norms may result in differential crowding responses (cf. Section IV, I).

Studies of proximity and nonverbal communication have consistently shown how nonverbal cues, affective arousal, and interpersonal spacing are inter-related (cf. Allgeier & Byrne, 1973; Argyle & Dean, 1965; Kleck, 1970). Data collected by McBride, King, and James (1965) even suggest that changes in galvanic skin response accompany invasion of the subject's personal space by the experimenter. Efran and Cheyne (1974) propose that overcrowding represents an end point on a continuum in which crowding reactions reflect the cumulative effect of mundane interpersonal encounters which are engaged in everyday. They demonstrated that although differences in intrusion were not mirrored by changes in cardiovascular activity, subjects who were forced to intrude on the shared space of others displayed more agonistic facial responses and later reported less positive mood responses than did control subjects.

A number of experiments have confirmed the importance of appropriate interpersonal spacing in determining the quality of interpersonal interaction and reactions to the setting. Baxter and Rozelle (1975) found reliable changes in speech patterns and nonverbal behavior as a function of interaction distance. Worchel and Teddlie (1976) found that violations of personal space led subjects to feel more crowded, to overestimate the length of the experiment, and to attribute more nervousness and aggressiveness to other subjects. In a study by Sundstrom (1975a), manipulations of dyadic interaction distance and eye contact (referred to as "intrusion" by Sundstrom) led to lower levels of facial regard and to initial discomfort that decreased with time.

Kutner (1973) argues that, because of the primary role of the exchange of visual information in the accurate assessment of and reaction to the environment, one of the major concomitants of close proximity is an increase in the visual exposure to others. While individuals can exercise some control over their own visual scanning and generally look at each other less at close proximities (Argyle & Dean, 1965; Goffman, 1963; Goldberg, Kiesler, & Collins, 1969), they have little control over other people's looking behavior. Kutner's laboratory study offers some support for the view that visual overexposure contributes to crowding stress. The pattern of factor loadings suggests that individuals exposed visually to others feel physically closer, more distracted, more nervous, and not only attempt to conform to normal social expectations, but also try to increase privacy by showing more signs of bodily protection.

The importance of considering all sources of stimulation is highlighted by Hall (1966) who observed that as two individuals come closer to one another, they perceive and experience each other more intensely. Accordingly in an environment providing a high degree of stimulation it might be expected that individuals would stand further apart in an attempt to regulate total stimulus input (cf. Little, 1965; Nesbitt & Steven, 1974). Distance from another is seen as one factor in a homeostatic relationship designed to regulate stimulus input. Regulation of interaction distance provides some control over the stimulus environment and deprived of this control, or alternative opportunities for environmental modification, the individual will show signs of crowding stress.

H. TERRITORIAL BEHAVIOR

The use of territorial behavior to regulate behavioral intrusion emerges in more recent analyses of territoriality which extrapolate findings and concepts derived from animal studies to humans (cf. Altman, 1970; Edney, 1974; Sommer, 1966; Stea, 1965).

Following an extensive analysis of definitional and conceptual issues of territoriality, Altman (1975) has defined territoriality as a self/other boundary regulation mechanism involving personalization or marking of a geographical area or object and the communication of "ownership" by its users. He classifies territories as primary, secondary, or public depending on their degree of importance and permanence of use by occupants. The number of empirical studies of territoriality is relatively small and comprises mainly naturalistic observations and field experiments. Such studies show that territorial behavior is affected by individual characteristics such as personality traits, normal–psychotic conditions (Esser, Chamberlaine, Chapple, & Kline, 1965; Horowitz, Duff, & Stratton, 1965), by interpersonal relationships of dominance and social-need compatability (Altman & Haythorn, 1967), and by situational and environmental determinants such as expectations of long versus short commitments to live with another person (Altman, Taylor, & Wheeler, 1971). These antecedent conditions may be seen as determining the degree of perceived control over the environment which is a major determinant of subsequent behavior. If the degree of environmental control is less than expected, or if it is predicted that environmental expectations will not be met, some form of adaptive response will be enacted. When these responses involve the explicit use and control of space, they may be regarded as territorial behavior. Such behavior is a major defensive and preventive reaction in relation to feelings of crowding. Sommer (1966) showed that people using the public reading areas of a university library exhibited a variety of strategies to minimize the impact of the environment—particularly the presence of others.

Territorial behavior may also be viewed as a social regulation mechanism that helps to preserve a viable social system and assists in regulating interpersonal events (Edney, 1976). The stabilizing function of territories applies both to family groups (e.g., Altman, Nelson, & Lett, 1972) and to a variety of other groups, including small experimental groups (e.g., Altman et al., 1971) and more unusual populations such as retarded boys resident in an institution (e.g., O'Neill & Paluck, 1973; Paluck & Esser, 1971a, 1971b). The absence or ineffectiveness of territories is used by Newman (1972) as one contributing factor to crime in low-cost urban housing developments. He explains crime rates in terms of the presence or absence of "defensible space," in part determined by the existence of territories and an individual's perceived control over space.

I. SEX DIFFERENCES

The extent to which the situation provides the level of stimulation and behavioral freedom preferred or needed by the individual is determined not only by the physical and social environment and task demands, but also by individual characteristics. For example, males and females exhibit different normative patterns of spatial behavior; these may account for their differential response to crowding (cf. Freedman *et al.*, 1972; Ross *et al.*, 1973). There is evidence that females have smaller zones of personal space and so are able to tolerate closer interpersonal contacts than males (Baxter, 1970; Hartnett, Bailey & Gibson, 1970; Leibman, 1970). Violation of personal space norms is likely to be more acute for males than females under high-density conditions and males will experience a greater lack of perceived environmental control than females. This difference is reflected in both perceptions of crowding and behavioral response. A considerable number of studies have demonstrated sex differences in social behavior as a function of interaction distance and spatial density (e.g., Baum & Koman, 1976; Epstein & Karlin, 1975; Fisher & Byrne, 1975), but these differences do not appear to be attributable to differences in arousal, for behavioral differences do not appear to be paralleled by differences in arousal (Aiello *et al.*, 1975).

J. E. Marshall and Heslin (1975) revealed a significant modifying effect of the sex of subject and of composition of the group (same vs. mixed sex) on the effects of spatial density and group size on affective reactions and participants' wish to remain in the group. Density, regardless of group size, depressed general feelings of members of all groups and interacted with the composition and sex of the group in its effect on feelings toward individuals, but in the reverse direction to that previously demonstrated (cf. Freedman *et al.*, 1972; Ross *et al.*, 1973). In single-sex groups men and women reacted very differently; women did not like the other members as much under high density as under low density, whereas men made a more positive evaluation of their co-members under high spatial density. Stokols proposed that participation in a 1½ hour task demanding involvement and cooperation makes achievement-related performance the salient dimension for the evaluation of comembers. It is postulated that this generates a successful "team" approach in the high-density setting for the males which leads to positive evaluation, but that among women these conditions raise feelings of ambivalence toward success, achievement, and leadership (cf. Horner, 1972a, 1972b) and so generate negative interpersonal feelings. Although an ingenious explanation of the discrepant findings on the interaction between density and sex of subject, it would seem appropriate to explore these assumptions more fully.

As predicted, members were more attracted to other members in the small (4-person) groups than in the large (16-person) groups (cf. Cartwright, 1968) but this effect was more pronounced for males than for females. Also whereas males' wish to remain in group was unaffected by the size or composition of the group, females wished to remain in the group when it was small if it was an all-female group but wished to remain in a large group when it was mixed. A consistent pattern in the results was that men appear to be sensitive primarily to group composition, whereas women seem to react to all combinations of the independent variables. This could reflect the greater sensitivity of women to environmental cues than men (Silverman, 1970). Specifically, mixed-sex groups produced a more positive response among males than single-sex groups, while the response of females to the composition of the group depended on group size. Marshall & Heslin suggest this may reflect the perceived limitation in choice for interaction and high vulnerability to unwanted advances from males in the small mixed-sex group.

J. PERSONALITY DIFFERENCES

The extent to which the presence of others is perceived as interfering or as a source of excessive stimulation will also depend on the personality of the participants. There is evidence that personality differences are reflected in personal space measures (cf. Frede, Gantney, & Baxter, 1968; Patterson & Holmes, 1966; Patterson & Sechrest, 1970), and observed differences in perceived crowding and behavioral response may partially derive from violation of these differential spacing norms. In particular it can be predicted that subjects with personality characteristics which create the need for distant interpersonal spacing will react less favorably to high density than subjects whose personalities permit smaller interaction distances. Cozby (1973) showed personal space to be significantly related to four personality variables: self-esteem (Coopersmith, 1967), dominance (Jackson, 1967), the need for change and variety in one's social and physical environment, and social avoidance and distress (SAD) (Watson & Friend, 1969). Close personal space which correlated with high self-esteem, dominance, desire for change, and low SAD was found to be associated with high-density preferences. Far personal space subjects showed an opposite preference pattern but this was restricted to a party situation.

According to the control view of crowding, a major personality correlate of subjective crowding will be the degree to which individuals typically feel they have personal control over their social environment. This perceived internality–externality of control (Rotter, 1966) was shown by Duke and Nowicki (1972) to be related to personal space, with external subjects, who do not feel they exert personal control over others, displaying greater interpersonal distance needs in interactions with an imaginary stranger than internal subjects who typically expect to control their environment. It has also been argued that externals will be more susceptible to noncontingencies in their environment in that their expectancies of lack of control over outcomes will be more extensive. "Learned helpless," which has been hypothesized as one outcome of chronic exposure to high density (Rodin, 1976), should therefore be a more general phenomenon for externals than for internals (S. Cohen, Rothbart, & Phillips, 1976). Schopler *et al.* (1977) argue that because interference potential is augmented when participants are perceived as unpredictable or uncontrollable, externals should feel more vulnerable than internals and should feel more crowded than internals and that this difference should be greater under conditions of spatial limitation. Their results showed that internality–externality did affect crowding but in interaction with another of their manipulated variables—the imposition of structure. In a regular discussion condition externals felt somewhat more crowded than internals in both a small and large room. The imposition of structure reduced feelings of crowding for externals in the small room but increased subjective crowding for internals in the small room.

A second experiment examined differential effects upon subjective crowding of maximizing either within-group or outside interference. In common with the imposition of structure, which was intended to lower interference, the creation of outside interference served to increase subjective crowding for internals. Schopler *et al.* argue that the common element in both manipulations is the preemption of personal control for initiating solutions to interference problems. This removal of personal control appears to increase feelings of crowding for internals, who expect to retain environmental control but not for externals, who have low expectations of control. There is evidence that internals are more cognitively active (Lefcourt, 1972) and adopt a more active, alert, and calculated posture with respect to their world (Phares, 1973) than is the case for externals, and differential sensitivity to preemption of personal control options therefore may be a potent determinant of individual differences in crowding reactions.

K. COPING RESPONSES

Success in coping with excessive stimulus input and with output limitations is a critical mediator between crowding stress and behavioral consequences. Some variables already examined as determinants of crowding and crowding stress, for example interpersonal spacing and territoriality, may also be seen as potentially compensatory mechanisms which may enable the individual to gain a degree of control over his interactions. However, there are other individual coping responses such as perceptual–cognitive filtering reactions as well as group-based mechanisms that guide increased coordination and synchronization of responses.

According to Milgram's (1970) analysis, one adaptive mechanism invoked by overload is a decrease in the concern for and involvement with others. The general observation that people in small towns are more friendly and less suspicious than those in large cities has often been noted (Hamburg, 1971), but studies that have compared the helpfulness of urban residents with their less urban counterparts have provided only partial support. Requests for assistance have been observed to receive a more favorable response in small towns than in large cities (cf. Korte & Kerr, 1975; McKenna & Morgenthau, 1970; Milgram, 1970), but Merrens (1973) failed to find any differences between Midwestern cities and towns in responses to small questions and favors, although he did find New York City residents less helpful than Midwestern residents. Using the lost-letter technique, Forbes and Gromoll (1971) also failed to find any differences between large cities, medium cities, and small towns. Support for Milgram's analysis derives from the finding that students in higher-density housing demonstrated less altruistic behavior (Bickman, Teger, Gabriele, McLaughlin, Berger, & Sunaday, 1973). Also Sherrod and Downs (1974) demonstrated that increased input levels arising from simultaneous exposure to visual and auditory laboratory tasks resulted in decreased helpfulness.

An examination of the "urban incivility" hypothesis in a different cultural setting was reported by Korte, Ypma, and Toppen (1975). Their study sought to compare the helpfulness shown toward a stranger in areas of the Netherlands differing with respect to degree of urbanization (cities vs. towns) and input level (high vs. low volume of inputs in the immediate surroundings). None of the three measures provided any evidence of city–town differences, or differences among four neighborhoods of Amsterdam with contrasting stereotypes of friendliness and helpfulness. Korte et al. consider a number of reasons for the absence of city–town differences but point out that urbanization effects may be partially dependent upon the culture in which they occur (Hauser, 1965). Two of the three helpfulness measures showed lower input levels to be associated with a higher degree of helpfulness, but the fact that differences in input level between high-input settings in cities and towns were not reflected in differences in helpfulness indicates that input levels are not necessarily the prepotent determinant.

Other responses which may be successful in decreasing stimulus input and interference from others are evident in a number of studies. In high spatial density and therefore reduced interpersonal distance subjects show low facial regard (Ross et al. 1973) and decreased willingness to discuss personal topics. Subjects expecting a high level of social density assume more peripheral seat positions (Baum & Greenberg, 1975; Baum & Koman, 1976). Also, Valins and Baum (1973) found that residents of corridor dormitories tended to initiate fewer interactions with a stranger and looked at him less often than suite residents. One way of coping with a high interactive demand is simply to avoid interactions.

The analysis of crowding in terms of behavioral interference focuses attention on the role of both individual and group-based strategies in minimizing the impact of physical and social environment on goal attainment. An individual who feels that the setting is not conducive to goal attainment may adjust his aspiration level by lowering his expected achievement level or creating more realistic time scales for task completion. The potential for cooperation inherent in any group is crucial in determining the consequences of crowding stress. If norms can be evolved for the use of scarce resources and for interpersonal interaction, these will help to provide that structure necessary for minimizing the impact of behavioral interference on both the individual and the group (Macdonald & Oden, 1973). However, the consequences of group-based solutions may not be comparable for all group members. The effectiveness of the coping response may well depend upon the status of the individual relative to other group members.

The formation of subgroups is another group response that may serve to reduce the amount and severity of interference. Some physical environments are more conducive to such a solution than others. Schopler and Stockdale (1977) argue that if the physical environment provides only limited protection against interference from others individuals will engage in strategies to compensate for this. It was found that corridor residents disclosed less intimate information to their roommates, knew less about their neighbors' feeling toward themselves, and felt less control over events nearby. These results are interpreted as cognitive distancing strategies to compensate for the lack of protection from interference in the corridor design.

Stokols (1976) argues that the availability of adaptive responses will depend upon the type of crowding experienced and proposes that crowding experiences involving a violation of social and spatial expectations will be of greater intensity, persistence, and be more difficult to resolve than those deriving solely from perceived deficiencies of the physical (spatial) environment. For example, if an individual's sense of frustration is attributed to unintentional environmental circumstances, the opportunity for ameliorating the perceived constraints by group coordination is not precluded, whereas in the personal crowding situation the number of adaptive options is reduced. The current analysis also points to differences in the type and range of adaptive responses potentially available. The strategies adopted will depend on the source of perceived lack of control, the flexibility inherent in the social and physical environment, and the ability of the individual or group to initiate and implement appropriate solutions.

L. CONCLUSIONS

The multidimensional approach to crowding initiated by the control-attribution analysis views the induction of crowding and crowding stress as a causal network of antecedent factors and behavioral and affective responses. The antecedents of crowding derive from a combination of situational variables and personal, interpersonal, and cultural characteristics which determine the perceived level of stimulus input and range of behavioral options. An inappropriate type of stimulus input or experience of behavioral interference will induce a perceived lack of environmental control which will lead to attempts to initiate adaptive responses to restore it. The consequences of crowding depend on the ability of the individual or group to remove the source of crowding stress or to cope with that stress through the use of behavioral, affective, and cognitive coping responses. The empirical work supports this analysis but future research must identify what setting characteristics define control opportunities and link such setting characteristics to the transient and long-term consequences experienced by the participants.

V. Overview

Any analysis of crowding must bear in mind the need to answer two questions: "What are the determinants of crowding?" and "What are the consequences of crowding?" The current analysis, by adopting a broad conceptual orientation, has attempted to provide preliminary answers to these questions which it is hoped will provide a basis for future research.

Examination of the difficulties associated with the density model indicated that a narrow definition of crowding in terms of density is inadequate. Both input and output approaches to crowding have recognized that crowding is a subjective state with multiple antecedent factors. Empirical studies within the input framework have examined the effect of variables assumed to increase perceptual and social input including group size, high interactive task demands, inappropriate interpersonal spacing, and an open physical environment. To restore the amount and rate of stimulus input to more acceptable levels the individual uses various coping responses, including perceptual and cognitive filtering, adjustment of personal space, and marking of territory. Output analyses have focused on those factors which contribute to increased behavioral interference, for example increased group size, task demands, low resource availability, inappropriate environmental design features, and lack of group structure. To minimize the impact of potential interference the individual (or group) utilizes differing strategies, and the interference approach emphasizes individual cognitive strategies and group-based solutions in achieving this.

These approaches recognize that crowding stress will depend not only on interpersonal processes, but also on individual and cultural expectations. Individual differences appear to be primarily a function of the personality characteristics and sex of the individual and their past experience. We might also expect differential vulnerability to crowding stress as a function of status and seek the effects of such stress in children or less dominant group members.

Although experimental studies have provided support for a variety of predictions about determinants and effects of crowding, they have rarely provide unambiguous support for any one theoretical position. For example, the subjective experience of crowding, indications of crowding stress, and the incidence of coping responses have been found to be inversely related to the anticipated degree of group structure (cf. Baum & Koman, 1976; Schopler et al., 1977). This finding has been interpreted in terms of behavioral interference, group structure being assumed to represent a regulating mechanism for interaction within the group, so a high degree of expected structure should lessen concern about possible interference with goal attainment. However, increases in group structure might also be expected to reduce social stimulation levels (Desor, 1972), reduce the necessity for unwanted interaction with others (Valins & Baum, 1973), and increase the ability of individuals to control their interpersonal interaction (Zlutnick & Altman, 1972). These views are compatible with analyses of group processes and task performance in terms of structural variables such as status, leadership, and communication networks, whereby structure may be seen both as a means of achieving and as a product of control.

These formulations recognize the multidimensional nature of crowding but differ with respect to the identity of the prepotent psychosocial stimuli. The division of the theoretical approaches into input views which emphasize stimulus dimensions of the physical and social environment, and output perspectives which focus on the behavioral implications of that environment, is valuable in imposing order on the conceptual confusion which exists in crowding research. However, this division implies that the approaches are mutually exclusive. In my view, it is more profitable to attempt a rapprochement between the theoretical positions.

The current analysis argues that perceived lack of control is fundamental to crowding stress and that this is the key concept in the development of an integrated framework for crowding research. The perceived lack of control arises from an incongruence between the needs and preference of the individual or group and those features of the physical and social environment which define the stimulus input and behavioral options. Crowding stress may be reduced by individual and group-based coping responses which minimize the impact of interactional demand and behavioral limitations. The effectiveness of these coping responses in restoring perceived environmental control is the critical mediator between stress and behavioral consequences. This will depend on the range of available coping responses, which will be a function of the prepotent stimulus inducing crowding stress, the magnitude of the associated psychological and physiological costs, and the ability of the individual to deal with socially complex situations.

Any satisfactory analysis of crowding must account for a wide spectrum of apparently contradictory phenomena. A prominent example in any informal discussion of crowding is the assertion that on many occasions people actively seek out situations which would commonly be described as crowded (e.g., football matches, art exhibitions, theater bars). These may be not merely situations of high density but may also potentially involve high levels of physical and social contact and/or behavioral interference. It is argued that these situations may be labeled as "crowded," but will be stressful and aversive only to the extent that their properties are incompatible with the desires, needs, and goals of the individual. For example, the individual who chooses to attend a football game wishes to be there, expects to be one of a large number of people, and assumes that the spatial constraints of the stadium and the spectators will result in a comparatively high level of physical contact, perceptual and social stimulation, and noise. There would be little point in attending such an event if these factors were missing. The individual who does not expect or desire interaction and whose behavioral goals are contrary to the rest of the group will experience crowding stress. Thus crowding stress is context-dependent, where the context is defined in terms of characteristics of both the behavioral setting and the individual.

Although this analysis identifies crowding stress as the outcome of failure to control interpersonal processes, it does not demand that others be personally present in the situation. It requires only that the negative feelings associated with lack of environmental control be attributable to the output from others or to the behavioral demands and limitations they create. According to this view an individual can feel crowded if the quantity and rate of stimulus input is higher than desired. The sources of this input may include telephone calls and memoranda, as well as physically present group members. Equally, crowding stress may result from excessive perceived behavioral demands and constraints such as a high work load with a time limitation.

The progress of crowding research rests upon an adequate conceptualization of crowding and a systematic examination of the relationship among the antecedent conditions and between these conditions and their effects. I believe the current analysis is valuable in a number of ways. By conceptualizing crowding stress in terms of perceived lack of environmental control, it provides an opportunity for linking a number of previously disparate variables. It focuses on a range of multiple predeterminants of crowding, a closer analysis of which is essential to develop an adequate predictive model of crowding. It must be recognized that environmental input and behavioral demands and limitations are a function of various physical, social, cultural, and personal variables. These variables are not independent and their specific interrelationships must be detailed by future research. Also, the implications of the majority of these variables must be explored more fully. For example, an increase in group size has implications over and above a decrease in average interpersonal distance and an increase in the interactional input and behavioral interference. Increased group size potentially means less time per individual for expressing and validating opinions and decreased knowledge of behavioral intentions. Such changes that decrease the level of environmental predictability and potentially reduce the individual's perceived control may reasonably be expected to contribute to the level of crowding stress.

The concept of environmental control also focuses attention on a range of situations which are not typified by high levels of physical density but which may induce crowding stress. The analysis permits the concept of crowding to be extended to dyadic interactions in which there is a high interactive demand, behavioral interference, or inappropriate interpersonal spacing. Inappropriate interpersonal spacing will be accentuated and the level of crowding increased if there are minimal spatial constraints and low density. Furthermore, the analysis points to the importance of examining other determinants of perceived control. These may include the degree to which an individual feels a member of or has a role within a group, whether he is being evaluated by other group members (Stokols & Resnick, 1975), and whether the individual is a stranger or knows others group members and so has some basis for predicting the behaviors of others.

The model has emphasized the role of coping mechanisms in mediating the consequences of crowding. It is obviously necessary to examine what factors expand the range of viable coping mechanisms and to examine their development, in both experimental and field settings, and as a function of the individual's past experience.

Successful explication of the interrelations among the predeterminants of crowding, and between these predeterminants and the consequences of crowding stress, will depend on the development of adequate mapping rules between the concepts defined by the model and the observable facets of behavior. For the current analysis to aid the integration and growth of crowding research, adequate operationalizations of the independent and dependent variables must be sought. Studies must be carried out to develop adequate indices of such concepts as environmental control, behavioral interference, crowding stress, and coping. Ideally these indices would include subjective reports, behavioral measures, and, where appropriate, physiological measures. Verbal assessments of crowding will obviously reflect not only the attributional processes involved in the perception of crowding but also the availability of verbal labels. It is likely that attributional processes and the appropriateness of available labels will be influenced by sociocultural factors, and it is therefore essential that these interrelations are evaluated if we are to understand crowding and its effects. Furthermore, measures must be developed that are applicable to the study of both short- and long-term effects of crowding and that are flexible enough to permit the study of crowding in field situations.

It is clear that the rapidly developing body of crowding research and theoretical analyses represent an increasingly firm basis for understanding the determinants and effects of crowding. The broad but integrative framework offered by this analysis highlights the prepotent determining variables and conceptual and methodological problems which must be overcome in future research. The test of this analysis of crowding will be the extent to which it contributes to future theoretical development and empirical research in crowding.

REFERENCES

Aiello, J. R., Epstein, V. M., & Karlin, R. A. Effects of crowding on electrodermal activity.

Sociological Symposium, 1975, **14**, 42–57.

Allgeier, A. R., & Byrne, D. Attraction toward the opposite sex as a determinant of physical proximity. *Journal of Social Psychology,* 1973, **90**, 213–219.

Altman, I. Territorial behavior in humans: An analysis of the concept. In L. A. Pastalan & D. H. Carson (Eds.), *Spatial behavior of older people.* Ann Arbor: University of Michigan Press, 1970. Pp. 1–24.

Altman, I. *The environment and social behavior.* Monterey, Calif.: Brooks, Cole, 1975.

Altman, I., & Haythorn, W. W. The effects of social isolation and group composition on performance. *Human Relations,* 1967, **4**, 313–340.

Altman, I., Nelson, P. A., & Lett, E. E. The ecology of home environments. *Catalog of Selected Documents in Psychology,* 1972, **2**, 65.

Altman, I., Taylor, D. A., & Wheeler, L. Ecological aspects of group behavior in social isolation. *Journal of Applied Social Psychology,* 1971, **1**, 76–100.

Argyle, M., & Dean, J. Eye contact, distance and affiliation. *Sociometry,* 1965, **28**, 289–304.

Baldassare, M. The effects of density on social behavior and attitudes. *American Behavioral Scientist,* 1975, **18**, 815–825.

Barker, R. G. Ecology and motivation. In M. R. Jones (Ed.), *Nebraska Symposium on Motivation.* Vol. 8. Lincoln: University of Nebraska Press, 1960. Pp. 1–50.

Barker, R. G. On the nature of the environment. *Journal of Social Issues,* 1963, **19**, 17–38.

Barker, R. G. Explorations in ecological psychology. *American Psychologist,* 1965, **20**, 1–14.

Barker, R. G. *Ecological psychology: Concepts and methods for studying the environment of human behavior.* Stanford, Calif.: Stanford University Press, 1968.

Barker, R. G., & Wright, H *Mid-west and its children: The psychological ecology of an American town.* New York: Harper, 1955.

Baron, R. M., Mandel, D. R., Adams, C. A., & Griffin, L. M. Effects of social density in University residential environments. *Journal of Personality and Social Psychology,* 1976, **34**, 434–446.

Baum, A., & Davis, G. E. Spatial and social aspects of crowding perception. *Environment and Behavior,* 1976, **8**, 527–544.

Baum, A., & Greenberg, C. I. Waiting for a crowd: The behavioral and perceptual effects of anticipated crowding. *Journal of Personality and Social Psychology,* 1975, **32**, 671–679.

Baum, A., Harpin, R. E., & Valins, S. The role of group phenomena in the experience of crowding. *Environment and Behavior,* 1975, **7**, 185–198.

Baum, A., & Koman, S. K. Differential response to anticipated crowding: Psychological effects of social and spatial density. *Journal of Personality and Social Psychology,* 1976, **34**, 526–536.

Baum, A., Riess, M., & O'Hara, J. Architectural variants of reactions to spatial invasion. *Environment and Behavior,* 1974, **6**, 91–100.

Baum, A., & Valins, S. Residential environments, group size and crowding. Proceedings of the 81st Annual Convention of the American Psychological Association, 1973, pp. 211–212.

Baxter, J. Interpersonal spacing in natural settings. *Sociometry,* 1970, **33**, 444–456.

Baxter, J. C., & Rozelle, R. M. Nonverbal expression as a function of crowding during a simulated police-citizen encounter. *Journal of Personality and Social Psychology,* 1975, **32**, 40–54.

Bickman, L., Teger, A., Gabriele, T., McLaughlin, C., Berger, M., & Sunaday, E. Dormitory density and helping behavior. *Environment and Behavior,* 1973, **5**, 464–491.

Biderman, A. D., Louria, M., & Bacchus, J. *Historical incidents of extreme overcrowding.* Washington, D.C.: Bureau of Social Science Research, 1963.

Booth, A. *Final Report: Urban crowding project.* Ottawa: Ministry of State for Urban Affairs, 1975.

Booth, A., & Cowell, J. Urban crowding and health. *Journal of Health and Social Behavior,* 1978, in press.

Booth, A., & Johnson, D. R. The effect of crowding on child health and development. *American Behavioral Scientist,* 1975, **18**, 736–749.

Booth, A., Welch, S., & Johnson, D. R. Crowding and urban crime rates. *Urban Affairs Quarterly,* 1976, **11,** 291–307.

Brain, P. F. Mammalian behavior and the adrenal cortex—a review. *Behavioral Biology,* 1972, **7,** 453–477.

Calhoun, J. B. The social aspects of population dynamics. *Journal of Mammalogy,* 1952, **33,** 139–159.

Calhoun, J. B. A behavioral sink. In E. L. Bliss (Ed.), *Roots of behavior.* New York: Harper, 1962. Pp. 295–315. (a)

Calhoun, J. B. Population density and social pathology. *Scientific American,* 1962, **206,** 139-148. (b)

Calhoun, J. B. *The ecology and sociology of the Norway rat.* Publ. No. 1008. Washington, D.C.: U.S. Public Health Service, 1963. (a)

Calhoun, J. B. The social use of space. In W. V. Mayer & R. G. Van Gelder (Eds.), *Physiological mammalogy.* Vol. 1. New York: Academic Press, 1963. Pp. 1–187. (b)

Carey, G. W. Density, crowding, stress and the ghetto. *American Behavioral Scientist,* 1972, **15,** 495–508.

Cartwright, D. The nature of group cohesiveness. In D. Cartwright & A. Zander (Eds.), *Group dynamics.* New York: Harper, 1968. Pp. 91–109.

Cassell, J. *Rapid population growth: Consequences and policy-implications.* Baltimore: Johns Hopkins Press, 1971.

Chandler, M. J., Koch, D., & Paget, K. F. Developmental changes in the response of children to conditions of crowding and congestion. In H. McGurk (Ed.), *Ecological factors in human development.* Amsterdam: North-Holland Publ., 1976. Pp. 111–123.

Chapin, F. S. The relationship of housing to mental health. Working paper for the Expert Committee on the Public Health Aspects of Housing of the World Health Organization, June 1961.

Choi, S. C., Mirjafari, A., & Weaver, H. B. The concept of crowding: A critical review and proposal of an alternative approach. *Environment and Behavior,* 1976, **8,** 345–362.

Chombert de Lauwe, P., & Chombert de Lauwe, M. *Famille et habitation* Paris: Editions du Centre Nationale de la Recherche Scientifique, 1959.

Christian, J. J. The adreno-pituitary system and population cycles in mammals. *Journal of Mammalogy,* 1950, **31,** 247–259.

Christian, J. J. The role of endocrine and behavioral factors in the growth of mammalian populations. In A. Gorbman (Ed.), *Comparative endocrinology.* New York: Wiley, 1959. Pp. 71–97.

Christian, J. J. Endocrine adaptive mechanisms and the physiologic regulation of population growth. In W. V. Mayer & R. G. Van Gelder (Eds.), *Physiological mammalogy.* New York: Academic Press, 1963. Pp. 189–353.

Christian, J. J., & Davis, D. E. Social and endocrine factors are integrated in the regulation of growth of mammalian populations. *Science,* 1964, **18,** 1550–1560.

Christian, J. J., Flyger, V., & Davis, D. C. Factors in the mass mortality of a herd of sika deer, Cervus nippon. *Chesapeake Science,* 1960, **1,** 79–95.

Christian, J. J., Lloyd, J. A., & Davis, D. E. The role of endocrines in the self-regulation of mammalian populations. In G. Pincus (Ed.), *Recent progress in hormone research.* Vol. 21. New York: Academic Press, 1965. Pp. 501–578.

Clarke, J. R. Influence of numbers on reproduction and survival in two experimental vole populations. *Proceedings of the Royal Society of London, Series B,* 1955, **144,** 68–85.

Cohen, J. L., Sladen, B., & Bennett, B. The effects of situational variables on judgements of crowding. *Sociometry,* 1975, **38,** 273–281.

Cohen, S., Rothbart, M., & Phillips, S. Locus of control and the generality of learned helplessness in humans. *Journal of Personality and Social Psychology,* 1976, **34,** 1049–1056.

Coopersmith, S. *Antecedents of self-esteem.* San Francisco: Freeman, 1967.

Cozby, P. G. Effects of density, activity and personality on environmental preferences. *Journal of Research in Personality,* 1973, **7,** 45–60.

Crew, F. A., & Mirskaia, L. Effect of density on adult mouse populations. *Biologia Generalis*, 1931, **7**, 239–250.

D'Atri, D. Psychophysiological responses to crowding. *Environment and Behavior*, 1975, **7**, 237–252.

Day, A. T., & Day, L. H. Cross-national comparison of population density. *Science*, 1973, **181**, 1016–1023.

Deevey, E. S. The hare and the haruspex: A cautionary tale. *American Scientist*, 1960, **48**, 415–429.

Department of the Environment. The social effects of living off the ground. *Housing Development Directorate Occasional Papers 1/75*. London: HM Stationery Office, 1975.

Desor, J. A. Toward a psychological theory of crowding. *Journal of Personality and Social Psychology*, 1972, **21**, 79–83.

Draper, P. Crowding among hunter gatherers: The !Kung Bushmen. *Science*, 1973, **182**, 301–303.

Dubos, R. The social environment, In H. M. Proshansky, W. H. Ittleson, & L. G. Rivlin (Eds.), *Environmental psychology*. New York: Holt, 1970. Pp. 202–208.

Duke, M., & Nowicki, S. A new measure and social-learning model for interpersonal distance. *Journal of Experimental Research in Personality*, 1972, **6**, 119–132.

Edney, J. J. Place and space: The effects of experience with a physical locale. *Journal of Experimental Social Psychology*, 1972, **8**, 124–135.

Edney, J. J. Human territoriality. *Psychological Bulletin*, 1974, **81**, 959–975.

Edney, J. J. Human territories: Comment on functional properties. *Environment and Behavior*, 1976, **8**, 31–47.

Efran, M. G., & Cheyne, J. A. Affective concomitants of the invasion of shared space: Behavioral, physiological and verbal indications. *Journal of Personality and Social Psychology*, 1974, **29**, 219–226.

Eisenberg, J, F. A comparative study in rodent ethology with emphasis on the evolution of social behavior. *Proceedings of the United States National Museum*, 1967, **122**, No. 3597, 1–51.

Epstein, Y. M., & Karlin, R. A. Effects of acute experimental crowding. *Journal of Applied Social Psychology*, 1975, **5**, 34–53.

Esser, A. H. A biosocial perspective on crowding. In J. Wohlwill & D. Carson (Eds.), *Environment and the social sciences: Perspectives and applications*. Washington, D.C.: American Psychological Association, 1972. Pp. 15–28.

Esser, A. H., Chamberlaine, A. S., Chapple, E. D., & Kline, N. S. Territoriality of patients on a research ward. In J. Wortis (Ed.), *Recent advances in biological psychiatry*. Vol. 7. New York: Plenum, 1965. Pp. 36–44.

Evans, G. W., & Eichelman, W. Preliminary models of conceptual linkages among proxemic variables. *Environment and Behavior*, 1976, **8**, 87–116.

Evans, G. W., & Howard, R. B. Personal space. *Psychological Bulletin*, 1973, **80**, 334–344.

Fanning, D. M. Families in flats. *British Medical Journal*, 1967, **18**, 382–386.

Fisher, J. D., & Byrne, D. Too close for comfort: Sex differences in response to invasions of personal space. *Journal of Personality and Social Psychology*, 1975, **32**, 15–53.

Forbes, G., & Gromoll, H. The lost-letter technique as a measure of social variables: some exploratory findings. *Social Forces*, 1971, **50**, 113–115.

Frede, M. C., Gantney, D. B., & Baxter, J. C. Relationships between body image boundary and interaction patterns on the maps test. *Journal of Consulting and Clinical Psychology*, 1968, **32**, 575–578.

Freedman, J. L. The effects of population density on humans. In J. T. Fawcett (Ed.), *Psychological perspectives on population*. New York: Basic Books, 1973. Pp. 209–238.

Freedman, J. L. *Crowding and human behavior*. San Francisco: Freeman, 1975.

Freedman, J. L., Heshka, S., & Levy, A. Population density and pathology: Is there a relationship? *Journal of Experimental Social Psychology*, 1975, **11**, 539–552.

Freedman, J. L., Klevansky, S., & Ehrlich, P. R. The effect of crowding on human task performance. *Journal of Applied Social Psychology,* 1971, **1,** 7–25.

Freedman, J. L., Levy, A. S., Buchanan, R. W., & Price, J. Crowding and human aggressiveness. *Journal of Experimental Social Psychology,* 1972, **8,** 528–548.

Galle, O. R., Gove, W. R., & McPherson, J. M. Population density and pathology: What are the relations for man? *Science,* 1972, **176,** 23–30.

Gillis, A. R. Population density and social pathology: The case of building type, social allowance and juvenile delinquency. *Social Forces,* 1974, **53,** 306–314.

Glass, D. C., & Singer, J. E. *Urban stress.* New York: Academic Press, 1972.

Goeckner, D. J., Greenough, W. T., & Mead, W. R. Deficits in learning tasks following chronic overcrowding in rats. *Journal of Personality and Social Psychology,* 1973, **28,** 256–261.

Goffman, E. *Presentation of self in everyday life.* New York: Doubleday, 1959.

Goffman, E. *Behavior in public places.* New York: Plenum, 1963.

Goldberg, G. N., Kiesler, C. A., & Collins, B. E. Visual behavior and face-to-face distance during interaction. *Sociometry,* 1969, **32,** 42–53.

Green, H. W. *Persons admitted to Cleveland State Hospital.* Cleveland: Cleveland Health Council, 1939.

Griffitt, W., & Veitch, R. Hot and crowded: Influences of population density and temperature on interpersonal affective behavior. *Journal of Personality and Social Psychology,* 1971, **17,** 92–98.

Hall, E. T., *The hidden dimension.* Garden City, N.Y.: Doubleday, 1966.

Hamburg, D. A. Crowding, stranger contact, and aggressive behavior. In L. Levi (Ed.), *Society, stress and disease.* Vol. 1. London and New York: Oxford University Press, 1971. Pp. 209–218.

Hanson, L., & Wicker, A. Effects of overmanning on group experience and task performance. Paper presented at the Western Psychological Association Convention, Anaheim, California, April, 1973.

Hartnett, J. J., Bailey, K. G., & Gibson, F. W. Personal space as influenced by sex and type of movement. *Journal of Psychology,* 1970, **76,** 139–144.

Hauser, P. Application of the ideal-type constructs to the metropolis in the economically less-advanced area. In P. Hauser & L. Schnor (Eds.), *The study of urbanization.* New York: Wiley, 1965.

Hird, J. P. Vertical living: Health aspects. *Royal Society of Health Journal,* 1967, **86,** 171–172.

Horner, M. S. The motive to avoid success and changing aspirations of college women. In J. Bartwick (Ed.), *Readings on the psychology of women.* New York: Harper, 1972. Pp. 62–67. (b)

Horner, M. S. Toward an understanding of achievement-related conflicts in women. *Journal of Social Issues,* 1972, **28,** 157–176. (b)

Horowitz, M. J., Duff, D. F., & Stratton, L. O. Human spatial behavior. *American Journal of Psychotherapy,* 1965, **19,** 20–28.

Hutt, C., & Vaizey, M. J. Differential effects of group density on social behavior. *Nature (London),* 1966, **209,** 1371–1372.

Ittleson, W. H., Proshansky, H. M., & Rivlin, L. G. The environmental psychology of the psychiatric ward. In H. M. Proshansky, W. H. Ittleson, & L. G. Rivlin (Eds.), *Environmental psychology: Man and his physical setting.* New York: Holt, 1970. Pp. 419–439.

Jackson, D. *Personality research form manual.* Goshen, N.Y.: Research Psychologists Press, 1967.

Jourard, S. M. Some psychological aspects of privacy. *Law and Contemporary Problems,* 1966, **31,** 307–318.

Kelley, H. N., & Thibaut, J. Group problem solving. In G. Lindzey & E. Aronson (Eds.), *The handbook of social psychology.* Vol. 4. Reading, Mass.: Addison-Wesley, 1969, Pp. 1–101.

Kelvin, P. *The bases of social behavior: An approach through order and value.* New York: Holt, 1970.

Kelvin, P. A social-psychological examination of privacy. *British Journal of Social and Clinical Psychology,* 1973, **12,** 248–261.

Kessler, A. *Interplay between social ecology and physiology, genetics and population dynamics of mice.* (Doctoral dissertation, Rockefeller University) Ann Arbor, Mich.: University Microfilms, No. 67-9869. 1966.

Kleck, R. E. Interaction distance and non-verbal agreeing responses. *British Journal of Social and Clinical Psychology,* 1970, **9,** 180–182.

Knowles, E. S. Boundaries around group interaction: The effect of group size and member status on boundary permeability. *Journal of Personality and Social Psychology* 1973, **20,** 327–331.

Knowles, E. S., & Bassett, R. L. Groups and crowds as social entities: Effects of activity, size, and member similarity on non-members. *Journal of Personality and Social Psychology,* 1976, **34,** 837–845.

Korte, C., & Kerr, N. Response to altruistic opportunities under urban and rural conditions. *Journal of Social Psychology,* 1975, **95,** 183–184.

Korte, C., Ypma, I., & Toppen, A. Helpfulness in Dutch society as a function of urbanization and environmental input level. *Journal of Personality and Social Psychology,* 1975, **32,** 996–1003.

Kutner, D. A., Jr. Overcrowding: Human responses to density and visual exposure. *Human Relations,* 1973, **26,** 31–50.

Landis, C., & Page, J. D. *Modern society and mental disease.* New York: Farrar & Rinehart, 1938.

Lazarus, R. S. *Psychological stress and the coping process.* New York: McGraw-Hill, 1966.

Lefcourt, H. M. Recent developments in the study of locus of control. In B. A. Maher (Ed.), *Progress in experimental personality research.* Vol. 6. New York: Academic Press, 1972.

Lefcourt, H. M. The function of the illusions of control and freedom. *American Psychologist,* 1973, **28,** 417–425.

Leibman, M. The effects of sex and race norms on personal space. *Environmental Behavior,* 1970, **2,** 208–246.

Levi, L., & Andersson, L. *Psychosocial stress: Population, environment and quality of life.* New York: Halsted Press, 1975.

Levy, L., & Herzog, A. N. Effects of population density and crowding on health and social adaptation. *Journal of Health and Social Behvaior,* 1974, **15,** 228–240.

Little, K. B. Personal space. *Journal of Experimental Social Psychology,* 1965, **1,** 237–247.

Lloyd, J. A. Effects of crowding among animals: Implications for man. *Sociological Symposium,* 1975, **14,** 6–23.

Loo, C. M. The effects of spatial density on the social behavior of children. *Journal of Applied Social Psychology,* 1972, **2,** 372–381.

Loo, C. Important issues in researching the effects of crowding in humans. *Representative Research in Social Psychology,* 1973, **4,** 219–226.

Loo, C. The psychological study of crowding: Some historical roots and conceptual developments. *American Behavioral Scientist,* 1975, **18,** 826-842.

Macdonald, W., & Oden, C. W., Jr. Effects of extreme crowding on the performance of five married couples during twelve weeks of intensive training. *Proceedings of the 81st Annual Convention of the American Psychological Association,* 1973, Pp. 209–210.

Mandler, G. The interruption of behavior. In D. Levine (Ed.), *Nebraska Symposium on Motivation.* Lincoln: University of Nebraska Press, 1964. Pp. 163–219.

Mandler, G., & Watson, D. L. Anxiety and the interruption of behavior. In C. D. Spielberger (Ed.), *Anxiety and behavior.* New York: Academic Press, 1966. Pp. 263–287.

Marsden, J. M. Crowding and animal behavior. In J. F. Wohlwill & D. H. Carson (Eds.), *Environment and the social sciences: Perspectives and applications.* Washington, D.C.: American Psychological Association, 1972. Pp. 5–14.

Marshall, N. J. Orientations towards privacy: Environmental and personality components. Unpublished doctoral dissertation in Psychology, University of California, Berkeley, 1971.

Marshall, J. E., & Heslin, R. Boys and girls together: Sexual composition and the effect of density and group size on cohesiveness. *Journal of Personality and Social Psychology,* 1975, **31,** 952–961.

McBride, G., King, M. G., & James, J. W. Social proximity effects on galvanic skin responsiveness in adult humans. *Journal of Psychology,* 1965, **61,** 153–157.

McCarthy, J. D., Galle, O. R., & Zimmern, W. Population density, social structure and interpersonal violence. *American Behavioral Scientist,* 1975, **18,** 771–789.

McClelland, L., & Auslander, N. Perceptions of crowding and pleasantness in public settings. *Environmental Psychology and Non-Verbal Behavior,* 1977, in press.

McGrew, P. L. Social and spatial density effects on spacing behavior in preschool children. *Journal of Child Psychology and Psychiatry,* 1970, **11,** 197–205.

McGrew, W. C. *An ethological study of children's behavior.* New York: Academic Press, 1972.

McKenna, W., & Morgenthau, S. Unpublished research. Graduate Center, City University of New York, 1970.

McPherson, J. M. Population density and social pathology: A re-examination. *Sociological Symposium,* 1975, **141,** 76–90.

Melbin, M. Time territoriality. Unpublished manuscript, Boston University, 1976.

Merrens, M. Nonemergency helping behavior in various sized communities. *Journal of Social Psychology,* 1973, **90,** 327–328.

Milgram, S. The experience of living in cities. *Science,* 1970, **167,** 1461–1468.

Mitchell, R. E. Some social implications of high density housing. *American Sociological Review,* 1971, **36,** 18–29.

Munroe, R. L. & Munroe, R. H. Population density and affective relationships in three East African societies. *Journal of Social Psychology,* 1972, **88,** 15–18.

Murray, R. The influence of population density upon the behavior and personality of school children. Unpublished doctoral dissertation, University of Dundee, 1973.

Murray, R. The influence of crowding on children's behavior. In D. Canter & T. Lee (Eds.), XX New York: Academic Press, 1974. Pp. 112–117. (a)

Murray, R. Overcrowding and aggression in primary school children. In C. M. Morrison (Ed.), *Educational priority, EPA, a Scottish study.* Edinburgh: HM Stationery Office, 1974. (b)

Nesbitt, P. D., & Steven, G. Personal space and stimulus intensity at a Southern California Amusement Park. *Sociometry,* 1974, **37,** 105–115.

Newman, O. *Defensible space.* New York: Macmillan, 1972.

Nogami, G. Y. Crowding: Effects of group size, room size or density? *Journal of Applied Social Psychology,* 1976, **6,** 105–125.

O'Neill, S. M., & Paluck, R. J. Altering territoriality through reinforcement. *Proceedings of the 81st Annual Convention of the American Psychological Association,* 1973, **8,** 901–902.

Paluck, R. J., & Esser, A. H. Controlled experimental modification of aggressive behavioral condition of severely retarded boys. *American Journal of Mental Deficiency,* 1971, **76,** 23–29. (a)

Paluck, R. J., & Esser, A. H. Territorial behavior as an indicator of changes in clinical behavior condition of severely retarded boys. *American Journal of Mental Deficiency,* 1971, **76,** 284–290. (b)

Pastalan, L. A. Privacy as an expression of human territoriality. In L. A. Pastalan and P. H. Carson (Eds.), *Spatial behavior of older people.* Ann Arbor: University of Michigan Press, 1970. Pp. 89–101.

Patterson, M. L., & Holmes, D. S. Social interaction correlates of the M.P.I. extraversion-introversion scale. *American Psychologist,* 1966, **21,** 724–725.

Patterson, M. L., & Sechrest, L. B. Interpersonal distance and impression formation. *Journal of Personality,* 1970, **38,** 161–166.

Paulus, P. B., Annis, A. B., Seta, J. J., Schkade, J. K., & Matthews, R. W. Density does affect task performance. *Journal of Personality and Social Psychology,* 1976, **34,** 248–253.

Paulus, P., Cox, V., McCain, G., & Chandler, J. Some effects of crowding in a prison environment. *Journal of Applied Social Psychology,* 1975, **5,** 86–91.

Paulus, P., McCain, G., & Cox, V. Note on the use of prisons as environments for the investigation of crowding. *Bulletin of the Psychonomic Society,* 1973, **1,** 427–428.

Phares, E. J. *Locus of control: A personality determinant of behavior.* New York: General Learning Press, 1973.

Pollock, H. M., & Furbush, A. M. Mental disease in 12 states, 1919. *Mental Hygiene,* 1921, **5,** 353–389.

Pressman, I., & Carol, A. Crime as a diseconomy of scale. *Review of Social Economy,* 1971, **29,** 227–236.

Proshansky, H. M., Ittleson, W., & Rivlin, L. G. Freedom of choice and behavior in a physical setting. In H. M. Proshansky, W. H. Ittleson, & L. G. Rivlin (Eds.), *Environmental psychology: Man and his physical setting.* New York: Holt, 1970. Pp. 173–183.

Rapoport, A. Toward a redefinition of density. *Environment and Behavior,* 1975, **7,** 133–158.

Rodin, J. Density, perceived choice and response to controllable and uncontrollable outcomes. *Journal of Experimental Social Psychology,* 1976, **12,** 564–578.

Roncek, D. W. Density and crime. A methodological critique. *American Behavioral Scientist,* 1975, **18,** 843–860.

Ross, M., Layton, B., Erickson, B., & Schopler, J. Affect, facial regard, and reactions to crowding. *Journal of Personality and Social Psychology,* 1973, **28,** 67–76.

Rotter, J. Generalised expectancies for internal versus external control of reinforcement. *Psychological Monographs,* 1966, **80,** 1–28.

Saegert, S., Mackintosh, E., & West, S. Two studies of crowding in urban public spaces. *Environment and Behavior,* 1975, **7,** 159–184.

Schmid, C. Completed and attempted suicides. *American Sociological Review,* 1955, **20,** 273–283.

Schmidt, D. E., Goldman, R. D., & Feimer, N. R. Physical and psychological factors associated with perceptions of crowding: An analysis of subcultural differences. *Journal of Applied Psychology,* 1976, **61,** 279–289.

Schmitt, R. C. Density, delinquency and crime in Honolulu. *Sociology and Sociological Research,* 1957, **41,** 274–276.

Schmitt, R. C. Density, health and social disorganization. *American Institute of Planners Journal,* 1966, **32,** 38–40.

Schopler, J., McCallum, R., & Rusbult, C. E. Behavioral interference and internality—Externality as determinants of subject crowding. Unpublished paper, University of North Carolina, Chapel Hill, 1977.

Schopler, J., & Stockdale, J. E. An interference analysis of crowding. *Environmental Psychology and Non-Verbal Behavior,* 1977, **1,** 81–88.

Schwartz, B. The social psychology of privacy. *American Journal of Sociology,* 1968, **73,** 741–752.

Shaw, C. R., & McKay, H. D. *Juvenile delinquency and urban areas.* Chicago: University of Chicago Press, 1942.

Sherrod, D. R. Crowding, perceived control and behavioral after-effects. *Journal of Applied Social Psychology,* 1974, **4,** 171–186.

Sherrod, D. R., & Downs, R. Environmental determinants of altruism: The effects of stimulus overload and perceived control on helping. *Journal of Experimental Social Psychology,* 1974, **10,** 458–479.

Silverman, J. Attentional styles and the study of sex differences. In D. Mostofsky (Ed.), *Attention: Contemporary theory and analysis.* New York: Appleton, 1970. Pp. 61–98.

Simmel, A. Privacy is not an isolated freedom. In J. R. Pennock & J. W. Chapman (Eds.), *Privacy.* New York: Atherton Press, 1971. Pp. 71–87.

Simmel, G. The metropolis and mental life. In G. Simmel, *The sociology of Georg Simmel.* Glencoe, Ill.: Free Press, 1950. Pp. 409–424.

Smith, P. K., & Connolly, K. J. Toys, space and children. *Bulletin of the British Psychological Society,* 1973, **26,** 167.

Smith, S., & Haythorn, W. W. Effects of compatability, crowding, group size and leadership seniority on stress, anxiety, hostility and annoyance in isolated groups. *Journal of Personality and Social Psychology,* 1972, **22,** 67–79.

Snyder, R. L. Reproduction and population pressures. In E. Stellar & J. M. Sprague (Eds.), *Progress in physiological psychology.* Vol. 2. New York: Academic Press, 1968. Pp. 119–160.

Sommer, R. Man's proximate environment. *Journal of Social Issues,* 1966, **22,** 59–70.

Southwick, C. H. The population dynamics of confined house mice supplied with unlimited food. *Ecology,* 1955, **36,** 212–225.

Southwick, C. H. An experimental study of intragroup agonistic behavior in rhesus monkeys *Behavior,* 1967, **28,** 182–209.

Stea, D. Space, territory and human movements. *Landscape,* 1965, **15,** 13–16.

Stockdale, J. E., & Schopler, J. The effects of spatial density and resource scarcity on subjective crowding. Unpublished manuscript, London School of Economics, 1976.

Stockdale, J. E., & Zallik, S. The effects of room size, competition and grouping on the perception of crowding. Unpublished manuscript, London School of Economics, 1976.

Stockdale, J. E., Wittman, L. S., Jones, L. E. & Greaves, D. A. A multidimensional analysis of subjective crowding. Paper presented at Human Consequences of Crowding Symposium, Antalya, Turkey, 1977.

Stokols, D. On the distinction between density and crowding: Some implications for further research. *Psychological Review,* 1972, **79,** 275–277 (a).

Stokols, D. A social-psychological model of human crowding phenomena *American Institute of Planners Journal,* 1972, **38,** 72–83 (b).

Stokols, D. The experience of crowding in primary and secondary environments. *Environment and Behavior,* 1976, **8,** 49–85.

Stokols, D., Rau, M., Pinner, B., & Schopler, J. Physical, social and personal determinants of the perception of crowding. *Environment and Behavior,* 1973, **5,** 87–116.

Stokols, D., & Resnick, S. An experimental assessment of neutral and personal crowding experiences. Paper presented at the Southeastern Psychological Association Convention, Atlanta, Georgia, 1975.

Stokols, D., Smith, T. E., & Prostor, J. J. Partitioning and perceived crowding in a public space. *American Behavioral Scientist,* 1975, **18,** 792–814.

Sundstrom, E. An experimental study of crowding: Effects of room size, intrusion and goal blocking on nonverbal behavior, self-disclosure and self-reported stress. *Journal of Personality and Social Psychology,* 1975, **35,** 645–654 (a).

Sundstrom, E. Towards an interpersonal model of crowding. *Sociological Symposium,* 1975, **14,** 129–144 (b).

Thiessen, D. D., & Rodgers, D. A. Population density and endocrine function. *Psychological Bulletin,* 1961, **58,** 441–451.

Thomas, E. J., & Fink, C. F. Effects of group size. *Psychological Bulletin,* 1963, **60,** 371–384.

Valins, S., & Baum, A. Residential group size, social interaction and crowding. *Environment and Behavior,* 1973, **5,** 421–439.

Van den Haag, E. On privacy. In J. R. Pennock & J. W. Chapman (Eds.), *Privacy.* New York: Atherton Press, 1971. Pp. 149–168.

Veno, A., & Peeke, H. U. S. Research on crowding in prisons: Methodological problems and ethical concerns. *Bulletin of the Psychonomic Society,* 1974, **3,** 183–184.

Vine, I. Social spacing in animals and man. *Social Science Information (Animal and Human Ethology),* 1973, **12,** 7–50.

Watson, E., & Friend, R. Measurement of social evaluative anxiety. *Journal of Consulting and Clinical Psychology,* 1969, **33,** 448–457.

Webb, S. D. The meaning, measurement and interchangeability of density and crowding indices. *Australian and New Zealand Journal of Sociology,* 1975, **11**, 60–62.

Webb, S. D., & Collette, J. Urban ecological and household correlates of stress-alleviative drug use. *American Behavioral Scientist,* 1975, **18**, 750–770.

Weinstein, M. A. The uses of privacy in the good life. In J. R. Pennock & J. W. Chapman (Eds.), *Privacy.* New York: Atherton Press, 1971. Pp. 88–104.

Westin, A. *Privacy and freedom.* New York: Atheneum, 1967.

White, R. W. Motivation reconsidered: The concept of competence. *Psychological Review,* 1959, **66**, 297–333.

Wicker, A. Undermanning theory and research: Implications for the study of psychological and behavioral effects of excess populations. *Representative Research in Social Psychology,* 1973, **4**, 185–206.

Wicker, A. Too many, too few: Effects of overmanning and undermanning on human behavior. Colloquium presented at the University of California, Irvine, May 1974.

Wicker, A. W., McGrath, J. E., & Armstrong, G. E. Organization size and behavior setting capacity as determinants of member participation. *Behavioral Science,* 1972, **17**, 499–513.

Willems, E. P., & Campbell, D. E. One path through the cafeteria. *Environment and Behavior,* 1976, **8**, 125–140.

Winsborough, H. H. The social consequences of high population density. *Law and Contemporary Problems,* 1965, **30**, 120–126.

Wirth, L. Urbanism as a way of life. *American Journal of Sociology,* 1938, **44**, 1–44.

Wohlwill, J. F. Human adaptation to levels of environmental stimulation. *Human Ecology,* 1974, **2**, 127–147.

Worchel, S., & Teddlie, C. The experience of crowding: A two-factor theory. *Journal of Personality and Social Psychology,* 1976, **34**, 30–40.

Wortman, C., & Brehm, J. Responses to uncontrollable outcomes. In L. Berkowitz (Ed.), *Advances in experimental social psychology.* Vol. 8. New York: Academic Press, 1975. Pp. 278–336.

Wynne-Edwards, V. C. *Animal dispersion in relation to social behavior.* New York: Hafner, 1962.

Wynne-Edwards, V. C. Self regulating systems in populations of animals. *Science,* 1965, **147**, 1543–1548.

Zlutnik, S., & Altman, I. *Environment and the social sciences: Perspectives and applications.* Washington, D.C.: American Psychological Association, 1972. Pp. 44–58.

SALIENCE, ATTENTION, AND ATTRIBUTION: TOP OF THE HEAD PHENOMENA[1]

Shelley E. Taylor

and

Susan T. Fiske

HARVARD UNIVERISTY
CAMBRIDGE, MASSACHUSETTS

[1]Research described in this chapter and preparation of the chapter itself were supported by research grants from NIMH (25827, 26460, and 26919) and from NSF (BNS77-009922) to the senior author. The junior author was supported by a National Science Foundation Graduate Fellowship. The suggestions and contributions of those who commented on earlier drafts of the chapter are gratefully acknowledged, and we are especially grateful for the extended comments of Leslie McArthur, Richard Nisbett, David Sears, Mark Snyder, Michael Storms, and Joachim Winkler.

249

I. Introduction

The last 20 years of research in social psychology testify to an enduring interest in issues of causal perception. How does an individual take in information about the social environment and put it together to make inferences about what causes things to happen as they do and what causes people to behave as they do? How thorough is the social perceiver's search of the environment and how sophisticated is this causal analysis? Heider (1958) first raised these issues systematically in his *Psychology of Interpersonal Relations*. He suggested that an understanding of how people assess causality and infer the dispositions of the people around them could be elucidated by uncovering the naive epistemology of the social perceiver. He drew upon Brunswik (1934) "lens" model of perception as a model of social perception, maintaining that the object of scientific study should be how the mind selects, organizes, and imputes meaning to the many social stimuli that impinge upon it. Heider assumed that the goal of the naive perceiver is to develop and stabilize perceptions of the enduring properties of persons and things through an examination of action, intention, ability, and environment.

As testimony to the heuristic value of Heider's ideas, two general lines of research evolved from his initial writings. One has likened the social perceiver to a naive scientist (Kelley, 1967, 1971). According to Kelley, the lay attributor "generally acts like a good scientist, examining the covariation between a given effect and various possible causes" (Kelley, 1971, p. 2). The perceiver assesses the distinctiveness of an outcome and the extent to which it covaries across time, persons, and modalities, in attempting to reach an explanation for the outcome. Though Kelley acknowledged that the attributor must occasionally make inferences on the basis of incomplete or faulty data, he concluded that with a few exceptions, "the lay attributor still uses [these data] in a reasonable and unbiased manner" (Kelly, 1971, p. 2). The research generated by Kelley's model (e.g., Garland, Hardy, & Stephenson, 1975; McArthur, 1972) has found some support for its predictions.

A second position, which also derives in part from Heider's work, has been slower to develop, at least within social psychology. This position maintains that instead of using the "scientific-like" processes outlined by Kelley, many perceivers seek a single, sufficient, and salient explanation for behavior, often the first satisfactory one that comes along (Jones & Davis, 1965; Kanouse, 1972). Within cognitive psychology, for example, judgment researchers have found that instead of employing base rate or consensus information logically, people are often more influenced by a single, colorful piece of case history evidence (Kahneman & Tversky, 1973; Nisbett, Borgida, Crandall, & Reed, 1976). Instead of using correlational evidence appropriately, subjects' subjective estimates of correlation magnitudes are often determined largely by positive instances (Jenkins & Ward, 1965; Smedslund, 1963). Instead of reviewing all the evidence that bears upon a particular problem, people frequently use the information which is most salient or available to them, that is, that which is most easily brought to mind (Tversky & Kahneman, 1974).

Within social psychology, the evidence that salient stimuli are used as a basis for causal inference has come largely from research on self-perception. In a study by Kiesler, Nisbett, and Zanna (1969), for example, a subject who has just agreed to proselytize against air pollution hears another subject say, "I'll proselytize for auto safety because it is important to me" (belief-relevant condition) or "I'll do it because this is a worthwhile study" (belief-irrelevant condition). The subject's anti-air-pollution beliefs are correspondingly strengthened by the "belief" manipulation, but not by the "belief-irrelevant" condition, thus testifying to the impact of a logically irrelevant but salient stimulus upon the expression of personal and, one would have thought, strongly held attitudes. A large number of studies fits this salience format, and in most cases the conclusion to be drawn is that making almost any cognition or behavior salient will influence the subject's attitudes and behavior (e.g.,Bandler, Madaras, & Bem, 1968; Davison & Valins, 1969; Nisbett & Schachter, 1966; L. Ross, Rodin, & Zimbardo, 1969; Schacter & Singer, 1962; Storms & Nisbett, 1970; Valins, 1966; Valins & Ray, 1967).

The fact that salient stimuli have such seemingly important effects on perceptions of causality has led theorists explicitly to acknowledge and generalize this principle. Jones and Davis (1965), for example, stated that:

> The perceiver seeks to find sufficient reason why the person acted and why the act took a particular form. Instead of the potentially infinite regress of cause and effect which characterizes an impersonal, scientific analysis, the perceiver's explanation comes to a stop when an intention or motive has the quality of being reason enough [p. 220].

Kanouse (1972) hypothesized that:

> Individuals may be primarily motivated to seek a single, sufficient, or satisfactory explanation for any given event, rather than one which is the best of all possible explanations...when more than one explanation is potentially available to an individual, which one he adopts may depend primarily on which of the various possible explanations is most salient [p. 131].

Our own position, which we will develop in this chapter, is that individuals frequently respond with little thought to the most salient stimuli in their environment. We believe that the causal attributions people make, the opinions people express, and the impressions they form of others in work or social situations are often shaped by seemingly trivial but highly salient information and that, accordingly, such attitudes and impressions show relatively little cross-situational consistency (e.g., Schuman & Johnson, 1976; Wicker, 1969).

We will call these kinds of attributions, opinions, and impressions "top of the head" phenomena. When someone says, "I gave you an answer off the top of my head," that person means that the answer or observation has very little thought behind it and that the person has responded with the first thing that came to mind. A "top of the head" answer implies that the respondent has spent little time on the matter, gathered little or no data beyond that of the immediate situation, and responded with an opinion nonetheless. The further implication is that the individual is not be be blamed, should the opinion be changed or forgotten.

The thesis of this chapter is, in part, that social psychologists study "top of the head" phenomena in their experimental investigations. They create artificial, isolated moments in time, in which the subject is invited to participate. By developing a relatively bland environment which contains only one or two interesting, attention-getting stimuli (the manipulations), the experimenter is able to predict and control the reactions of the subjects in that environment. In the experimental world, then, what is made salient becomes the basis of the subjects' opinions and impressions. This characterization of experimentation is scarcely new and constitutes the basis of much criticism of experimental social psychology. Our position, however, is quite different from that of such critics. We believe that this experimental portrait of a fragmented world, in which individuals respond with little thought to the most salient stimuli in their environment, mirrors reality.

One of the authors recently took part in a survey of women's professional experiences at Harvard. Questions included such items as, "Are your committee assignments heavier, lighter, or the same as other people's?" "Have you ever been the victim of overt sex discrimination?" "Are your colleagues appreciative of your work?" Six months later, when the tallied results were distributed, and this author looked them over, she realized she had no idea how she had responded to a majority of the items. Had it been a good day or a bad day? Was it a semester with lots of committee assignments or not? Had anyone recently complimented her on her work? Had she been mistaken for a secretary on that particular day?

Before we are accused of a radically situationist approach to behavior, let us hasten to add that we are attempting to explain the behavior of, at best, all of the people some of the time, or perhaps more modestly, some of the people some of the time. It is patently obvious that there are issues, decisions, and opinions to which we direct a substantial amount of attention, effort, and time, and while the product of such extensive rumination may not be perfectly rational using some objective criterion, one can demonstrate an information search, a consideration of alternatives, and other characteristics of what we call "good decisions" in the process the individual goes through. These are not the kinds of situations we are attempting to describe. We are characterizing that tremendous number of unself-conscious opinion statements and impressions that form the substance of our chatter, rather than our reflections, and of our unthinking reactions, rather than our thoughts.

Our chapter is an analysis of this "top of the head" phenomenon particularly as it relates to self-perception and the perception of others. We will maintain that "top of the head" phenomena are far more common than we would like to admit, that they can be predicted quite reliably, that they account for an enormous amount of our experimental findings, and that they bear a significant impact on our causal attributions, learning, memory, evaluations, and imputation of personal characteristics to others.

We will make the claim that causal perception is substantially determined by where one's attention is directed within the environment and that attention itself is a function of what information is salient. In this context, we will suggest that the Jones–Nisbett actor–observer effect is substantially a manifestation of perceptual salience, and we will then broaden this conclusion to suggest that causal agents are seen as efficacious to the extent that information about them is salient. We will then review evidence suggesting that whether the social perceiver attributes causality to the dispositional attributes of actors or to situational factors in the environment can also be predicted by focus of attention: Observers will perceive situations as more causally important to the extent that situations are made salient; observers will perceive dispositions of actors as more important to the extent that actors are made salient.

In the fifth section, we will review the effects that differential attention has on social perceptions other than causal perceptions. We will show that when the salient stimulus is a person, differential attention affects evaluations of attitudinal and behavioral consistency, affective judgments, and perceived representativeness.

Sixth, we will examine the literature which assesses how these effects are mediated. We will suggest that information about salient stimuli is both more plentiful and more available, but that this latter factor—availability—is what mediates the attention–causality relationship. We propose that what may make information more available is either (a) encoding through more than one mode, specifically both iconic and semantic encoding, or (b) encoding which differs from the encoding of other stimuli, that is, images as opposed to semantic encoding. We will then apply some of these ideas to the question of what makes particular cognitions salient.

In the seventh section, we will examine the generalizability of salience

effects. Are they reserved for situations that are redundant, unsurprising, unarousing, uninvolving, and uninformative, or do they also arise in more involving,
engrossing, arousing, informative situations as well? In short, we will be ad-
dressing the question: Are salience effects engaged not only by certain cues, but
by certain situations as well? Finally, we will raise the question: Is there a style of
processing information that is reflected in these salience effects? Social perceivers experience salience effects as absurd, since they fly in the face of our beliefs
about self-conscious, intentional, rational choice behavior. We will attempt to
salvage both views of the information processor—the salience viewpoint and the
naive scientist viewpoint—by suggesting that they reflect two qualitatively different kinds of information processing.

II. Salience and Causality

The hypothesis that causal analysis is affected by what is salient originated
with Heider (1958). In explaining how the naive perceiver construes meaning
from the social environment, Heider (1958) noted that the perceiver is prone to
certain biases, as a function of some bits of information being more salient than
other bits of information.

> It seems that behavior in particular has such salient properties it tends to engulf the total
> field rather than be confined to its proper position as a local stimulus whose interpretation
> requires additional data of a surrounding field—the situation in social perception [p. 54].

Partly on the basis of these observations, Jones and Nisbett (1972) developed
what can be interpreted as a perceptual theory of actor–observer differences in
perceived causality. Jones and Nisbett hypothesized a chronic difference in actors'
and observers' accounts of the causes of behavior. Specifically, they suggested
that actors interpret their own behavior largely in situational terms (e.g., I yelled
because everyone caused me trouble today), whereas observers interpret an actor's behavior in dispositional terms (e.g., he yelled because he is a hostile
person). Though Jones and Nisbett proposed several possible mediators of their
actor–observer effect, the one that has received the most attention is the
hypothesized differences in what information is perceptually prominent.

Actors' sensory receptors are directed outward away from their own behavior and toward the environment. Accordingly, actors should have available to
them more information and more salient information about their environment
than about themselves, since they literally cannot see themselves behaving.
When asked the reasons why they engaged in a particular behavior, actors should
think back over their store of information and attribute causality to their environment, since environmental information is most salient, plentiful, and available.

The sensory receptors of observers viewing an actor, on the other hand, are focused on the actor who is a dynamic figure against a situational ground. As Heider noted, for an observer, the actor's behavior is salient. The observer's attention is drawn to the actor, and accordingly the observer gathers more information about the actor's behavior than about the actor's environment. When asked the reasons why the actor engaged in a particular behavior, observers should think back over their store of information and attribute causality to the actor, since actor information is most salient, plentiful, and available. In summary, then, both actors and observers overrepresent that information which is perceptually salient in order to make a causal explanation of an event.

If it is the case that actor–observer differences are mediated by perceptual salience, then it should be possible to alter perceptions of causality by manipulating what information is salient. Storms (1973) developed a test of the perceptual explanation of the actor–observer effect. He created a situation where two (actor) subjects exchanged information about themselves, while two other subjects acted as observers; each observer watched only one actor, A or B. Following the interaction some subjects saw a videotaped playback of only one subject's behavior; the other groups were controls and saw no videotape. Actors then rated themselves (and observers rated their matched actor) on a series of scales in which they were asked how much of the actor's behavior was due to situational factors and how much to dispositional qualitites of the actor. The actor–observer hypothesis predicts that observers would attribute the actor's behavior to his dispositions and that actors would attribute their own behavior to situational factors. In support of this, actors saw themselves as more influenced by situational factors than did their matched observers. More significantly, the test of the salience explanation is in the videotape condition. When the group observed a playback of one actor's behavior (e.g., actor A), this information was redundant for two people, actor B and observer A, since they had observed actor A throughout the initial interaction. Hence, these two people should retain or strengthen their expected attributions. For two other people, however, this was relatively new information; actor A had not seen himself, nor had observer B watched actor A during the earlier interaction. Storms found that with this new information, actor A was less situational in describing himself, and observer B was more situational in describing actor B, as compared with the subjects for whom the information was redundant. The Storms study, then, provides strong evidence that the differences in actors' and observers' attributions are mediated by what information is perceptually salient.

III. Salience and Perception of Causal Agents

We can extend the perceptual salience interpretation of Jones and Nisbett to make a more general statement about the relationship between perception and causality. Such an extension would maintain that causal agents are seen as efficacious in proportion to their perceptual salience. That is, if the differences between actors' and observers' attributions are mediated by the information that engulfs one's visual field, then whatever one attends to within one's environment should influence the perceptions of causality. If one attends to a part of the environment to the relative exclusion of another, the information from that part should be most salient. This information, in turn, should provide a basis for the explanation one adopts in deciding who caused what in the situation. Our overall hypothesis, then, is that point of view or attention determines what information is salient; perceptually salient information is then overrepresented in subsequent causal explanations. This hypothesis extends the salience principle both beyond the dispositional–situational distinction and beyond the actor–observer comparison. Evidence for this hypothesis comes from studies on both the perception of others and the perception of self.

A. EVIDENCE FOR PERCEPTION OF OTHERS

A perceiver will regard another as causal to the extent that the person's behavior is salient, and what is salient depends on attention. Perceptions of a person's relative causality should depend, then, on the perceiver's focus of attention. To demonstrate this general link, Taylor and Fiske (1975) conducted two studies. In the first study, perceptual salience was manipulated by seating position (see Fig. 1). Six observers watched a dialogue, seated so that for two observers, one actor was salient, for two, the other was salient, and for two, the actors were equally salient. Since all subjects watched the conversation simultaneously, the only informational differences were the actors' relative visual salience. Dependent measures included estimates of how much the actor set the tone of the conversation, determined the kind of information exchanged, and caused his partner to behave as he did. Dispositional–situational causality scales also were included. Consistent with the hypotheses, the actor who engulfed the visual field was rated as more causal. The same results were obtained in a second operationalization of salience. In study 2, subjects observed two actors on a split screen video playback, so that both actors were equally visible; differential attention was manipulated by telling some subjects to pay particular attention to the actor on the left and others, to pay particular attention to the actor on the right. Although the dispositional–situational causality measures yielded no results in either study, again, the general causality results provided strong support for the salience–causality link. Subjects attributed causality to the salient stimulus person.

Taking the hypothesis to less contrived, more common settings, one would predict that any salient individual in a group would be perceived as dispropor-

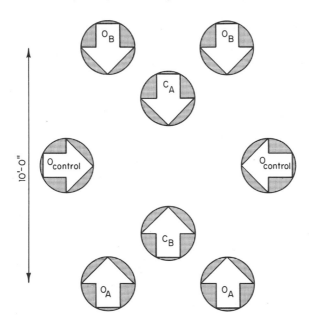

Fig. 1.   Seating arrangement for confederates (C) and observers (O), with arrows indicating visual orientation. A and B indicate matched actors and observers. From Taylor and Fiske (1975).

tionately causal. Rather than relying on direct control of observers' attention, that is, by seating arrangement or by instruction, one can manipulate salience by relying on principles of spontaneous selective attention. Novelty elicits spontaneous attention, as research in cognitive psychology has shown consistently (e.g., Berlyne, 1960; Jeffrey, 1968). Thus, a novel individual within a small group should be salient to observers and subsequently perceived as disproportionately causal in the group.

In order to test the effects of person novelty on observers' perceptions of causality, Taylor, Fiske, Close, Anderson, and Ruderman (1977) investigated perceptions of solo blacks, women, and men. An individual who is the only X (e.g., black) in an otherwise all Y (e.g., white) group should draw off a disproportionate amount of attention, since this solo X is novel. Accordingly, the solo X should be perceived as disproportionately causal. Similarly, the only male or female in an opposite-sex group is novel, should elicit attention, and consequently be perceived as particularly influential. In the first study, Taylor *et al.* manufactured a small group. Six men were tape-recorded in a brainstorming session for a publicity campaign. The number, timing, and quality of their suggestions were carefully controlled. College-age men of approximately equal attractiveness were photographed. Their photographs were then paired with the taped voices to create a coordinated slide and tape presentation. The result was an engrossing and movielike experience. By changing the race of one or more of the faces one could vary the perceived racial composition of the group without altering the content of the discussion. Three experimental conditions were developed, consisting of a group of six whites, an integrated group of three blacks and three whites, and another group with five whites and a solo black. The test of the novelty hypothesis comes in comparing perceptions of the solo black and perceptions of the same black in an integrated group, that is, when he was not novel. The data supported the hypotheses. A solo black was perceived as talking more, being more influential, and giving a clearer impression than was the same person when he was not a solo or when he was part of the majority.

The results of that study were fleshed out by a replication of the novelty-causality effect. Another group discussion was recorded, with three men and three women participating. To change the group's sex composition, not only the slides had to change but also the voices. Accordingly, opposite-sex people mimicked the exact phrasing and tone of voice of the original speeches. When a natural-sounding imitation was obtained, it was spliced in and substituted for the original voice, leaving the discussion intact. Upon completion of this painstaking process, subjects could be shown a slide and tape show depicting one man and five women, three men and three women, five men and one woman, or any other sex composition of a six-person group. The discussion ostensibly took place among colleagues in a teachers' lounge, and the topics ranged from unionization to gossip. The test of the novelty hypothesis compared perceptions of the solo male and solo female with perceptions of the same individual when she/he was not a solo. As in the first study, the solo was perceived as disproportionately influential, talkative, and prominent, whether male or female. These studies combine to show strong support for the salience–causality link in person perception.

B.   EVIDENCE FOR SELF-PERCEPTION

Similarly, the attention–causality effect holds for self-perception. An impressive quantity of data collected by Duval, Wicklund, and their associates (Duval & Hensley, 1977; Duval & Wicklund, 1972, 1973; Wicklund, 1975b) shows that when the self is salient, self-attributions of causality are exaggerated. For example, Duval and Wicklund (1973, study 2) manipulated self-attention by placing a large mirror in front of some subjects and not others. Subjects were read a series of ten hypothetical situations, all having positive outcomes or all having negative outcomes. The situations involved fairly serious consequences, such as a traffic accident, a drastic change in class grades, or making a profit on stocks. In all situations, either the subject or another person was potentially responsible for the hypothetical outcomes. The test of the attention hypothesis hinged on the percentages of causality which subjects assigned to themselves in the self-attending (mirror) and control (no mirror) conditions. For both positive and negative situations, self-attending subjects assigned disproportionate causality to themselves.

Other manipulations of self-attention cover a wide range of techniques, although the mirror is most common (Table II, to be discussed later, gives examples). Consistently, these studies find that self-attending subjects overrate their causal role on a variety of tasks (see Duval & Hensley, 1977, for a review). Thus, studies in self- and other-perception indicate that attributions of causality follow from differential attention.

IV. Salience and Attributions for Causes of Behavior

In further support of a salience interpretation of causal attribution, one would predict that relative prominence determines perceived locus of causality. Earlier, we examined actor–observer differences from this perspective. In that case, the situation is prominent for the actor, and the actor is prominent for the observer. Then we demonstrated the general principle that relative salience determines attributions of causality in self- and other-perception. Following a salience framework, one would predict further that observers attribute to the situation, to the extent that it is salient, and to the actor's dispositions, the more the actor is salient. This hypothesis has been investigated in a variety of contexts.

A. MANIPULATIONS OF RELATIVE SALIENCE

Before assessing the support for this hypothesis, it is worth noting that salience has been operationalized in a variety of different ways. First, there is a set of studies which depend on the principles of spontaneous selective attention. Cognitive psychology has shown that bright, moving, complex, and novel objects elicit attention (e.g., Berlyne, 1958; Koffka, 1935; Titchener, 1908/1966). Social psychologists have applied these principles to social manipulations of salience, and Table I summarizes these applications of spontaneous attention.[2]

---

[2]The efforts to relate the determinants of figural emphasis to differential attention have produced consistent results thus far. That is, the conditions that lead to differential attention to objects within a visual field, namely brightness, motion, complexity, and novelty, also produce differential attention to persons within a visual field. In most of these studies, however, differential attention has been inferred from experimental condition differences on dependent measures, rather than measured directly. Only Langer, Taylor, Fiske, and Chanowitz (1976, studies 1 and 2) and Taylor and Langer (1977, study 2) actually measured attentional differences as a function of novelty. The results of studies in which attention is spontaneously directed could be improved upon and strengthened by tapping attention directly, as for example through looking time, assessed using subject-controlled presentation periods (e.g., Berscheid, Graziano, Monson, & Dermer, 1976; Fiske, 1978), a corneal reflector, or a videotape of a subject's eye movements.

TABLE I
SOCIAL MANIPULATIONS OF SPONTANEOUS ATTENTION

Manipulation	Results	Reference
Brightness	Salient actor less situational Salient actor more causally prominent Salient actor more positively evaluated Differential recall for salient actor	McArthur & Post (1977, study
Motion	Salient actor less situational	McArthur & Post (1977, study
Complexity	Salient actor less situational	McArthur & Post (1977, study
Novelty		
Contextual novelty (i.e., solo status)	Salient actor more situational	McArthur & Post (1977, study 4–5)
	Salient actor more situational Salient actor more causally prominent Salient actor evaluatively exaggerated Salient actor more representative More recall for salient actor	Taylor, Fiske, Close, Anderson & Ruderman (1977, study 1
Statistical novelty (visual rarity of other)	Differential attention to salient person	Langer, Taylor, Fiske, & Chanowitz (1976, study 1
	Salient person more positively evaluated Attentional interpretation of discomfort from social novelty	Langer, Taylor, Fiske, & Chanowitz (1976, study 3
	Novelty elicits staring and avoidance	Taylor & Langer (1977)
(false feedback about self)	Self-novelty increases conformity	Duval (1976)

A second approach to the social manipulation of attention involves directly restricting the range of cues available to the subject. Table II summarizes the wide range of research using this method. We will draw upon a number of these studies in the next few sections.

B. ATTRIBUTIONS OF DISPOSITIONAL AND SITUATIONAL CAUSALITY

To reiterate, the perceptual salience hypothesis predicts that observers will perceive the actor's dispositions as causal to the extent that the actor is salient. Similarly, observers will perceive the situation as causal, to the extent that it is salient.

Clear support for this prediction comes from a series of studies conducted by McArthur and Post (1977). In their experiments, subjects observed two individuals, who had just met each other, talking together casually. One of the two individuals was highlighted while the other was not. Specifically, brightness was manipulated by having one stimulus person seated in a bright light and another in

TABLE I

SOCIAL MANIPULATIONS OF DIRECTED ATTENTION

Manipulation	Results	Reference
Visual perspective		
Seating position	Salient actor more causally prominent	Taylor & Fiske (1975, study 1)
Videotape playback	Self-salience increases conformity	Duval (1976)
	Self-salience decreases situational causality	Storms (1973)
	Environment salience (i.e., other actor) increases situational causality	
Mirror	Self-salience increases attitude–behavior consistency	Carver (1975)
	Self-salience increases self-relevant cognitions	Davis & Brock (1975)
	Self-salience decreases attitude–behavior consistency	Liebling, Seiler, & Shaver (1974, 1975)
	Self-salience inhibits aggression	Scheier, Fenigstein, & Buss (1974, study 1)
	Self-salience facilitates performance	Wicklund & Duval (1971, study 3)
	Self-salience increases equity restoration	Chase & Gibbons (1977)
	Self-salience increases altruism, if salience "content-free"	Gibbons, Rosenfield, & Wicklund (1977)
	Self-salience increases dispositional and attitudinal self-attributions	Pryor, Gibbons, Wicklund, Fazio, & Hood (1977)
	Self-salience inhibits or facilitates performance depending on level of evaluation anxiety	Liebling & Shaver, 1973

Continued

TABLE II—*Continued*

Manipulation	Results	Reference
Auditory perspective		
Audiotape playback	Self-salience exaggerates self-evaluation	Ickes, Wicklund, & Ferris (1973)
	Self-salience increases conformity to positive reference group	Wicklund & Duval (1971, study 1)
	Self-salience increases information search in difficult decisions	Wicklund & Ickes (1972)
Experimenter instruction	Self-salience increases attitude–behavior consistency for women	Cupchik & Leventhal (1974)
	Environment salience increases situational, decreases dispositional causality	Regan & Totten (1975)
	Salient actor causally prominent	Taylor & Fiske (1975, study 2)
	More recall for salient actor	
Placement of props		
Camera present	Self-salience increases self-relevant cognitions	Davis & Brock (1975)
	Self-salience increases self-relevant cognitions	Geller & Shaver (1976)
	Self-salience increases dissonance	Insko, Worchel, Songer, & Arnold (1973)
	Self-salience increases conformity to counterattitudinal behavior	Wicklund & Duval (1971, study 2)
Audience present	Self-salience worsens performance, more so if evaluation apprehension and mirror present	Innes & Young (1975)
	Self-salience inhibits aggression, when audience salient	Scheier, Fenigstein, & Buss (1974, study 2)

a dim light. Movement was manipulated by having one person rocking in a rocking chair, while the other person remained motionless. Pattern complexity was manipulated by having one person wearing a boldly patterned shirt, and the other, a solid gray shirt. Novelty was manipulated by having one male in a group wearing a shirt different in color from those of the other persons in the group. In a fifth study, they also looked at how a solo male in an otherwise female group and how a solo female in an otherwise male group were perceived. In studies 1–3, McArthur and Post found that a salient actor was viewed less situationally than a nonsalient actor, when the operationalizations were relative brightness and movement. The effect held partially for the complexity manipulation as well.

Manipulations of novelty, however, produce the opposite pattern: A novel individual's behavior is viewed more situationally than that of the nonnovel person. McArthur and Post (1977) found that the person in the novel shirt (study 4) and the solo male and female (study 5) were all seen as influenced by the situation rather than by dispositional factors. Taylor *et al.* (1977) also found a trend such that solo blacks' behavior was regarded as under the influence of situational factors. McArthur and Post (1977) attempted a resolution to this apparent contradition. They suggested that in attention experiments, one must consider the salience of the actor's background in addition to the salience of the actor's behavior. In the "novelty" studies, the actor is distinctive solely by virtue of the context. As such, we would expect a more situational interpretation of the actor's behavior, and indeed these are the cases where the reversals are found. Research by Arkin and Duval (1975) makes a similar point. The salience of the situation was manipulated by making items in the environment either stationary or moving. When the situation was dynamic, both actors and observers made high situational attributions, whereas when the situation was stable, the usual actor–observer differences emerged. [Interestingly, in a different context, Kelley (1971) and Snyder and Frankel (1976) make a similar argument.] In sum, the McArthur and Post effort at resolution seems to explain the apparent reversals within the salience findings quite satisfactorily: Causality is attributed to dispositions when attention is focused upon an actor and to situational factors when the situation is salient.

However, there are cases in which items assessing dispositional and situational causality simply fail to show effects at all (e.g., Taylor & Fiske, 1975). We can summarize by saying that we do not yet know what conditions are necessary to demonstrate the relationship between attention and attributions of differential dispositional or situational causality. There are psychometric problems with the dispositional–situational distinction. Taylor and Koivumaki (1976) found that the dispositional–situational distinction failed to fulfill the requirements of end points of a single continuum. The two sources of causality failed to operate in an hydraulic fashion. Taylor and Fiske (1975) found that many subjects failed to understand the distinction and/or did not perceive it as meaningful. There is some evidence that natural language causal inferences cannot easily be coded into dispositional or situational categories (Garland *et al.*, 1975). Bell (1975) has suggested that the dispositional–situational distinction may mean different things to actors than to observers. Observers may be answering the question, ''Why did *X* happen,'' whereas actors may be answering the question, ''Given that I caused *X*, what were my reasons.'' Miller, Smith, and Uleman (1977) have found extremely low and nonsignificant correlations among variables purportedly measuring the same thing, measures which included a single continuum with dispositional and situational at the two ends, two separate continua, and open-ended measures coded into dispositional and situational categories. Future research efforts to examine causal attribution should seek less confusing and cumbersome measurement procedures.

V. Salience and Noncausal Perception

Generally, causal attribution has been the focus of empirical investigations of the effects of differentially salient stimuli. However, some other perceptions than causal ones have been investigated and appear to be affected by differential attention as well, most notably evaluations of personal qualities, perceived representativeness, and attitudinal consistency. The evidence bearing on these perceptions will be covered in the following sections.

A. ATTENTION AND EVALUATION

The evidence relating attention to evaluations suggests that attributes are evaluated more extremely in either a positive or a negative direction when one overattends to a stimulus. However, the evidence is largely inferential, rather than direct, since research in person perception has, for the most part, not been designed to examine the relationship between attention and evaluation (Fiske, 1977). Requirements for such a test are, first, a comparison person or condition against which to evaluate a salient other and, second, behavior which is clearly positive or negative. In most of the studies on attention and person perception, actors' behaviors have ranged from neutral to fairly pleasant, leading one to predict either positive exaggeration of attributes or possibly greater variance in ratings on evaluations.

For the most part, positive exaggeration has been the rule when exaggeration has been found. McArthur and Post (1977) found that the brightly lit actor was rated more positively than the dimly lit one, but the effect was not found with their other manipulations of figural emphasis. Likewise, Storms (1973) and Taylor and Fiske (1975), using the same questions, found no evaluative exaggeration of the salient person. However, in all three experiments, the behaviors were bland and the conversations rather uninteresting, and thus these nonresults are predictable.

Some of the studies of novelty (statistical or contextual rarity) have found extremity in evaluations. Langer *et al.* (1976), for example, found that evaluations of both a physically crippled person and a pregnant woman were positively inflated compared with ratings of the same individual in "normal" attire; this trend toward artificially high ratings of the physically stigmatized has been noted by others as well (Kleck, Ono, & Hastorf, 1966). Though this effect has not previously been interpreted in attentional terms (Kleck, 1969), the appropriateness of such an interpretation should be clear, given that research demonstrates high differential attention to the physically stigmatized (Langer *et al.*, 1976). Taylor *et al.* (1977, study 1) found that a solo black was rated more positively than was a black in a mixed group or a comparable white. In their study 2, Taylor *et al.* (1977) found that a person perceived positively or negatively in a sex-integrated group was viewed even more positively or negatively when he or she was the only member of that sex in the group. This is the only effort thus far to examine divergent evaluations of others in both directions (positive and negative) within a single study, but together with the other supportive data, it strengthens the viability of the attention-extremity hypothesis.

Self-perception research also supports the hypothesis that attention increases the strength of evaluations. Duval and Wicklund (1972) hypothesized and found that under conditions of objective self-awareness, that is, self-focused attention, negative self-relevant thoughts increased (see also Ickes, Wicklund, & Ferris, 1973). However, more recently (Wicklund, 1975b) evidence has accumulated that positive self-relevant thoughts can be increased by self-focused attention too, that is, after a success experience or other form of positive feedback (McDonald, 1976; Gibbons, Rosenfield, & Wicklund, 1977).

The effects of attention upon evaluations are not confined to the person–perception and self-perception arena. There is evidence that attention to other kinds of stimuli, such as cognitions, increases their evaluative strength as well. Tesser, in a series of studies summarized in Tesser (1978), has in some cases instructed subjects to think about a particular stimulus (e.g., an object such as a picture or an attitude) and in other cases, he has prevented subjects from so doing through a distraction task (e.g., Sadler & Tesser, 1973; Tesser & Cowan, 1977). He finds that the more time a subject has to think about the stimulus, the more extreme evaluation of the stimulus becomes (e.g., Tesser & Conlee, 1975; Tesser & Leone, 1977). The experiments he reports range across a wide variety of stimulus items. Similar effects have been observed by M. Ross (1975); Zajonc, Markus, and Wilson (1974); Perlman and Oskamp (1971); Brickman, Redfield, Harrison, and Crandall (1972); and Grush (1976). In sum, the evidence is strongly supportive of the hypothesis that attention increases the strength of evaluations.

B. ATTENTION AND PERCEIVED REPRESENTATIVENESS

Tversky and Kahneman (1974) define a stimulus as representative if it is perceived as a typical instance of its class. For example, Franco might be perceived as a typical instance of a dictator. Most of the studies relating person perception and attention do not lend themselves to a test of the hypothesis that attention increases perceived representativeness, in that it is not clear of what class the salient stimulus person might be representative. A few studies do lend themselves to examination of the question, specifically those which manipulate novelty by means of membership in a particular social category (e.g., sex), and the results suggest that attention does indeed increase perceived representativeness.

Taylor *et al.* (1977), in their study 1, found that subjects viewed black stimulus persons in somewhat stereotyped terms; when asked if the stimulus persons had played any particular roles in the group, subjects reported that blacks were more likely to be the group comedian and less likly to be the group leader. These attributes were somewhat more likely to be true of the solo black than blacks in the mixed group, though largely by dint of sheer frequency of being cast in a special role. That is, a solo black was seen as playing a special role in the group by 75% of the subjects, compared with 50% role ascription to blacks in the mixed group. The role that distinguished the solo black from other group members was most often that of "group organizer," an assistant who kept the group rolling and brought it back to its topic.

In their study 2, Taylor *et al.* (1977) found similar and stronger effects with perceptions of solo men and women in work groups. As in study 1, solos were more likely to be cast in special roles than were men and women in mixed groups, and again these roles often had sex-typed content, that is, "She was motherly," "He was a typical macho type." Consistent with these experiments are data from field studies by Kanter (1977) and Wolman and Frank (1975) on solo women in work organizations. They found that solo women were perceived as playing out highly sex-typed social roles in groups *vis-à-vis* their male colleagues. Kanter also found, and the personal experiences of tokens (Taylor, 1977) bears out the observation, that solo women or blacks are often cast as spokespersons for their entire sex or race. Overall, then, there is some support for the proposition that salience by virtue of category membership increases perceptions of category representativeness.

C. ATTENTION AND CONSISTENCY

Attitude change researchers of the 1960s noted with some alarm the striking lack of consistency between attitudes and the behaviors they presumably predict, as well as between attitudes expressed in one situation and attitudes expressed in another. Current research on attention and social perception indicates that the problem might be rephrased. Attitudes are indeed consistent, with each other and with behavior, but to varying degrees, depending on where the subject's attention is directed. Research suggests that directing attention to a person's attitudes or behavior will increase attitude–attitude or attitude–behavior consistency respectively, but that directing attention to social norms or situational variables which are irrelevant to the subject's attitudes will reduce interattitudinal or attitude–behavior consistency. For example, when an experimental manipulation makes salient certain of the subjects' cognitions, subjects will evidence new attitudes consistent with those cognitions (Salancik & Conway, 1975). Further evidence for this principle comes from dissonance research. When subjects are distracted, little dissonance reduction occurs (Allen, 1965), but when subjects' self-attention is increased, dissonance reduction is greater (Brehm & Wicklund, 1970; Insko, Worchel, Songer, & Arnold, 1973). Research from objective self-awareness theory indicates that self-awareness makes subjects' attitudes more consistent across situations (Pryor, Gibbons, Wicklund, Fazio, & Hood, 1977), presumably because self-attention makes salient one's own cognitions (see also Wicklund, 1975a). However, when the disagreeing attitudes of others are made salient, self-aware subjects are *more* likely than others to conform (Duval, 1976; Wicklund & Duval, 1971).

Turning to the effect of self-attention on attitude–behavior consistency, Wicklund (1975b) argues that self-awareness focuses subjects' attention on any inconsisteny between their ideal and actual selves. An impressive array of studies shows that self-attending subjects are especially likely to behave in more ideal or desirable ways, for example, less physical aggression (Scheier, Fenigstein, & Buss, 1974), greater bystander intervention (Gibbons *et al.,* 1977), more restoration of equity (Chase & Gibbons, 1977), and better task performance (McDonald, 1976; Wicklund & Duval, 1971).

Overall, the data on attitudes, cognitive sets, and self-attention indicate that attitude–behavior and attitude–attitude consistencies and inconsistencies can be explained by focus of attention.

D. COMMENT ON NONCAUSAL PERCEPTIONS

To summarize, this section has reviewed evidence showing that differential attention exaggerates evaluations of a person, increases perceived representativeness, and can increase attitudinal and behavioral consistency. While these kinds of perceptions may not be as central to the perceiver's analysis of a social situation as are causal perceptions, they are important nonetheless. Perceptions of another person's friendliness or representativeness of some category can provide an inferential data base, which itself provides a basis for subsequent causal analysis. For example, having decided that a person is truly nasty will influence the probability of one's interacting with that person in the future and the perceptions of the person's motives for any subsequent behavior. Judging a person as representative of some category (such as blacks) rather than as an individual is likely to lead to stereotyped interpretations of any subsequent behavior, other attributes, and personal motives. One's own attitude–behavior consistency leads to others drawing inferences about one, which in turn shape one's subsequent behavior. We would hope that in the future more attention will be paid to perceptions in addition to explicitly causal ones, since these other kinds of judgments do influence behavior and are likely to produce subsequent causal analyses.

VI. Salience, Attention, and Attribution: Mediating Processes

Why engulfment of one's attention should produce such a splendid array of effects, ranging from overrated prominence to exaggerated evaluation, is not entirely clear. Accordingly, some attempt to specify the mediating process is clearly warranted. In this section, we will examine various candidates for the mediation of the attention–causality link. We will explore the results from studies on amount and availability of recall, as well as distraction during encoding and decoding. The evidence suggests that memorial availability may be determined by encoding modality and that availability, in turn, has a direct effect upon perceptions of causality.

A. ATTENTION AND VOLUME OF RECALL

One effort to specify the mediating processes for the effects of attention on social perception is Taylor and Fiske (1975). Taylor and Fiske reasoned that differential attention might lead to differential volume of encoded information about a salient stimulus; when a perceiver was subsequently asked to record impressions, for example, ''Who caused the conversation to proceed as it did?'' the perceiver might simply have more data stored on the salient actor and, therefore, overrepresent that actor as the causal agent.

The evidence that differential recall accompanies differential salience is weak, but in the predicted direction. Taylor and Fiske (1975, study 2) found that more was recalled about an attended-to actor than about an unattended-to actor in two separate operationalizations of attention. In study 1, because of a ceiling effect, there was no differential recall. McArthur and Post (1977) measured recall in all five of their figural emphasis studies, and found that only in the ''brightness'' experiment was there differential recall of the figurally prominent individual's statements. In study 1, Taylor et al. (1977) examined recall of blacks' and whites' suggestions in a racially integrated situation versus a situation with a solo black person in an otherwise white group. There was a marginal effect for subjects to remember more of what the solo black said in comparison with the other group members. Berscheid et al. (1976) found that more was recalled about the attended-to person (i.e., a future dating partner). In sum, of the ten efforts to measure volume of recall, five showed the predicted effect, five showed no effect, and there were no reversals. If these results are tabulated by taking the standard normal deviates of their respective probabilities (Rosenthal, 1978), the combined probability level for such a pattern is $p < .0001$. Thus, the overall pattern of recall effects supports the hypothesis. However, the failures to find the attention–recall effects are somewhat surprising.

Thus, differential attention can covary with differential recall, but is does not do so reliably. Furthermore, biased causal attributions have been obtained in studies that have not found differential recall. Accordingly, the hypothesis that differential amounts of encoded information mediate perceived causality is rendered an unlikely candidate for the process.

B. ATTENTION AND AVAILABILITY OF RECALL

Pryor and Kriss (1977) investigated whether or not availability of information might mediate between differential attention and biased attributions. They reasoned that, whereas subjects may well take in equivalent amounts of information about the salient and nonsalient aspects of their environment, they may have information about the salient part of the environment stored in a more easily retrieved form. To test this hypothesis, Pryor and Kriss first demonstrated that more salient stimuli (sentence subjects, as opposed to sentence objects) are more available (more quickly identified in a reaction time task). In study 2, they showed that the more salient stimuli were also more likely to be viewed as causes, thus confirming the tenability of their hypothesis. Consistent with previous studies, volume of recall was unaffected by the salience manipulation, clarifying that ease of retrieval and not amount of information encoded is the important variable. While the Pryor and Kriss investigation does not resolve the issue of mediation entirely—first, because the design does not test mediation (as will be discussed), and second, because the stimuli involved are limited to words in sentences rather than social stimuli—the study is nonetheless inventive and highly suggestive (see also Geller & Shaver, 1976).

Rholes (1977) conducted a study which is also consistent with the Pryor–Kriss argument. In a first study he had subjects learn word lists containing certain critical words (priming words), for example, "doctor." In a second and ostensibly unrelated study, the same subjects were asked to assign causality in descriptive passages, for example, "the physician chastised the patient." When particular words had been made available to subjects (e.g., doctor, in study 1), their synonyms were more often cited as causes (e.g., physician, in study 2). Higgins, Rholes, and Jones (1977) and Salancik (1974), using similar formats, found similar results.

Taken together, these studies suggest that total amount of information taken in need not be affected by differential attention (though it can be). What the availability explanation suggests is that somehow the information connected with the salient person or attribute is stored at the top of the mental heap or in some easily retrieved form. What form this might take has yet to be addressed; some speculations will be offered later on. In conclusion, the evidence for selective retrieval in the attention studies is stronger than that for selective encoding, although the latter, as we have already seen, can occur, too.

C. COMMENT ON MEDIATION STUDIES

The mediation studies, while inventive and highly suggestive, also point out how underdeveloped our tests of mediation are. In their research, social psychologists have constructed demonstration studies, sets of antecedent conditions which produce anticipated effects, which are not inconsistent with particular hypothesized processes. However, rarely is any independent evidence gathered which makes the imputed process more tenable than any of several other process models which are consistent with the same data (Taylor, 1976).

While the studies cited above are certainly superior to the average method of assessing mediation, they do not enable us to choose among the causal paths in Fig. 2. Although Pryor and Kriss make a good argument against (b) in their study, they cannot distinguish between (a) and (c), (c) being the mediational path that is proposed. A superior methodology would be to demonstrate that the independent variable → dependent variable link disappears when the mediating process is interfered with, and some procedures appropriate to testing this point are partial correlations, covariance analysis, and path analytic techniques.

D. DISTRACTION AND MEDIATION

To return to the mediation issue, one possibility regarding the effects of attention upon perceptions of causality is that the relationship can be made to disappear under either of two sets of conditions: distraction during encoding or distraction during retrieval. That is, if little information gets in in the first place,

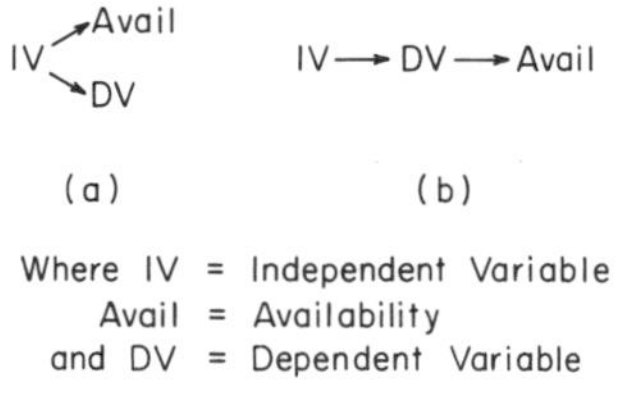

$$IV \begin{array}{c} \nearrow \text{Avail} \\ \searrow \text{DV} \end{array} \qquad IV \longrightarrow DV \longrightarrow \text{Avail} \qquad IV \longrightarrow \text{Avail} \longrightarrow DV$$

$$(a) \qquad\qquad (b) \qquad\qquad (c)$$

Where IV = Independent Variable
Avail = Availability
and DV = Dependent Variable

Fig. 2.   (a–c) Range of possible relations among availability, manipulated independent variables, and measured dependent variables.

subjects should have little to go on for their ascriptions of prominence and causality. And if salient information is not available because retrieval is blocked by distraction, again there should be little opportunity for bias to manifest itself.

Fiske and Taylor (1977) accordingly reran their point-of-view experiment with two additional manipulations. Subjects took part in the standard point-of-view procedure, with half the subjects receiving a distraction task while they observed the interaction (e.g., counting the number of pronouns used by both speakers) and half receiving no distraction. Crossed with this variable was a second variable of availability–no availability; for half the subjects, as they filled out the dependent measures, there was an engaging video presentation going on, a manipulation which should harm the ability to retrieve aspects of the prior conversation. The remaining half of the subjects were not distracted as they filled out the dependent measures (perceived causality). Fiske and Taylor found, somewhat to their surprise, that neither distraction manipulation eliminated the point-of-view effect. The video distraction task simply resulted in subjects' spending more time recording their impressions of the conversation. However, data from the pronoun distraction condition revealed some suggestive points about mediation. Subjects who performed the distraction task remembered virtually nothing about the content of the conversation they observed. Yet they manifested the point-of-view effect as strongly as the nondistracted subjects. The results of this study strongly suggest that the point-of-view effect depends upon visual and not verbal information. The next section pursues this argument further.

E. FURTHER PERSPECTIVES ON MEDIATION: IMAGING AND DIFFERENTIAL ATTENTION

A brief digression is now necessary. As noted earlier, Jones and Nisbett posited several possible mediators of actor–observer effects. In addition to the attentional explanation, they suggested that actors and observers have differing levels and kinds of information about their own versus another's behavior which may mediate whether dispositional or situational attributions are made. Taylor and Koivumaki (1976) and Nisbett, Caputo, Legant, and Maracek (1973), however, found that neither degree of acquaintanceship nor affective involvement predicted differential dispositional or situational attributions. Taylor and Achitoff (1974) found that perceived similarity to the actor also did not reduce observers' inclination to make dispositional attributions for an actor's behavior.

Two studies (Regan & Totten, 1975; Taylor & Achitoff, 1974) have successfully altered observers' attributions about actors' behaviors. In both cases, observers were encouraged to take the role of the actor and try to see the world as the actor saw it. Under these circumstances observers do make situational attributions for actors' behavior. Taylor (1975b) has argued that what subjects in the

Regan and Totten and Taylor and Achitoff studies did was to adopt the actor's point of view in the mind's eye. They constructed a visual image and scanned it in a fashion similar to what subjects do when they scan their actual environment. When it came to attributing causality, they, like subjects in real perspective experiments, overattributed the information which had been salient to them.

This conjectural explanation has some supportive evidence behind it. Kosslyn (1973, 1975; Kosslyn, Holyoak, & Huffman, 1976; Kosslyn & Pomerantz, 1977) has demonstrated that many of the properties of constructed images are analogous to those of percepts. He showed, for example, that it takes longer to identify an attribute of an image that is small than one that is large. It takes longer to identify a property of the left side of an image if one is attending to the right side than if one is attending to the left side. Social material is also affected by the imaging process. Pinto and Abelson (1976, unpublished observations; Abelson, personal communication) asked people to imagine that they were observing a series of actions from a balcony, as the actor in the story, or with no particular vantage point. They were read a series of actions including ones that were best seen from far away, as well as ones which could be best experienced by the main character (or actor) in the story. Vantage point influenced recall of the story with balcony subjects remembering more "far visual" details and actor subjects remembering more "body sensation" details. Taylor, Etcoff, Fiske, and Laufer (1978) asked people to imagine that they were one of four persons in a story: a cab driver, his passenger, a motorcyclist, or a Toyota driver positioned behind the motorcyclist. In essence, this is an imaged point-of-view manipulation. The story contained a large amount of information, variously best "seen" by particular characters. At the end of the story, the cab and motorcycle crashed into each other. Taylor et al. found that subjects remembered the information best "seen" from their particular vantage point, and this was true regardless of whether subjects were actors (cabbie or motorcyclist) or observers (passenger or Toyota driver). Furthermore, subjects tended to attribute blame in the accident to the person who had engulfed their imaged field, that is, the cabbie and passenger to the motorcyclist and the motorcyclist and Toyota driver to the cabbie.

What is intriguing about this image explanation is that not only might it explain the discrepencies among the actor–observer studies, it might also elucidate the attention → availability → causality links. It may well be that when attention is manipulated, though verbal material is stored in a relatively unbiased fashion, only the salient aspects of the environment are encoded in image form. When it comes time to attribute causality or evaluate attributes, the subject is able to retrieve visual instances of only the salient portions of the environment and thus they become overrepresented in the informational basis of the explanation. Thus, for example, when asked "Who talked more?" the subject can bring to mind more pictures of the salient actor's talking than instances of the other person's talking. Likewise, when asked "How pleasant was this person?," the subject can bring to mind more instances of the salient person's behavior (if the individual was pleasant) or more instances of unpleasant behavior (if the individual was unpleasant), thus creating evaluative extremity. It should be possible to test this hypothesis by demonstrating biased recollection of visual material in the absence of biased recollection of semantic material. Additionally, reaction times for recognition of portions of the salient environment should be faster than reaction times for the nonsalient portions of the environment.

Alternatively, it may be that the effects of differential attention upon social cognitions are jointly mediated by visual and verbal information. We have already seen that somewhat more verbal information is retained about salient than nonsalient stimuli. It is also likely that more visual information is retained about a salient than a nonsalient stimulus. Accordingly, it may be the case that information about a salient stimulus is more available than information about a nonsalient stimulus because it has been doubly encoded, in both words and images. That is, information may be more easily brought to mind if it is retrievable through more than one mode.

To summarize, what are the possible relationships between differential attention and attributions of causality? The relationship may be direct (nonmediated); it may be mediated by differential verbal recall; it may be mediated by differential visual information; or it may be doubly mediated, by both visual and verbal recall. We are not yet in a position to select an explanation. However, preliminary results from path analytic models suggest that dual mediation, rather than either single path or the direct (nonmediated) path, may be the best explanation (Fiske, Taylor, & Kenny, 1978).

F. COGNITIVE SALIENCE AND MEDIATION

These alternative explanations help fill out the mediational path between salient visual stimuli and their effects upon various dependent variables, but the explanation obviously applies only for visual manipulations of salience. It does not explain how salient cognitions operate upon perceptions of causality and related dependent variables. We, like Nisbett and Valins (1972), propose that a cognition, once made salient, functions as an hypothesis. A search, however sketchy, is then made for data. This search is undoubtedly biased in predictable ways.

An overuse of confirming evidence is one such bias. In the L. Ross, Lepper, and Hubbard (1975) study, for example, subjects were given false feedback leading them to believe that they were either very good or very bad at a social sensitivity task. Later, after subjects were told that the feedback was false, the authors found that subjects nonetheless imputed to themselves attitudes consistent with the feedback. L. Ross *et al.* (1975) reasoned that once subjects had received the false feedback, they retrieved previous incidents which were consistent with the feedback. When they were told the feedback was false, they simply erased one piece of what was now a highly buttressed opinion; this opinion was consistent with the feedback and based on evidence which was true and salient, but only as a result of the biased search (see also Taylor, 1975a).

These conjectures are also consistent with the literature on perceived covariation. Smedslund (1963) and Jenkins and Ward (1965) suggest that in estimating degree of correlation + + instances are the primary sources of data considered, with + −, − +, and − − instances going relatively ignored. An explanation for this pattern is that hits are easier to see or are more salient than are nonoccurences of events. That is, as L. Ross (1977) notes, we do not chronically attend to things that do *not* happen; rather, we are biased in favor of effects.

A second prominent bias in search behavior is that sample size goes substantially ignored as a basis for evaluating the quality of data (Kahneman & Tversky, 1973). Indeed, people's judgments are often more influenced by colorful and immediate bits of case history information than they are by objectively better, but relatively pallid statistical information (Nisbett *et al.*, 1976). Nisbett *et al.* argued that this is due to the fact that individual instances are concrete, vivid, and salient. We agree with this position and would carry the argument one step further. Case history information is more imageable than statistical information. Accordingly, it may well be encoded both iconically and in verbal form, whereas statistical information may be encoded only in verbal form. When an individual must then use information to make a judgment, the information which has been encoded through more than one mode will be more available. This again suggests the general point that salient information may be encoded through more than one channel, with the result that it will subsequently be more easily brought to mind, since it is retrievable through more than one mode. Accordingly, the dual encoding hypothesis may explain the results of experiments that manipulate the salience of cognitions, as well as those that manipulate perceptual salience.

VII.   Generalizability of Salience Effects

The salience-attention literature that we have just reviewed presents a dismally simplistic view of the human thinker. This nonthinker seems to be subject to the arbitrary and whimsical manipulations of an experimenter, drawn in by whatever information is made salient. There is a very real and important question of under what circumstances salient information does have an impact on explanation and understanding. Do salient stimuli have an impact in high information situations? Under conditions where the perceiver is involved in the scenario?

Under conditions of perceiver arousal? Each of these questions has some evidence which bears on the predictions.

A.   SALIENCE AND INFORMATION LEVEL

One might hypothesize that salient information would have an impact on attribution only under the most bland and uninvolving of conditions. That is, if the scene is boring and generally highly redundant, subjects' attention might be easily diverted by informationally irrelevant but salient cues, such as movement or color, but not if the situation is generally higher in information level. In the point-of-view setting, for example, we might expect that causal attribution to the person who engulfs one's visual field would be obviated if a more engrossing conversation were taking place. The only evidence on this point is a pilot study by Gartrell (1975) in which, instead of a bland conversation between two persons who participated about equally, subjects viewed a conversation in which one actor's behavior (talkativeness) was clearly determined by the reticence of the other. The more talkative actor became increasingly anxious during the conversation, as he tried to fill up the silences. Under these conditions, there was a clear main effect for which actor had caused the situation to evolve as it had, but the point of view manipulation nonetheless strongly predicted the degree to which this was true. Preliminary evidence, then, suggests that even in high-information situations, salience affects attributions, but more data and different manipulations of information level are clearly needed.

B.   SALIENCE AND INVOLVEMENT

A second issue raises the question of whether or not subject involvement in the situation would reduce the impact of salience manipulations. There are many ways, of course, of manipulating involvement. One might, for example, manipulate point of view (Fig. 1) in a situation in which subjects have a strongly held position on the issue or a personal relationship with one of the participants. Alternatively, one might manipulate whether or not the outcome of the situation has any personal relevance for the subject. On this latter point there is some data from the field of self-perception. Taylor (1975a) presented false feedback to subjects suggesting that they were attracted to men they had previously rated as medium (less preferred) in attractiveness. She found that subjects rated the less preferred picture much higher than previously, and the initially preferred photo somewhat lower following the feedback. However, in a second experimental condition, the subjects were told that they would actually be meeting and interacting with some of the men in the pictures. Under these circumstances, false feedback not only did not show up as a determinant of the picture ratings, but subjects actively refuted the implications of the feedback. The false feedback model was quite successful in predicting to a situation of low subject involvement and quite unsuccessful when the level of involvement was higher. In this experiment, then, personal involvement, as operationalized through anticipated future consequences, reduced the impact of the salient stimulus (the false feedback). Whether this would be true of visual salience effects or of other manipulations of involvement is unknown.

C. SALIENCE AND AROUSAL

A third variable of interest in this context is arousal. The effect of arousal on attention is to reduce the range of cues attended to (Easterbrook, 1959; Kahneman, 1973). Attention becomes more focused. Both Hull's and Spence's theories of learning predict that under conditions of arousal, the most obvious or familiar cues will be utilized. Thus we would expect that under conditions of high arousal, attention to salient information should be greater than under conditions of low arousal. The treatment of certain emotional disorders draws on some of these assumptions. For example it is believed that part of the problem experienced by both chronically test-anxious people and stutterers is that their own shortcomings and worries about their disorder are salient to them, rather than appropriate environmental cues, such as the task itself (for test-anxious people) or the words that they are communicating (for stutterers). Under conditions of anxiety, these tendencies may be increased. Wine (1971), for example, found that this was precisely the case in an investigation of task performance anxiety. Chronically self-focused subjects, under conditions of anxiety arousal, further narrowed their self-attention to the detriment of task-related cues. Storms and McCaul (1976) proposed that anxiety exacerbates stuttering and other emotional disorders because the disorder (e.g., stuttering) is the dominant mode of responding in the situation. Liebling and Shaver (1973) also found that self-focused attention interfered with task performance at high levels of evaluation anxiety. One might expect that, for these subjects, self-attributions of blame and responsibility would also increase under conditions of arousal, since self-focused attention is increased. Although there is no direct data as yet on the arousal–causality relationship in attributions, the relationship between arousal and increased attention to salient stimuli is reasonably clear. Whether attributions are similarly affected by arousal should be a focus of subsequent research.

What is interesting about the predictions ventured above is that they are somewhat contradictory. Under most circumstances, we would expect level of information, subject involvement, and subject arousal to be highly correlated, and yet the implications of each variable for the effects of salience are different. Be that as it may, these findings will fill an important gap in a literature which has, until now, examined the impact of salient stimuli only in relatively uninvolving settings.

D. SALIENCE AND INDIVIDUAL DIFFERENCES

Increased involvement in a situation may, instead of increasing or decreasing the strength of salience effects, merely change the determinants of what is salient. That is, in addition to principles of figural emphasis provoking differential attention, it may be that under conditions of enhanced involvement, differences in individual need states, personality, prior reinforcement schedules, or schema use predict differential attention without necessarily changing the effects of salience upon attributions and evaluations. What might some of these individual differences be (cf., McGuire & Padawer-Singer, 1976)?

Temporary need states clearly influence direction of attention. A thirsty person scans the environment for drinking fountains, while a driver running out of gas looks for gas stations. When people are lonely, they seek familiar faces, while bored people look for novel stimulation. People who are anticipating future interaction with someone spend more time looking at that person than they do to people with whom they anticipate no future interation (e.g., a date versus nondate; Berscheid et al., 1976).

Chronic individual difference orientations may influence attentional behavior. Snyder (1976) has presented convincing evidence that individuals differ consistently in the extent to which they monitor their own behavior and environment. This dimension, termed self-monitoring, may well be one of attentional style, or differential receptivity to cues which call for directed attention to the environment and the self (see also Berscheid et al., 1976). Other chronic individual differences also affect attention style, such as anxiety (Wine, 1971), need for stimulation (Sales, 1971), locus of control (Baker, 1974), and obesity (e.g., Kozlowski & Schachter, 1975).

A previous history of positive or negative reinforcement in an environment either from persons or from objects should influence direction of attention. Individuals can be expected to attend to objects and persons who have positively reinforced them in the past so as to approach them and increase the chance of subsequent reinforcement. Conversely, individuals should attend to those who have negatively reinforced them in the past, presumably for the purpose of avoiding them.

Individual cognitive schemas can affect what information is attended to. Markus (1977) has presented convincing evidence that people take in and process information about themselves faster if it fits a schema they hold about themselves than if it does not (see also Tesser, 1978).

Finally, personal and often long-term interests influence what information people seek out. The literature on selective exposure (Sears, 1968) indicates that individuals seek out information consistent with their positions on issues if it will be useful to them. Although Sears' review examines primarily selective exposure to written persuasive messages, the principle can be expected to apply to other kinds of search behavior as well, for example, visual exploration of a new environment. That is, we direct our own attention intentionally to seek out information for a given purpose or goal, and one of the main determinants of intentional attention is enduring interests.

It should be clear from the conjectural nature of this section that little research has attempted to interrelate perceiver variables, environmental stimuli, and focus of attention. In our opinion, this area merits investigation, and research should focus on individual differences in sensitivity to certain classes of cues and temporary need states which restrict, enlarge, or specify the kinds of information individuals will attend to, especially under conditions of high involvement.

E. COMMENT ON GENERALIZABILITY OF SALIENCE EFFECTS

Overall, there is no strong basis for predicting that salience effects will disappear under conditions of high involvement. However, even if it is found that salience effects are most likely to emerge under conditions of low involvement, this does not trivialize the effects. Low-involvement behavior is more characteristic of our daily activities than we would like to admit. For example, false feedback studies have real-world analogs in the influence of hormones, blood sugar level, and the like on mood and the course of social interactions. Cocktail party opinions, lunch arguments, and bus ride debates can probably be elucidated by knowledge of what cues or attitudes are made salient in the situation. Langer (1978) has chronicled the astonishing wealth of situations in which we fail to evidence any thinking at all.

Critics of the attentional approach may be right in saying that salience effects pertain to superficial processing. We would argue, by way of rebuttal, that our daily judgments often are superficial, and second that, once formed, an opinion tends to be buttressed rather than reconsidered. A judgment based on attentional phenomena takes on a life of its own, regardless of the fallibility of the original perception. Carefully considered thoughts may well be based on phenomena such as the seemingly trivial salience effects we describe here.

Furthermore, as the data come in, the generality of salience effects is more and more apparent. If people indeed conduct a biased search for cognitions supporting a preliminary attitude, as L. Ross, Lepper, & Hubbard (1975) and we have hypothesized, then the effects of seizing on salient data should actually increase over time. For example, Tesser (1978) finds that thinking about a stimulus polarizes its initial evaluations. Thus in-depth processing, rather than attenuating salience effects, may in fact increase them.

In sum, we are suggesting that the array of situations in which salience effects have been demonstrated thus far is sufficient to justify its status as a research problem and to demonstrate its applicability to real-world situations. Any research which demonstrates that salient stimuli have an impact in more involving, arousing, or informative situations will simply increase the range of already substantial generalization.

VIII. Implications of a Psychology of Salience

The psychology of salience is embarrassing because it suggests first that people commonly utilize irrelevant and trivial social cues for drawing what would seem to be sophisticated inferences, and furthermore that they do so without awareness. Nisbett and Wilson (1977) report a series of experiments which leads one to a similar conclusion. They demonstrated that subjects are consistently unable to report what stimuli had an impact on their behavior. Rather, they report consensually appropriate, plausible explanations for their behavior. The conclusion reached by Nisbett and Wilson is that people may well have no direct access to their thought processes. Further evidence for the unaware social perceiver comes from research on "scripts." Langer (1978) has suggested that people react to many social situations with overlearned, almost reflexive, cognitive reactions, what Abelson (1976) terms well-rehearsed "scripts." For example, when people first meet each other, they exchange a variety of social pleasantries; yet, if they were forced to reconstruct precisely what they did and said to each other, they would probably not be able to do so. Langer's general point is that some of what we call thought may turn out to be as automatic as most of our overlearned motor behavior, like driving or riding a bike.

Despite such evidence, the notion of automatic reactions to salient cues remains unaccepted. Researchers who obtain salience effects or who comment on others' salience effects go to great pains to impute to subjects a more rational, conscious information-processing strategy than we believe is actually occurring or certainly than there is evidence for. Subjects likewise find salience hypotheses absurd, and during debriefs they vehemently deny that their impressions and causal attributions could have been shaped by trivial but salient stimuli. Reasons for such negative reactions seem to be based on several factors. First, the phenomenal self experiences its reactions to social situations as thought out and mulled over, not as automatic. Second, the thought processes one imputes to oneself do not bear any similarity at all to the strategies salience studies suggest one is actually using. Finally, one can conjure up many cases in which it is only through the intentional application of rational thought processes that one has succeeded in solving a problem. These all contribute to a belief in thoughtful processing.

It is possible, however, to salvage both viewpoints of the social perceiver. Though limitations of space preclude a complete discussion of this issue here, we will offer a few speculations as to how this salvaging operation might proceed. A number of researchers in cognitive psychology have suggested that there may be two modes of processing information, an automatic process and a controlled process (e.g., Atkinson & Shiffrin, 1968; Deutsch & Deutsch, 1963; LaBerge, 1975; Neisser, 1967; Schneider & Shiffrin, 1977; Shiffrin & Schneider, 1977). In the most recent version of this argument, Schneider and Shiffrin (1977) have delineated these processes as follows:

> Automatic processing is activation of a learned sequence of elements in long-term memory that is initiated by appropriate inputs and then proceeds automatically—without subject control, without stressing the capacity limitations of the system, and without necessarily demanding attention. Controlled processing is a temporary activation of a sequence of elements that can be set up quickly and easily but requires attention, is capacity-limited (usually serial in nature), and is controlled by the subject [p. 1].

They further note that controlled processing is used in difficult, unpracticed situations, whereas automatic processing, which does not require attention, develops "following consistent mapping of stimuli to responses over trials" (p. 1), for example, after a lot of practice.

The psychology of salience with which we have been concerned in this chapter may well reflect automatic processing. We would argue that selective attention to movement, brightness, complexity, and novelty (all factors which, as we have seen, influence social perception) lies within the province of automatic processing. They may well be stimulus qualities which the perceiver has never had to learn to respond to, but to which one's attention is instead drawn naturally. Not all automatic processing is unlearned. Selective attention as a function of individual differences, instructional set, and temporary need states may be learned modes of automatic processing. That is, over a lifetime, the perceiver acquires ways of acting upon the environment (selecting out particular cues, scanning for certain attributes) which, after practice, become part of automatic processing as well. Accordingly, these automatic ways of searching out and abstracting meaning from social situations come to occur spontaneously and without awareness, when the appropriate inputs occur. Individual needs and certain social schemas or scripts seem to fall into this category in that they are overlearned and well-practiced. To take a slightly different approach, certain social situations which are frequent, redundant, and boring may be more likely than others to elicit in subjects the automatic mode of processing. As we noted earlier, these characteristics have been true of most of the experimental tests of salience hypotheses. They include conversations in which little happens, discussions in which the social perceiver has little personal investment, or situations engaging low levels of arousal.

It is important not to overstate the relationship between the cognitive formulations just discussed and the social perceptions we are attempting to explain. Social perception does not consist of a single automatic or controlled process, but rather a set of activities, some of which are controlled and others of which are automatic. For example, just reading the experimenter's questions involves some automatic and some controlled processes (Shiffrin & Schneider, 1977). In the salience phenomena, what we are hypothesizing is that the search of the social environment is automatic, though not necessarily the process of putting together the information that search yields to produce a social judgment. Hence, the evaluation of a social situation seems to the social perceiver to be a rational, conscious process, when the information on which it is based may be a function of salient cues.

If these conjectures are accurate, it would explain both why salience effects are counterintuitive (because the social perceiver is not aware of them) and why perceivers are so certain that they have access to many of their thought processes (because much of the time they in fact do). Approaches like Kelley's Analysis of Variance model may be instances of controlled processing, whereas automatic social processing may be fleshed out by salience effects and by social scripts.

If these speculations are borne out, they further suggest that the role of naive epistemology in theory derivation must be altered. That is, while naive epistemology may continue to play an important theory-generating role (Heider, 1958), its evidentiary role in the verification of hypotheses would seem to be limited to situations in which we are assured that some controlled processing is going on. Automatic processes necessitate the use of measures of reaction time, scanning, recall, and the like—ones that do not rely on the perceiver's awareness of internal processes. Controlled processing, on the other hand, can be elucidated by subject protocols and open-ended dependent measures in which the perceiver may have some insight into the processing.

IX. Summary

Attention within the social environment is selective. It is drawn to particular features of the environment either as a function of qualities intrinsic to those features (such as light or movement) or as a function of the perceiver's own dispositions and temporary need states. These conditions are outlined in Table III. As a result of differential attention to particular features, information about those features is more available to the perceiver. Relative to the quantity of information retained about other features, more is retained about the salient features. Information about salient features (stimuli) may be encoded in more

TABLE III

EFFECTS OF SALIENT INFORMATION ON SOCIAL PERCEPTION

Determinants of selective attention	Mediation	Social perceptions
Properties of stimuli	Higher volume of recall	Heightened learning
Brightness		
Contrast		
Movement		
Novelty		Greater prominence and causality
Properties of situation	Greater availability of information (possibly in image form)	Intraindividual consistency
Environmental cues		
Instructional set		
Properties of perceiver	Possible multimodal encoding of information (semantic and iconic)	Exaggerated evaluations
Temporary need states		Perceived representativeness
Enduring individual differences in traits, reinforcement schedules, schemas		Effects on dispositional and situational causality (unclear)

than one manner, for example, both semantically and iconically. And the information may be encoded in more accessible form, for example, as images in the visual salience studies. Accordingly, when the perceiver is asked to make a judgment about a particular stimulus, one accesses recall to see what kind of information is available. The more instances of a particular behavior one can find, the more confident one is that the behavior reflects an attribute of the stimulus. Accordingly, persons, when they are salient, are seen as more causally prominent (because the perceiver has more instances of their behavior overall), more evaluatively extreme, and possibly more representative of the class of which they are a member. When the salient person is the self, the same effects occur, and the individual is also found to show more consistency in attitudes and behaviors. These processes may occur primarily in situations which are redundant, unsurprising, uninvolving, and unarousing. They seem to occur automatically and substantially without awareness, and as such, they differ qualitatively from the intentional, conscious, controlled kind of search which we like to think characterizes all our behavior.

REFERENCES

Abelson, R. P. Script processing in attitude formation and decision making. In J. Carroll & J. Payne (Eds.), *Cognition and social behavior*. Hillsdale, N.J.: Lawrence Erlbaum Associates, 1976.

Allen, V. L. Effect of extraneous cognitive activity on dissonance reduction. *Psychological Reports*, 1965, **16**, 1145–1151.

Arkin, R., & Duval, S. Focus of attention and causal attribution of actors and observers. *Journal of Experimental Social Psychology*, 1975, **11**, 427–438.

Atkinson, R. C., & Shiffrin, R. M. Human memory: A proposed system and its control processes. In K. W. Spence & J. T. Spence (Eds.), *The psychology of learning and motivation: Advances in research and theory*. Vol. 2. New York: Academic Press, 1968.

Baker, J. Individual differences, point of view, and perceptions of causality. Unpublished senior thesis, Harvard University, 1974.

Bandler, R. J., Madaras, G. R., & Bem, D. J. Self-observation as a source of pain perception. *Journal of Personality and Social Psychology*, 1968, **9**, 205–209.

Bell, L. G. Comments on measuring the attribution of causality. Paper presented at the American Psychological Association Convention, Chicago, September, 1975.

Berlyne, D. W. The influence of complexity and novelty in visual figures on orienting responses. *Journal of Experimental Psychology*, 1958, **55**, 289–296.

Berlyne, D. W. *Conflict, arousal, and curiosity*. New York: McGraw-Hill, 1960.

Berscheid, E., Graziano, W., Monson, T., & Dermer, M. Outcome dependency: Attention, attribution, and attraction. *Journal of Personality and Social Psychology*, 1976, **34**, 978–989.

Brehm, J. W., & Wicklund, R. A. Regret and dissonance reduction as a function of post-decision salience of dissonant information. *Journal of Personality and Social Psychology*, 1970, **14**, 1–7.

Brickman, P., Redfield, J., Harrison, A. A., & Crandall, R. Drive and predisposition as factors in the attitudinal effects of mere exposure. *Journal of Experimental Social Psychology*, 1972, **8**, 31–44.

Brunswik, E. *Wahrnemung und gegenstandweit*. Leipzig and Vienna: Deuticke, 1934.

Carver, C. S. Physical aggression as a function of objective self-awareness and attitudes toward punishment. *Journal of Experimental Social Psychology,* 1975, **11**, 510–519.

Chase, T. C., & Gibbons, F. X. Objective self-awareness and the standard of equity: Restoration after overpayment. Unpublished manuscript, University of Texas, 1977.

Cupchik, G. C., & Leventhal, H. Consistency between expressive behavior and the evaluation of humorous stimuli: The role of sex and self observation. *Journal of Personality and Social Psychology,* 1974, **30**, 429–442.

Davis, D., & Brock, T. C. Use of first person pronouns as a function of increased objective self-awareness and performance feedback. *Journal of Experimental Social Psychology,* 1975, **11**, 381–388.

Davison, G. G., & Valins, S. Maintenance of self-attributed and drug-attributed behavior change. *Journal of Personality and Social Psychology,* 1969, **11**, 25–33.

Deutsch, J. A., & Deutsch, S. Attention: Some theoretical considerations. *Psychological Review,* 1963, **70**, 80–90.

Duval, S. Conformity on a visual task as a function of personal novelty on attitudinal dimensions and being reminded of the object status of self. *Journal of Experimental Social Psychology,* 1976, **12**, 87–98.

Duval, S., & Hensley, V. Extensions of objective self-awareness theory: The focus of attention-causal attribution hypothesis. In J. H. Harvey, W. J. Ickes, & R. F. Kidd (Eds.), *New directions in attribution research.* Vol. 1. Hillsdale, N.J.: Lawrence Erlbaum Associates, 1977.

Duval, S., & Wicklund, R. A. *A theory of objective self-awareness.* New York: Academic Press, 1972.

Duval, S., & Wicklund, R. A. Effects of objective self-awareness on attribution of causality. *Journal of Experimental Social Psychology,* 1973, **9**, 17–31.

Easterbrook, J. A. The effect of emotion on cue utilization and the organization of behavior. *Psychological Review,* 1959, **66**, 183–200.

Fiske, S. T. How do I know thee: A review of interpersonal information processing. Unpublished manuscript, Harvard University, 1977.

Fiske, S. T. Attention and the weighting of behavior in person perception. Unpublished doctoral thesis, Harvard University, 1978.

Fiske, S. T., & Taylor, S. E. Salience, attention, and availability. Paper presented at the annual meeting of the Eastern Psychological Association, Boston, April 1977.

Fiske, S. T., Taylor, S. E., & Kenny, D. A. Path analysis of attentional mediation in attribution. In preparation, 1978.

Garland, H., Hardy, A., & Stephenson, L. Information search as affected by attribution type and response category. *Personality and Social Psychology Bulletin,* 1975, **1**, 612–615.

Gartrell, D. Dominance–submissiveness of actor, point of view of observer, and the attribution of causality in interactions. Paper presented at the annual meeting of the Canadian Sociology and Anthropology Association, Edmonton, Alberta, May 1975.

Geller, V., & Shaver, P. Cognitive consequences of self-awareness. *Journal of Experimental Social Psychology,* 1976, **12**, 99–108.

Gibbons, F. X., Rosenfield, D., & Wicklund, R. A. Self-focused attention, self-concern, and bystander intervention. Unpublished manuscript, University of Texas, 1977.

Grush, J. E. Attitude formation and mere exposure phenomena: A non-artifactual explanation of empirical findings. *Journal of Personality and Social Psychology,* 1976, **33**, 281–290.

Heider, F. *The psychology of interpersonal relations.* New York: Wiley, 1958.

Higgins, E. T., Rholes, W. S., & Jones, C. R. Category accessibility and impression formation. *Journal of Experimental Social Psychology,* 1977, **13**, 141–154.

Ickes, W. J., Wicklund, R. A., & Ferris, C. B. Objective self-awareness and self-esteem. *Journal of Experimental Social Psychology,* 1973, **9**, 202–219.

Innes, J. M., & Young, R. F. The effect of presence of an audience, evaluation apprehension, and objective self-awareness on learning. *Journal of Experimental Social Psychology*, 1975, **11**, 35–42.

Insko, C. A., Worchel, S., Songer, E., & Arnold, S. E. Effort, objective self-awareness, choice, and dissonance. *Journal of Personality and Social Psychology*, 1973, **28**, 262–269.

Jeffrey, W. E. The orienting reflex and attention in cognitive development. *Psychological Review*, 1968, **75**, 323–334.

Jenkins, H. M., & Ward, W. C. Judgment of contingency between responses and outcomes. *Psychological Monographs*, 1965, **79**,(1, Whole No. 594).

Jones, E. E., & Davis, K. E. From acts to dispositions: The attribution process in person perception. In L. Berkowitz (Ed.), *Advances in experimental social psychology*. Vol. 2. New York: Academic Press, 1965.

Jones, E. E., & Nisbett, R. E. The actor and the observer: Divergent perceptions of the causes of behavior. In E. E. Jones, D. E. Kanouse, H. H. Kelley, R. E. Nisbett, S. Valins, and B. Weiner (Eds.), *Attribution: Perceiving the causes of behavior*. Morristown, N.J.: General Learning Press, 1972.

Kahneman, D. *Attention and effort*. Englewood Cliffs, N.J.: Prentice-Hall, 1973.

Kahneman, D., & Tversky, A. On the psychology of prediction. *Psychological Review*, 1973, **80**, 237–251.

Kanouse, D. E. Language, labeling, and attribution. In E. E. Jones, D. E. Kanouse, H. H. Kelley, R. E. Nisbett, S. Valins, and B. Weiner (Eds.), *Attribution: Perceiving the causes of behavior*. Morristown, N.J.: General Learning Press, 1972.

Kanter, R. M. Some effects of proportions on group life. Skewed sex ratios and responses to token women. *American Journal of Sociology*, 1977, **82**, 965–990

Kelley, H. H. Attribution theory in social psychology. In D. Levine (Ed.), *Nebraska Symposium on Motivation*. Vol. 15. Lincoln: University of Nebraska Press, 1967.

Kelley, H. H. Attribution in social interaction. In E. E. Jones, D. E. Kanouse, H. H. Kelley, R. E. Nisbett, S. Valins, and B. Weiner (Eds.), *Attribution: Perceiving the causes of behavior*. Morristown, N.J.: General Learning Press, 1972.

Kiesler, C. A., Nisbett, R. E., & Zanna, M. P. On inferring one's beliefs from one's behavior. *Journal of Personality and Social Psychology*, 1969, **11**, 321–327.

Kleck, R. Physical stigma and task oriented instructions. *Human Relations*, 1969, **22**, 53–60.

Kleck, R., Ono, H., & Hastorf, A. H. The effects of physical deviance upon face-to-face interaction. *Human Relations*, 1966, **19**, 425–436.

Koffka, K. *Principles of Gestalt psychology*. New York: Harcourt, 1935.

Kosslyn, S. M. Scanning visual images: Some structural implications. *Perception & Psychophysics*, 1973, **14**, 90–94.

Kosslyn, S. M. Information representation in visual images. *Cognitive Psychology*, 1975, **7**, 341–370.

Kosslyn, S. M., Holyoak, K. J., & Huffman, C. S. A processing approach to the dual coding hypothesis. *Journal of Experimental Psychology: Human Learning and Memory*, 1976, **2**, 223–233.

Kosslyn, S. M., & Pomerantz, J. R. Imagery, propositions, and the form of internal representations. *Cognitive Psychology*, 1977, **9**, 52–76.

Kozlowski, L. T., & Schachter, S. Effects of cue prominence and palatability on the drinking behavior of obese and normal humans. *Journal of Personality and Social Psychology*, 1975, **32**, 1055–1059.

La Berge, D. Acquisition of automatic processing in perceptual and associative learning. In P. M. A. Rabbit & S. Dornic (Eds.), *Attention and performance*. Vol. 5. New York: Academic Press, 1975.

Langer, E. J. Rethinking the role of thought in social interaction. In J. H. Harvey, W. J. Ickes, & R. F. Kidd (Eds.), *New directions in attribution research*. Vol. 2. Hillsdale, N.J.: Lawrence Erlbaum Associates, 1978.

Langer, E. J., Taylor, S. E., Fiske, S. T., & Chanowitz, B. Stigma, staring and discomfort: A novel stimulus hypothesis. *Journal of Experimental Social Psychology*, 1976, **12**, 451–463.

Liebling, B. A., Seiler, M., & Shaver, P. Unsolved problems for self-awareness theory: A reply to Wicklund. *Journal of Experimental Social Psychology*, 1975, **11**, 82–85.

Liebling, B. A., & Shaver, P. Evaluation, self-awareness, and task performance. *Journal of Experimental Social Psychology*, 1973, **9**, 297–306.

Liebling, B. A., Seiler, M., and Shaver, P. Self-awareness and cigarette-smoking behavior. *Journal of Experimental Social Psychology*, 1974, **10**, 325–332.

Markus, H. Self-schemata and processing information about the self. *Journal of Personality and Social Psychology*, 1977, **35**, 63–78.

McArthur, L. The how and what of why: Some determinants and consequences of causal attribution. *Journal of Personality and Social Psychology*, 1972, **22**, 171–193.

McArthur, L., & Post, D. Figural emphasis and person perception. *Journal of Experimental Social Psychology*, 1977, XX

McDonald, P. G. Reactions to objective self-awareness. Unpublished doctoral dissertation, Tulane University, 1976.

McGuire, W. J., & Padawer-Singer, A. Trait salience in the spontaneous self-concept. *Journal of Personality and Social Psychology*, 1976, **33**, 743–754.

Miller, F. D., Smith, E. R., & Uleman, J. F. Problems in assessing dispositional and situational attributions. Unpublished manuscript, New York University, 1977.

Neisser, U. *Cognitive psychology*. New York: Appleton, 1967.

Nisbett, R. E., Borgida, E., Crandall, R., & Reed, H. Popular induction: Information is not necessarily informative. In J. S. Carroll & J. W. Payne (Eds.), *Cognition and social behavior*. Hillsdale, N.J.: Lawrence Erlbaum Associates, 1976.

Nisbett, R. E., Caputo, C., Legant, P., & Maracek, J. Behavior as seen by the actor and as seen by the observer. *Journal of Personality and Social Psychology*, 1973, **27**, 154–164.

Nisbett, R. E., & Schachter, S. Cognitive manipulation of pain. *Journal of Experimental Social Psychology*, 1966, **2**, 227–236.

Nisbett, R. E., & Valins, S. Perceiving the causes of one's own behavior. In E. E. Jones, D. E. Kanouse, H. H. Kelley, R. E. Nisbett, S. Valins, and B. Weiner (Eds.), *Attribution: Perceiving the causes of behavior*. Morristown, N.J.: General Learning Press, 1972.

Nisbett, R. E., & Wilson, T. D. Telling more than we can know: Verbal reports on mental processes. *Psychological Review*, 1977, **84**, 231–259.

Perlman, D., & Oskamp, S. The effects of picture content and exposure frequency on evaluations of Negroes and whites. *Journal of Experimental Social Psychology*, 1971, **7**, 503–514.

Pryor, J. B., Gibbons, F. X., Wicklund, R. A., Fazio, R. H., & Hood, R. Self-focused attention and self-report validity. *Journal of Personality*, 1977, **45**, 513–527.

Pryor, J. B., & Kriss, M. The cognitive dynamics of salience in the attribution process. *Journal of Personality and Social Psychology*, 1977, **35**, 49–55.

Regan, D., & Totten, J. Empathy and attribution: Turning observers into actors. *Journal of Personality and Social Psychology*, 1975, **32**, 850–856.

Rholes, W. S. The influence of availability on causal attribution. Paper presented at the meeting of Eastern Psychological Association, Boston, April 1977.

Rosenthal, R. Combining results of independent studies. *Psychological Bulletin*, 1978, **85**, 185–193.

Ross, L. The intuitive psychologist and his shortcomings: Distortions in the attribution process. In L. Berkowitz (Ed.), *Advances in experimental social psychology*. Vol. 10. New York: Academic Press, 1977.

Ross, L., Lepper, M., & Hubbard, M. Perseverance in self-perception and social perception: Biased attributional processes in the debriefing paradigm. *Journal of Personality and Social Psychology,* 1975, **32,** 880–892.

Ross, L., Rodin, J., & Zimbardo, P. G. Toward an attribution therapy: The reduction of fear through induced cognitive–emotional misattribution. *Journal of Personality and Social Psychology,* 1969, **12,** 279–288.

Ross, M. Salience of reward and intrinsic motivation. *Journal of Personality and Social Psychology,* 1975, **32,** 245–254.

Sadler, O., & Tesser, A. Some effects of salience and time upon interpersonal hostility and attraction during social isolation. *Sociometry,* 1973, **36,** 99–112.

Salancik, J. R. Inference of one's attitude from behavior recalled under linguistically manipulated cognitive sets. *Journal of Experimental Social Psychology,* 1974, **10,** 415–427.

Salancik, J. R., & Conway, C. Attitude inferences from salient and relevant cognitive content about behavior. *Journal of Personality and Social Psychology,* 1975, **32,** 829–840.

Sales, S. M. Need for stimulation as a factor in social behavior. *Journal of Personality and Social Psychology,* 1971, **19,** 124–134.

Schachter, S., & Singer, J. E. Cognitive, social and physiological determinants of emotional state. *Psychological Review,* 1962, **69,** 379–399.

Scheier, M. F., Fenigstein, A., & Buss, A. H. Self-awareness and physical aggression. *Journal of Experimental Psychology,* 1974, **10,** 264–273.

Schneider, W., & Shiffrin, R. M. Controlled and automatic human information processing: I. Detection, search, and attention. *Psychological Review,* 1977, **84,** 1–66.

Schuman, H., & Johnson, M. P. Attitudes and behavior. *Annual Review of Sociology,* 1976, **2,** 161–207.

Sears, D. O. The paradox of de facto selective exposure without preference for supportive information. In R. P. Abelson, E. Aronson, W. J. McGuire, T. M. Newcomb, M. J. Rosenberg, and P. H. Tannenbaum (Eds.), *Theories of cognitive consistency: A sourcebook.* Chicago: Rand McNally, 1968.

Shiffrin, R. M., & Schneider, W. Controlled and automatic human information processing: II. Perceptual learning, automatic attending, and a general theory. *Psychological Review,* 1977, **84,** 127–190.

Smedslund, J. The concept of correlation in adults. *Scandinavian Journal of Psychology,* 1963, **4,** 165–173.

Snyder, M. Attribution and behavior: Social perception and social causation. In J. H. Harvey, W. J. Ickes, & R. F. Kidd (Eds.), *New directions in attribution research.* Hillsdale, N.J.: Lawrence Erlbaum Associates, 1976.

Snyder, M., & Frankel, A. Observer bias: A stringent test of behavior engulfing the field. *Journal of Personality and Social Psychology,* 1976, **34,** 857–864.

Storms, M. D. Videotape and the attribution process: Reversing actors' and observers' point of view. *Journal of Personality and Social Psychology,* 1973, **27,** 165–175.

Storms, M. D., & McCaul, K. D. Attribution processes and emotional exacerbation of dysfunctional behavior. In J. H. Harvey, W. J. Ickes, & R. F. Kidd (Eds.), *New directions in attribution research.* Vol. 1. Hillsdale, N.J.: Lawrence Erlbaum Associates, 1976.

Storms, M. D., & Nisbett, R. E. Insomnia and the attribution process. *Journal of Personality and Social Psychology,* 1970, **16,** 319–328.

Taylor, S. E. On inferring one's attitudes from one's behavior: Some delimiting conditions. *Journal of Personality and Social Psychology,* 1975, **31,** 126–131. (a).

Taylor, S. E. A social psychology of salience: Perspectives in attribution processes. Paper presented at the meeting of the New England Social Psychological Association, Boston, October 1975. (b).

Taylor, S. E. The development of cognitive social psychology. In J. Carroll & J. Payne (Eds.),

Cognition and social behavior. Hillsdale, N.J.: Lawrence Erlbaum Associates, 1976.

Taylor, S. E. Structural aspects of prejudice reduction: The case of token integration. In J. Sweeney (Ed.), *Psychology and politics.* New Haven, Conn.: Yale University Press, 1977.

Taylor, S. E., & Achitoff, P. To see ourselves as others see us: Empathy, role-taking, and actor-observer effects. Unpublished manuscript, Harvard University, 1974.

Taylor, S. E., Etcoff, N. L., Fiske, S. T., & Laufer, J. K. Imaging, empathy, and attributions of causality. Unpublished manuscript, Harvard University, 1978.

Taylor, S. E., & Fiske, S. T. Point of view and perceptions of causality. *Journal of Personality and Social Psychology,* 1975, **32,** 439–445.

Taylor, S. E., Fiske, S. T., Close, M., Anderson, C., & Ruderman, A. Solo status as a psychological variable: The power of being distinctive. Unpublished manuscript, Harvard University, 1977.

Taylor, S. E., & Koivumaki, J. H. The perception of self and others: Acquaintanceship, affect, and actor–observer differences. *Journal of Personality and Social Psychology,* 1976, **33,** 403–408.

Taylor, S. E., & Langer, E. J. Pregnancy: A social stigma? *Sex Roles,* 1977, **3,** 27–35.

Tesser, A. Self-generated attitude change. In L. Berkowitz (Ed.), *Advances in experimental psychology.* Vol. II. New York: Academic Press, 1978.

Tesser, A., & Conlee, M. C. Some effects of time and thought on attitude polarization. *Journal of Personality and Social Psychology,* 1975, **31,** 262–270.

Tesser, A., & Cowan, C. L. Some attitudinal and cognitive consequences of thought. *Journal of Research in Personality,* 1977, **11,** 216–226.

Tesser, A., & Leone, C. Cognitive schemas and thought as determinants of attitude change. *Journal of Experimental Psychology,* 1977, **13,** 340–356.

Titchener, E. B. Attention as sensory clearness. In *Lectures on the elementary psychology of feeling and attention.* New York: Macmillan. 1908. Pp. 171–206. (Reprinted in P. Bakan (Ed.). *Attention: An enduring problem in psychology.* Princeton, N.J.: Van Nostrand, 1966.)

Tversky, A., & Kahneman, D. Judgment under uncertainty: Heuristics and biases. *Science,* 1974, **185,** 1124–1131.

Valins, S. Cognitive effects of false heart-rate feedback. *Journal of Personality and Social Psychology,* 1966, **4,** 400–408.

Valins, S., & Ray, A. Effects of cognitive desensitization on avoidance behavior. *Journal of Personality and Social Psychology,* 1967, **7,** 345–350.

Wicker, A. W. Attitudes versus actions: The relationship of verbal and overt behavioral responses to attitude objects. *Journal of Social Issues,* 1969, **25,** 41–78.

Wicklund, R. A. Discrepancy reduction or attempted distraction? A reply to Liebling, Seiler, and Shaver. *Journal of Experimental Social Psychology,* 1975, **11,** 78–81. (a).

Wicklund, R. A. Objective self-awareness. In L. Berkowitz (Ed.), *Advances in experimental social psychology.* Vol. 8. New York: Academic Press, 1975. (b).

Wicklund, R. A., & Duval, S. Opinion change and performance facilitation as a result of objective self-awareness. *Journal of Experimental Social Psychology,* 1971, **7,** 319–342.

Wicklund, R. A., & Ickes, W. J. The effect of objective self-awareness on predecisional exposure to information. *Journal of Experimental Social Psychology,* 1972, **8,** 378–387.

Wine, J. Test anxiety and direction of attention. *Psychological Bulletin,* 1971, **76,** 92–104.

Wolman, C., & Frank, H. The solo woman in a professional peer group. *American Journal of Orthopsychiatry,* 1975, **45,** 164–171.

Zajonc, R. B., Markus, H., & Wilson, W. R. Exposure effects and associative learning. *Journal of Experimental Social Psychology,* 1974, **10,** 248–263.

SELF-GENERATED ATTITUDE CHANGE[1]

Abraham Tesser

UNIVERSITY OF GEORGIA
ATHENS, GEORGIA

Much current attitude change research is addressed to some aspect of the question of "Who says what to whom with what effect?" This question implies

[1]Preparation of this chapter was partially supported by grants from the National Science Foundation (SOC 74-13925) and the National Institutes of Mental Health (1 F32 MH05802-01). Some of the work was completed while the author was a Visiting Fellow at Yale University. I am indebted to Robert Abelson and Claudia Cowan for reading and commenting on preliminary versions of this chapter.

that attitude change is the result of receiving information from some external source. In this chapter, attitude change is viewed from a different perspective. The emphasis is on how simply thinking about some attitude object dynamically alters one's beliefs and feelings.

I.   Theoretical Overview

A broad-brush sketch of the approach taken here shows it to employ constructs that enjoy a long history in social psychology as well as a strong contemporary appeal. We suggest that: (a) for various stimulus domains persons have naive theories or *schemas* which make some attributes of the stimuli salient and provide rules for inferences regarding other attributes; (b) thought, under the direction of a schema, produces changes in beliefs, and these changes are often in the direction of greater schematic and evaluative consistency; (c) attitudes are a function of one's beliefs. Since thought tends to make beliefs more evaluatively consistent and attitudes are a function of beliefs, thought will tend to polarize attitudes. The immediately following sections are intended to review prior research which bears on these ideas as well as to amplify our line of reasoning.

A.   COGNITIVE SCHEMAS

Sir Frederick Bartlett (1932) is generally credited with introducing the schema construct to social psychology in his monograph, "Remembering." By schema he meant

> an active organisation of past reactions, or of past experiences, which must always be supposed to be operating in any well-adapted organic response. . . . What is very essential to the whole notion, [is] that the organised mass results of past changes . . . are actively *doing* something all the time; are, so to speak, carried along with us, complete, though developing, from moment to moment [p. 201].

The view taken here has the same general thrust as that of Bartlett and is laid out most explicitly by Rumelhart and Ortony (1976). A schema is a naive theory of some stimulus domain and the individual using it a "naive scientist" (Kelley, 1967; Ross, 1977). Even relatively simple stimuli have associated with them a large number of attributes. Additionally, we often have a great deal of knowledge about the stimulus domain and the particular object. Obviously, we cannot attend to all this information simultaneously (Broadbent, 1958; G. A. Miller, 1956). When we apply a particular schema for thinking about some stimulus object it does two things. First, it tells us what to attend to. Like a scientific theory, it makes some attributes relevant, that is salient, while allowing others to be ignored. Second, a schema contains the network of associations that is believed to hold among the attributes of the stimulus and thereby provides rules for making inferences about the stimulus. Thus, if information conveying some relevant attribute is unavailable from the stimulus itself or is ambiguous or is unavailable from memory, the schema allows for the "filling in" of such information with "default options." We have various *causal* schemas which we use to make inferences about what produces particular effects in physical (Piaget, 1960) as well as social domains (Kelley, 1972; Stotland & Canon, 1972). Entities which function like schemas have been described under the name of personal constructs (Kelly, 1955), scripts (Abelson, 1976), and inferential sets (Jones & Thibaut, 1958).

In addition to delineating what is attended to and providing inference rules, schemas have other noteworthy properties. Following Rumelhart and Ortony (1976), schemas vary in levels of abstraction and can embed themselves one within the other. Lower level schemas can serve as "data" for higher level schemas. Thus, objects can be understood in terms of their major constituents without reference to the detail associated with lower level, embedded sub-schemas. Schemas represent knowledge rather than simple dictionary definitions: They are not necessarily linguistic entities but may include other symbolic representations; they not only define the object but embed it in a large knowledge network which allows comprehension even when formal definitional criteria are not met.

There are data to suggest that persons do develop and use implicit schemalike knowledge structures. Such structures seem to be important in understanding, remembering, and thinking about things as diverse as simple visual patterns and meaningful stories (Neisser, 1976). For example, Posner and Keele (1968, 1970) presented subjects with distortions of schematic or prototypic dot patterns without presenting the prototypes themselves. They found that subjects were as likely to recall seeing the prototype (which they hadn't seen) as the patterns they had seen. Further, "recognition" of the prototypes was less subject to loss over time than were the actually seen instances. Focusing on naturally occurring schemas, it takes less time to process information which is clearly consistent or clearly inconsistent with the schema. For example, with the natural category "mammal," it takes subjects longer to verify the statement, "A whale is a mammal" than to verify the statement "A dog is a mammal" (Rosch, 1973). On the other hand, subjects respond faster to "Is a collie a refrigerator?" than to "Is a collie a cat?" (Smith, Shoben, & Rips, 1974). The importance of schemas in processing stories has been discussed for a long time. Bartlett (1932) found that memory for a story from a different culture tended to be systematically distorted. He argued that the distortions made the story more consistent with the schema provided by the subjects' own culture. Rumelhart (1975) and Schank and Abelson (1975) have also argued persuasively for the necessity of a schema or cognitive script construct to explain how people understand stories.

Persons appear to have well-developed schemas for processing information about other persons. Traits of others seem to be well-organized in the perceiver's head. This organization, which has come to be known as "implicit personality theory" (Schneider, 1973), is very strong and pervasive. The same structure emerges, for example, not only in rating fictitious persons, but also in rating recent and better known acquaintances (Passini & Norman, 1966). In a paradigm similar to that of Posner and Keele, Cantor and Mischel (1977) showed that traits such as "introvert" and "extrovert" can function as prototypes. They found that subjects exposed to prototypic adjective descriptions were biased toward recognizing as presented, nonpresented adjectives that were consistent with the prototype.

There is evidence that schemas also affect our behavior and perceptions of our selves. Let us term persons who sort behavioral and perceptual situations into equivalence classes that are consistent with a particular trait "schematics" and persons who do not "aschematics." Thus, while both "schematics" and "aschematics" may obtain the same score on a paper-and-pencil measure of the trait, the aschematics' responses will be highly variable across items while the schematics' responses will have little variability. Bem and Allen (1974) found that, compared with aschematics, schematics exhibited considerable cross-situational consistency in behavior over a variety of situations. Norman (1975) did a conceptually similar study with the same general results. Hazel Markus (1977) identified persons who had self-schemas organized around the trait "independent" or around the trait "dependent" or who had neither schema. She found that persons with a particular self-schema endorsed more schema-consistent adjectives as self-descriptive and did so with shorter latencies than did aschematics or persons with a different schema. They were also able to supply more examples of schema-consistent behavior; they indicated that they were more likely to engage in such behavior in the future, and they were more resistent to counterschema information about themselves.

Different schemas may be used to think about the same object. Recall our characterization of a schema as a "naive theory." Depending on his purpose, a scientist may find one or another theory more useful for thinking about a particular phenomenon. Under some circumstances he may think about light using a wave theory; under other circumstances, he may think about light using a particle theory. Similarly, as situations change, an individual may "tune in" different schemas for thinking about the same stimulus.

There are some data to show that tuning in different schemas for thought affects the cognitive representation of the object. For example, Carmichael, Hogan, and Walter (1932) gave their subjects simple line drawings. Some subjects were told that each drawing represented one thing, while the remaining subjects were told it represented something else. When the two groups of subjects were asked to reproduce the original drawing, their drawings were quite different. Each group tended to distort the original drawing in the direction of the label they had been provided. More recently, Pinto and Abelson (cited in Abelson, 1976) had subjects listen to a story. Some subjects were to assume the role of the protagonist while listening; others were to imagine themselves watching the action from a balcony. When subjects were asked to reproduce the story, the balcony group had better recall of far visual details and the protagonist group had better recall of body sensation detail.

In sum, persons have and use organized knowledge structures, which we term schemas, in a variety of contexts—for perceiving visual arrays; for understanding meaningful prose; for processing information about the natural world; for understanding and perceiving other persons; and for perceiving and guiding their own behavior. It is also the case that different schemas can be tuned in for thinking about the same object. Below we examine in a more focused way the function of such structures in thought.

B. IMPACT OF THOUGHT

> For thinking, in the proper psychological sense, is never the mere reinstatement of some suitable past situation produced by a crossing of interests, but is the utilisation of the past in the solution of difficulties set by the present [Bartlett, 1932, p. 225].

1. Thought Makes Beliefs More Schemalike

According to William James (1907), voluntary attention to or thought about a particular thing

> ... is a repetition of successive [very brief] efforts which bring back the topic to the mind ... however, note that it is not an identical *object* in the psychological sense, but a succession of mutually related objects forming an identical *topic* only ... [pp. 420–421].

In short, thought does not involve a passive review of a static object but, rather, a dynamic process which alters the salient cognitive representation of that object. Furthermore, we suggest that cognitive schemas provide the necessary blueprints for such alteration.

It is not difficult to find evidence for the constructive role of thought. Bartlett (1932) had persons attend to a story from a different culture by having them repeatedly attempt to reproduce the story. Although responses quickly became stereotyped, there was some evidence that a detail which

> ... fits in with a subject's pre-formed interests and tendencies ... tends to take a progressively earlier place in successive reproduction [p. 93].

Furthermore,

> ... in all successive remembering, rationalisations, the reduction of material to a form that can be readily and "satisfyingly" dealt with, is very prominent [p. 94].

The method of serial reproduction involves exposing a stimulus to an individual who describes it to a second individual who, in turn, describes it to a third, and so on. Changes in the description over the chain of reproductions can tell us something about the way in which thought affects the cognitive representation of the stimulus. This method was introduced by Bartlett (1932) and used extensively by Allport and Postman (1947) in their studies of rumor. In general, the representation of the sitmulus, as indexed by its reproduction, becomes assimilated to the presumed schema of the subject. Following Allport and Postman (1947), this occurs in several ways: (a) *assimilation to principle theme*—reproduction is made more consistent with the main point; (b) *good continuation*—the adding of detail to complete a meaningful unit, production of closure; (c) *assimilation by condensation*—the combining of elements into fewer units; (d) *assimilation to expectation*—the reproduction is changed to be consistent with things as they usually are; (e) *assimilation to interest*—sharpening with respect to a detail of particular interest to the subject; (f) *assimilation to prejudice*—message is made consistent with subject's own hatreds.

More recently, Rips (1975) found that schemalike structures operate in inductive judgments. For example, *robin* is a more representative exemplar of a "bird" schema than is *duck*. His results indicate that information about an exemplar is inferred to be true of other exemplars to the extent that the given exemplar is representative of the schema.

The evidence supports the conclusion that thought biases or changes the cognitive representation of objects so as to make them more like the individual's relevant schema. In order for this to happen, however, an individual's schema must be engaged. For example, Spiro (1975) has shown that if subjects are required to memorize information, they tend to set up brand new schemas especially for that information, and the information tends not to be distorted over time. On the other hand, if people are asked simply to "react" to the information, then over time the information tends to be distorted systematically in the direction of well-developed, already extant schemas. Similarly, Ebbesen, Cohen, and Lane (1975) had subjects view short sequences of other persons' behavior under "memory" instructions or "impression" instructions. They found that subsequent trait ratings were more highly organized and the organization was more like a well-developed schema (i.e., implicit personality theory) for the "impression" subjects than for the "memory" subjects.

The discussion to this point has been concerned with the assimilative character of schemas—the tendency for thought to make the cognitive representations of the object more like the schema—because it is this aspect of schemas with which we are primarily concerned. Schemas, however, also exhibit accomodation. That is, they change as a function of experience with a stimulus domain. Accommodation often results in making the schema a more complete and veridical "theory" of the stimulus domain. If thought occurs in the absence of the object, it is not possible to "reality test" schematic inferences. Under such conditions, we would expect assimilation tendencies to be relatively strong and accommodation tendencies relatively weak.

In sum, there is evidence to suggest that thought, at least under some conditions, tends to result in a set of cognitions more consistent with the schema. Below we suggest that an evaluative consistency principle plays a role in these changes as well.

2. Thought Makes Beliefs More evaluatively Consistent[2]

Schemas provide a blueprint for thought-generated changes in belief. Without such a blueprint, we would expect little and rather unsystematic change. Thus, schemas are crucial to the cognitive changes discussed here. Furthermore, there is evidence to suggest that schema-directed changes often follow an evaluative consistency principle. That is, thought results in a more evaluatively consistent set of beliefs—more univalent, less ambivalent.

Some of the research on interpersonal impression formation is relevant to the hypothesis that thought produces consistent changes in cognition. Asch (1946) found that if he asked subjects who had been exposed to a list of adjectives describing another's personality to describe that person, they tended to go beyond the information given. This inferred linkage of one trait to another is so pervasive that it has been noted as a problem by psychometricians seeking valid ratings of personality (e.g., Mischel, 1968). Many of these trait linkages are organized around an affective or evaluative dimension. That is, if a person is liked, he is seen to have an overabundance of "good" traits and a paucity of "bad" traits. This is the well-known "halo effect" (Thorndike, 1920; Wells, 1907).

Some researchers (e.g., Phillips, 1967; Rosenberg & Abelson, 1960) have found that, as a function of thought, one's cognitions within a particular domain tend to become more "balanced," that is, positively evaluated entities become positively associated with other positively evaluated entities and negatively associated (dissociated) with negative entities; negatively evaluated entities become associated with other negative entities.

Spiro (1975) presented subjects with either a balanced or imbalanced (Heider, 1958) story about a couple that was contemplating marriage. Subjects were then given ancillary information either consistent or inconsistent with the story they heard. Subjects who were instructed to think and react to the story later

---

[2]There is a substantial body of literature which suggests that thought also makes beliefs more consistent with formal logic (e.g., McGuire, 1960; Wyer & Goldberg, 1970). Although such changes can result in cognitions that are more evaluatively consistent, this need not necessarily be the case. It is interesting to note in this context, however, that persons' *subjective* judgments of what is logical are, to some extent, influenced by their own attitudes (e.g., Feather, 1964).

reconstructed it to be more balanced with the ancillary information. (Subjects who were instructed to memorize the story did not show this distortion.)

It is *not* suggested that a blanket consistency principle is operating. Rather, consistency tends to operate locally, within a schema. Not any evaluatively consistent inference will be made but only one that is ''semantically'' consistent with the schema. Thus, depending upon the schema tuned in for thinking about the object, the same initial cognition could lead to *different* inferences. Further, although schematic changes in belief are usually in the direction of greater evaluative consistency, this need *not always* be the case.

C. RELATIONSHIP BETWEEN BELIEFS AND ATTITUDES[3]

Thought under the direction of a schema tends to alter salient cognitions. There is much evidence to suggest that one's overall attitude or affect is at least partially determined by one's salient cognitions and that changes in such cognitions will result in attitude change.

Rosenberg (1956), for example, has suggested that an individual's feeling toward some object is causally dependent on his cognitions or beliefs that the object blocks ($-$) or facilitates ($+$) attainment of his positive and negative values. If, for example, an individual believes that the attitude object tends to facilitate the realization of his positive values and block the attainment of negative values, he should feel positively about that object. There are data consistent with the hypothesis that beliefs and affect are positively correlated (e.g., Fishbein & Ajzen, 1975; Rosenberg, 1956). Further Norman (1975) measured beliefs and affect at two points in time and found that the correlation was stronger the second time. The suggested causal relationship, that an alteration in beliefs produces an alteration in affect, also has empirical support within this particular means–end framework (Carlson, 1956).

One's immediate thoughts have also been shown to bear a significant relationship to one's feelings. Love (described in Greenwald, 1968) had subjects list the thoughts that occurred to them when they were confronted with a persuasive message. Each thought was classified in terms of its favorability to the attitude issue. An index based on these thoughts bore a significant relationship to attitudes following the communication even when the influence of pretest attitudes was statistically held constant.

In sum, while there are a number of ways in which cognitions have been conceptualized, measured, and put into a single index, this index has invariably been shown to bear a significant positive relationship to the overall affect exhibited toward the object. If our analysis is correct, if thought, under the guidance of

[3]In general, for purposes of this chapter, the terms attitude, evaluation, and affect are used interchangeably to denote one's feeling about an object.

a cognitive schema, tends to make beliefs more evaluatively consistent, and if affect is related to beliefs, then thought should tend to polarize feelings.

D. SUMMARY

Persons have organized knowledge structures called schemas. During thought schemas make some beliefs salient and provide rules for making inferences. Schema-directed thought tends to result in a set of cognitions more consistent with the schemas and also more evaluatively consistent. Since affect is dependent on salient cognitions, this greater evaluative consistency leads to attitude polarization.

An example might help concretize the argument. We have suggested that an implicit personality theory is a schema. Suppose an individual has the following initial set of beliefs about another: Gregarious, physically attractive, honest, impolite, comes from Peoria, etc. Suppose now he has occasion to think about this person as a friend. Application of his schema for thinking may make salient the fact that the other is "gregarious," "honest," and "impolite" while the fact that he "comes from Peoria" is not considered. Further, his schema may lead him to infer or generate new beliefs. It might predict that persons who are "gregarious" have "many acquaintances," that "physically attractive" persons are "good athletes," etc. According to the individual's schema, "impolite" may be inconsistent with "gregarious." Therefore, he might reinterpret "impolite" to mean "open in expressing feelings," which would follow from "honest." Or, he may simply assume that he was wrong about the other's being "impolite." Note that with the aid of a schema, thought produces a total set of salient cognitions that make the initially likable person even more likable. If the individual did not have a schema, all initial information would be equally relevant. There would be no rules about what the information implies and, hence, no selective adding, reinterpreting, or ignoring of information. Without a schema, thought would produce little systematic attitude change.

In the example, all the schema-produced changes were in an evaluatively consistent direction. We assume that evaluative consistency will be an important and pervasive information-processing rule in many schemas. But this need not always be the case. Further, we assume that the thought-induced changes are not the result of a simple associational system. Rather, the same initial beliefs will lead to different changes depending upon the particular schema being used. We will have more to say on these points below.

This theorizing forces the adoption of a nontraditional view of attitudes. If feelings toward an object change simply as a result of thinking about the object with a new schema, then attitudes are not as fixed and relatively enduring as we typically suppose. An attitude at a particular point in time is the result of a constructive process (Anderson, 1978). And, *there is not a single attitude toward an object* but, rather, any number of attitudes depending on the number of schemas available for thinking about the objects. The implications of construing attitudes in this way are obviously far-reaching, and I shall explore one of these in Section IV,A.

II. Theory-Inspired Research

The analysis presented here suggests that thought about some particular object in the absence of any new information will tend to produce attitude polarization. This hypothesis and its corollary, the more time spent thinking about the object (up to a point) the greater the polarization, are examined in Section II,A. The cognitive changes underlying self-generated attitude change are presumed to be directed by a cognitive schema. This implies that, in the absence of a cognitive schema or with a poorly developed schema, the effects of thought on attitude change will be attenuated. This hypothesis is tested in Section II,B. Systematic schema-directed changes of beliefs (assimilation) should be easier in the absence of the object. That is, the presence of the object provides "reality constraints" that reduce the possibilities for distortion and hence should attenuate self-generated attitude change (Section II,C). The notion that attitudes and attitude changes are dependent on cognitive schemas implies that thinking about a particular object with different schemas will result in different attitudes and that these different attitudes will become more intensified with thought (Section II,D). In Section II,E we shall explore the presumed microprocess underlying self-generated attitude change; that is (*a*) thought-induced changes in belief are schema specific rather than *generally* consistent; (*b*) thought results in the addition of; and (*c*) reinterpretation of cognitions. Finally in Section II,F we shall deal with some interpretational issues.

A.   THOUGHT INTENSIFIES FEELING

According to Aristotle, "The brain tempers the heat and seething of the heart" (p. 652b). This suggests that thought moderates feelings. However, consider for a moment the child who is expecting a brand new, fire-engine red bicycle for Christmas. He thinks of that bicycle often, and each time he thinks about it, it becomes more attractive to him. Consider the student who is nervous about an upcoming statistics final. He thinks about it often, and each time he thinks about it, the exam becomes more odious and frightening. These examples as well as a number of studies conducted in our laboratories suggest that Aristotle's hypothesis, at least under some conditions, is wrong. We have found that, rather than reducing the strength of one's feelings, thinking about some person, idea, or thing often intensifies or *polarizes* one's initial feelings about it; ". . . a sensation attended to becomes stronger than it otherwise would be" (James, 1907, p. 425).

Our first experiment (Sadler & Tesser, 1973) was concerned with "how people form impressions of one another." Each subject and his experimental "partner" in an adjoining cubicle were to tell something about themselves to one another. After the subject spent 2 minutes describing himself, it was his "partner's" turn to tell about himself. Unknown to the subject, his "partner" was, in actuality, simulated with one of two tape recordings. By random assignment, half the subjects were exposed to a recording simulating a likable "partner." This "partner" complimented the subject on his self-presentation and described himself in positive terms without appearing to brag. The remaining subjects were exposed to a simulated dislikable "partner" who criticized the subject and who was smug, arrogant, and insulting. Following this, half of the subjects were given an irrelevant task intended to distract them from thinking about their partner, while the remaining subjects were instructed to think about their partner. Finally, subjects were asked to record their impressions of their partner in evaluative terms on a series of scales.

As expected, subjects evaluated the likable "partner" positively and the dislikable "partner" negatively. More importantly, this difference was *more* pronounced when subjects were given an opportunity to think about their partner ($p < .01$ for interaction). In other words, rather than becoming less extreme as suggested by Aristotle, subjects who were exposed to a likable "partner" felt more positive and subjects exposed to a dislikable "partner" felt more negative about him after thought than after distraction.

If thought has an impact on feelings, then the longer one thinks about something, the greater should be the impact on his feelings. Since a time manipulation in the Sadler and Tesser study had no systematic impact, we undertook an additional set of experiments (Tesser & Conlee, 1975) to examine more closely the effects of time spent thinking. The first study in this set concerned feelings about a heterogeneous set of attitude issues such as: prostitution should be legalized; in many cases, revolution is the best way to correct political and social problems; etc. When subjects arrived for the experiment, each was given a booklet containing a sample item and seven other items (randomly selected for each subject from a pool of 60 such items). For the practice issue, subjects scaled their initial feelings. They were instructed to think about the issue (jotting down notes if they so desired), and to scale their feelings about it again. The same procedure was followed for each of the remaining issues. The major independent variable was amount of time spent in thought, and subjects were randomly assigned to think about each issue for either 30, 60, 90, or 180 seconds.

The results of this study are shown in Fig. 1 (the curve labeled Experiment 1). On the ordinate is the mean percentage of issues on which feelings become polarized, that is initially negative feelings that become more negative and initially positive feelings that become more positive (see Section II,F,1 for a discus-

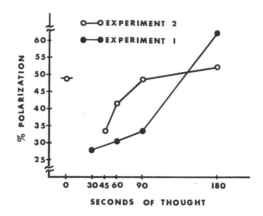

Fig. 1.   Percentage of attitudes changing in the direction of polarization as a function of time spent thinking about the attitude object. (From Tesser and Conlee, copyright 1975, by the American Psychological Association. Reprinted by permission.)

sion of this dependent variable). The abscissa indicates the amount of time spent in thought. The results are as predicted and clear—polarization of attitudes in a monotonic function of time spent thinking about the issue ($p < .01$). (Note: Wherever specific predictions are tested, the reported significance levels are one-tailed.)

The next experiment was designed to replicate the results of the previous experiment as well as to explore more systematically the effects of initial attitude direction (positive or negative) and initial attitude extremity on polarization. At a first session, subjects scaled their feelings toward each of the 62 items in the pool of issues. For each subject, eight issues were selected: two issues on which he was moderately positive, two slightly positive, two slightly negative, and two moderately negative. In a second session, some 1–4 weeks after the first, subjects were asked to write down their thoughts while thinking about each issue. By random assignment, some subjects thought about each issue for 45 seconds, some for 60 seconds, some for 90 seconds, and some for 180 seconds before scaling their attitude a second time. One final group of subjects was given neither an opportunity to think nor to list their thoughts before rescaling their attitude.

Initial attitude direction and extremity had no systematic effect on percentage of issues toward which attitudes polarized but, as can be seen in Fig. 1 (Experiment 2), the results of Experiment 1 were replicated. Given at least some time to think, the mean percentage of attitudes becoming polarized is a monotonic function of time spent in thought ($p < .05$). Still, there was one anomalous result. Subjects not given an opportunity to think did not, as expected, have the lowest level of polarization. Recall, however, that subjects in the various thought conditions were required to write down their thoughts. If they interpreted this requirement to be a kind of defense of their attitude, they may have moderated their position so as to make it appear more defensible (Cialdini, Levy, Herman & Evenbeck, 1973). The result of this would be to lower the polarization curve in the various thought conditions relative to the No Thought (and No Thought listing) condition.

The third experiment in this series therefore eliminated the thought listing requirement. Subjects indicated their initial feelings about a number of photojournalistic-type slides. Each subject was briefly shown a slide toward which he felt moderately positive (or negative) and was then given a distraction task to work on. Subjects in the No Thought condition next rescaled their feelings. Subjects in the Short Thought condition were given an additional 28 seconds; and subjects in the Long Thought condition were given an additional 60 seconds to think about the slide before rescaling their feelings. As expected, fewer subjects' feelings polarized in the No Thought condition (5%) compared with the Combined Thought conditions (24%, $p < .03$). Further, the feelings of subjects in the Long Duration condition were about twice as likely to become polarized (32%) as those in the Short Duration condition (16%, $p < .07$).

In the studies described above we have found that thought polarized feelings about other persons, general attitudinal issues, and photojournalistic pictures. And, this thought-polarization effect occurred regardless of whether the initial attitude direction was positive or negative. Other studies have produced similar results with feelings about others who have been described to subjects (Tesser & Cowan, 1975, 1977) feelings about paintings (Tesser, 1976), feelings about risky actions (Bateson, 1966), and even feelings about oneself (Ickes, Wicklund, & Ferris, 1973). While there have been some failures to obtain the effect (e.g., Anderson, 1971; Simpson & Ostrom, 1975), the weight of evidence suggests the generalization that thought does have an impact on feelings and that the nature of the impact is to intensify or polarize feelings.

We assume that thought will not continue to polarize attitudes indefinitely. Thoughtful people simply don't walk around with more and more extreme attitudes. Although Tesser and Paulhus (1976) found a positive relationship between amount of self-reported thought and attitude polarization over a period of 2 weeks, the relationship was slightly negative over 4 weeks. Konecni (1975) found that angered subjects who were given the opportunity to think were more aggressive than distracted subjects after 7 minutes, but this difference vanished by 11 minutes. We expect the thought-polarization effect to be of rather short duration but the reason for this is unclear. We assume that the process is dependent on evaluatively consistent changes in cognitions. Perhaps all the changes that can be made are done so rather rapidly, and further thought can do little more in that direction and may even produce inconsistent changes. Perhaps, after some time, sustained thought becomes difficult. According to William James (1907), *"No one can possibly attend to an object that does not change"* (p. 421). Thus, perhaps as potential changes are exhausted, attention flags. On the other hand, persons may, over time, adapt to the changed level of affect in a kind of mini "flooding." It is also possible that this increasing affect may act as a kind of danger signal that causes the individual to engage in a "reality search," that is, check his beliefs about the object, thus attenuating the polarization process.

B. SCHEMAS ARE NECESSARY FOR THOUGHT-INDUCED CHANGE

The research just described suggests that thought can polarize attitudes. We have argued that this effect is a result of cognitive changes under the direction of a cognitive schema. A schema provides rules for changing beliefs and, thus, the feeling. However, without implicit rules of inference (i.e., a schema) it is unclear how thought can systematically change the beliefs. If this line of speculation is correct, we would expect that the better developed one's cognitive schema for thought, the greater the likelihood that thought will result in attitude change.

There are some data to support this hypothesis. Cromwell and Caldwell (1962) had subjects make judgments of acquaintances. The judgments were made using constructs that the judge typically used [as determined by the Kelly (1955) Role Rep Test] or using constructs that the judge does not typically use. A schema (i.e., construct) that is more frequently used should become more fully developed—articulated and complex—and its use should result in more polarized judgments. This is precisely what Cromwell and Caldwell found.

We (Tesser & Leone, 1977) completed two additional studies to test the hypothesis further that thought with a well-developed schema results in greater attitude change than thought with a less well-developed schema. The first experiment used trait-adjective descriptions of persons and of groups as stimuli. We assumed that subjects have well-developed schemas for thinking about the personality of other persons (i.e., implicit personality theories; Schneider, 1973) but less well-developed schemas for thinking about the "personality" of groups. The explicit predictions were that: (a) thought would result in greater attitude polarization than distraction; (b) this difference would be more pronounced with persons as stimuli than groups; and (c) the difference between persons and groups would be more pronounced given an opportunity for thought than given distraction.

For each subject, we selected, from a set of adjective descriptions the subject had previously rated, two moderately likable and two moderately dislikable *person* descriptions. From another set of previously rated adjective descriptions, we selected two moderately likable and two moderately dislikable *group* descriptions. Half our subjects were encouraged to think for 90 seconds and then (re)rate each description in turn (in counterbalanced order). The remaining subjects were distracted from thinking about each description for 90 seconds before rerating. The results were entirely consistent with the hypothesis. First, subjects indicated that it was easier to think about the person stimuli than the group stimuli, thus validating our assumption that subjects have better developed schemas for thinking about the former. Second, as can be seen in Fig. 2, thought resulted in greater polarization than distraction ($p < .001$); person descriptions were associated with more polarization than group descriptions ($p < .005$); and person/group interacted with thought/distraction ($p < .05$) in precisely the form predicted. The difference between thought and distraction was more pronounced with "persons" ($p < .001$) than "groups" ($p \cong .05$), and the difference between "persons" and "groups" was more pronounced given thought ($p < .001$) than given distraction (n.s.). Furthermore, these results were recently replicated by Valenti (1975).

This study demonstrates that polarization as a function of thought is less likely when the attitude object is one for which subjects are presumed to have a less well-developed schema (i.e., groups). Given the centrality of the schema hypothesis, another experiment was performed. In this experiment, the stimulus domains sampled were women's fashions and football plays. Holding the stimulus constant, we would expect women to have better developed schemas for thinking about fashions than for thinking about football; we would expect men to have better developed schemas for thinking about football than for thinking about fashions.

Our specific predictions concerning polarization were that distraction would result in less overall polarization than thought; within distraction, sex and stimulus domain variables should have minimal effect; within thought, males with football stimuli and females with fashion stimuli should show a higher probability of polarization than males with fashion stimuli and women with football stimuli.

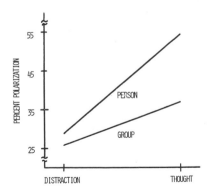

Fig. 2.   Percentage of attitudes changing in the direction of polarization as a function of thought and stimulus (person descriptions vs. group descriptions). From Tesser and Leone (1977).

The procedure was similar to that used in previous studies. Subjects were either given an opportunity to think (90 seconds) about or were distracted from thinking (90 seconds) about video-taped sequences of football tackles and women's fashions. The particular taped sequences were selected for each subject from a number of sequences which he/she had previously rated on an evaluative dimension (e.g., did they like the dress; did they think it was a good tackle). The selected sequences were either moderately positive (+4) or moderately negative (−4) on a scale that ranged from +7 to −7.

Postexperimental questionnaires validated the assumed schema differences. Again, the attitude change results also supported the theoretical predictions (see Fig. 3). Each of the specific expectations were supported. Sex and stimuli made relatively little difference within distraction (n.s.); within thought, the simple interaction of sex of subject and stimulus domain was significant ($p < .01$) and of the expected form—the most polarization was associated with male subjects with sport stimuli and female subjects with fashion stimuli.

The results of the two studies, group versus person descriptions, and sports versus fashions sequences, provide dovetailing support for the thesis that the better developed a cognitive schema for thought, the greater the probability that thought will result in attitude polarization.

C. THOUGHT, REALITY CONSTRAINTS, AND ATTITUDE CHANGE

Simply thinking about some object can result in attitude change. There is some evidence that this process is under the control of a cognitive schema.

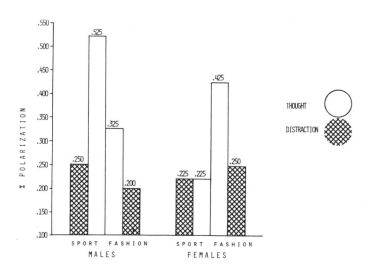

Fig. 3.   Percentage of attitudes changing in the direction of polarization as a function of subject sex and stimulus (sports vs. fashions). From Tesser and Leone (1977).

Presumably, thought results in schema-directed cognitive changes which in turn affect attitudes. In the absence of the object, with no opportunity for reality testing, there is no constraint on such assimilative changes. On the other hand, we assume that persons are responsive to reality and in most instances, specific objects are not perfect embodiments of an individual's schema. Thus, the presence of the object acts as a "reality constraint" on the kinds of changes that can be made. This being the case, it follows that thought in the presence of the object should produce less polarization than thought in the absence of the object.

In order to test this hypothesis, we (Tesser, 1976) had subjects initially evaluate slides of paintings. Following this, each subject was briefly shown one of the paintings which he had rated as likable (or dislikable). He was then randomly assigned to one of three period conditions: *Distraction*—Solved problems designed to distract him from thinking about the painting; *Object Present*—Thought about the painting while the painting was displayed; *Object Absence*—Thought about the painting while the painting was not displayed. Period 1 lasted 90 seconds, after which subjects were randomly assigned to one of three period 2 conditions. Period 2 also lasted 90 seconds and was composed of the same three conditions as the first period. Finally, subjects rerated their feelings toward the selected painting. (Subjects went through this whole procedure twice—once for a painting initially rated as moderately likable; once for a painting initially rated as moderately dislikable.)

Since sex of subject interacted significantly with the experimental manipulations, I shall discuss the results for males and females separately. Our female subjects behaved just as predicted by the hypothesis (see Fig. 4). Regardless of

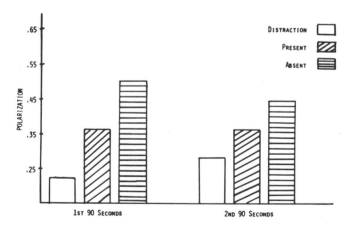

Fig. 4.   Percentage of attitudes changing in the direction of polarization as a function of distraction, thinking with the object present, and thinking with the object absent. Data based on female subjects only. Adapted from Tesser (1976).

whether their initial feelings were positive or negative, the feelings of those in the Distraction condition during the first 90 seconds (period 1) were less likely to become more extreme ($p < .05$) than the feelings of those in the Object Present condition which, in turn, were less likely to become more extreme ($p < .05$) than those in the Object Absent condition. The second 90 seconds (period 2) produced the same ordering: Object Absent produced the most polarization followed by Object Present, followed by Distraction. However, the differences were not as pronounced as they were in period 1 and the only one to approach significance was that between Distraction and Object Absent ($p < .10$).

These data suggest that the aphorism ''Absence makes the heart grow fonder'' is true but only under very limited conditions. Absence makes the heart grow fonder if the absent object was initially liked *and* the individual thinks about it. If the object is initially disliked, then thought will produce even greater *dislike*. Under conditions where it is true that ''out of sight is out of mind'' (i.e., distraction), we would expect relatively little polarization regardless of initial attitude.

In contrast to the females, there was little discernible pattern in the results for males. How might we account for this sex difference? Sex differences in information processing (Tyler, 1965) are a possibility, but the fact that thought resulted in polarization for men (as well as women) in every other study reported here tends to rule that out. Further, questionnarie data from this study also seem to rule out differences in emotional responses to or interest in the *particular* picture stimuli used.

In general, however, women have a greater interest in art (Tyler, 1965). We would also guess that women are more likely to have contact with aesthetic objects *qua* aesthetic objects and to be more concerned with making formal aesthetic judgments. Such exposure should produce more differentiated and articulated cognitive structures or schemas for dealing with such objects. As noted in the previous section (II,B), self-generated attitude change appears to be dependent on a well-developed schema and perhaps that is why the predicted results held for females and not males.

D. TUNING IN COGNITIVE SCHEMAS

We have suggested that attitudes are dependent on one's salient cognitions, that thought results in changes in one's salient cognitions about an object, and that these changes are dependent upon a cognitive schema. Often the thought-generated set of cognitions is more consistent with the initial attitude direction than is the initial set of cognitions, and the attitude polarizes. However, attitude polarization need not be an inevitable result of thought. Whether an individual's attitude polarizes or not depends upon the specific changes in his cognitions. Those changes depend, in turn, on the particular schema used for thinking about the object.

We propose that persons can—and often do—use different schemas. Just as different theories call our attention to different aspects of a phenomenon, tuning in different schemas should make salient different cognitions about the object. If one's feelings are causally dependent on one's salient cognitions, the tuning in of different schemas would immediately result in different feelings about the attitude object. Furthermore, if thought consists of the application of a schema to one's cognitions—with the result that those cognitions become more consistent with the schema—we would expect that the thought would result in the polarization of feelings in the direction of the tuned in schema. In summary, persons do not have a *single* feeling or evaluation of an object. Feelings vary depending upon the particular cognitive schema we "tune in" (see also Abelson, 1976). And further, the more we think about the object (generally), the more extreme our attitude will become in the direction of the *tuned in* schema.

There is a good deal of systematic research consistent with the hypothesis that feelings are a function of the particular schema tuned in. In a relatively early study, Jones & deCharms (1958) had their Navy subjects tune in different schemas for thinking about a well-adjusted and a poorly adjusted sergeant who, while a prisoner, had collaborated with the enemy. Subjects found the well-adjusted sergeant less acceptable, idealistic, and patriotic than the poorly adjusted sergeant. And this was true to a greater extent for subjects who thought about the stimulus persons using a schema concerned with appropriateness of his behavior than for subjects who thought about the stimulus persons using other schemas.

Hanno and L. E. Jones (1973) provide evidence that tuning in different schemas changes the rules of inference. They had their subjects estimate the probability of the occurrence of one trait from the existence of another trait over 120 possible pairs of 16 traits. Using these inferences as input to a multidimensional scaling routine, they found that the resulting configurations differed as a function of the schema the subjects used in making their inferences—that is, the configurations were different when the traits were those of a family doctor than when they were those of a politician.

A study by Salancik (1974) provides even stronger evidence for the hypothesis that an individual's attitude depends on the schema tuned in. Subjects rated the extent to which they participated in a number of behaviors in a recently completed course. Some of the behaviors were relevant to intrinsic aspects of the course (e.g., did nonrequired reading; discussed material with friends) and some were related to extrinsic aspects of the course (e.g., generally did the homework). Some subjects were then induced to tune in an "intrinsic motivational schema" and others an "extrinsic motivational schema" in evaluating the course. If attitudes are a function of the schema tuned in, we would expect the following: With an "intrinsic motivational schema," the correlation between intrinsic behavior recalled and evaluation should be *higher* than that between extrinsic behavior recalled and evaluation; with an "extrinsic motivational schema," the correlation between intrinsic behaviors recalled and evaluation should be *lower* than that between extrinsic behavior recalled and evaluation. Both of these predictions were significantly confirmed. This work has recently been extended by Salancik and Conway (1975).

These studies seem consistent with the notions that persons can tune in different schemas for thinking about objects and that these schemas have consequences for attitude change. However, none of these studies was designed with the schema hypothesis in mind and their support for the theory depends upon *post hoc* reinterpretation. Therefore, an experiment explicitly designed to test these hypotheses appeared necessary. The experiment we (Tesser & Danheiser, 1978) ran to fill this void was based on the assumption that the particular schema used to think about another person would be determined by one's relationship to that person (Jones & Thibaut, 1958). The schema one tunes in to think about a competitor makes salient negative aspects of the competitor and leads to negatively evaluated inferences about him. On the other hand, the schema one tunes in to think about a cooperating partner makes salient positive aspects of the partner and leads to positively evaluated inferences (Deutsch, 1968; Lerner, Dillehay, & Sherer, 1967). These assumptions lead to the prediction that *regardless of initial attitude direction,* the introduction of a competitive relationship should lead to a decrease in attraction, while the introduction of a cooperative relationship should lead to an increase in attraction. Further, this difference in attitude change should be more pronounced given an opportunity for thought than given distraction. The first part of the procedure closely followed that of Sadler and Tesser (1973). Subjects described themselves and then listened to the self-description of a bogus partner who was either likable or dislikable. Following this, they gave their initial impression of the other on a 10.5 mm line anchored with the labels "very positive"/"very negative" (MM scale), a series of six evaluative semantic differential scales (S-D scale), and Byrne and Nelson's (1965) interpersonal judgment scale (I.J.S). They were then led to believe that they would either be cooperating or competing with the other and were either instructed to think about the other or were distracted from thinking about the other. Finally, they again evaluated the other on the three scales.

The change in attraction scores for each measure were analyzed with a single planned comparison reflecting the theoretical predictions. As can be seen in Table I, the planned comparison was significant for each measure. The obtained means were ordered exactly as expected in every instance but one. (There was a nonsignificant reversal on the I.J.S.—the change was more positive under cooperation-low thought than under cooperation-high thought.)

We suggested earlier that thought need not invariably lead to attitude polarization, but should lead to change in the direction of whatever particular schema was tuned in. In this study, thought did *not* result in polarization. In fact, initial attitude direction had no consistent effect on attitude change. Rather, as ex-

TABLE I
MEAN CHANGE IN ATTITUDE TOWARD OTHER

Scales	High opportunity for thought		Low opportunity for thought		$F(1,114)$ for planned comparison
	Cooperative schema	Competitive schema	Cooperative schema	Competitive schema	
MM	.67	− .12	.21	−.06	12.80[a]
S-D	.33	−1.05	.08	−.73	5.87[b]
I.J.S.	−.20	− .90	.24	−.03	5.27[b]

Note: Adapted from Tesser and Danheiser (1978).
[a] $p < .05$.
[b] $p < .001$.

pected, the subject's relationship to his "partner," which presumably tuned in a schema, controlled the direction and magnitude of attitude change. In sum, it appears that the tuning in of different schemas for a particular object results in different feelings about the object. Furthermore, increased thought with a particular schema results in feeling more extreme in the direction of that schema.

At this point, it should be clear that the phenomenon we are dealing with cannot be explained by simply assuming that there is, associated with the attitude object, a simple set of beliefs that is indiscriminately accessed when the object is thought about. First, an individual's attitude is not a function of all his beliefs about some object but only of his salient beliefs (e.g., Kaplan & Fishbein, 1969). The beliefs that are salient for a particular object are not necessarily invariant. Thus, there has to be some mechanism for making particular beliefs salient and a simple associational network does not provide for such a mechanism. Second, a simple associational network implies that the associations or implications of each belief are invariant. However, in this section, we have reviewed evidence suggesting that this is not the case.

If it is true that different schemas can be tuned in to deal with the same stimulus, then the question of what determines which schema will be tuned in becomes important. Our account is highly speculative. We presume that the tuning process is one in which control passes back and forth between stimulus and schema, each having an impact on the other. The initially salient aspects of the stimulus are matched against potential schemas. Furthermore, we assume that what is initially salient in the stimulus is not invariant. Particular attributes may become more salient as a function of their intensity, change, unexpectedness, etc., and the subject's own motivational state (cf. Stotland & Canon, 1972;

Taylor & Fiske, 1978). When there is a reasonable fit with a particular schema, that schema takes over information processing. The stimulus is examined for confirmation of the schema. In this examination, new aspects of the stimulus may become salient and there may be assimilative changes in the perception and cognition of the stimulus and accommodative changes in the schema. If the stimulus continues to provide information reasonably consistent with the current schema, the current schema continues to control information processing. If examination reveals large discrepancies between the current schema and the stimulus object, the current schema is abandoned and a new one which is better able to handle the now salient information is recruited and takes over control of information processing.

Most instances of thought-generated change have been in the direction of polarization. In the absence of changes in attribute salience, motivational state, interpersonal relationships, etc., we would expect thought to make an individual's feelings more extreme in the direction of the previous attitude, that is, polarization. There are two reasons for this expectation. First, continued use of the same schema should result in polarization. And we would expect no change in schema without change in salience or motivation. Second, one attribute of an object that tends to be generally salient is one's previous evaluation of, or feelings about, the object. Osgood and his colleagues (e.g., Osgood, Suci, & Tannenbaum, 1957) have conducted numerous factor analytic studies of judgments of various objects. In general, they find that the most important factor to emerge is evaluative. When this is coupled with the fact that all of us have schemas concerning evaluation (Abelson & Rosenberg, 1958; Heider, 1958; Zajonc, 1968b) which lead us to expect liked objects to have/be associated with likable attributes and objects and disliked objects to have/be associated with dislikable attributes and objects, it is not surprising that thought often results in polarization. Furthermore, if the evaluation or feeling is somehow fixed, and that evaluation can tune in a schema, then over time we would expect one's cognitions to change in the direction of the affect. In an ingenious study, Rosenberg (1960) hypnotically altered subjects' affect toward a particular attitude object and found that over time their beliefs about the attitude object did change to be consistent with the affect.

E. THE MICROPROCESS

Until now, we have looked at attitude change as a function of thought without paying much attention to the details of the specific ways in which thought might change an individual's underlying beliefs. It has been suggested that although such changes result in greater evaluative consistency, these changes are schema-specific. That is, the changes are not simply "balanced" but must conform to the "semantics" of the schema in use. This point is explored in

Section II,E,1. Section II,E,2 through Section II,E,4 examine the specific ways in which cognitions are made more evaluatively consistent. That is, are consistent cognitions added? Are inconsistent cognitions reinterpreted? Are there other possibilities?

1. Thought Produces Schema-Specific Changes

To test the hypothesis that thought produces schema-specific changes in beliefs, we (Clary, Tesser, & Downing, 1978) attempted to get measures of schema content and then measure people's beliefs as a result of thought. In this case, we assumed that persons had a well-developed and shared schema for *salesman* and one for *bookkeeper*. To provide a gross measure of schema content, 100 subjects listed the characteristics that they thought an ideal salesman would possess, while another 100 subjects listed the characteristics that an ideal bookkeeper would possess. The most frequently mentioned characteristics served as a "salesman key" and a "bookkeeper key."

As usual, we expected that compared to distraction, thought about an individual initially seen as a moderately good prospect for salesmen bookkeeper should lead to a more extreme evaluation (i.e., polarization) of that person as a salesman/bookkeeper. Let us focus on the salesman key. Since cognitive changes are under the direction of a schema, focusing on a prospect for salesman should produce a set of beliefs more consistent with the salesman schema, that is, a higher score on the salesman key. On the other hand, while thought about a moderately good prospect for a bookkeeper should lead to polarization, since a different schema is being used, thought should *not* necessarily lead to a set of *cognitions* more consistent with the salesman schema. A complementary set of expectations exists for the bookkeeper key.

To test these expectations, 80 subjects were recruited for an experiment in "Personnel Decisions." Half the subjects were assigned to the Bookkeeper condition and half to the Salesman condition. Each subject rated the resumes of 15 "applicants" on a 15-point scale (Outstanding Salesman [Bookkeeper] +7 to Very Poor Salesman [Bookkeeper] −7). The subjects in each condition were then given 90 seconds in which they either thought about or were distracted from thinking about one of the candidates to which they had initially given a moderately favorable rating (+4). After rerating the candidate, subjects were asked to write a paragraph describing why they might hire the candidate (including their impressions of the candidate's personal attributes). These paragraphs were scored with both the salesman key and the bookkeeper key.

As expected, regardless of whether the focus was on salesman or bookkeeper, there was a greater probability of polarization in the Thought condition ($\bar{X}$ = .35) than in the Distraction condition ($\bar{X}$ = .175; $p < .05$). More important for present purposes are the scores on the salesman and bookkeeper keys. Although scores on the bookkeeper key were unaffected by thought, scores on the salesman key were affected by thought. As can be seen in Fig. 5, in addition to the obvious Focus main effect, Thought interacted with Focus in precisely the predicted way ($p < .05$) on the salesman key. When subjects thought about an applicant in terms of his being a salesman, their beliefs about the applicant became more consistent with a "good salesman schema" as indexed by the salesman key ($p < .07$). On the other hand, thought produced no differences on the salesman key when an applicant was being considered for a bookkeeper job.

Since the same effect was *not* present for people who thought about the applicant in terms of his being a bookkeeper, a number of alternative explanations are eliminated and the schema interpretation strengthened. For example, one alternative may be that thought results in more cognitions and the greater the number of cognitions, the greater the likelihood of having a higher score on the salesman key. However, "bookkeeper focus" subjects experienced the same opportunity for thought manipulation and wrote the same length descriptions but did not exhibit the effect. Perhaps, since the salesman key contains positively evaluated attributes and thought leads to a more positive evaluation of the prospect, subjects simply write more positive things after thought. However, with thought, the bookkeeper subjects also had a more positive evaluation of the prospect but they did not have a higher score on the salesman key. It appears that "salesman focus" and "bookkeeper focus" produced different thought-induced cognitive changes. Recall that schemas direct cognitive changes. Different schemas, "good salesman" versus "good bookkeeper," should produce different changes.

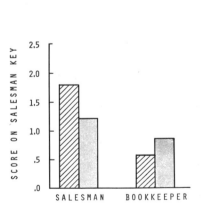

Fig. 5.   Score on "salesman key" as a function of whether subjects thought or were distracted from thinking about an applicant for a salesman's job or a bookkeeper's job. From Clary *et al.* (1978).

2. Thought Generates Consistent Cognitions

There are at least three different ways in which thought can change cognitions to result in attitude polarization. The individual can add or *generate* new cognitions which make his set of salient cognitions more evaluatively consistent. He can block, suppress, or *lose* inconsistent cognitions. Or he can shade the meaning of, or *reinterpret,* cognitions so that they become more evaluatively consistent. Some individuals might show a greater proclivity for generation while others show a greater proclivity for loss or reinterpretation. Others might favor two out of the three while still others would tend to use all three processes equally. It might also be the case that the kind of process used is a function of properties of the attitude itself, that is, its initial consistency, complexity, familiarity, etc. What this suggests is that the demonstration of any one process will not necessarily rule out the operation of the other processes. Furthermore, we have no way of directly observing the thought process but must combine rational assumptions with the observation of antecedent conditions and subsequent behavior to make inferences about what the intervening processes might have been.

Our first study (Sadler & Tesser, 1973) yielded some relevant results. In addition to indicating their feelings about their partner, subjects listed their thoughts concerning him and their evaluations of each thought. The thought-loss hypothesis would lead us to expect fewer inconsistent cognitions with thought than with distraction. There was no difference. The data are, however, consistent with the thought-generation hypothesis. Regardless of whether the partner was likable or dislikable, thought resulted in the listing of a greater number of cognitions consistent with the attitude than did distraction ($p < .01$; .05, respectively; see Fig. 6).

Given the design of the Sadler and Tesser study, it is impossible to know whether the thought-associated differences in feeling are a result of the differences in the number of consistent cognitions generated as hypothesized, or whether the difference in number of cognitions is, in some way, a result of or justification of the thought-related change in feelings. Suppose, however, that we set up conditions which make it either easy or difficult for the subject to generate consistent cognitions. If polarization is causally dependent on the generation of consistent cognitions, we would expect a greater thought-polarization effect (i.e., difference between thought and distraction) where generation is relatively easy rather than where it is more difficult. Such a result would provide clearer evidence for the causal role of generation in the thought-polarization effect.

Claudia Cowan and I (Tesser & Cowan, 1975) reasoned that new cognitions would be generated to be consistent with one's initial cognitions. The greater the number of initial cognitions, the more difficult it would be to generate new cognitions consistent with all of them. Therefore, if thought polarizes attitudes by a process of generation and generation is facilitated with fewer initial cognitions, then we would expect a greater thought-polarization effect with fewer initial cognitions.

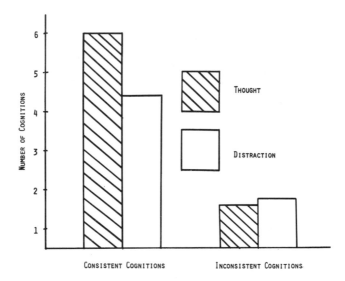

Fig. 6.   Number of cognitions produced by subjects who were given an opportunity for think-ing about their partner or who were distracted from thinking about their partner. Adapted from Sadler and Tesser (1973).

The attitude objects in this study were other persons described by lists of trait adjectives. To vary number of initial cognitions, half of the descriptions contained four adjectives (cognitions) and half contained eight adjectives (cogni-tions). After indicating their attraction to a number of such described persons, subjects were given 90 seconds in which they were distracted from thinking about, or were asked to think about, descriptions which they initially either liked or disliked. Finally, subjects again scaled their feelings about the described persons.[4]

The results were quite consistent with expectations (see Fig. 7). The thought-polarization effect (i.e., the difference between thought and distraction) is significantly more pronounced ($p < .05$) with four cognitions than with eight cognitions. Also as predicted, within the Thought condition four cognitions produced more polarization than eight cognitions ($p < .05$). Number of cogni-tions was expected to have little effect within Distraction and, although there appears to be such an effect, it is in the direction opposite to Thought and is not significant.

[4]In this study, subjects were also asked to list their thoughts concerning the described person. The number of cognitions listed, however, proved quite insensitive in this study and was not affected by the Thought manipulation or even the Number of Cognitions manipulation. The problems with the index in this study are discussed by Tesser and Cowan (1975), and the problems with thought list measures in general are discussed by N. Miller and Baron (1973) and Anderson (1978).

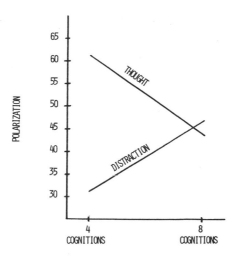

Fig. 7. Percentage of attitudes changing in the direction of polarization as a function of thought and number of initial cognitions. From Tesser and Cowan (1975).

The results of the Sadler and Tesser study and the "number of cognitions" study provide dovetailing support for the generation hypothesis. In the first case, thought produced more attitude polarization and a greater number of consistent cognitions than distraction. In the second, the thought-polarization effect was clear under conditions which were expected to facilitate the generation of consistent cognitions and that effect was nonexistent under theoretically less favorable conditions.

3. Reinterpretation

As noted above, evidence of the operation of one process such as generation does not, in itself, rule out the possibility of the operation of other processes. In a recently completed pair of studies, Tesser and Cowan (1977) found some evidence that the reinterpretation of inconsistent cognitions to make them more consistent may also be implicated in the production of the thought-polarization effect.

In the first of these studies, subjects, after making some initial ratings, were given either 25 or 90 seconds to think about persons described by a list of trait adjectives. Half of the descriptions contained three likable traits and half contained three dislikable traits. All contained a fourth, neutral trait to be used as a kind of "tracer." Subjects rerated their feelings about each of the described persons and indicated the meaning of the "tracer" adjective on a series of six semantic differential evaluative scales (e.g., good/bad, positive/negative, optimistic/pessimistic).

If subjects' attitudes polarize because they reinterpret inconsistent cognitions (in this case the neutral "tracer") to be more consistent with the initial attitude, not only would we expect the "tracer" to have a more positive evaluation when associated with the likable description than a negative description (i.e., a well-documented context effect which need not be explained in terms of a reinterpretation hypothesis, e.g., Anderson, 1971) but, more importantly, we would expect this difference to be more pronounced with 90 seconds of thought than with 25 seconds of thought.

The results were encouraging. First, as expected, 90 seconds of thought produced greater polarization of feelings about the described persons than 25 seconds of thought ($p < .06$). Also, on each of the semantic differential scales, the "tracers" were evaluated more positively in association with the likable descriptions than with the dislikable descriptions ($p < .01$). Finally, as predicted by the reinterpretation hypothesis, the latter difference was more pronounced with 90 seconds of thought than with 25 seconds of thought on two of the scales ($p < .06$).

The results of this study were promising but not as conclusive as one might hope. First, the predicted effect of thought duration on the evaluation of the "tracer" emerged on only two of the six scales. Second, demonstrating that the polarization of feelings and the reinterpretation of cognitions is related does not establish the direction of causality. That is, polarization may be a function of thought-induced reinterpretation of cognitions as hypothesized, or reinterpretation may be a function of attitude polarization. Our strategy for disentangling these possibilities, as before, was to try to establish conditions which vary in the extent to which they are facilitative of the hypothesized process—in this case, reinterpretation—and then to see if they affect polarization.

We reasoned that the *ambiguity* of an inconsistent cognition should affect the ease with which reinterpretation could take place. Let us define an ambiguous cognition as one that, when considered by itself, has a large number of interpretations. Then, compared to an unambiguous cognition, it should be easier to reinterpret the meaning of an ambiguous cognition so as to make it consistent with either a set of positive cognitions or a set of negative cognitions. Therefore, we would expect greater attitude polarization as a result of thought with an ambiguous inconsistent cognition than with an unambiguous inconsistent cognition.

Fortunately, Wyer (1974) had scaled personality trait adjectives in terms of ambiguity. For our next study, we selected those that were matched in terms of being evaluatively neutral but differing in ambiguity to be used as "tracers." Four types of personality descriptions were constructed by combining three likable and three dislikable traits with an ambiguous "tracer" and three likable and three dislikable traits with an unambiguous "tracer." Subjects initially rated the likability of a number of these four adjective descriptions. Two descriptions of each of the four types were selected for each subject. Half the subjects thought about each of the selected descriptions for 90 seconds, rerated their feeling toward the person described, and then evaluated the meaning of the "tracer" on six evaluative semantic differential scales. The remaining subjects were shown the eight selected descriptions but were distracted from thinking about each for 90 seconds before making their ratings.

The reinterpretation hypothesis was fully supported by the polarization of feelings results. As predicted, thought produced more polarization of feelings than distraction *and* this effect was more pronounced with an ambiguous "tracer" than with an unambiguous "tracer" ($p < .01$). These means are shown in Fig. 8. The evaluations of the "tracers" over all six semantic differential scales also tended to support the reinterpretation hypothesis. Not only was there a significant ($p < .01$) context effect (i.e., the "tracer" was evaluated more positively when associated with a likable description than with a dislikable description), but this context effect was stronger under thought than distraction ($p < .05$). It was also stronger with ambiguous "tracers" than with unambiguous "tracers" ($p < .01$).

The last two studies were intended to address the reinterpretation of inconsistent cognitions explanation, and the results consistently supported this explanation. However, the studies do not unequivocally rule out other possibilities. For example, it may not be easier only to reinterpret an ambiguous cognition, but it may be easier to generate new consistent cognitions given an ambiguous one. Thus, we must conclude that although the reinterpretation hypothesis has survived several experimental tests and remains a plausible possibility, its validity has not been unambiguously demonstrated.

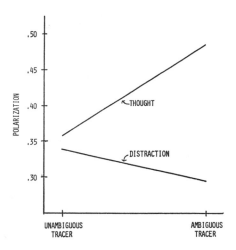

Fig. 8. Percentage of attitudes changing in the direction of polarization as a function of thought and ambiguity of initial cognitions. From Tesser and Cowan (1977).

4. Other Possibilities

Above we have provided some data supporting the hypotheses that thought results in the addition of consistent cognitions and the reinterpretation of inconsistent cognitions. There is a third possibility. Thought can result in the functional loss of inconsistent cognitions. The cognitions' implications may not change, but their weight or importance to the attitude may decline. For example, Davidson and Kiesler (1964) observed subjects choosing between job candidates. The more time subjects were given to deliberate, the more they tended to exaggerate the importance of attributes on which their favored candidate was strong and to minimize the importance of attributes on which their favored candidate was weak. Another possibility is that nonrehearsal of the inconsistent cognition during thought may make it more difficult to retrieve the inconsistent cognition from memory. There is some evidence that, compared with consistent cognitions, people have a harder time retrieving inconsistent cognitions over time (e.g., Levine & Murphy, 1943). However, we could find no demonstration indicating that this effect is more pronounced with *thought* about the object.

A final possibility emerges from the two studies described in connection with the reinterpretation hypothesis. It will be recalled that the "tracer" was rated on six evaluative semantic differential scales. In addition to the difference in means on these scales as a function of thought (the difference reported earlier), there appeared to be a systematic difference in the intercorrelations among the six scales. On the average, the intercorrelations were higher as a function of thought[5] and this difference was significant in the first study. This indicates that if one were to factor analyze the correlation matrix at increasing levels of thought, a single factor would account for a greater proportion of the rating variance. Since the scales themselves are evaluative, the factor would be evaluative. One implication of all this is that thought results in greater cognitive organization around an evaluative factor. It is not difficult to see how such a process could affect attitude polarization.

F. SOME INTERPRETATIONAL ISSUES

1. The Polarization Index

Much of the data presented in support of our hypotheses are based on a binary measure of attitude polarization: If an individual's attitude became more polarized, he received a score of "1"; if his attitude did not change or became

---

[5]A finding that is tantalizingly similar in some ways was reported by Ebbesen *et al.* (1975). Earlier we suggested that persons are less likely to engage currently extant, well-developed schemas under memory instructions. Ebbesen *et al.* found that subjects viewing others' behavior sequences under "impression" instructions generated trait ratings that were more highly intercorrelated than subjects viewing the same sequence under "memory" instructions.

less polarized, he received a score of "0." The mean of this index can be interpreted as the percent of attitudes polarizing. In every instance in which this index has been used, an index based on the algebraic difference between pre- and posttest scores has also been computed. In each case (some 11 independent studies), the binary index has provided stronger support for the theoretical predictions. Since the construct validity of a measure is a function of its behavior *vis-à-vis* theoretical expectations (Cronbach & Meehl, 1955), the binary index appears to have greater validity than the algebraic measure.

The greater validity of the binary index may be due to its relative insensitivity to "errors." In order to elaborate this point, it would be useful to look at an actual change score distribution. For purposes of illustration we show, in Fig. 9, change score distributions for the three stimuli presumed to be associated with well-developed schemas in the pair of studies by Tesser and Leone (1977) (Section II,B). Recall that the specific experimental stimuli selected for each subject were originally rated as +4 or −4 on a scale that ranged from +7 to −7. In the figure, this point is shown as 0 change. From this point there are three levels of

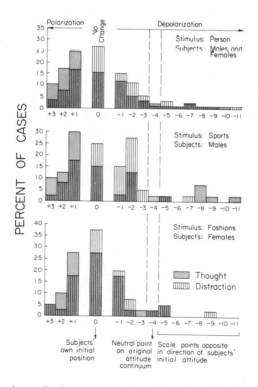

Fig. 9.   Attitude change distribution as a function of thought, subject sex, and stimulus. From Tesser and Leone (1977).

change in the direction of polarization possible: $+1$, $+2$, or $+3$ and potentially 11 levels of change in the direction of depolarization: -1 to -11.

Thought is more likely to produce polarization, that is, $+1$, $+2$, $+3$, than is distraction. On the other hand, distraction is more frequently associated with "no change," 0, and the first three levels of depolarization, that is, -1, -2, -3 than is thought. Looking only at these cases, regardless of whether one indexes polarization by the binary index or an algebraic change measure, thought clearly produces more polarization than distraction.

Look now at the cases in which the subject has abandoned his initial attitude direction by becoming neutral (-4) or adopting a new position opposite in direction $(-5$ to $-11)$ to his original position. There are relatively few such cases and since there is no thought/distraction difference among them, they do not add to the separation of the Thought versus Distraction condition means. However, they do increase the within-condition variability (i.e., error variance). Clearly, this increase in error variance will be much more pronounced with the algebraic index (which takes into account the entire range of scores) than with the binary index. In sum, it appears that the binary index has been more responsive to experimental manipulations because the change score distributions are skewed and the binary index is less affected by instances in the tails of the distribution.

There is another issue concerning the binary index that needs to be dealt with—the meaning of a score in terms of polarization/depolarization. The binary index can be interpreted as the percentage of attitudes in a condition that becomes more polarized so it is tempting to assume that anything above 50% is polarization and anything below 50% is depolarization. However, even under those experimental conditions where polarization is presumed to be maximal, the binary index barely reaches or surpasses .5. One might conclude that (a) thought does not do anything but, on the other hand, distraction produces depolarization, or (b) thought does not produce polarization but merely retards depolarization. A careful analysis does not support either of these conclusions.

First, 50% is not an appropriate dividing line for polarization/ depolarization. It is too high because it doesn't allow for the fact that a large proportion of attitudes exhibit no change at all (see Fig. 9). For example, if 60% of the attitudes exhibited no change and every change that occurred was in the direction of polarization, the index would be .40—less than 50%. Also, in every case in which this index has been used, the initial attitude was selected because it was different from the theoretical neutral point on the scale. To the extent that the population mean is close to the neutral point, one would expect *depolarization* on the basis of a regression artifact. Thus, it is clear that some theoretical, *absolute* criterion of polarization is very difficult to construct and clearly it is not 50%. Polarization must be defined on a relative basis in terms of comparisons among relevant treatment conditions. Let us deal with the conclusions in the above paragraph in those terms.

If it is the case that thought is the inert condition but distraction produces depolarization, then differences between thought and distraction conditions should be associated with differences in the effects of distraction. That is, thought, being inert, should produce little variability over conditions while distraction should produce differences between conditions. In fact, just the opposite is the typical result (e.g., Fig. 3). Differences between conditions are usually associated with thought while distraction produces little between-condition variability. Thus, the action appears to be with thought, not distraction.

If thought does not polarize attitudes but merely retards a "natural" depolarization process, we would expect decreasing polarization over time, with thought reducing the slope of that function. Thought would not change the *direction* of the slope; at most, if thought was 100% effective, the slope would be zero. However, in some four separate experiments, polarization *increased* over time with thought (Tesser & Conlee, 1975; Tesser & Cowan, 1977). This implies that, rather than retarding depolarization, thought actually increases polarization. Whenever different levels of thought are examined, either over time or, holding time constant, over distraction versus thought instructions, there is a positive association between thought and attitude change.

2. Experimental Demand

The basic manipulation in these studies involves instructions to think about a particular attitude object. Perhaps this instruction suggests to subjects that attitude polarization is appropriate and they behave accordingly. If this were the case, the attitude polarization phenomenon would be an artifact, a result of experimental demand (Orne, 1962) rather than thought-dependent processes.

Several converging lines of evidence render the "experimental demand" hypothesis implausible. First, it is unclear why the thought instruction should lead subjects to believe that exhibiting attitude polarization is the expected or socially desirable thing to do. It is at least equally plausible that subjects who are asked to think about their opinions in a psychological experiment would give a more moderate opinion since such a stance is more rational, indicates less bias, and is easier to defend (Cialdini *et al.*, 1973). It is also more plausible to assume that subjects would see increased agreement/positivity as more desirable than polarization (Jones & Sigall, 1971).

To the extent that subjects are unaware of the independent variable, guessing the true hypothesis and behaving in accord with it are more difficult. In every study in this series, thought/distraction has been a between-subject variable and, thus, subjects have been unaware of this manipulation. Further, in every study, subjects have been thoroughly interviewed in a postexperimental debriefing session. In these interviews, almost none of the subjects has been able to verbalize the thought polarization relationship. (Nor, in almost every instance, have they been able to articulate the particular experimental hypotheses.)

Other results are also inconsistent with a demand interpretation. Several studies have not used a thought/distraction manipulation, but have used *identical* thought instructions while varying, *between* subjects, the time permitted for thought (Tesser & Conlee, 1975; Tesser & Cowan, 1977). Attitudes polarized as a function of time, not instructions. In the Tesser and Danheiser (1978) study, the usual thought/distraction manipulation was used but thought did not result in the attitude polarization expected from the "demand" hypothesis. Thought resulted, as predicted, in attitude change in the direction of the tuned in schema.

Many of the experiments reported in this chapter involve interactions difficult to explain with a "demand" hypothesis. Why should the thought manipulation "demand" polarization with four initial cognitions but not eight; why should the thought manipulation "demand" polarization with an ambiguous "tracer" but not with an unambiguous "tracer"; why should the thought manipulation "demand" polarization for women's fashion but not football plays for women (and just the opposite for men)?

In short, the hypothesis that thought-induced attitude change is a function of experimental demand appears implausible. It has no compelling rationale; subjects' self-reports are inconsistent with it; and it has a difficult time accounting for a variety of experimental outcomes.

3. Some Other Interpretations

One alternative explanation holds that thought retards forgetting about various aspects of the stimulus, and forgetting produces depolarization. This is a variant of the proposition that distraction produces depolarization while thought retards depolarization. This general proposition has already been examined (Section II,F,1) and found wanting. The evidence is even stronger against this particular variant. We would expect persons to be more prone to forget stimuli from less familiar domains than from more familiar domains. If thought affects attitude change by preventing forgetting, then its effects should be more pronounced in less familiar domains than in more familiar domains. In fact, just the opposite result has been obtained (Section II,B).

Perhaps, in thinking about the object, our subjective feelings of uncertainty regarding what we know about the object are somehow reduced. When we feel more certain in our knowledge about the object, our feelings concerning the object become more extreme. The presence of the object during thought should increase subjective feelings of certainty about what is known about the object. Therefore, the "uncertainty reduction" hypothesis would predict greater thought polarization with the object present than with it absent. What data we have suggest just the opposite. The absence of the object *facilitates* polarization (Section II,C).

Another possibility is that polarization is really an "energized" version of the initial (dominant) response. Perhaps thought simply increases general arousal which in turn "energizes" the performance of dominant responses. This hypothesis accounts for much of the data reported. Assume, for example, that the initial response is more "dominant" for stimuli associated with a well-developed schema (familiar) than with a less well-developed schema. One would expect, and we have obtained (Section II,B), a greater polarization effect with a well-developed schema. It is also reasonable to assume a more "dominant" initial response with a fewer number of initial cognitions and we have found a stronger thought-polarization affect with fewer initial cognitions. However, if we assume that response competition is increased with an ambiguous stimulus, the hypothesis appears to be contradicted by the finding that the effect is stronger with an ambiguous element in the stimulus than with no ambiguous element (Section II,E,3). In spite of this contradiction, given the simplicity of the hypothesis, its relation to a large and established body of psychological literature, and its ability to account for so much of the present data, it should not be summarily dismissed. It and other simple mechanisms such as the salience effects discussed by Taylor and Fiske (1978) deserve increased attention.

III.   Some Implications for Other Lines of Research

Below, the implications of the self-generated attitude change formulation for the relationship between attitudes and behavior and for psychotherapy are explored. The relevance of the present formulation to "mere exposure" and "group polarization" research is also briefly touched upon.

A.   ATTITUDES AND BEHAVIORS

Social psychologists spend much of their time trying to understand how attitudes develop and change (McGuire, 1969). Presumably, they are thus occupied because attitudes are an important determinant of other behaviors. Naturally, then, when it is suggested that attitudes may have relatively little to do with other behaviors (Wicker, 1969), many of us feel compelled to show how this last assertion is based on inadequate evidence (Dillehay, 1973) or must be qualified (Norman, 1975).

The usual paradigm used in relating attitudes and behavior is to measure an individual's attitude or feeling about some object in a single situation on a single occasion and then to observe the extent to which he engages in a particular behavior *vis-à-vis* the object in a single situation on a single occasion. Use of such a paradigm relies on at least two questionable assumptions. First, it assumes that the observed behavior is interchangeable with any other behavior in the sense that all behavior is at least partially dependent on affect. However, Triandis (1964) has factor analyzed a number of social behaviors and found several *independent* factors. This implies that different behaviors have different determinants. Therefore, to presuppose that affect determines all behavior is simply naive (Kiesler, Collins, & Miller, 1969).

The standard paradigm also assumed that individuals have a *single attitude* toward the object. We have argued, however, that one's attitude at the moment is a constructive process generated from the *particular* schema tuned in. Even if one's affect concerning an object is a determinant of the particular behavior under study, the observed correlation between affect and behavior can be highly attenuated. Such a case will arise when the conditions present at the time of the behavioral measurement tune in a schema different from that operative when the measure of affect was taken. A different schema will make different cognitions salient and hence result in a different attitude. Therefore, the original measure of affect will be almost irrelevant.[6]

For example, in the classic study by LaPiere (1934), a Chinese couple was served in a variety of public places even though the proprietors of these places had responded negatively to a letter asking if they would serve Chinese persons. It seems reasonable to assume that "Chineseness" was more salient in the letter and "Customerness" when the persons showed up (see also Kutner, Wilkins, & Yarrow, 1952). The study by Minard (1952) of the Pocahontas coal mine workers is also often cited as an example of an attitude–behavior discrepancy. He found that most of the white workers were congenial in their relations with black co-workers in the mine but not on the surface. Suppose we assume that in the mine a "co-worker" schema is tuned in and on the surface a "friend" schema is tuned in. If we assume that blackness is negatively evaluated and race is less relevant to the "co-worker" schema than the "friend" schema, this behavior is easy to understand (see also Star, Williams, & Stouffer, 1958). These examples suggest that if we want to evaluate the proposition that attitudes determine behavior, we need a taxonomy of behaviors and schemas to determine which kinds of behaviors are affected by attitudes. We also need some way of assuring that the attitude measured is the same as that operating when the behavior is observed.

Some very recent research and theorizing about attitude–behavior relationships seem, in a broad sense, to be compatible with the present position. For example, there is evidence to suggest that manipulations designed to get persons to think about their attitudes or prior behavior tend to increase the relationship between attitudes and behavior (e.g., Carver, 1975; Snyder & Swann, 1976; Zanna & Fazio, 1977). On a theoretical level, Markus (1977) has suggested that behavioral consistency is a function of the schemas one has—self-schemas in her

---

[6]The attitude toward the same object tuned in by two different schemas will not be independent. Although different schemas make salient different *sets* of cognitions, for each individual those sets are drawn from the same pool.

particular case. If one does not have a self-schema that includes a particular behavioral dimension, then behavior on that dimension will be inconsistent. By implication, if one does not have a schema about some attitude object which includes a specific kind of behavior, then behavior toward the object will be inconsistent. Snyder (1977) has elaborated on this notion. He suggests that

> Beliefs will be translated into action to the extent that: (1) these beliefs are *available* in the form of a well-articulated *"cognitive structure"* [i.e., schema] containing clear behavioral implications, and (2) these beliefs are linked to an *"action structure"* that makes belief a *relevant* . . . guide to action . . . [p. 5].

The action structures are scriptlike entities containing guidelines or "rules of thumb" regarding the behavioral implications of beliefs. Similarly, Abelson (1976) argues that previous attempts to rationalize the disappointing relationship between attitudes and behaviors are not very compelling because they deal with generalized abstractions. He suggests that attitudes be conceptualized as the ensemble of scripts about the object. The scripts contain specific behavioral information. Since scripts develop from ". . . commerce the individual personally has had or anticipates with the object" (p. 41), it follows that attitude–behavior consistency should be greatest for objects that individuals have had personal experience with. In fact, Zanna and Fazio (1977), in a recent summary of relevant research, make an impressive case for the prediction

> . . . that attitudes based upon direct behavioral experience with an attitude object are more predictive of later behavior than are attitudes formed through indirect, non-behavioral experience [p. 2].

In sum, the theorizing and data reviewed in this section hold the promise that schemalike constructs and attentional mechanisms will prove useful in our attempt to understand attitude–behavior relationships.

B. PSYCHOTHERAPY

The work on self-generated attitude change has some obvious implications for clinical psychology. To the extent that there are self-generated changes that are the result of a nonlogical inference process with few "reality constraints," we would expect to find exaggerated affect (e.g., phobias). Obviously, phobias also develop in other ways, but construing the etiology of phobias in this way has some interesting implications for psychotherapy.

This approach suggests that under certain circumstances, exposure to the anxiety-arousing object or situation, either concretely or symbolically, will be therapeutic. For example, we have shown (Section II,C) that self-generated attitude polarization is attenuated in the presence of "reality constraints." Naturally, exposure will have this impact only to the extent that it contradicts the beliefs underlying the exaggerated affect. It is possible to interpret some contemporary approaches to therapy in these terms. For example, systematic desensitization (Wolpe, 1958) and modeling approaches (Bandura, 1969) all involve exposing the client to the feared object or situation under conditions which would seem to contradict his prior beliefs.

We have suggested that specific beliefs are abandoned because they are inconsistent with other evidence, for example, what one perceives the object really to be. Such "reality constraints" are only one form of belief constraint. Specific beliefs can be contradicted and thus abandoned without the presence of the object or any new information about the object. If the derivation of the belief is examined and found wanting, this too will cause the belief to be abandoned. For example, the individual might discover that the belief represents a faulty use of his accepted inferential rules; that he is implicitly using a premise which he believes is false; or that he is ignoring a premise which he believes is true. We might term this kind of belief constraint a *"process constraint."*

The sources of "reality constraints" are clear: They come from perceiving the object itself or from authoritative information about the object. What about "process constraints"? We assume that for the most part, implicit thought processes, that is, inferential rules, are not logical but psychological (Abelson & Rosenberg, 1958). At the same time, most of us within Western culture recognize and accept the appropriateness of formal logic in making inferences. Thus, forcing an individual to make explicit his implicit thought processes should make salient illogical inferences, thereby constraining the process and attenuating the exaggerated affect. This suggests that having a person with an exaggerated fear carefully describe *why* he believes what he does about the feared object will result in reduced fear.

A highly structured (constrained) form of therapy pushing the client toward making his inference process explicit (and, presumably, more logical) has just been suggested. Contrast this to the kind of approach that may be derived from abreaction or a catharsis process. This process assumes that focusing on or "reliving" the affect results in a reduction of the neurotic anxiety. It suggests a therapeutic approach in which the client is encouraged to focus on and to "experience" in an *un*constrained way the affect associated with the object. From our perspective, such an approach would not be recommended. Explicit focus on the affect should tune in a schema consistent with that affect and thought would be expected to result in affective polarization rather than moderation.

To test some of these speculations, we (Tesser, Leone, & Clary, 1978) conducted an experiment which included a Process Constraints condition, an Affective Focus condition (i.e., catharsis), and a Control condition. Twenty-six females who, on a preliminary questionnaire, indicated they were extremely anxious about public speaking were recruited in groups of three or four for the study. Within each group, one subject was randomly assigned to each of the three conditions (the fourth subject was also assigned to one of the conditions with the particular condition changing over groups).

When a group of subjects arrived, the experimenter explained that each person would be seen, individually, by another experimenter for a brief discussion. Following that discussion, they would return and give a brief talk to the rest of the group. When each subject went to see the second experimenter, the experimental manipulation was administered. If the subject was in the Process Constraints condition while she was asked to describe her feelings about public speaking, she was directed to focus on and make explicit *why* she feels that way; that is, she was to describe what her beliefs were and why she held those beliefs. If she was in the Affective Focus condition, she was asked to focus on and describe how she feels when making a public speech; to try to relive those emotions; to describe the physical sensations; etc. If she was in the Control condition, she was presented with a number of topics and asked how much anxiety would be produced by each during public speaking and why most people would or would not be anxious discussing these topics. Following the manipulation, each subject went through a short relaxation procedure (i.e., deep breathing exercises, muscle contraction/relaxation). Finally, she rated her present anxiety level, had a piece of test paper affixed to her index finger (to measure palmar sweat), and returned to the rest of the group.

When the subject returned to the rest of the group, she was given a couple of topics to use in an extemporaneous talk before the group (including the first experimenter). While the first subject was talking, the second subject was with the second experimenter receiving one of the treatments. When the second subject returned for her talk, the third subject was with the second experimenter, and so on. After each subject's talk, the test paper measuring palmar sweat was removed; the subject filled out a questionnaire concerning her anxiety during the talk; and the rest of the group (including the first experimenter) rated the subject's anxiety during the talk. Thus, we had three indices of treatment effectiveness: a physiological index (palmar sweat), a self-report index, and a behavioral index (ratings by the group members).

Recall our expectations. Process Constraints should reduce anxiety while Emotional Focus should, if anything, polarize feelings, that is, increase anxiety, and the Control condition should be between these two. First, there were no differences in reported anxiety after the treatment but before giving the talk. Using the group as the unit for statistical analysis, our hypothesis was confirmed on both the physiological and self-report measures. The palmar sweat index yielded a mean of 2.79 for Process Constraints, a mean of 2.86 for the Control condition, a mean of 3.50 for the Emotional Focus condition, and the planned comparison was significant ($p < .05$). Self-reported anxiety during the talk was lowest under Process Constraints ($\bar{\chi} = 4.03$), intermediate under the Control condition ($\overline{X}$ = 4.79), highest under Emotional Focus ($\overline{X}$ = 5.36) and, again, the planned comparison was significant ($p < .01$). The means for the behavioral ratings were not ordered as predicted, and neither the planned comparison nor an omnibus F-test indicated any difference.[7]

The physiological and self-report data supported our hypotheses. The imposition of process constraints seems to be effective in reducing anxiety. We have suggested that the process constraints treatment is effective because it forces awareness of illogical beliefs. In spite of the fact that other research using similar kinds of treatments has obtained similar results (e.g., Karst & Trexler, 1970; Trexler & Karst, 1972), more *analytic* research is clearly necessary. The catharsis or emotional focus treatment seemed to increase rather than decrease anxiety. Here, as in a number of studies previously discussed in this report, the result of attention has been affective polarization. Although other interpretations are possible, we suggest that focusing on the anxiety results in cognitive changes making one's beliefs more consistent with the feelings of anxiety.

This initial attempt to examine the implications of self-generated attitude change for clinical psychology is encouraging. A more comprehensive examination of its commonalities and differences with respect to other approaches such as Ellis' rational–emotive therapy appears called for. Additional research that examines effectiveness in a long-term treatment context with some follow-up is necessary. And, more research dealing with the comparative effectiveness of a "process constraints" approach and other approaches would be useful.

C. MERE EXPOSURE

In 1968, Zajonc (1968a) published a monograph in which he provided both correlational and experimental evidence for the proposition that simply increasing the frequency of exposure of a stimulus produces a more favorable attitude toward that stimulus. "Mere exposure" is like "mere thought" if we assume that when a subject is exposed to a stimulus, he focuses his attention upon it (i.e., thinks about it). The presence of the object during repeated exposures should, from the present perspective, create "reality constraints," making it more difficult to detect the results of thought-generated change. In a methodological vein (Stang, 1974), "mere exposure" is typically a within-subject variable, whereas all of our work manipulates thought as a between-subject factor. "Mere exposure" is typically manipulated in terms of frequency of exposure (with duration confounded), whereas our work has generally manipulated thought duration with one exposure (Tesser & Conlee, 1975).

The thesis that increasing exposure results in greater positivity regarding the

---

[7]A later study which included these same three conditions failed to replicate the palmar sweat results but did replicate the self-report results ($p < .01$).

object appears to be inconsistent with the prediction that thought usually results in polarization. The empirical outcomes of experiments have mostly yielded positivity effects (e.g., Zajonc, 1968a), sometimes polarization effects (e.g., Brickman, Redfield, Harrison, & Crandall, 1972), as well as other less frequent outcomes (see Harrison, 1977, for a comprehensive review). Earlier we suggested that thought-generated attitude change was a function of change in cognitions under the direction of a schema and that a schema was necessary for these changes. It turns out that positivity has generally been obtained with stimuli for which we would not expect subjects to have well-developed cognitive schemas; that is,

> ... stimuli that were novel and relatively neutral affect. Turkish-like words, Chinese ideographs, and nonsense syllables have consistently shown an increase in attractiveness with repeated exposures [Zajonc, Markus, & Wilson, 1974, p. 248].

Although we have found little evidence of positivity in our own studies using poorly developed schemas, the fact that such effects are commonly obtained is not inconsistent with the present approach. More germane is what happens with stimuli for which subjects are assumed to have well-developed schemas. It turns out that when such stimuli are not initially neutral, polarization has been found. For example, Brickman *et al.* (1972) found that disliked popular songs became even more disliked with increased exposure and that initially liked paintings increased in positivity and initially disliked paintings decreased in positivity with increased exposure.[8] Perlman and Oskamp (1971) found a shift to negativity with repeated exposure to a picture of someone in a negative role (e.g., a prisoner) and a shift to positivity with repeated exposure to a picture of someone in a positive role (e.g., a priest).

Furthermore, within the mere exposure paradigm, there are data documenting the mediational role of just the kind of cognitive changes we have talked about. In one study (Grush, 1976), positive words become more positive (n.s.) and negative words more negative ($p < .02$) with increasing exposure. More importantly, when subjects were asked to provide associations, the more frequently exposed words were associated with a larger number of cognitions ($p < .05$). Further, for the negative stimuli, increased exposure resulted in more negative evaluations of those associated cognitions.

It appears, then, that given stimuli for which subjects have a well-developed schema, even with exposure (i.e., object present) as a manipulation of thought, the predicted polarization effects can be detected. Further, Grush's work suggests that these changes are at least partially mediated by systematic changes

[8]Brickman *et al.* used both male and female subjects but they did not report using sex as a factor in the analysis of their data. Therefore, we do not know if the polarization effect was stronger for the females than the males as we would expect.

in beliefs about the object. The self-generated attitude change approach does not anticipate, nor can it explain, every outcome ever obtained within the mere exposure paradigm (Harrison, 1977). On the other hand, the fact that it can account for some of these outcomes suggests that it may be playing some role in producing them.

D. GROUP POLARIZATION

A phenomenon analogous to self-generated attitude change on the individual level seems to operate at the group level. The work started with issues on a risk dimension (Dion, Baron, & Miller, 1970) but has been generalized to a number of issues including attitudes, jury decisions, ethical decisions, judgments, person perception, and negotiation and conflict (see Myers & Lamm, 1976, for an excellent summary and integration of this research). Moscovici and Zavalloni (1969) coined the term "group polarization" to describe this tendency for the average group response, after discussion, to be more extreme in the direction of the average prediscussion response.

Two threads of evidence suggest that the self-generated attitude process as described here may play a mediational role in the group polarization process. First, there are some data indicating that simply giving an individual time to think about the issues on which groups polarize tends to result in the individual's attitude polarizing. Bateson (1966) found that both subjects who, without discussion, thought about and generated arguments concerning their initial position and subjects who discussed the issue exhibited a significant polarization effect, and there was no difference in the magnitude of the effect between the two groups. Flanders and Thistlethwaite (1967) used a 2 x 2 design: Subjects were either encouraged to think about the issues on their own or were given no opportunity to think about the issues; this was followed either by a group discussion or no group discussion. These two variables interacted in affecting polarization. Thought with and without discussion, and discussion without prior thought, resulted in significant and equivalent amounts of polarization; no thought/no discussion resulted in no polarization. [Although there have been a number of unsuccessful attempts to replicate these studies (e.g., Dion & Miller, 1971; Pruitt & Teger, 1967), there are some methodological possibilities which might account for the discrepancy (Burnstein & Vinokur, 1977).]

Some evidence suggests that just learning the initial positions of other group members results in a small degree of polarization (Myers, 1974). Earlier we suggested that instructions, a change in relationship, etc., could cause an individual to tune in a different schema for thinking about the same object. Similarly, Burnstein, Vinokur, and Trope (1973) suggest that

> ... knowledge that others' choices are discrepant from his own may induce the person to reconstruct a line of reasoning [i.e., tune in a schema] which he thinks could have produced

such choices. That is to say, knowing others have chosen differently stimulates the person to generate arguments which could explain [and thus would support] their choices [p. 244].

To test this hypothesis, Burnstein and Vinokur (1975) set up three conditions. In condition I, subjects learned of the others' preferences and then generated relevant arguments; in condition II, subjects learned of others' preferences but generated arguments for an unrelated issue; in condition III, subjects did not learn of the others' preferences and wrote arguments on both sides of the relevant issue. The results supported the hypothesis. The preferences of subjects in condition I polarized while this was not the case in the other two conditions.

In sum, "group thought" or discussion often results in attitude polarization as does individual thought. Further, there is some evidence to suggest that self-generated attitude change captures some of the variance in this effect (Burnstein & Vinokur, 1977).

IV. Some Unfinished Business

In this chapter we have examined in some detail the effects of thought on attitudes. We have taken a first step toward conceptualizing such effects, but much work needs to be done. Our central concept, the cognitive schema, needs greater theoretical specification and elaboration into types and levels—perhaps along the lines of Schank and Abelson (1977). We have suggested that different schemas can be used for thinking about the same object and much too briefly touched on the variables that might control such processes. Clearly these variables need to be elaborated lest the theory be one that can account for any possible outcome on a *post hoc* basis. We have suggested that thought, under the direction of a schema, makes cognitions more evaluatively consistent, but we have not indicated whether this was due to a motivational bias toward consistency or a simple cognitive bias perhaps reflecting the fact that it is often the case that good things tend to go together in the real world. Nor have we said anything about how the cognitions which presumably underly the expressed affect are valued and combined, although substantial progress on this problem is being made by Anderson (e.g., Anderson, 1974). Finally, future research with the schema construct is going to have to do a better job of *independently* assessing schemas as has been done by Markus (1977), for example.

We have focused on the effects of thought but, in a sense, any attempt to understand such effects is incomplete unless it also deals with the variables that control what is thought about. There are a couple of hints available. For example, Tesser and Paulhus (1976) found some support for the notion that the more extreme the initial attitude toward some object, the more an individual is likely to think about it. Freud has suggested that strong needs which are frustrated could lead to primary process thinking or dreaming about relevant objects. Indeed, in their study of semistarvation, Brozek, Guetzkow, Baldwin, and Cranston (1951) found that "during starvation the thoughts of food, in all its ramifications, came to dominate the men's minds" (p. 250), and Sanford (1936) found that subjects tended to give more food responses to a word association test before a regular meal than after it. It has also occurred to a number of investigators that thought about an object should be a function of the magnitude of the potential rewards and costs associated with the object. Thus Langer, Blank, and Chanowitz (1976, reported in Langer, 1978) found that the greater the cost of doing a favor, the more thoughtful was the response to the request for the favor. Although Tesser and Johnson (1974) found only a partial support for the hypothesis that dependence on another increases thought (and hence polarization) about the other, Berscheid, Graziano, Monson, and Dermer (1976) found that dependence on another affects a number of variables associated with thought (e.g., attention, memory, extremity of rating). Finally, one's evaluation of the object may determine how much it is thought about. Both James (1907) and Bartlett (1932), among others, have suggested that we tend to avoid thinking about dislikable things while we do not avoid thinking about likable things.

V. Summary

We have seen that thought about some nonneutral attitude object in the absence of any new external information or change in overt behavior often results in attitude *polarization*. Attitude polarization seems to be predicated on *cognitive changes* such as the addition of consistent cognitions and the reinterpretation of existing inconsistent cognitions. Such changes in cognitions and affect are expected to occur only to the extent that persons have a developed *cognitive schema* for thinking about the object. A schema is a "naive" theory about the object which makes salient selected cognitions and provides rules for making inferences. We have suggested that one's attitude is a function of those salient cognitions and inferences. The data also suggest that persons can tune in more than one schema for thinking about a particular object. Thus persons have the potential for more than one attitude toward the same object. Some implications for the relationship between attitudes and behavior and for psychotherapy were touched upon. The relationship between this research and group polarization research and mere exposure research were briefly explored. Finally, we have pointed out a number of aspects of the present approach that are in need of further elaboration.

REFERENCES

Abelson, R. P. Script processing in attitude formation and decision making. In J. S. Carroll & J. W.

Payne (Eds.), *Cognition and social behavior*. Potomac, Md.: Lawrence Erlbaum Associates, 1976.

Abelson, R. P., & Rosenberg, M. J. Symbolic psycho-logic: A model of attitudinal cognition. *Behavioral Science*, 1958, **3**, 1–13.

Allport, G. W., & Postman, L. *The psychology of rumor*. New York: Holt, 1947.

Anderson, N. H. Two more tests against change of meaning in adjective combinations. *Journal of Verbal Learning and Verbal Behavior*, 1971, **10**, 75–85.

Anderson, N. H. Cognitive algebra: Integration theory applied to social attribution. In L. Berkowitz (Ed.), *Advances in experimental social psychology*. Vol. 7. New York: Academic Press, 1974.

Anderson, N. H. Integration theory applied to cognitive responses and attitudes. In R. E. Petty, T. M. Ostrom, & T. C. Brock (Eds.), *Cognitive responses to persuasion*. New York: McGraw-Hill, 1978, in press.

Aristotle. *De partibus animalium*. Book 2, Chapter 7, 652b.

Asch, S. E. Forming impressions of personality. *Journal of Abnormal and Social Psychology*, 1946, **41**, 258–290.

Bandura, A. *Principles of behavior modification*. New York: Holt, 1969.

Bartlett, F. C. *Remembering: A study in experimental and social psychology*. London: Cambridge University Press, 1932.

Bateson, N. Familiarization, group discussion, and risk taking. *Journal of Experimental Social Psychology*, 1966, **2**, 119–129.

Bem, D. J., & Allen, A. On predicting some of the people some of the time: The search for cross-situational consistencies in behavior. *Psychological Review*, 1974, **31**, 506–520.

Berscheid, E., Graziano, W., Monson, T., & Dermer, M. Outcome dependency: Attention, attribution, and attraction. *Journal of Personality and Social Psychology*, 1976, **34**, 978–989.

Brickman, P., Redfield, J., Harrison, A. A., & Crandall, R. Drive and predisposition as factors in the attitudinal effects of mere exposure. *Journal of Experimental and Social Psychology*, 1972, **8**, 31–44.

Broadbent, D. *Perception and communication*. Oxford: Pergamon, 1958.

Brozek, J., Guetzkow, H., Baldwin, M. V., & Cranston, R. A quantitative study of perception and association in experimental semi-starvation. *Journal of Personality*, 1951, **19**, 245–264.

Burnstein, E., & Vinokur, A. What a person thinks upon learning he has chosen differently from others: Nice evidence for the persuasive-arguments explanation of choice shifts. *Journal of Experimental Social Psychology*, 1975, **11**, 439–458.

Burnstein, E., & Vinokur, A. Persuasive argumentation and social comparison as determinants of attitude polarization. *Journal of Experimental Social Psychology*, 1977, **13**, 315–332.

Burnstein, E., Vinokur, A., & Trope, Y. Interpersonal comparison versus persuasive argumentation: A more direct test of alternative explanations for group induced shifts in individual choice. *Journal of Experimental Social Psychology*, 1973, **9**, 236–245.

Byrne, D., & Nelson, D. Attraction as a linear function of proportion of positive reinforcements. *Journal of Personality and Social Psychology*, 1965, **1**, 659–663.

Cantor, N., & Mischel, W. Traits as prototypes: Effects on recognition memory. *Journal of Personality and Social Psychology*, 1977, **35**, 38–48.

Carlson, E. R. Attitude change through modification of attitude structure. *Journal of Abnormal and Social Psychology*, 1956, **52**, 256–261.

Carmichael, L., Hogan, H., & Walter, A. An experimental study of the effect of language on the reproduction of visually perceived form. *Journal of Experimental Psychology*, 1932, **15**, 73–86.

Carver, C. S. Physical aggression as a function of objective self-awareness and attitudes towards punishment. *Journal of Experimental Social Psychology*, 1975, **11**, 510–519.

Cialdini, R. B., Levy, A. C., Herman, C. P., & Evenbeck, S. Attitudinal politics: The strategy of moderation. *Journal of Personality and Social Psychology*, 1973, **25**, 100–108.

Clary, E. G., Tesser, A., & Downing, L. L. Influence of a salient schema on thought-induced cognitive change. *Personality and Social Psychology Bulletin,* 1978, **4,** 39–43.

Cromwell, R. L., & Caldwell, D. F. A comparison of ratings based on personal constructs of self and others. *Journal of Clinical Psychology,* 1962, **18,** 43–46.

Cronbach, L. J., & Meehl, P. E. Construct validity in psychological tests. *Psychological Bulletin,* 1955, **52,** 281–302.

Davidson, J. R., & Kiesler, S. B. Cognitive behavior before and after decisions. In L. Festinger (Ed.), *Conflict, decision, and dissonance.* Stanford, Calif.: Stanford University Press, 1964.

Deutsch, M. The effects of cooperation and competition upon group processes. In D. Cartwright & A. Zander (Eds.), *Group dynamics.* (3rd ed.) New York: Harper, 1968.

Dillehay, R. C. On the irrelevance of the classical negative evidence concerning the effect of attitudes on behavior. *American Psychologist,* 1973, **28,** 887–891.

Dion, K. L., Baron, R. S., & Miller, N. Why do groups make riskier decisions than individuals? In L. Berkowitz (Ed.), *Advances in experimental social psychology.* Vol. 5. New York: Academic Press, 1970.

Dion, K. L., & Miller, N. An analysis of the familiarization explanation of the risky-shift. *Journal of Experimental Social Psychology,* 1971, **7,** 524–533.

Ebbesen, E. B., Cohen, C. B., & Lane, J. L. Encoding and construction processes in person perception. Paper presented at the meeting of the American Psychological Association, Chicago, Aug. 1975.

Feather, H. T. Acceptance and rejection of arguments in relation to attitude strength, critical ability, and intolerance of inconsistency. *Journal of Abnormal and Social Psychology,* 1964, **69,** 127–137.

Fishbein, M., & Ajzen, I. *Belief, attitude, intention, and behavior: An introduction to theory and research.* Reading, Mass.: Addison-Wesley, 1975.

Flanders, J. P., & Thistlethwaite, D. L. Effect of familiarization and group discussion upon risk-taking. *Journal of Personality and Social Psychology,* 1967, **5,** 91–98.

Greenwald, A. G. Cognitive learning, cognitive response to persuasion, and attitude change. In A. G. Greenwald, T. C. Brock, & T. M. Ostrom (Eds.), *Psychological foundations of attitudes.* New York: Academic Press, 1968.

Grush, J. E. Attitude formation and mere exposure phenomena: A nonartifactual explanation of empirical findings. *Journal of Personality and Social Psychology,* 1976, **33,** 281–290.

Hanno, M. S., & Jones, L. E. Effects of a change in reference person on the multidimensional structure and evaluations of trait adjectives. *Journal of Personality and Social Psychology,* 1973, **28,** 368–375.

Harrison, A. A. Mere exposure. In L. Berkowitz (Ed.), *Advances in experimental social psychology.* Vol. 10. New York: Academic Press, 1977.

Heider, F. *The psychology of interpersonal relations.* New York: Wiley, 1958.

Ickes, W. J., Wicklund, R. A., & Ferris, C. B. Objective self-awareness and self-esteem. *Journal of Experimental Social Psychology,* 1973, **9,** 202–219.

James, W. *The principles of psychology.* Vol. 1. New York: Holt, 1907.

Jones, E. E., & de Charms, R. The organizing function of interaction roles in person perception. *Journal of Abnormal and Social Psychology,* 1958, **57,** 155–164.

Jones, E. E., & Sigall, H. The bogus pipeline: A new paradigm for measuring affect and attitude. *Psychological Bulletin,* 1971, **76,** 349–364.

Jones, E. E., & Thibaut, J. W. Interaction goals as bases of interference in interpersonal perception. In R. Tagiuri & L. Petrullo (Eds.), *Person perception and interpersonal behavior.* Stanford, Calif.: Stanford University Press, 1958.

Kaplan, K. J., & Fishbein, M. The source of beliefs, their saliency, and prediction of attitude.

Journal of Social Psychology, 1969, **78,** 63–74.

Karst, T. O., & Trexler, L. D. Initial study using fixed-role and rational-emotive therapy in treating public-speaking anxiety. *Journal of Consulting and Clinical Psychology,* 1970, **34,** 306–366.

Kelley, H. H. Attribution theory in social psychology. In D. Levine (Ed.), *Nebraska Symposium on Motivation.* Vol. 15. Lincoln: University of Nebraska Press, 1967. Pp. 192–238.

Kelley, H. H. *Causal Schemata and the attribution process.* New York: General Learning Press, 1972.

Kelly, G. A. *The psychology of personal constructs.* Vol. 1. New York: Norton, 1955.

Kiesler, C. A., Collins, B. E., & Miller, N. *Attitude change.* New York: Wiley, 1969.

Konecni, V. J. Annoyance, type and duration of postannoyance activity, and aggression: The "cathartic" effect. *Journal of Experimental Psychology: General,* 1975, **104,** 76–102.

Kutner, B., Wilkins, C., & Yarrow, P. R. Verbal attitudes and overt behavior involving racial prejudice. *Journal of Abnormal and Social Psychology,* 1952, **47,** 649–652.

Langer, E. J. Rethinking the role of thought in social interaction. In J. Harvey, W. Ickes, & R. Kidd (Eds.), *New directions in attribution research.* Vol. 2. Potomac, Md.: Laurence Erlbaum Associates, 1978, in press.

LaPiere, R. T. Attitudes vs. action. *Social Forces,* 1934, **13,** 230–237.

Lerner, M. J., Dillehay, R. C., & Sherer, W. C. Similarity and attraction in social contexts. *Journal of Personality and Social Psychology,* 1967, **5,** 481–486.

Levine, J. M., & Murphy, G. The learning and forgetting of controversial material. *Journal of Abnormal and Social Psychology,* 1943, **38,** 507–517.

Markus, H. Self-schemata and processing information about the self. *Journal of Personality and Social Psychology,* 1977, **35,** 63–78.

McGuire, W. J. A syllogistic analysis of cognitive relationships. In M. J. Rosenberg, C. I. Hovland, W. J. McGuire, R. P. Abelson, & J. W. Brehm (Eds.), *Attitude organization and change.* New Haven, Conn.: Yale University Press, 1960.

McGuire, W. J. The nature of attitudes and attitude change. In G. Lindzey & E. Aronson (Eds.), *The handbook of social psychology.* (2nd ed.) Vol. 3. Reading, Mass.: Addison-Wesley, 1969.

Miller, G. A. The magical number seven, plus or minus two: Some limits on our capacity for processing information. *Psychological Review,* 1956, **63,** 81–97.

Miller, N., & Baron, S. On measuring counterarguing. *Journal for the Theory of Social Behavior,* 1973, **3,** 101–118.

Minard, R. D. Race relationships in the Pocahontas coal field. *Journal of Social Issues,* 1952, **8,** 29–44.

Mischel, W. *Personality and assessment.* New York: Wiley, 1968.

Moscovici, S., & Zavalloni, M. The group as a polarizer of attitudes. *Journal of Personality and Social Psychology,* 1969, **12,** 125–135.

Myers, D. G. Social comparison processes in choice dilemma responding. *Journal of Psychology,* 1974, **86,** 287–292.

Myers, D. G., & Lamm, H. The group polarization phenomenon. *Psychological Bulletin,* 1976, **83,** 602–627.

Neisser, U. *Cognition and reality.* San Francisco: Freeman, 1976.

Norman, R. Affective-cognitive consistency, attitudes, conformity, and behavior. *Journal of Personality and Social Psychology,* 1975, **32,** 83–91.

Orne, M. T. On the social psychology of the psychological experiment: With particular reference to demand characteristics and their implications. *American Psychologist,* 1962, **17,** 776–783.

Osgood, C. E., Suci, G. J., & Tannenbaum, P. H. *The measurement of meaning.* Urbana: University of Illinois Press, 1957.

Passini, F. T., & Norman, W. T. A universal conception of personality structure. *Journal of*

Personality and Social Psychology, 1966, **4,** 44–49.

Perlman, D., & Oskamp, S. The effects of picture content and exposure frequency on evaluations of Negroes and whites. *Journal of Experimental Social Psychology,* 1971, **7,** 503–514.

Phillips, J. L. A model for cognitive balance. *Psychological Review,* 1967, **74,** 481–495.

Piaget, J. [*The child's conception of physical causality*] (M. Garbain, Ed. and trans.). London: Kegan Paul, 1960.

Posner, M. I., & Keele, S. W. On the genesis of abstract idea. *Journal of Experimental Psychology,* 1968, **77,** 353–363.

Posner, M. I., & Keele, S. W. Retention of abstract ideas. *Journal of Experimental Psychology,* 1970, **83,** 304–308.

Pruitt, D. G., & Teger, A. I. Is there a shift toward risk in group discussion? If so, is it a group phenomenon? If so, what causes it? Paper presented at the American Psychological Association Convention, 1967.

Rips, L. J. Inductive judgments about natural categories. *Journal of Verbal Learning and Verbal Behavior,* 1975, **14,** 665–681.

Rosch, E. H. Natural categories. *Cognitive Psychology,* 1973, **4,** 328–350.

Rosenberg, M. J. Cognitive structure and attitudinal affect. *Journal of Abnormal and Social Psychology,* 1956, **53,** 367–372.

Rosenberg, M. J. Cognitive reorganization in response to the hypnotic reversal of attitudinal affect. *Journal of Personality,* 1960, **28,** 39–63.

Rosenberg, M. J., & Abelson, R. P. An analysis of cognitive balancing. In M. J. Rosenberg, C. I. Hovland, W. J. McGuire, R. P. Abelson, & J. W. Brehm (Eds.), *Attitude organization and change.* New Haven, Conn.: Yale University Press, 1960.

Ross, L. The intuitive psychologist and his shortcomings: Distortions in the attribution process. In L. Berkowitz (Ed.), *Advances in experimental social psychology.* Vol. 10. New York: Academic Press, 1977.

Rumelhart, D. E. Notes on a schema for stories. In D. G. Bobrow & A. M. Collins (Eds.), *Representation and understanding: Studies in cognitive science.* New York: Academic Press, 1975.

Rumelhart, D. E., & Ortony, A. The representation of knowledge in memory. In R. C. Anderson, R. J. Spiro, & W. E. Montague (Eds.), *Schooling and the acquisition of knowledge.* Hillsdale, N. J.: Lawrence Erlbaum Associates, 1976.

Sadler, O., & Tesser, A. Some effects of salience and time upon interpersonal hostility and attraction during social isolation. *Sociometry,* 1973, **36,** 99–112.

Salancik, G. R. Inference of one's attitude from behavior recalled under linguistically manipulated cognitive sets. *Journal of Experimental Social Psychology,* 1974, **10,** 415–427.

Salancik, G. R., & Conway, M. Attitude inferences from salient and relevant cognitive content about behavior. *Journal of Personality and Social Psychology,* 1975, **35,** 829–840.

Sanford, R. N. The effect of abstinence from food upon imaginal processes. *Journal of Psychology,* 1936, **2,** 129–136.

Schank, R. C., & Abelson, R. P. Scripts, plans and knowledge. In *Advance Papers of the Fourth International Joint Conference on Artificial Intelligence.* Tbilisi, Georgia, USSR: 1975. Pp. 151–157.

Schank, R. C., & Abelson, R. P. *Scripts, plans, goals and understanding: An inquiry into human knowledge structures.* Hillsdale, N.J.: Laurence Erlbaum Associates, 1977.

Schneider, D. J. Implicit personality theory: A review. *Psychological Bulletin,* 1973, **79,** 294–309.

Simpson, D. D., & Ostrom, T. M. Effect of snap and thoughtful judgments on person impressions. *European Journal of Social Psychology,* 1975, **5,** 197–208.

Smith, E. E., Shoben, E. G., & Rips, L. G. Structure and process in semantic memory: A featural model for semantic decisions. *Psychological Review,* 1974, **81,** 214–241.

Snyder, M. When believing means doing: A cognitive social psychology of action. Paper presented at the annual meeting of the American Psychological Association, San Francisco, August 1977.

Snyder, M., & Swann, W. B., Jr. When actions reflect attitudes: The politics of impression management. *Journal of Personality and Social Psychology*, 1976, **34**, 1034–1042.

Spiro, R. J. *Inferential reconstruction in memory for connected discourse* (Tech. Rep. No. 2). Urbana-Champaign: University of Illinois, Laboratory for Cognitive Studies in Education, 1975.

Stang, D. J. Methodological factors in mere exposure research. *Psychological Bulletin,* 1974, **81**, 1014–1025.

Star, S. A., Williams, R. M., & Stouffer, S. Negro infantry platoons in white companies. In E. E. Maccoby, T. M. Newcomb, & E. L. Hartley (Eds.), *Readings in social psychology.* (3rd ed.) New York: Holt, 1958.

Stotland, E., & Canon, L. K. *Social psychology: A cognitive approach.* Philadelphia: Saunders, 1972.

Taylor, S. E., & Fiske, S. T. Salience, attention, and attribution: Top of the head phenomena. In L. Berkowitz (Ed.), *Advances in Experimental Social Psychology,* Vol. II. New York: Academic Press, 1978.

Tesser, A. Thought and reality constraints as determinants of attitude polarization. *Journal of Research in Personality,* 1976, **10**, 183–194.

Tesser, A., & Conlee, M. C. Some effects of time and thought on attitude polarization. *Journal of Personality and Social Psychology,* 1975, **31**, 262–270.

Tesser, A., & Cowan, C. L. Some effects of thought and number of cognitions on attitude change. *Social Behavior and Personality,* 1975, **3**, 165–173.

Tesser, A., & Cowan, C. L. Some attitudinal and cognitive consequences of thought. *Journal of Research in Personality,* 1977, **11**, 216–226.

Tesser, A., & Danheiser, P. Anticipated relationship, salience of partner and attitude change. *Personality and Social Psychology Bulletin,* 1978, **4**, 35–38.

Tesser, A., & Johnson, R. D. Thought and dependence as determinants of interpersonal hostility. *Bulletin of the Psychonomic Society,* 1974, **2**, 425–430.

Tesser, A., & Leone, C. Cognitive schemas and thought as determinants of attitude change. *Journal of Experimental Social Psychology,* 1977, **13**, 340–356.

Tesser, A., Leone, C., & Clary, G. Affect control: Process constraints versus catharsis. *Cognitive Therapy and Research,* 1978, in press.

Tesser, A., & Paulhus, D. L. Toward a causal model of love. *Journal of Personality and Social Psychology,* 1976, **34**, 1095–1105.

Thorndike, E. L. A constant error in psychological ratings. *Journal of Applied Psychology,* 1920, **4**, 25–29.

Trexler, L. D., & Karst, T. O. Rational-emotive therapy, placebo, and no-treatment effects on public-speaking anxiety. *Journal of Abnormal Psychology,* 1972, **79**, 60–67.

Triandis, H. C. Exploratory factor analyses of the behavioral component of social attitudes. *Journal of Abnormal and Social Psychology,* 1964, **68**, 420–430.

Tyler, L. E. *The psychology of human differences.* (3rd ed.) New York: Appleton, 1965.

Valenti, A. An analysis of the process of attitude polarization. Unpublished doctoral dissertation, University of Georgia, 1975.

Wells, F. L. A statistical study of literary merit. *Archives of Psychology,* 1907, **16**, No. 7.

Wicker, A. W. Attitudes versus actions: The relationship of verbal and overt behavioral responses to attitude objects. *Journal of Social Issues,* 1969, **25**, 41–78.

Wolpe, J. *Psychotherapy by reciprocal inhibition.* Palo Alto, Calif.: Stanford University Press, 1958.

Wyler, R. S. Changes in meaning and halo effects in personality impression formation. *Journal of*

Personality and Social Psychology, 1974, **29,** 829–835.

Wyer, R. S., Jr., & Goldberg, L. A. A probabilistic analysis of the relationships among beliefs and attitudes. *Psychological Review,* 1970, **77,** 100–120.

Zajonc, R. B. The attitudinal effects of mere exposure. *Journal of Personality and Social Psychology,* 1968, **9,** 1–27. (a)

Zajonc, R. B. Cognitive theories in social psychology. In G. Lindzey & E. Aronson (Eds.), *Handbook of social psychology.* (Rev. ed.) Vol. 1. Reading, Mass.: Addison-Wesley, 1968. (b).

Zajonc, R. B., Markus, H., & Wilson, W. R. Exposure effects and associative learning. *Journal of Experimental Social Psychology,* 1974, **10,** 248–263.

Zanna, M. P., & Fazio, R. H. Direct experience and attitude-behavior consistency. Paper presented at the annual meeting of the American Psychological Association, San Francisco, August 1977.

SUBJECT INDEX

A

Ability, demonstrated, choice and, 117–119
Absolute sleeper effect, 16–20
Achievement motivation, 135–137
  choice and, 131–135
  concept of, 126–131
Antisocial behavior, group polarization and, 151–152
Arousal, salience and, 276–277
Attention
  consistency and, 266–267
  differential, salience and, 271–273
  evaluation and, 264–265
  perceived representativeness and, 265–266
  recall and
    availability of, 269–270
    volume of, 268–269
Attitude
  group polarization of, *see* Group polarization
  validation of, 48–50
Attitude change, self-generated
  behavior and, 323–325
  beliefs and, 296–297
  cognitive schemas and, 290–293, 302–304, 306–310
  exposure and, 328–330
  group polarization and, 330–331
  impact of thought on, 293–296
  interpretational issues in, 318–323
  microprocess, 310–318
  psychotherapy and, 325–328
  reality constraints and, 304–306
  thought and, 298–302, 304–306
Attitude persistence
  compliance and, 10–12
  conceptualization of, 4–7
  consistency approaches, 30–31
    dissonance and related attribution theories, 36–39
    observation of discrepant behaviors, 39–42
    psychological approach, 32–33
    self-insight procedure, 35–36
    summary of, 42
    syllogistic theory, 31–32
    value discrepancies and, 33–35
  direct test of, 9–10
  discounting cue hypothesis and absolute sleeper effect and, 16–20
  dissociative cue hypothesis and, 16
  identification and, 12–13
  importance of study of, 2–4
  internalization and, 13–15
  predictions of, 43–48
  retention of message details and all details combined, 20–25
    specific details, 25–30
  time and, 7–8
Attribution
  for causes of behavior, 259
    dispositional and situational causality, 260–264
    manipulations of relative salience, 259–260
  choice and, 115–117
  persistence of attitude change and, 36–39

B

Behavior attitudes and, 323–325
Beliefs, self-generated attitude change and, 296–297

C

Causality, *see under* Salience
Choice(s)
  achievement motivation and, 126–137
  attribution theory and, 115–117
  decision theory and, 114–115
  in extraordinary circumstances, 137–141
  in ordinary circumstances, 124–126
  of others, group polarization and, 179–186
  utility and, 119–124
    achievement-related, 117
    in ordinary circumstances, 124–126
Compliance, persistence of attitude change and, 10–12
Conflict, group polarization and, 152–154, 159–162
Contingency model of leadership, 60
  motivational structure and, 60–62
  situational control and, 62–66

339

CONTENTS OF OTHER VOLUMES

A
B   8
C   9
D   0
E   1
F   2
G   3
H   4
I   5
J   6